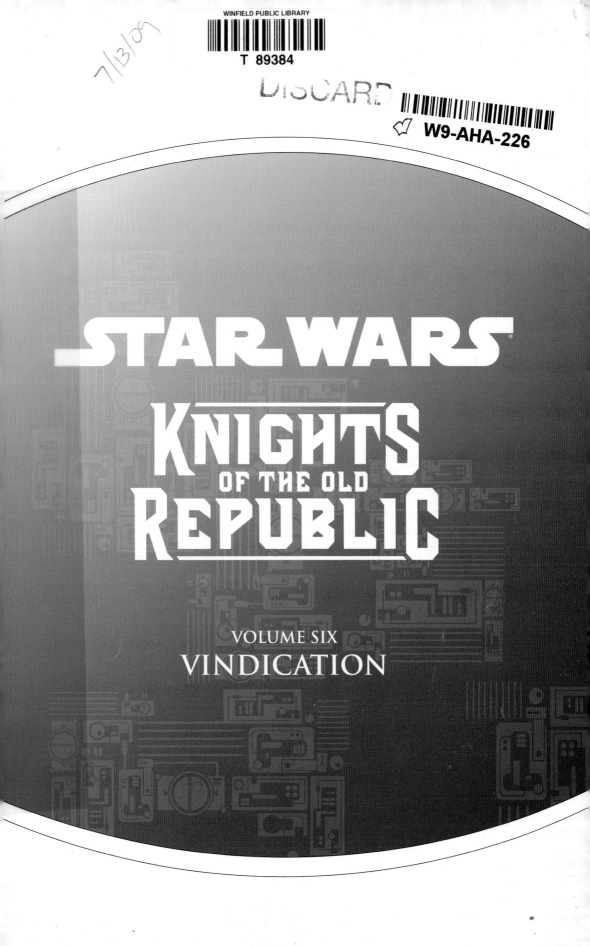

STAR WARS®

KNIGHTS OF THE OLD REPUBLIC

VOLUME SIX
VINDICATION

The Old Republic
(25,000–1,000 years before the Battle of Yavin)

The Old Republic was the legendary government that united a galaxy under the rule of the Senate. In this era, the Jedi are numerous, and serve as guardians of peace and justice. The **Tales of the Jedi** *comics series takes place in this era, chronicling the immense wars fought by the Jedi of old, and the ancient Sith.*

The events in this story take place approximately 3,963 years before the Battle of Yavin.

STAR WARS®

KNIGHTS OF THE OLD REPUBLIC

VOLUME SIX
VINDICATION

SCRIPT JOHN JACKSON MILLER

ART BONG DAZO, BRIAN CHING, ALAN ROBINSON & JOE PIMENTEL

COLORS MICHAEL ATIYEH

LETTERING MICHAEL HEISLER

COVER ART BRIAN CHING & MICHAEL ATIYEH

Dark Horse Books®

PUBLISHER   MIKE RICHARDSON

COLLECTION DESIGNER   STEPHEN REICHERT

ART DIRECTOR   LIA RIBACCHI

ASSISTANT EDITOR   FREDDYE LINS

EDITOR   DAVE MARSHALL

*Special thanks to Elaine Mederer, Jann Moorhead, David Anderman, Leland Chee,
Sue Rostoni, and Carol Roeder at Lucas Licensing.*

STAR WARS: KNIGHTS OF THE OLD REPUBLIC VOLUME SIX—VINDICATION

This volume collects issues twenty-nine through thirty-five
of the Dark Horse comic-book series *Star Wars: Knights of the Old Republic.*

Published by
Dark Horse Books
A division of Dark Horse Comics, Inc.
10956 SE Main Street
Milwaukie OR 97222

darkhorse.com
starwars.com

To find a comics shop in your area,
call the Comic Shop Locator Service toll-free at 1-888-266-4226

First edition: May 2009
ISBN 978-1-59582-274-1

1 3 5 7 9 10 8 6 4 2
Printed in China

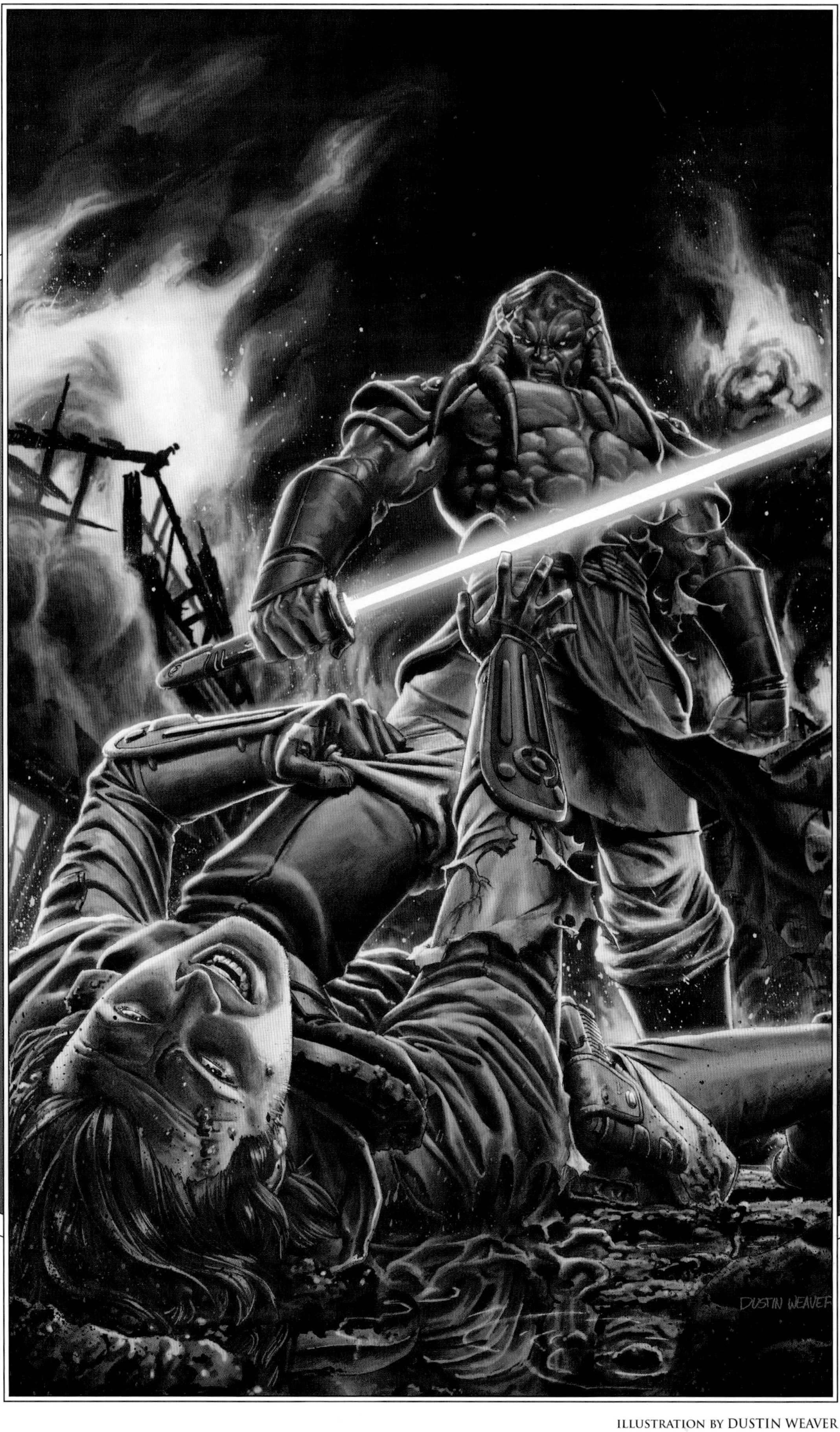
DUSTIN WEAVER
ILLUSTRATION BY DUSTIN WEAVER

EXALTED

art by Bong Dazo

While the Jedi Knights defend the galaxy, a secret cabal of Jedi seers known as the Covenant goes further, working to predict and prevent the return of the Sith. Their missions include efforts to find and quarantine dangerous Sith artifacts—and to capture the unlikely personification of their fears: Zayne Carrick.

Once the apprentice of Covenant cofounder Lucien Draay, Zayne becomes a fugitive when the group's seers suspect he might pose a future threat to the Jedi Order. Framed for murder, Zayne travels the galaxy with con artist Gryph, the mysterious Jarael, and others in a futile attempt to clear his name.

But Zayne's destiny changes when he crosses paths with Covenant agent Celeste Morne. Suspecting that her own organization framed Zayne, Celeste gives him a final gift before departing: the very key he needs to expose the Covenant. But using it means going directly into enemy territory . . .

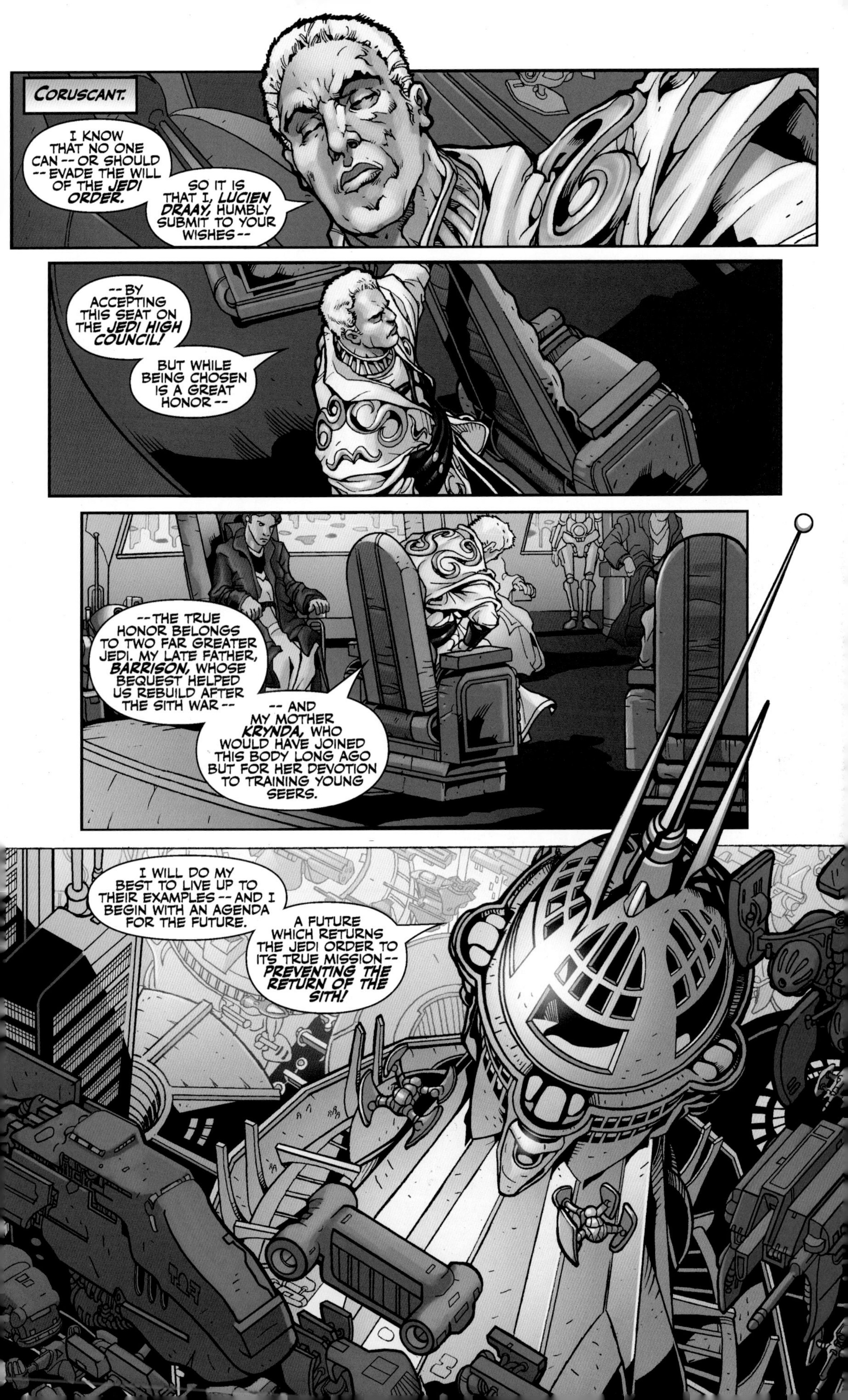
CORUSCANT.
I KNOW THAT NO ONE CAN -- OR SHOULD -- EVADE THE WILL OF THE JEDI ORDER.
SO IT IS THAT I, LUCIEN DRAAY, HUMBLY SUBMIT TO YOUR WISHES --
-- BY ACCEPTING THIS SEAT ON THE JEDI HIGH COUNCIL!
BUT WHILE BEING CHOSEN IS A GREAT HONOR --
-- THE TRUE HONOR BELONGS TO TWO FAR GREATER JEDI. MY LATE FATHER, BARRISON, WHOSE BEQUEST HELPED US REBUILD AFTER THE SITH WAR --
-- AND MY MOTHER KRYNDA, WHO WOULD HAVE JOINED THIS BODY LONG AGO BUT FOR HER DEVOTION TO TRAINING YOUNG SEERS.
I WILL DO MY BEST TO LIVE UP TO THEIR EXAMPLES -- AND I BEGIN WITH AN AGENDA FOR THE FUTURE.
A FUTURE WHICH RETURNS THE JEDI ORDER TO ITS TRUE MISSION -- PREVENTING THE RETURN OF THE SITH!

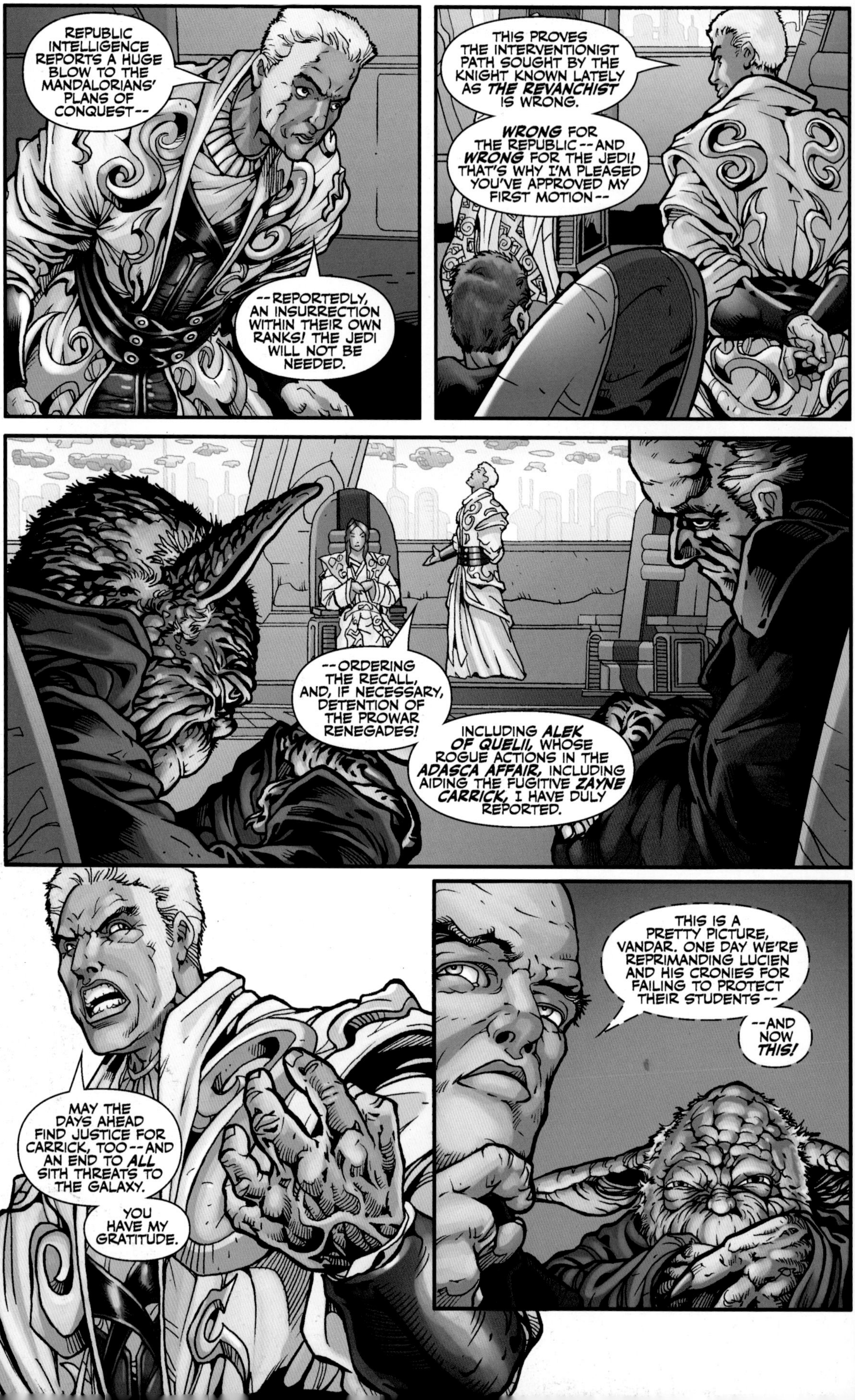
REPUBLIC INTELLIGENCE REPORTS A HUGE BLOW TO THE MANDALORIANS' PLANS OF CONQUEST--
--REPORTEDLY, AN INSURRECTION WITHIN THEIR OWN RANKS! THE JEDI WILL NOT BE NEEDED.
THIS PROVES THE INTERVENTIONIST PATH SOUGHT BY THE KNIGHT KNOWN LATELY AS THE REVANCHIST IS WRONG.
WRONG FOR THE REPUBLIC--AND WRONG FOR THE JEDI! THAT'S WHY I'M PLEASED YOU'VE APPROVED MY FIRST MOTION--
--ORDERING THE RECALL, AND, IF NECESSARY, DETENTION OF THE PROWAR RENEGADES!
INCLUDING ALEK OF QUELII, WHOSE ROGUE ACTIONS IN THE ADASCA AFFAIR, INCLUDING AIDING THE FUGITIVE ZAYNE CARRICK, I HAVE DULY REPORTED.
MAY THE DAYS AHEAD FIND JUSTICE FOR CARRICK, TOO--AND AN END TO ALL SITH THREATS TO THE GALAXY.
YOU HAVE MY GRATITUDE.
THIS IS A PRETTY PICTURE, VANDAR. ONE DAY WE'RE REPRIMANDING LUCIEN AND HIS CRONIES FOR FAILING TO PROTECT THEIR STUDENTS--
--AND NOW THIS!

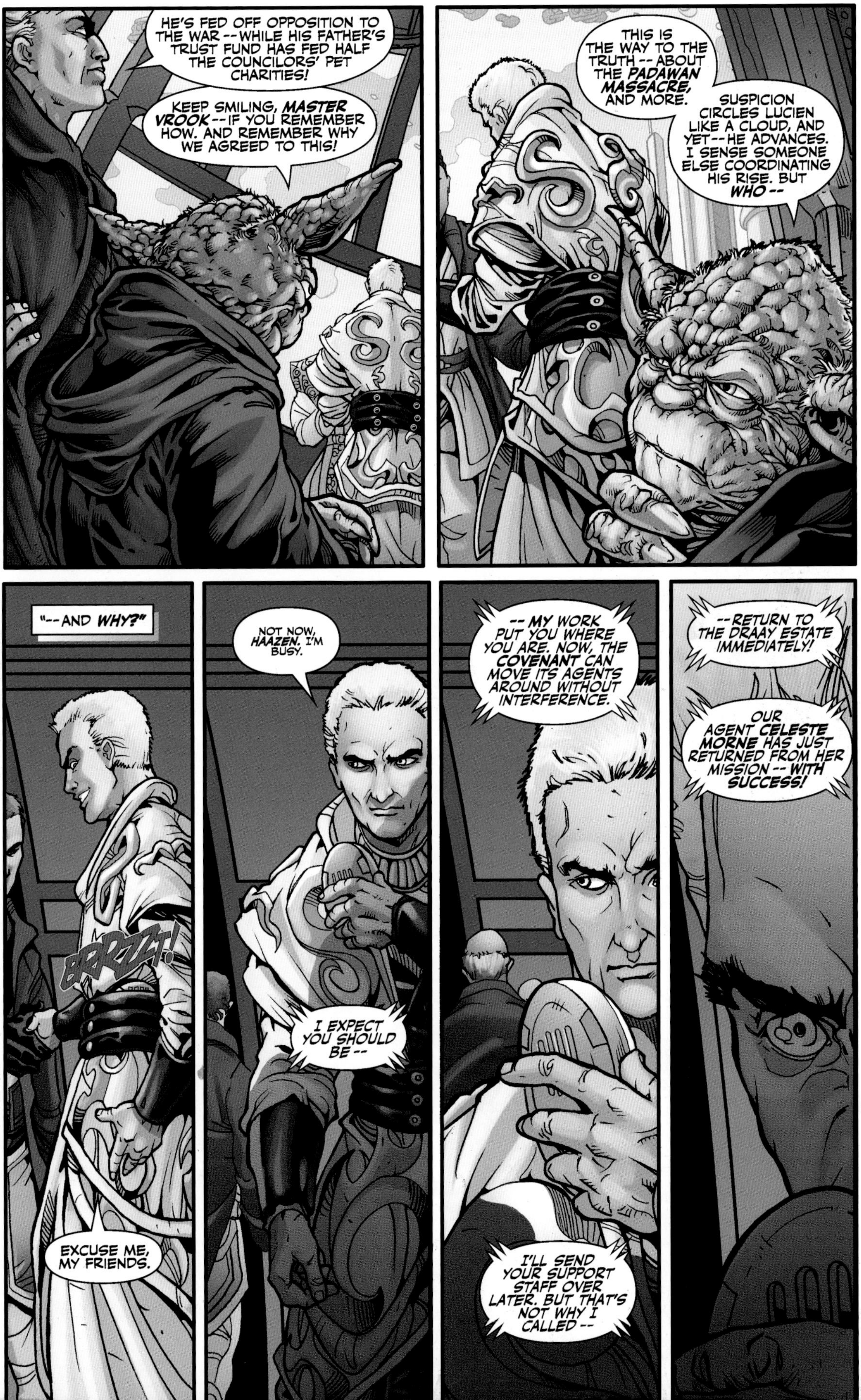
HE'S FED OFF OPPOSITION TO THE WAR--WHILE HIS FATHER'S TRUST FUND HAS FED HALF THE COUNCILORS' PET CHARITIES!
KEEP SMILING, MASTER VROOK--IF YOU REMEMBER HOW. AND REMEMBER WHY WE AGREED TO THIS!
THIS IS THE WAY TO THE TRUTH--ABOUT THE PADAWAN MASSACRE, AND MORE.
SUSPICION CIRCLES LUCIEN LIKE A CLOUD, AND YET--HE ADVANCES. I SENSE SOMEONE ELSE COORDINATING HIS RISE. BUT WHO--
"--AND WHY?"
BRRZZZT!
EXCUSE ME, MY FRIENDS.
NOT NOW, HAAZEN. I'M BUSY.
I EXPECT YOU SHOULD BE--
--MY WORK PUT YOU WHERE YOU ARE. NOW, THE COVENANT CAN MOVE ITS AGENTS AROUND WITHOUT INTERFERENCE.
I'LL SEND YOUR SUPPORT STAFF OVER LATER. BUT THAT'S NOT WHY I CALLED--
--RETURN TO THE DRAAY ESTATE IMMEDIATELY!
OUR AGENT CELESTE MORNE HAS JUST RETURNED FROM HER MISSION--WITH SUCCESS!

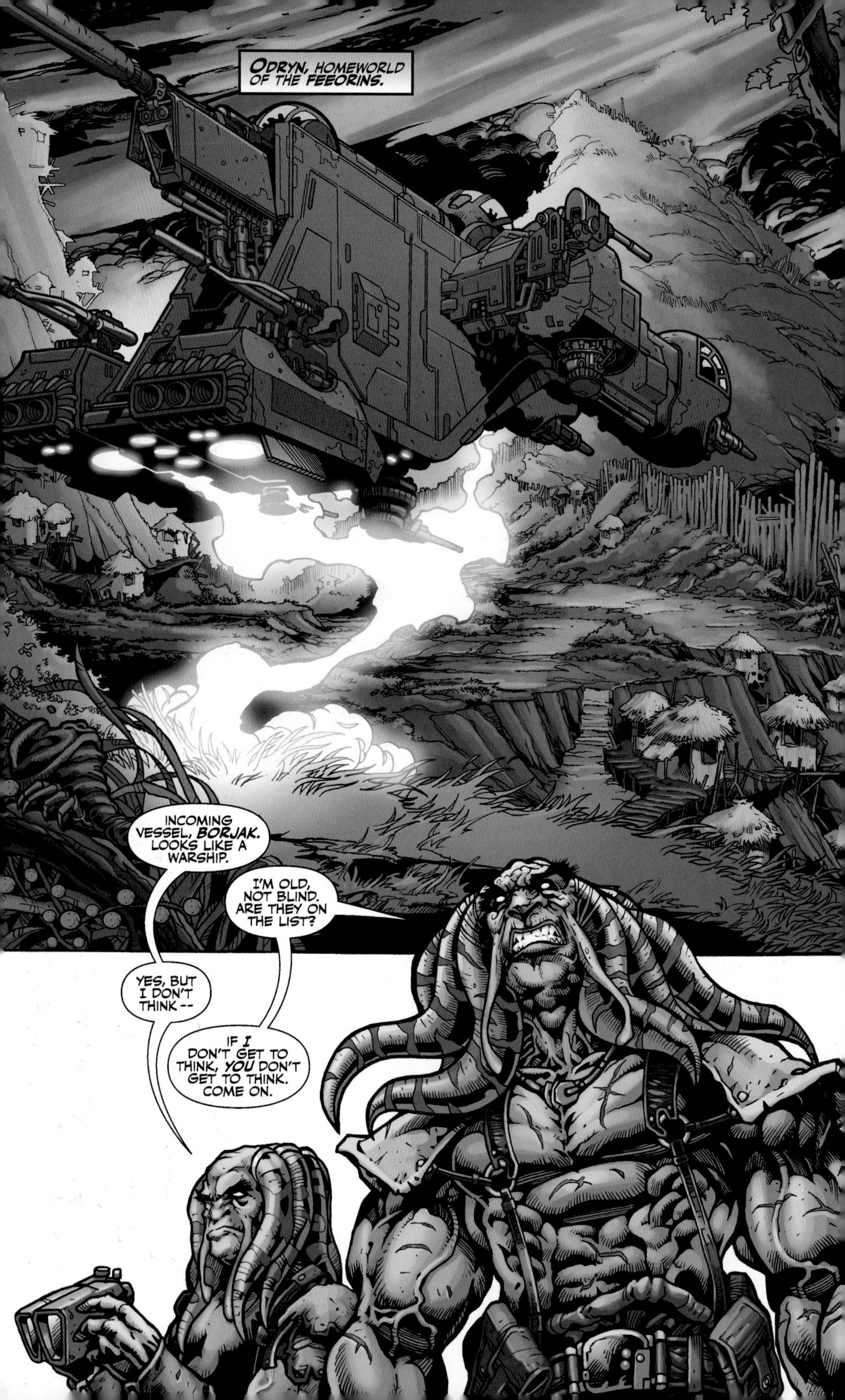
ODRYN, HOMEWORLD OF THE FEEORINS.
INCOMING VESSEL, BORJAK. LOOKS LIKE A WARSHIP.
I'M OLD, NOT BLIND. ARE THEY ON THE LIST?
YES, BUT I DON'T THINK--
IF I DON'T GET TO THINK, YOU DON'T GET TO THINK. COME ON.

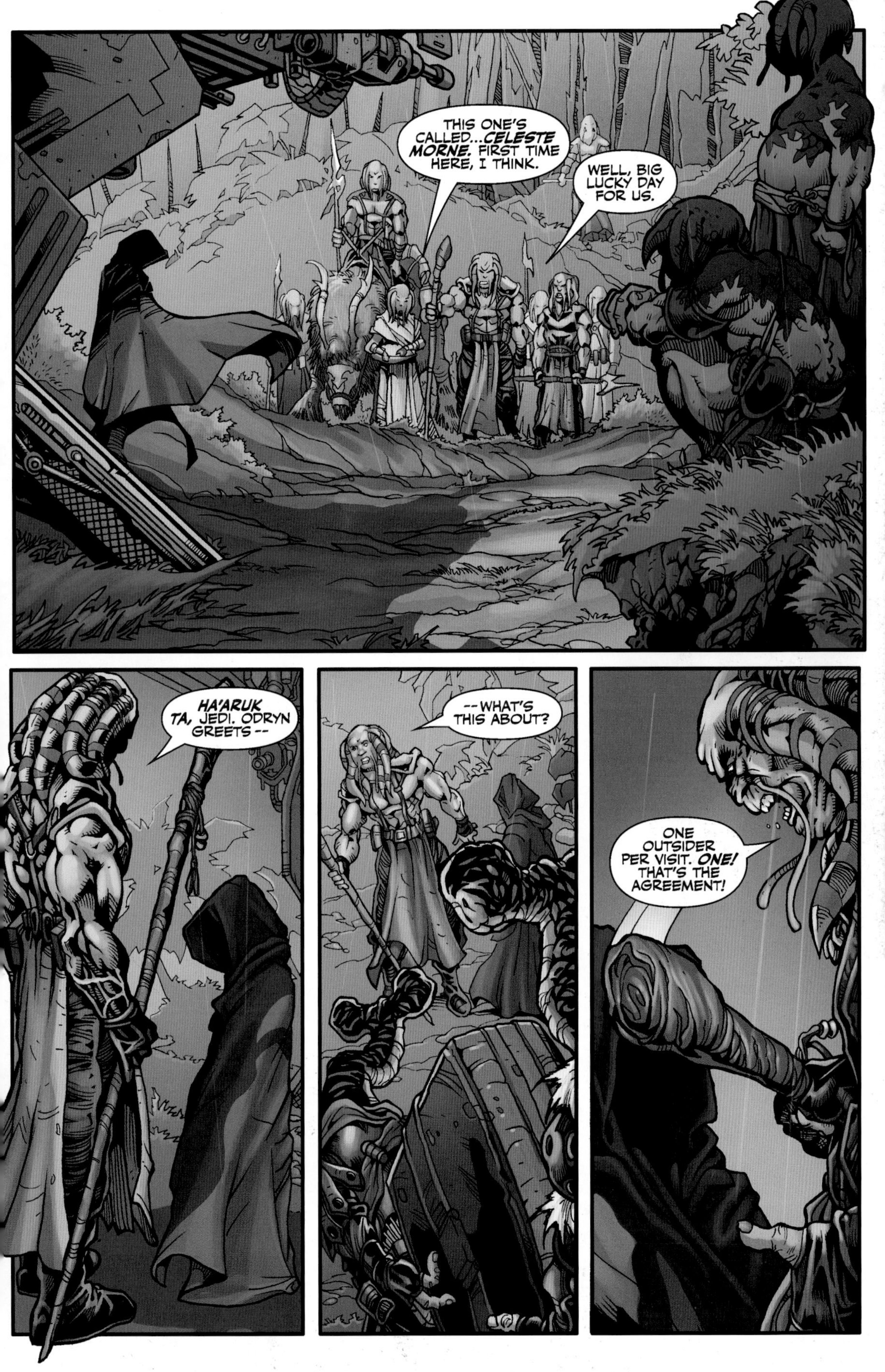
THIS ONE'S CALLED...CELESTE MORNE. FIRST TIME HERE, I THINK.
WELL, BIG LUCKY DAY FOR US.
HA'ARUK TA, JEDI. ODRYN GREETS--
--WHAT'S THIS ABOUT?
ONE OUTSIDER PER VISIT. ONE! THAT'S THE AGREEMENT!

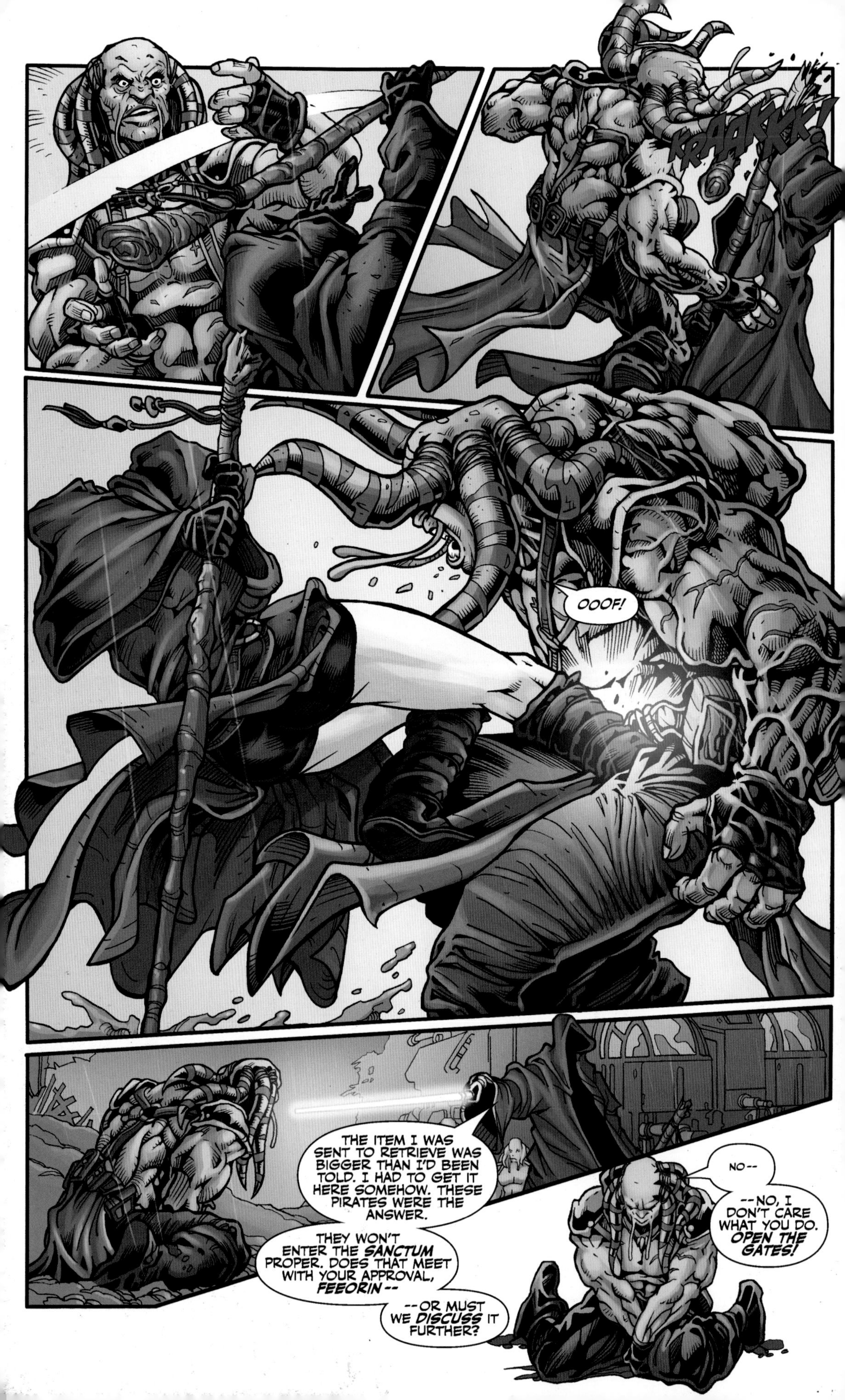
KRAAKKK!
OOOF!
THE ITEM I WAS SENT TO RETRIEVE WAS BIGGER THAN I'D BEEN TOLD. I HAD TO GET IT HERE SOMEHOW. THESE PIRATES WERE THE ANSWER.
THEY WON'T ENTER THE SANCTUM PROPER. DOES THAT MEET WITH YOUR APPROVAL, FEEORIN--
--OR MUST WE DISCUSS IT FURTHER?
NO--
--NO, I DON'T CARE WHAT YOU DO. OPEN THE GATES!

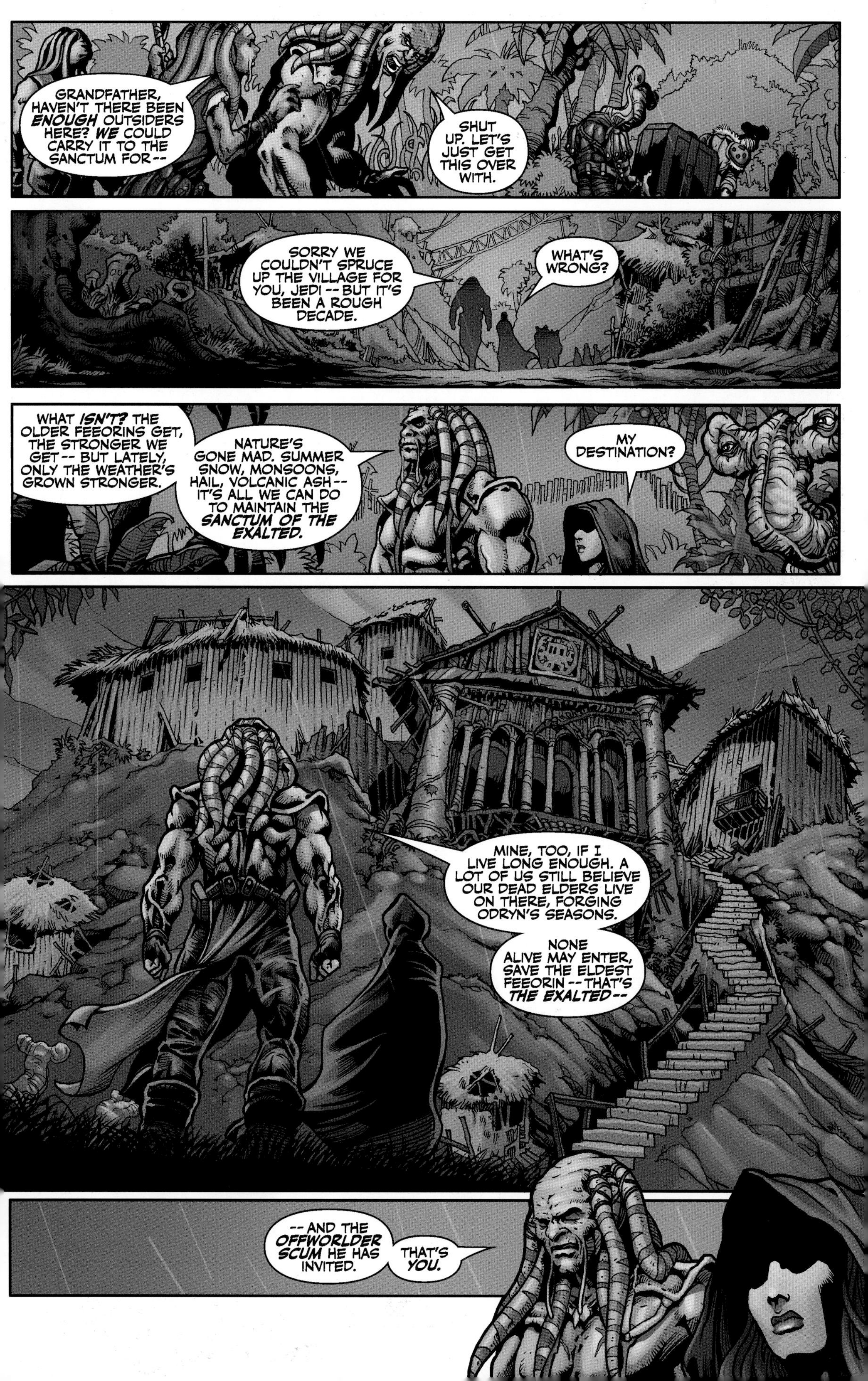
GRANDFATHER, HAVEN'T THERE BEEN ENOUGH OUTSIDERS HERE? WE COULD CARRY IT TO THE SANCTUM FOR--
SHUT UP. LET'S JUST GET THIS OVER WITH.
SORRY WE COULDN'T SPRUCE UP THE VILLAGE FOR YOU, JEDI--BUT IT'S BEEN A ROUGH DECADE.
WHAT'S WRONG?
WHAT ISN'T? THE OLDER FEEORINS GET, THE STRONGER WE GET--BUT LATELY, ONLY THE WEATHER'S GROWN STRONGER.
NATURE'S GONE MAD. SUMMER SNOW, MONSOONS, HAIL, VOLCANIC ASH--IT'S ALL WE CAN DO TO MAINTAIN THE SANCTUM OF THE EXALTED.
MY DESTINATION?
MINE, TOO, IF I LIVE LONG ENOUGH. A LOT OF US STILL BELIEVE OUR DEAD ELDERS LIVE ON THERE, FORGING ODRYN'S SEASONS.
NONE ALIVE MAY ENTER, SAVE THE ELDEST FEEORIN--THAT'S THE EXALTED--
--AND THE OFFWORLDER SCUM HE HAS INVITED.
THAT'S YOU.

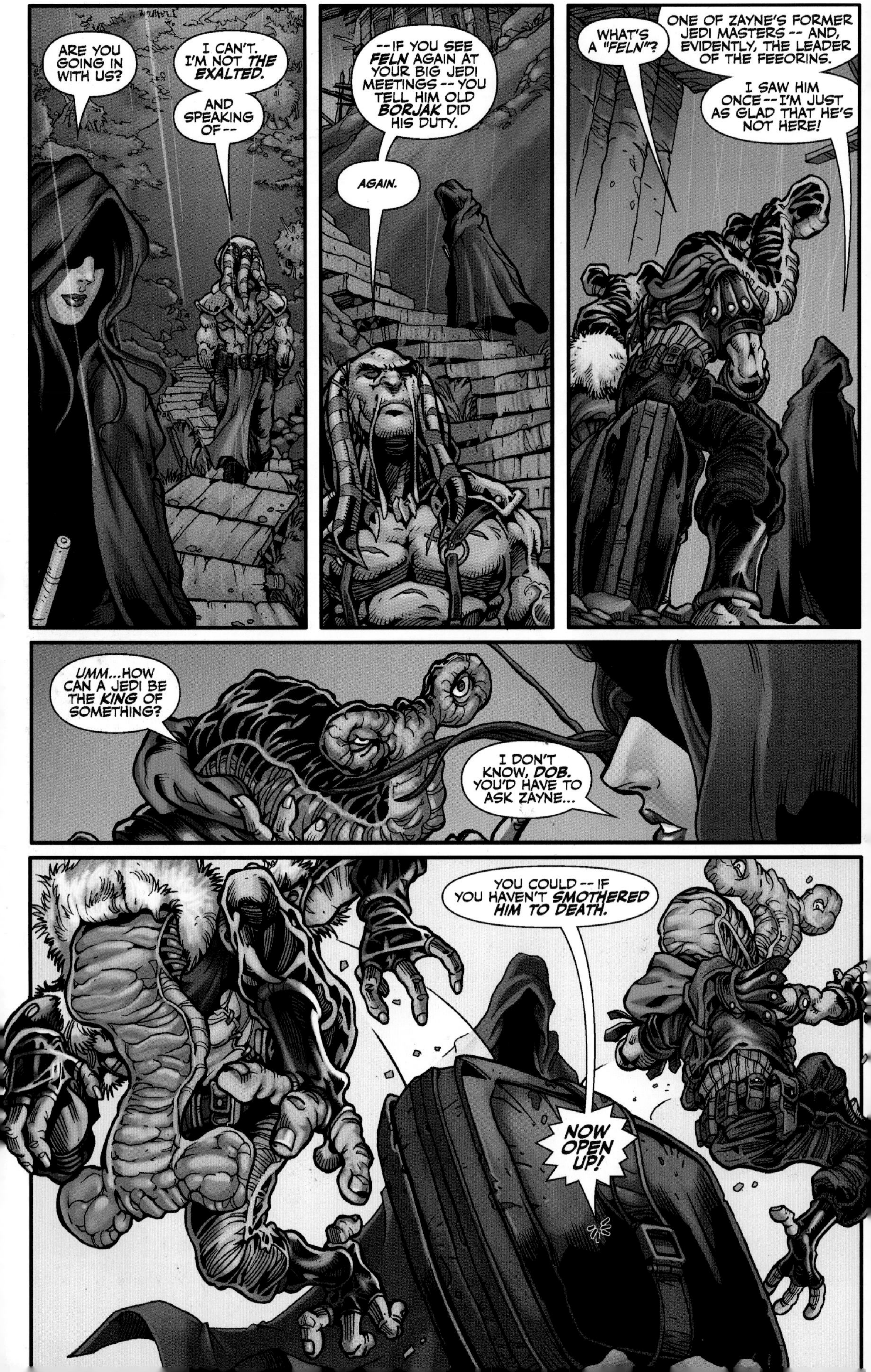
ARE YOU GOING IN WITH US?
I CAN'T. I'M NOT THE EXALTED.
AND SPEAKING OF--
--IF YOU SEE FELN AGAIN AT YOUR BIG JEDI MEETINGS--YOU TELL HIM OLD BORJAK DID HIS DUTY.
AGAIN.
WHAT'S A "FELN"?
ONE OF ZAYNE'S FORMER JEDI MASTERS--AND, EVIDENTLY, THE LEADER OF THE FEEORINS.
I SAW HIM ONCE--I'M JUST AS GLAD THAT HE'S NOT HERE!
UMM...HOW CAN A JEDI BE THE KING OF SOMETHING?
I DON'T KNOW, DOB. YOU'D HAVE TO ASK ZAYNE...
YOU COULD--IF YOU HAVEN'T SMOTHERED HIM TO DEATH.
NOW OPEN UP!

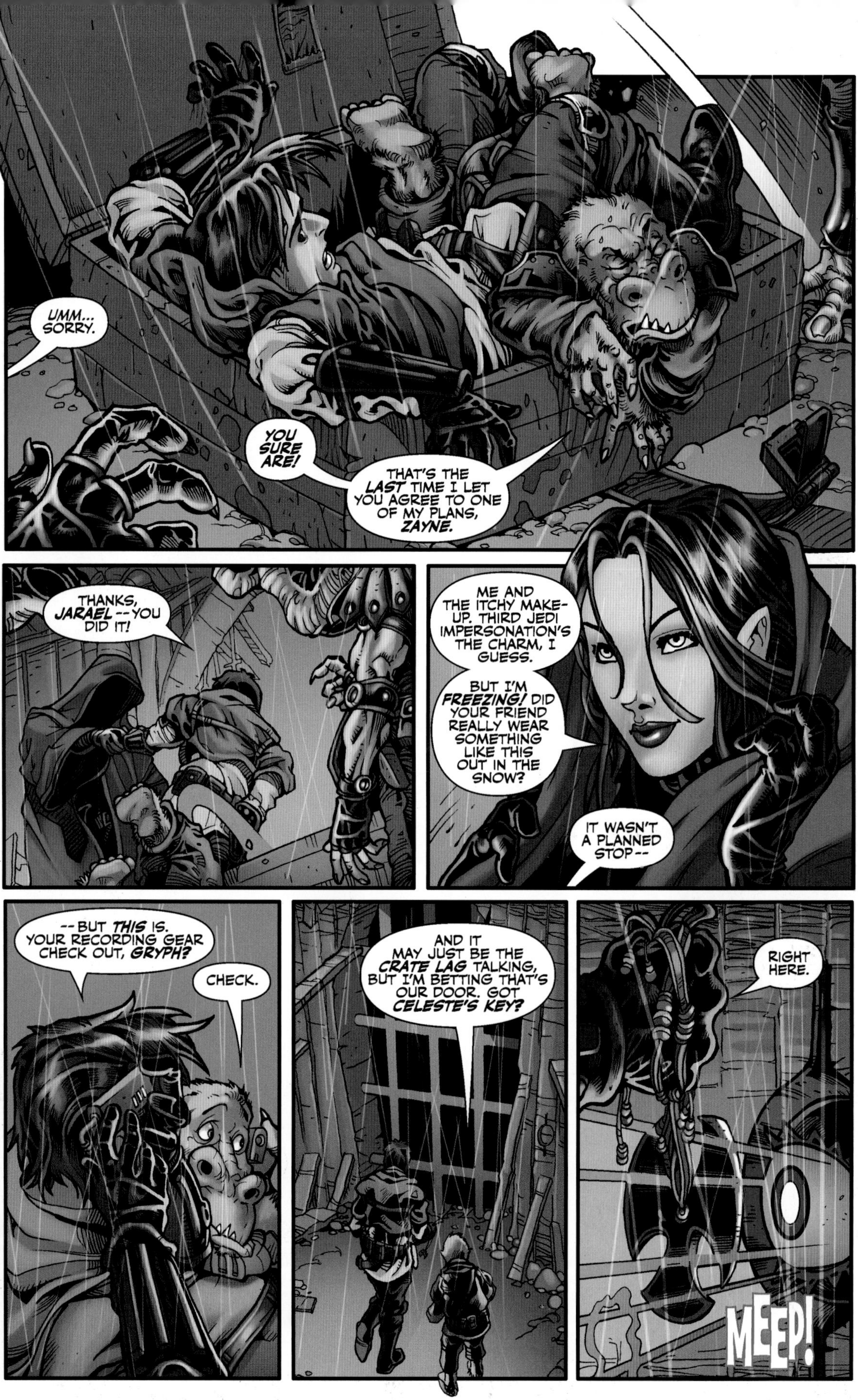
UMM... SORRY.
YOU SURE ARE!
THAT'S THE LAST TIME I LET YOU AGREE TO ONE OF MY PLANS, ZAYNE.
THANKS, JARAEL--YOU DID IT!
ME AND THE ITCHY MAKE-UP. THIRD JEDI IMPERSONATION'S THE CHARM, I GUESS.
BUT I'M FREEZING! DID YOUR FRIEND REALLY WEAR SOMETHING LIKE THIS OUT IN THE SNOW?
IT WASN'T A PLANNED STOP--
--BUT THIS IS. YOUR RECORDING GEAR CHECK OUT, GRYPH?
CHECK.
AND IT MAY JUST BE THE CRATE LAG TALKING, BUT I'M BETTING THAT'S OUR DOOR. GOT CELESTE'S KEY?
RIGHT HERE.
MEEP!

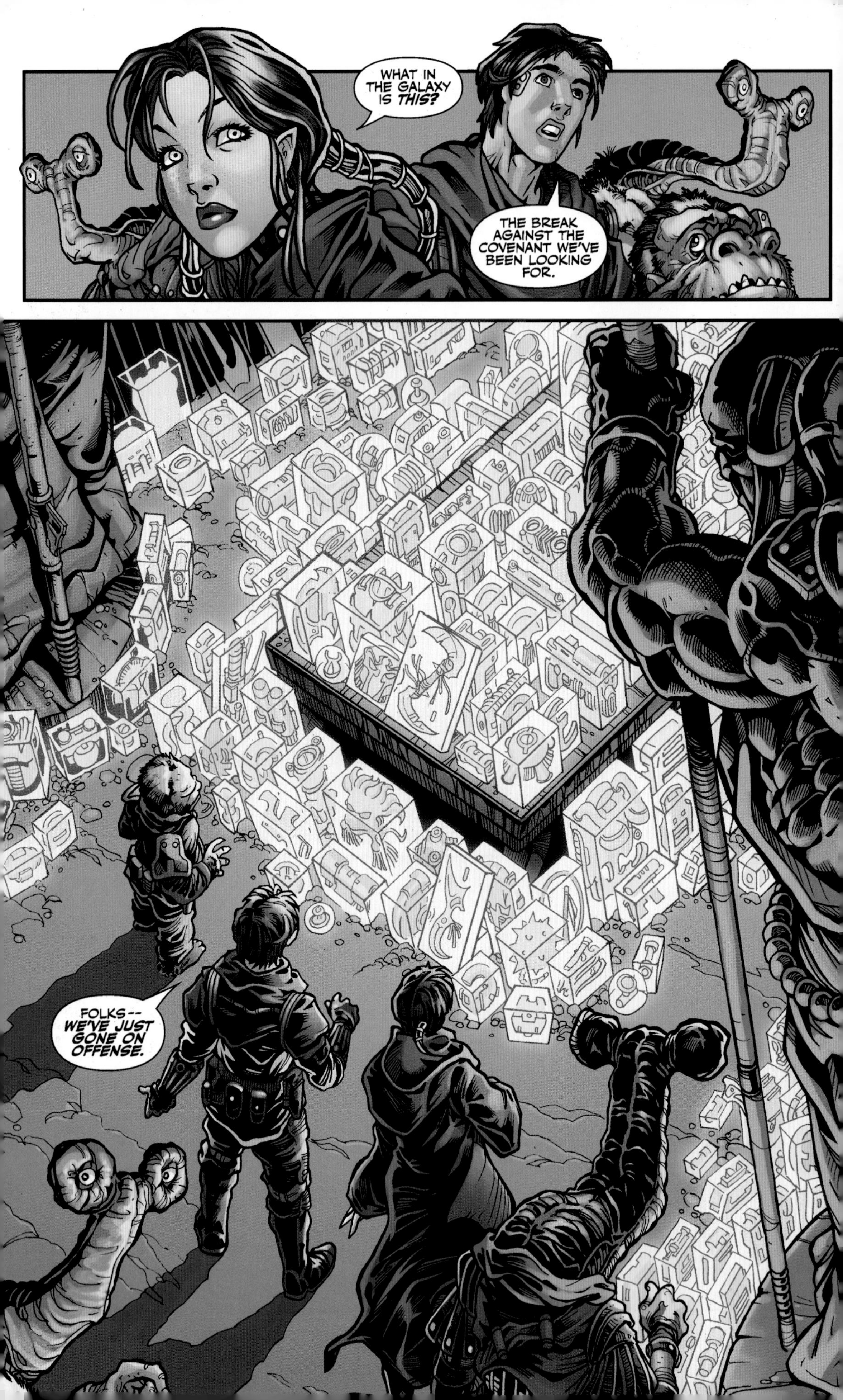
WHAT IN THE GALAXY IS *THIS?*
THE BREAK AGAINST THE COVENANT WE'VE BEEN LOOKING FOR.
FOLKS-- ***WE'VE JUST GONE ON OFFENSE.***

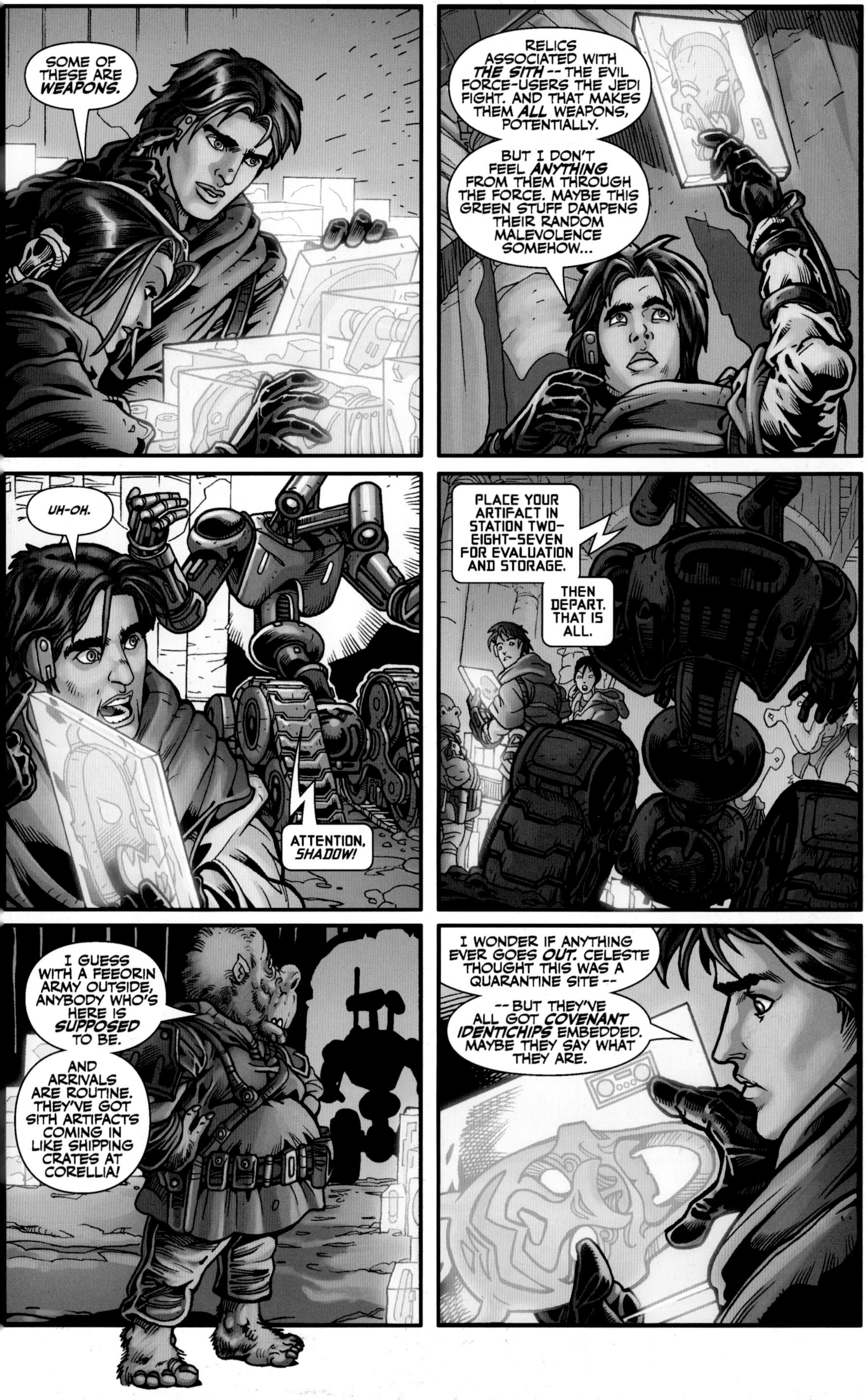
SOME OF THESE ARE *WEAPONS.*
RELICS ASSOCIATED WITH *THE SITH* -- THE EVIL FORCE-USERS THE JEDI FIGHT. AND THAT MAKES THEM *ALL* WEAPONS, POTENTIALLY.
BUT I DON'T FEEL *ANYTHING* FROM THEM THROUGH THE FORCE. MAYBE THIS GREEN STUFF DAMPENS THEIR RANDOM MALEVOLENCE SOMEHOW...
UH-OH.
ATTENTION, *SHADOW!*
PLACE YOUR ARTIFACT IN STATION TWO-EIGHT-SEVEN FOR EVALUATION AND STORAGE.
THEN DEPART. THAT IS ALL.
I GUESS WITH A FEEORIN ARMY OUTSIDE, ANYBODY WHO'S HERE IS *SUPPOSED* TO BE.
AND ARRIVALS ARE ROUTINE. THEY'VE GOT SITH ARTIFACTS COMING IN LIKE SHIPPING CRATES AT CORELLIA!
I WONDER IF ANYTHING EVER GOES *OUT.* CELESTE THOUGHT THIS WAS A QUARANTINE SITE --
-- BUT THEY'VE ALL GOT *COVENANT IDENTICHIPS* EMBEDDED. MAYBE THEY SAY WHAT THEY ARE.

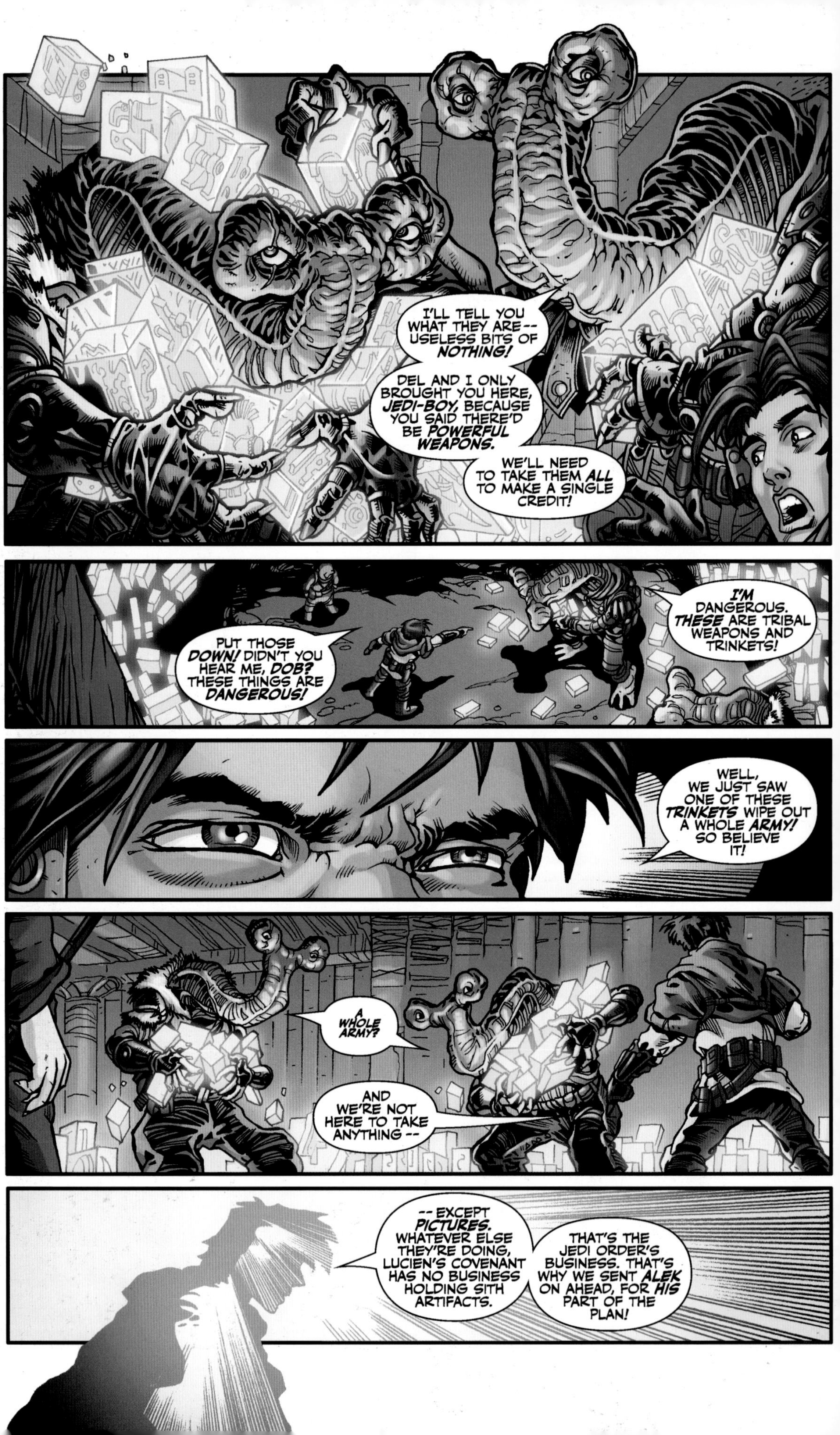

I'LL TELL YOU WHAT THEY ARE-- USELESS BITS OF NOTHING!
DEL AND I ONLY BROUGHT YOU HERE, JEDI-BOY, BECAUSE YOU SAID THERE'D BE POWERFUL WEAPONS.
WE'LL NEED TO TAKE THEM ALL TO MAKE A SINGLE CREDIT!
PUT THOSE DOWN! DIDN'T YOU HEAR ME, DOB? THESE THINGS ARE DANGEROUS!
I'M DANGEROUS. THESE ARE TRIBAL WEAPONS AND TRINKETS!
WELL, WE JUST SAW ONE OF THESE TRINKETS WIPE OUT A WHOLE ARMY! SO BELIEVE IT!
A WHOLE ARMY?
AND WE'RE NOT HERE TO TAKE ANYTHING --
-- EXCEPT PICTURES. WHATEVER ELSE THEY'RE DOING, LUCIEN'S COVENANT HAS NO BUSINESS HOLDING SITH ARTIFACTS.
THAT'S THE JEDI ORDER'S BUSINESS. THAT'S WHY WE SENT ALEK ON AHEAD, FOR HIS PART OF THE PLAN!

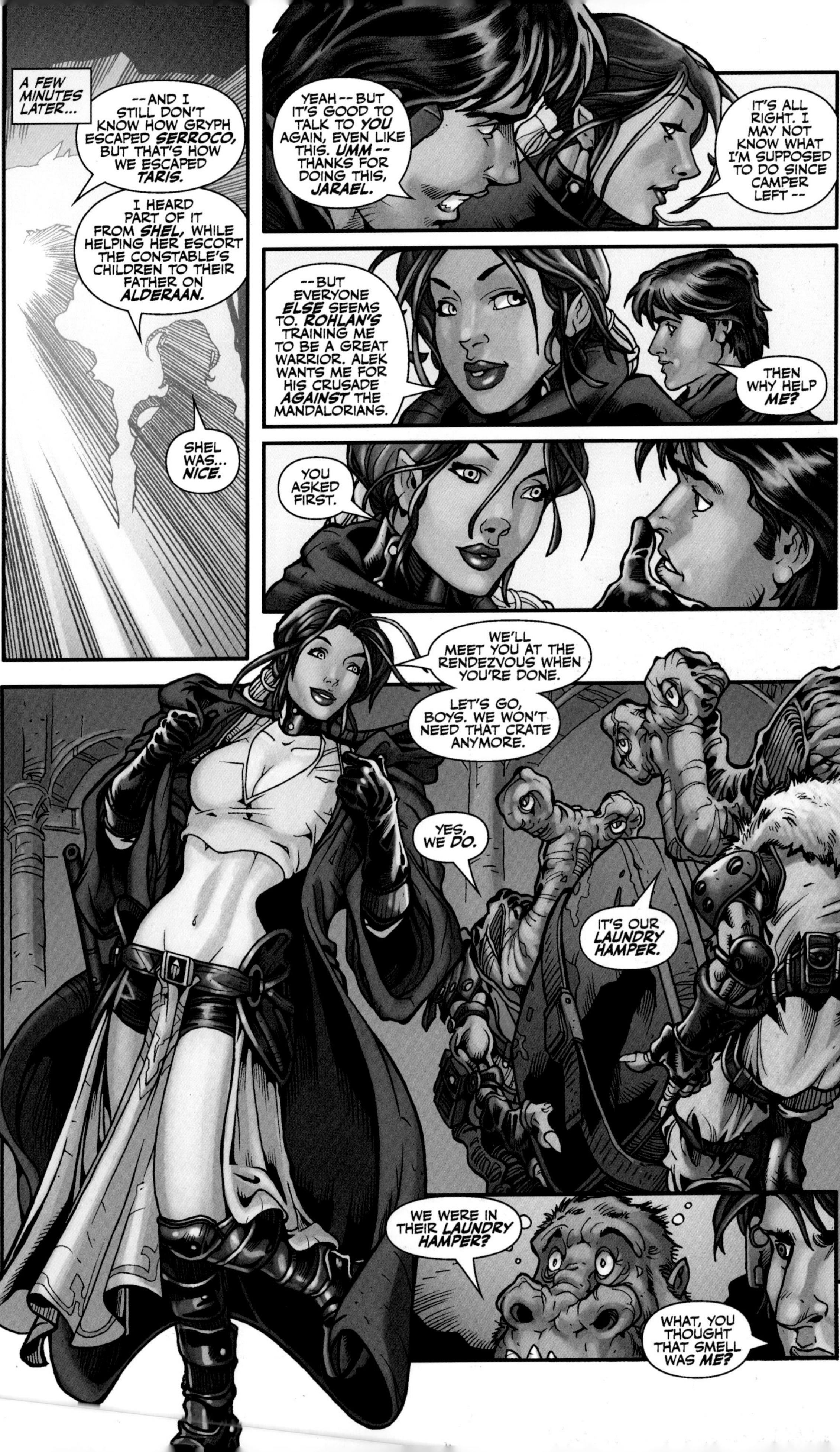
A FEW MINUTES LATER...
--AND I STILL DON'T KNOW HOW GRYPH ESCAPED SERROCO, BUT THAT'S HOW WE ESCAPED TARIS.
I HEARD PART OF IT FROM SHEL, WHILE HELPING HER ESCORT THE CONSTABLE'S CHILDREN TO THEIR FATHER ON ALDERAAN.
SHEL WAS... NICE.
YEAH-- BUT IT'S GOOD TO TALK TO YOU AGAIN, EVEN LIKE THIS. UMM -- THANKS FOR DOING THIS, JARAEL.
IT'S ALL RIGHT. I MAY NOT KNOW WHAT I'M SUPPOSED TO DO SINCE CAMPER LEFT --
--BUT EVERYONE ELSE SEEMS TO. ROHLAN'S TRAINING ME TO BE A GREAT WARRIOR. ALEK WANTS ME FOR HIS CRUSADE AGAINST THE MANDALORIANS.
THEN WHY HELP ME?
YOU ASKED FIRST.
WE'LL MEET YOU AT THE RENDEZVOUS WHEN YOU'RE DONE.
LET'S GO, BOYS. WE WON'T NEED THAT CRATE ANYMORE.
YES, WE DO.
IT'S OUR LAUNDRY HAMPER.
WE WERE IN THEIR LAUNDRY HAMPER?
WHAT, YOU THOUGHT THAT SMELL WAS ME?

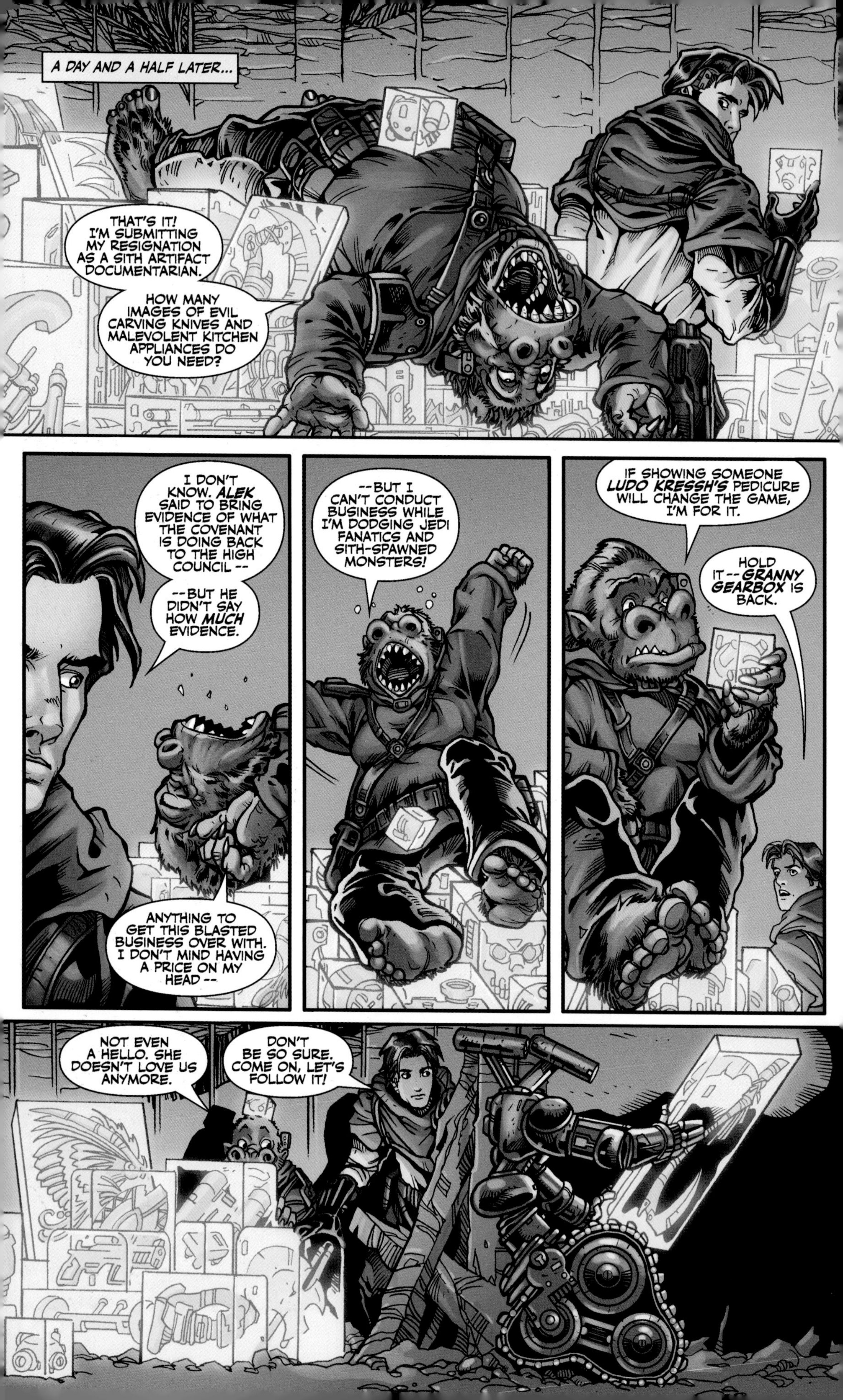
A DAY AND A HALF LATER...
THAT'S IT! I'M SUBMITTING MY RESIGNATION AS A SITH ARTIFACT DOCUMENTARIAN.
HOW MANY IMAGES OF EVIL CARVING KNIVES AND MALEVOLENT KITCHEN APPLIANCES DO YOU NEED?
I DON'T KNOW. ALEK SAID TO BRING EVIDENCE OF WHAT THE COVENANT IS DOING BACK TO THE HIGH COUNCIL --
--BUT HE DIDN'T SAY HOW MUCH EVIDENCE.
ANYTHING TO GET THIS BLASTED BUSINESS OVER WITH. I DON'T MIND HAVING A PRICE ON MY HEAD --
--BUT I CAN'T CONDUCT BUSINESS WHILE I'M DODGING JEDI FANATICS AND SITH-SPAWNED MONSTERS!
IF SHOWING SOMEONE LUDO KRESSH'S PEDICURE WILL CHANGE THE GAME, I'M FOR IT.
HOLD IT--GRANNY GEARBOX IS BACK.
NOT EVEN A HELLO. SHE DOESN'T LOVE US ANYMORE.
DON'T BE SO SURE. COME ON, LET'S FOLLOW IT!

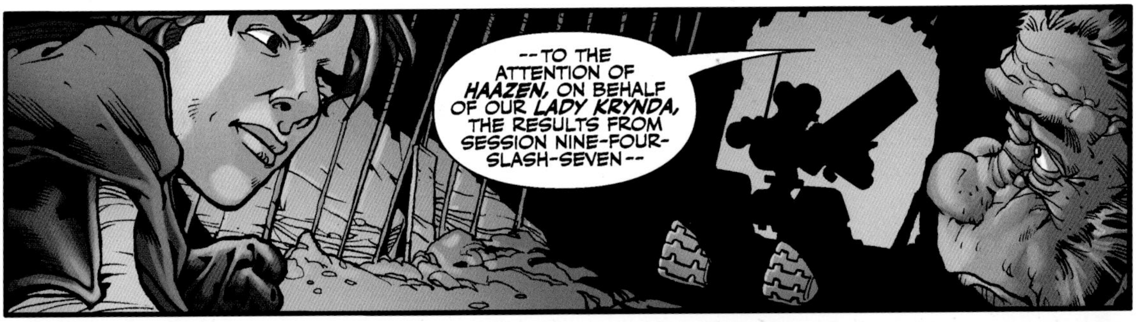
--TO THE ATTENTION OF HAAZEN, ON BEHALF OF OUR LADY KRYNDA, THE RESULTS FROM SESSION NINE-FOUR-SLASH-SEVEN--

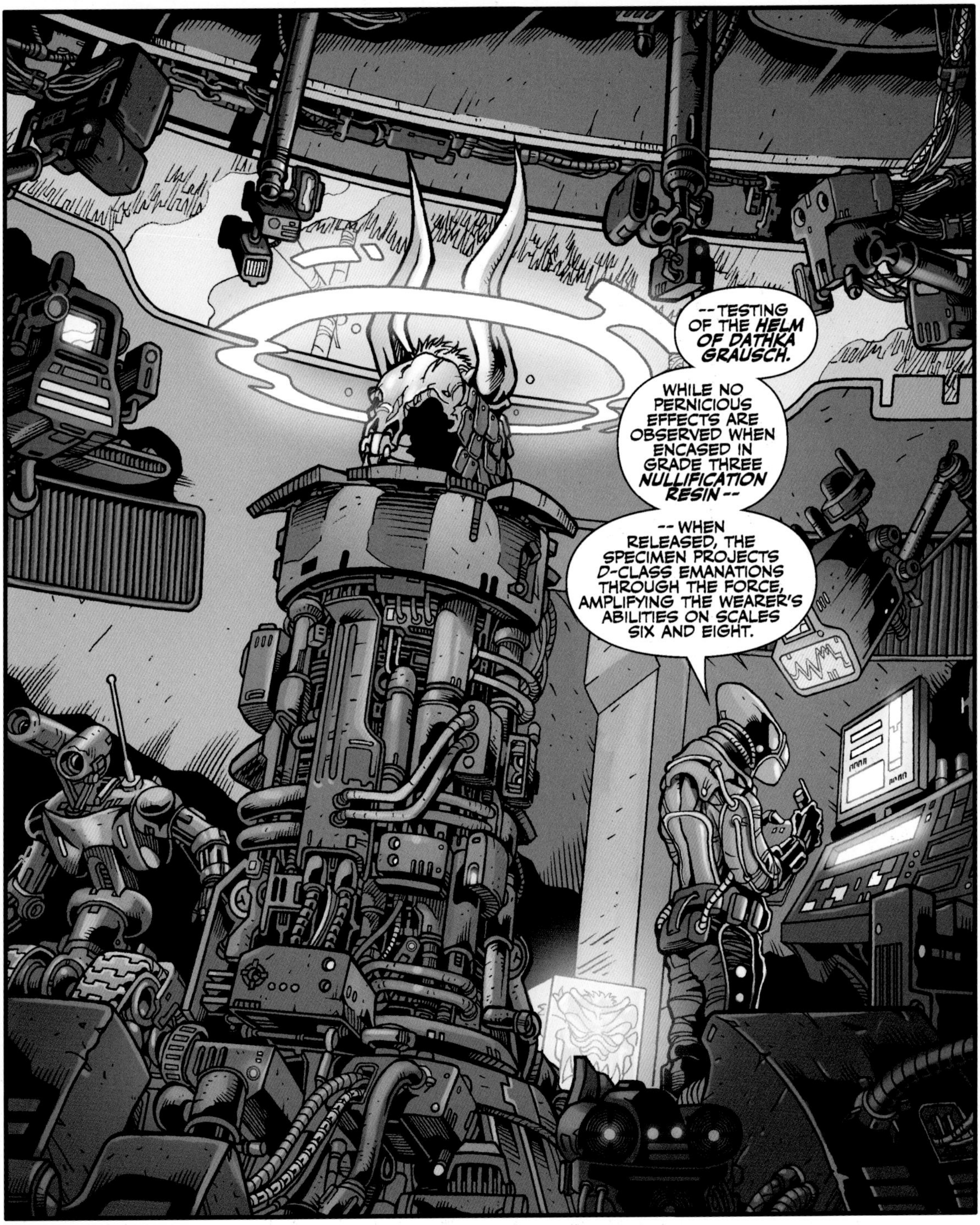
--TESTING OF THE HELM OF DATHKA GRAUSCH.
WHILE NO PERNICIOUS EFFECTS ARE OBSERVED WHEN ENCASED IN GRADE THREE NULLIFICATION RESIN--
--WHEN RELEASED, THE SPECIMEN PROJECTS D-CLASS EMANATIONS THROUGH THE FORCE, AMPLIFYING THE WEARER'S ABILITIES ON SCALES SIX AND EIGHT.

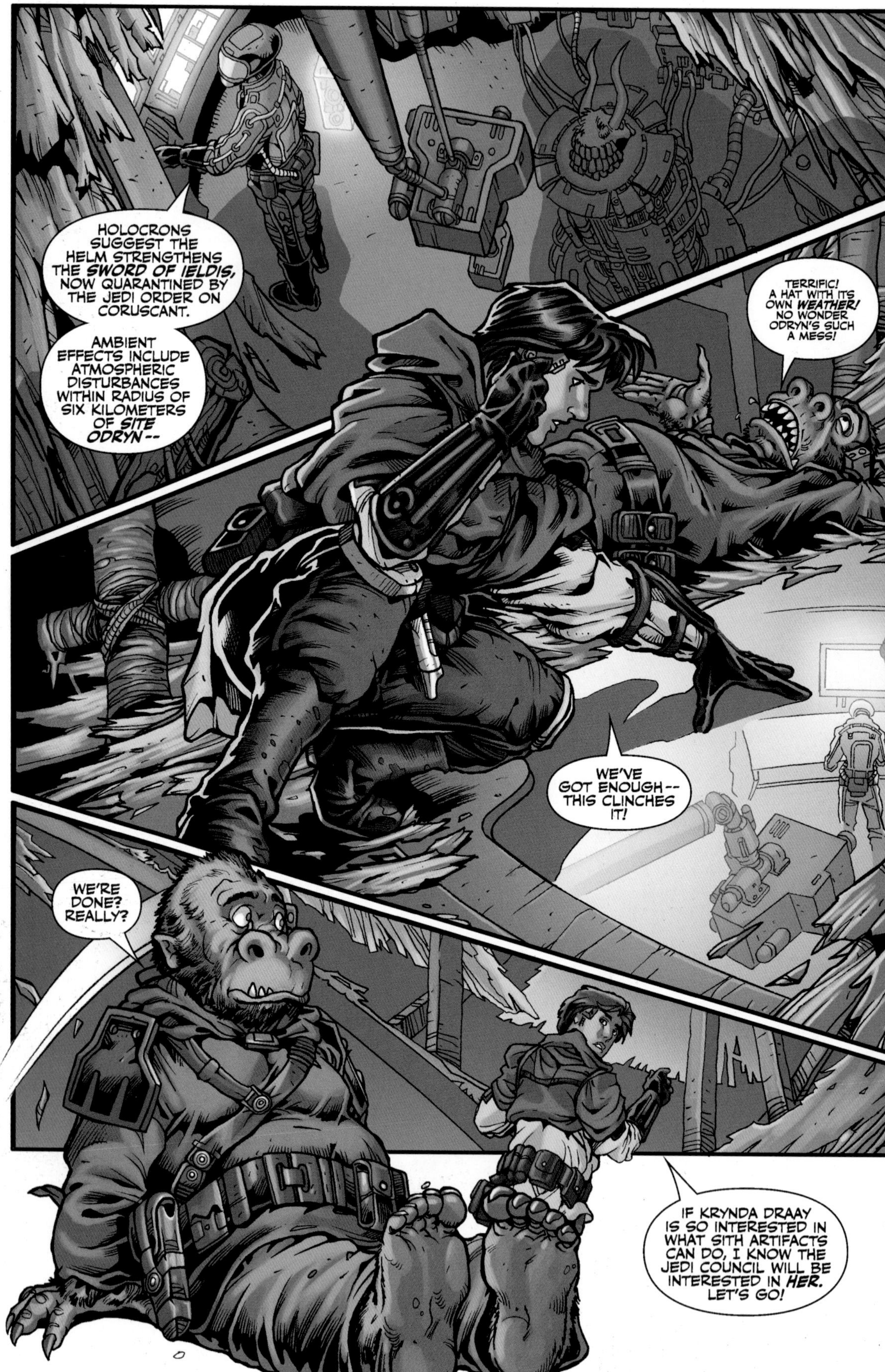

HOLOCRONS SUGGEST THE HELM STRENGTHENS THE SWORD OF IELDIS, NOW QUARANTINED BY THE JEDI ORDER ON CORUSCANT.
AMBIENT EFFECTS INCLUDE ATMOSPHERIC DISTURBANCES WITHIN RADIUS OF SIX KILOMETERS OF SITE ODRYN--
TERRIFIC! A HAT WITH ITS OWN WEATHER! NO WONDER ODRYN'S SUCH A MESS!
WE'VE GOT ENOUGH-- THIS CLINCHES IT!
WE'RE DONE? REALLY?
IF KRYNDA DRAAY IS SO INTERESTED IN WHAT SITH ARTIFACTS CAN DO, I KNOW THE JEDI COUNCIL WILL BE INTERESTED IN HER. LET'S GO!

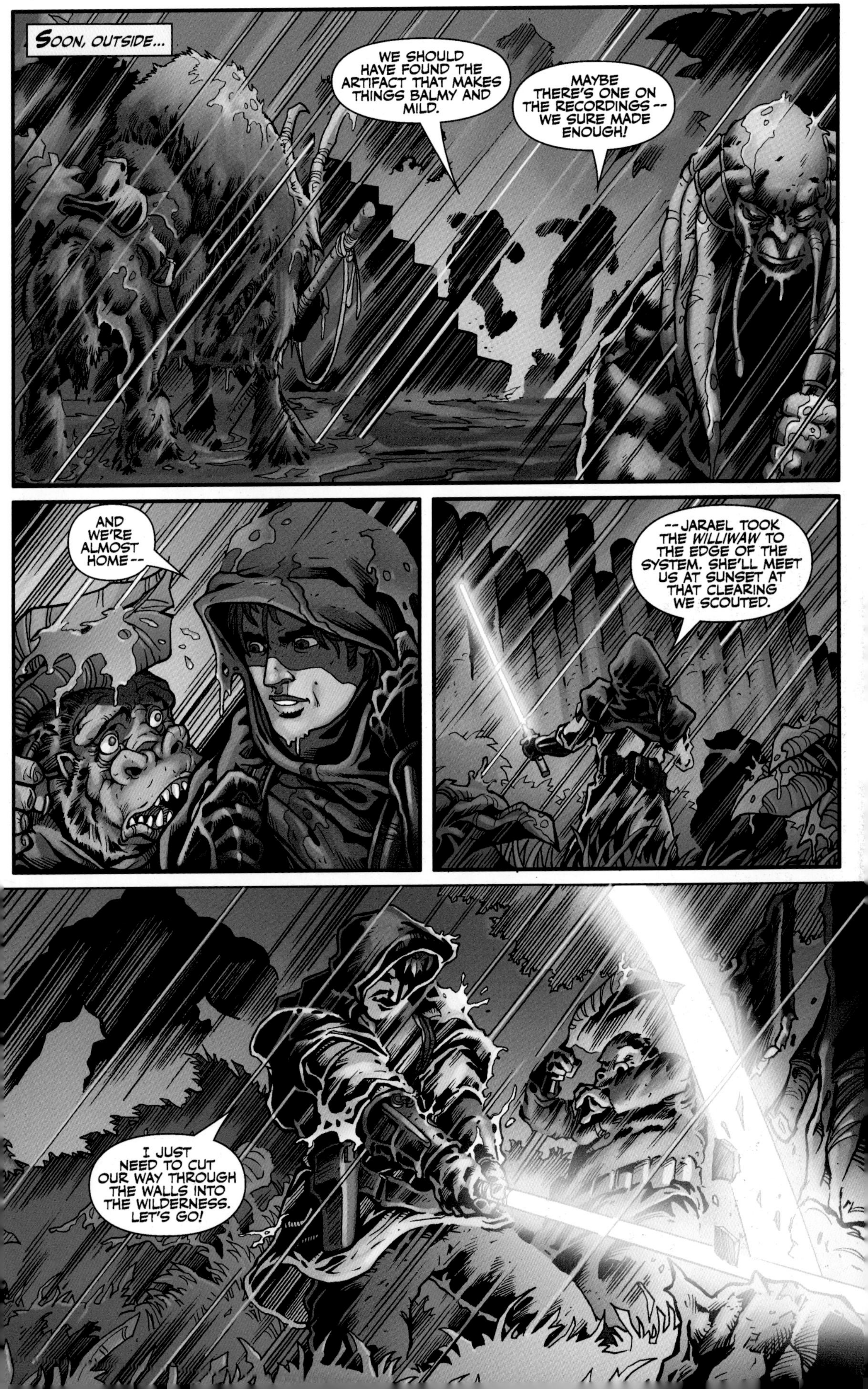
SOON, OUTSIDE...
WE SHOULD HAVE FOUND THE ARTIFACT THAT MAKES THINGS BALMY AND MILD.
MAYBE THERE'S ONE ON THE RECORDINGS -- WE SURE MADE ENOUGH!
AND WE'RE ALMOST HOME--
--JARAEL TOOK THE *WILLIWAW* TO THE EDGE OF THE SYSTEM. SHE'LL MEET US AT SUNSET AT THAT CLEARING WE SCOUTED.
I JUST NEED TO CUT OUR WAY THROUGH THE WALLS INTO THE WILDERNESS. LET'S GO!

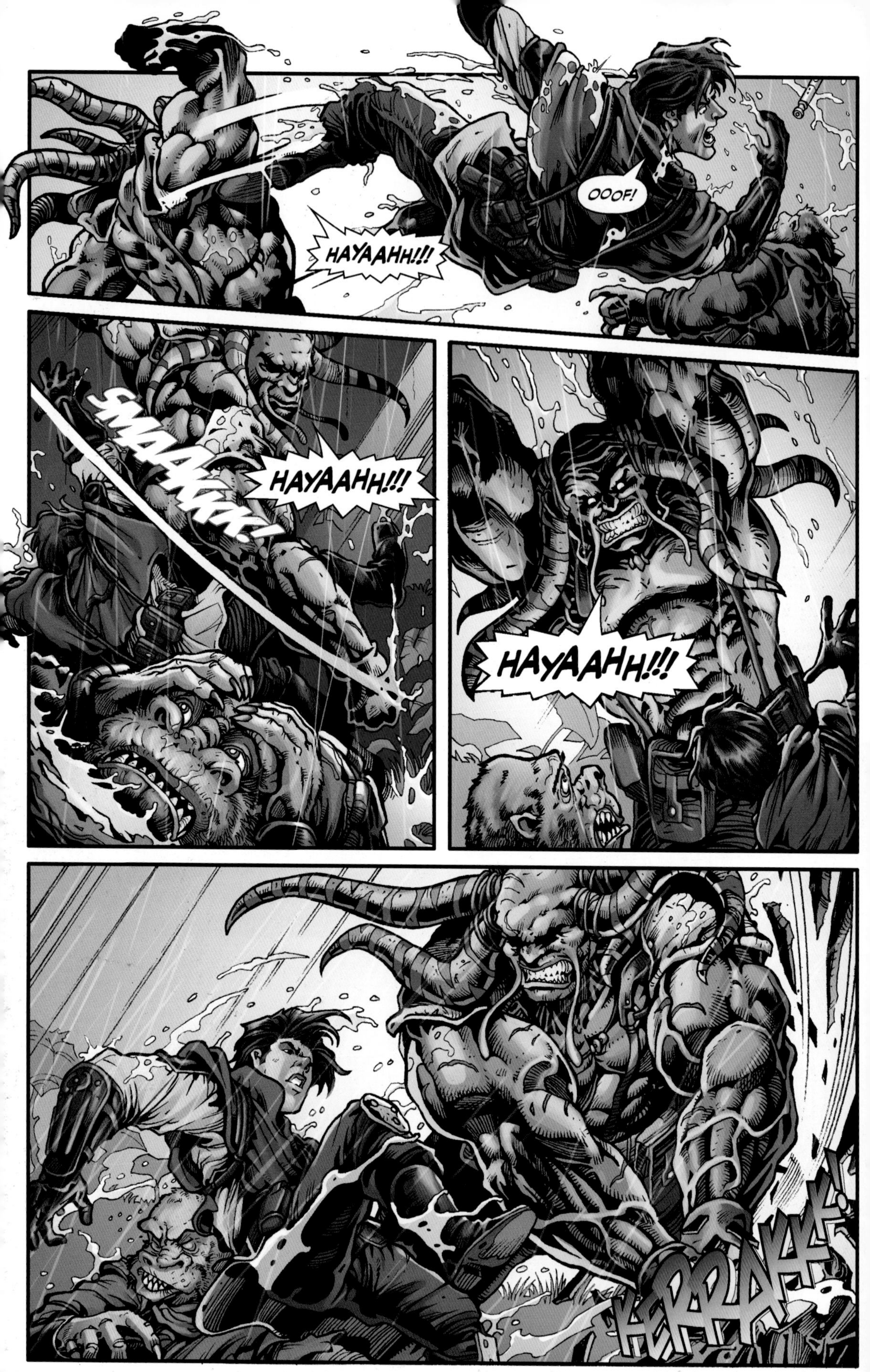

OOOF!
HAYAAHH!!!
SMAAKK!
HAYAAHH!!!
HAYAAHH!!!
KERRAK!

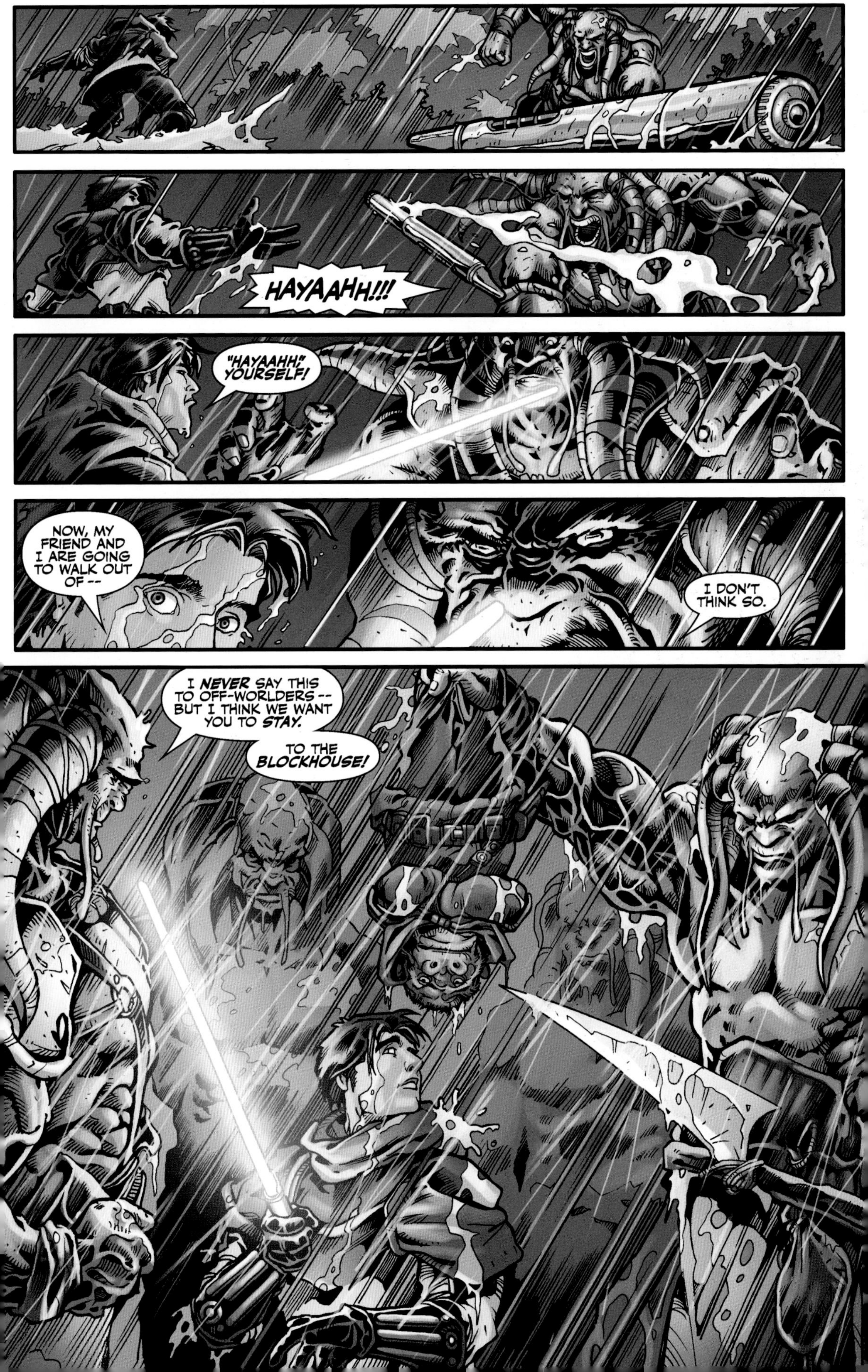
HAYAAHH!!!
"HAYAAHH," YOURSELF!
NOW, MY FRIEND AND I ARE GOING TO WALK OUT OF --
I DON'T THINK SO.
I NEVER SAY THIS TO OFF-WORLDERS -- BUT I THINK WE WANT YOU TO STAY.
TO THE BLOCKHOUSE!

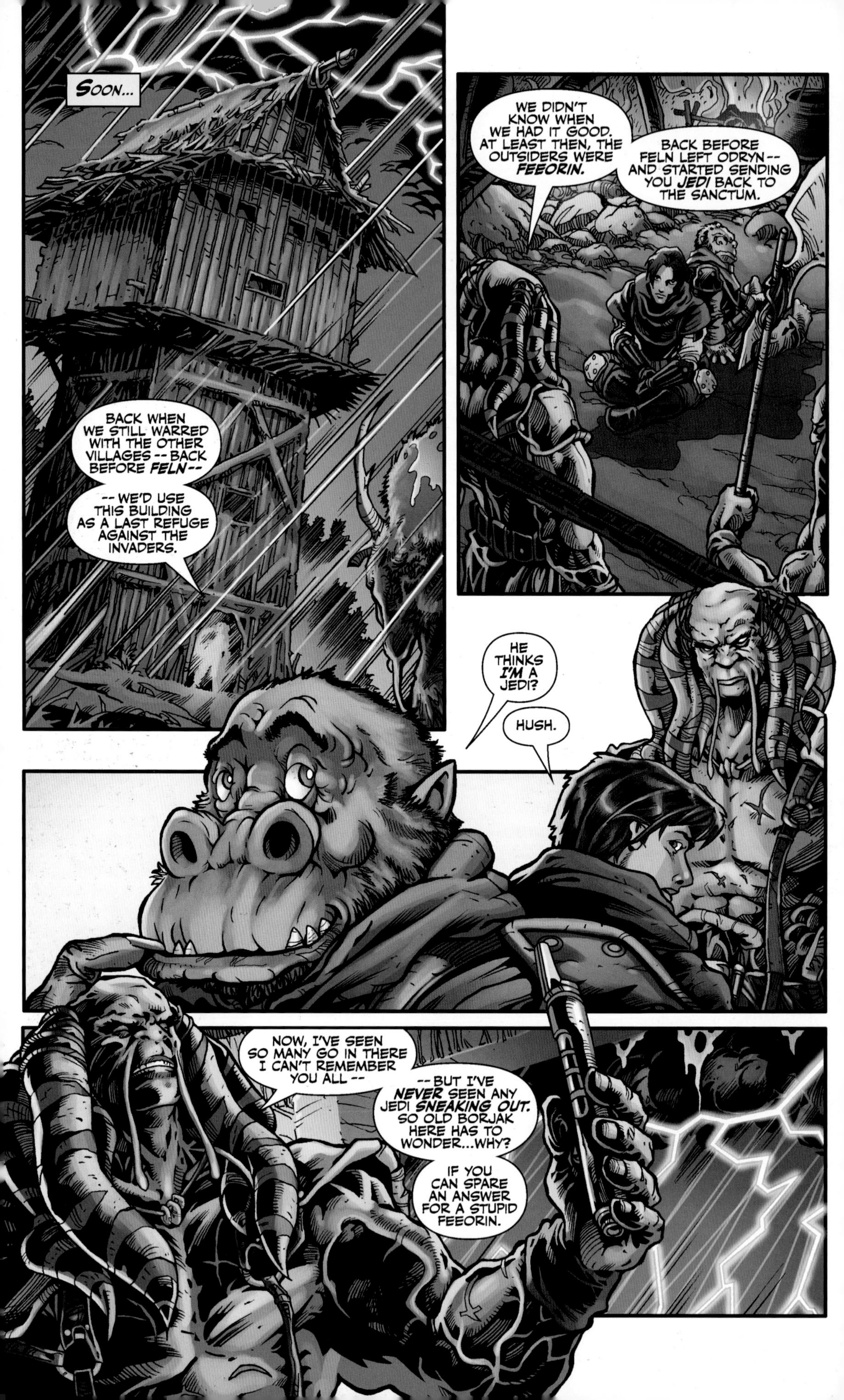
SOON...
BACK WHEN WE STILL WARRED WITH THE OTHER VILLAGES -- BACK BEFORE FELN--
-- WE'D USE THIS BUILDING AS A LAST REFUGE AGAINST THE INVADERS.
WE DIDN'T KNOW WHEN WE HAD IT GOOD. AT LEAST THEN, THE OUTSIDERS WERE FEEORIN.
BACK BEFORE FELN LEFT ODRYN -- AND STARTED SENDING YOU JEDI BACK TO THE SANCTUM.
HE THINKS I'M A JEDI?
HUSH.
NOW, I'VE SEEN SO MANY GO IN THERE I CAN'T REMEMBER YOU ALL --
-- BUT I'VE NEVER SEEN ANY JEDI SNEAKING OUT. SO OLD BORJAK HERE HAS TO WONDER...WHY?
IF YOU CAN SPARE AN ANSWER FOR A STUPID FEEORIN.

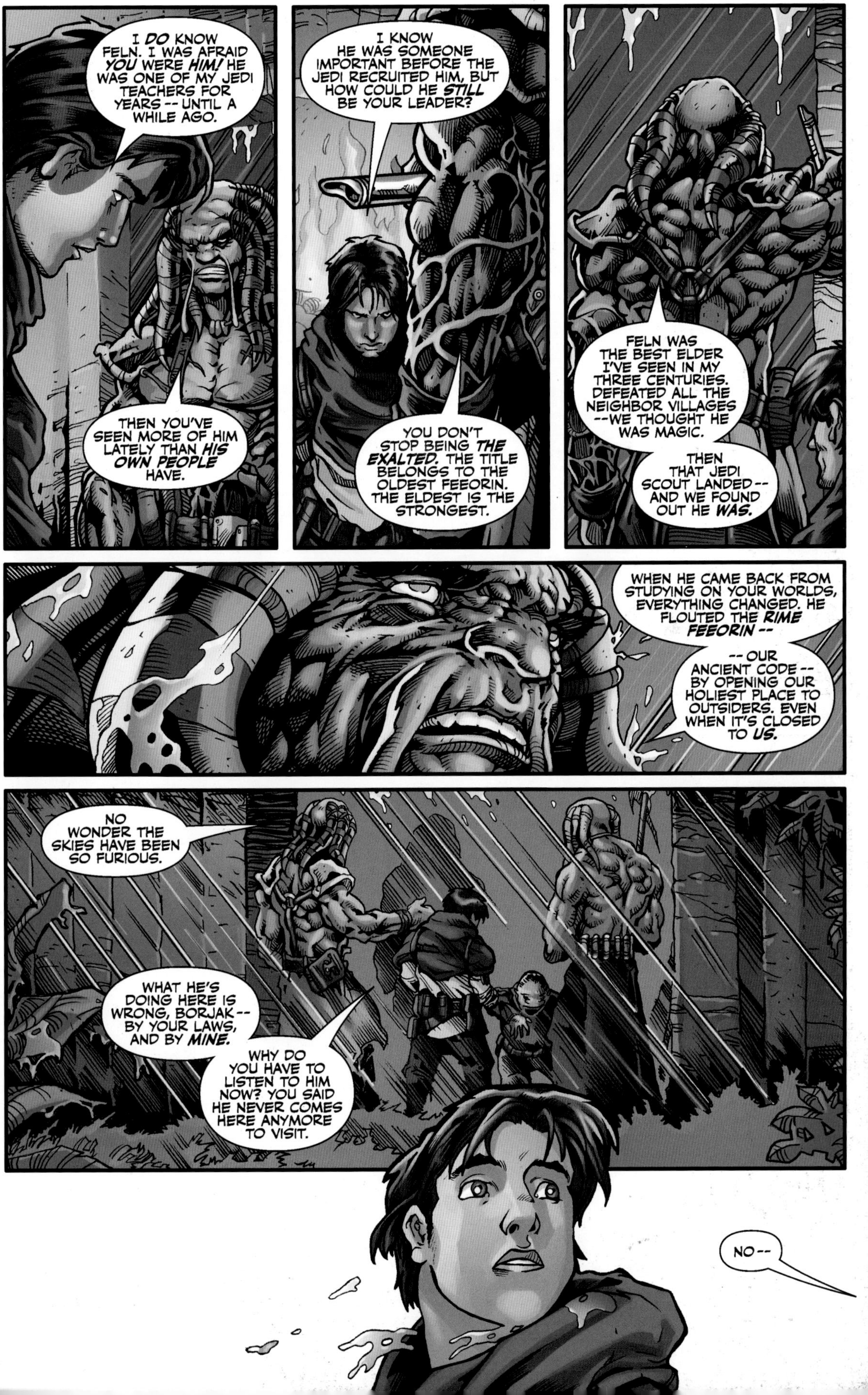
I DO KNOW FELN. I WAS AFRAID YOU WERE HIM! HE WAS ONE OF MY JEDI TEACHERS FOR YEARS -- UNTIL A WHILE AGO.
THEN YOU'VE SEEN MORE OF HIM LATELY THAN HIS OWN PEOPLE HAVE.
I KNOW HE WAS SOMEONE IMPORTANT BEFORE THE JEDI RECRUITED HIM, BUT HOW COULD HE STILL BE YOUR LEADER?
YOU DON'T STOP BEING THE EXALTED. THE TITLE BELONGS TO THE OLDEST FEEORIN. THE ELDEST IS THE STRONGEST.
FELN WAS THE BEST ELDER I'VE SEEN IN MY THREE CENTURIES. DEFEATED ALL THE NEIGHBOR VILLAGES --WE THOUGHT HE WAS MAGIC.
THEN THAT JEDI SCOUT LANDED -- AND WE FOUND OUT HE WAS.
WHEN HE CAME BACK FROM STUDYING ON YOUR WORLDS, EVERYTHING CHANGED. HE FLOUTED THE RIME FEEORIN --
-- OUR ANCIENT CODE -- BY OPENING OUR HOLIEST PLACE TO OUTSIDERS. EVEN WHEN IT'S CLOSED TO US.
NO WONDER THE SKIES HAVE BEEN SO FURIOUS.
WHAT HE'S DOING HERE IS WRONG, BORJAK -- BY YOUR LAWS, AND BY MINE.
WHY DO YOU HAVE TO LISTEN TO HIM NOW? YOU SAID HE NEVER COMES HERE ANYMORE TO VISIT.
NO --

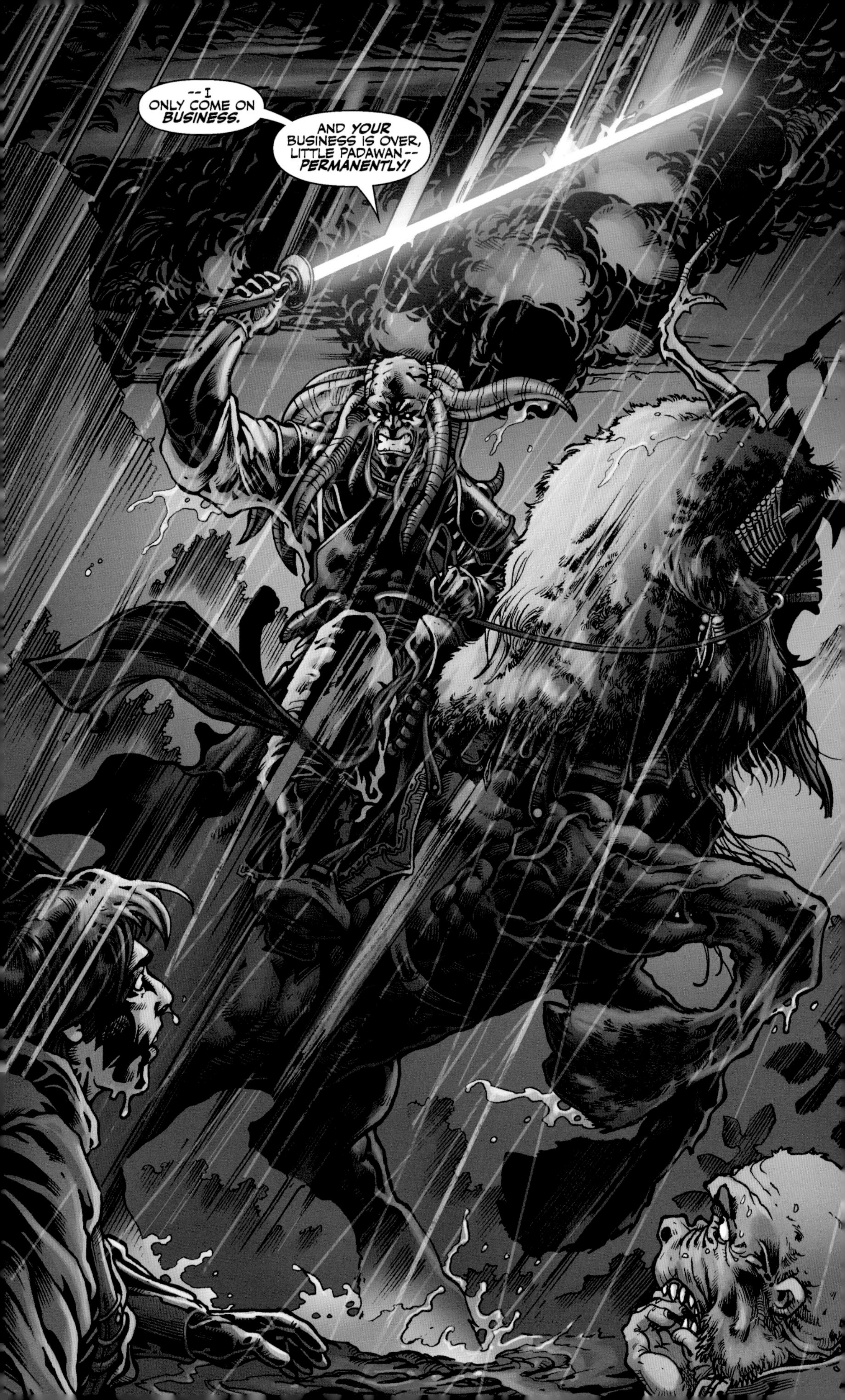
--I ONLY COME ON BUSINESS.
AND YOUR BUSINESS IS OVER, LITTLE PADAWAN-- PERMANENTLY!

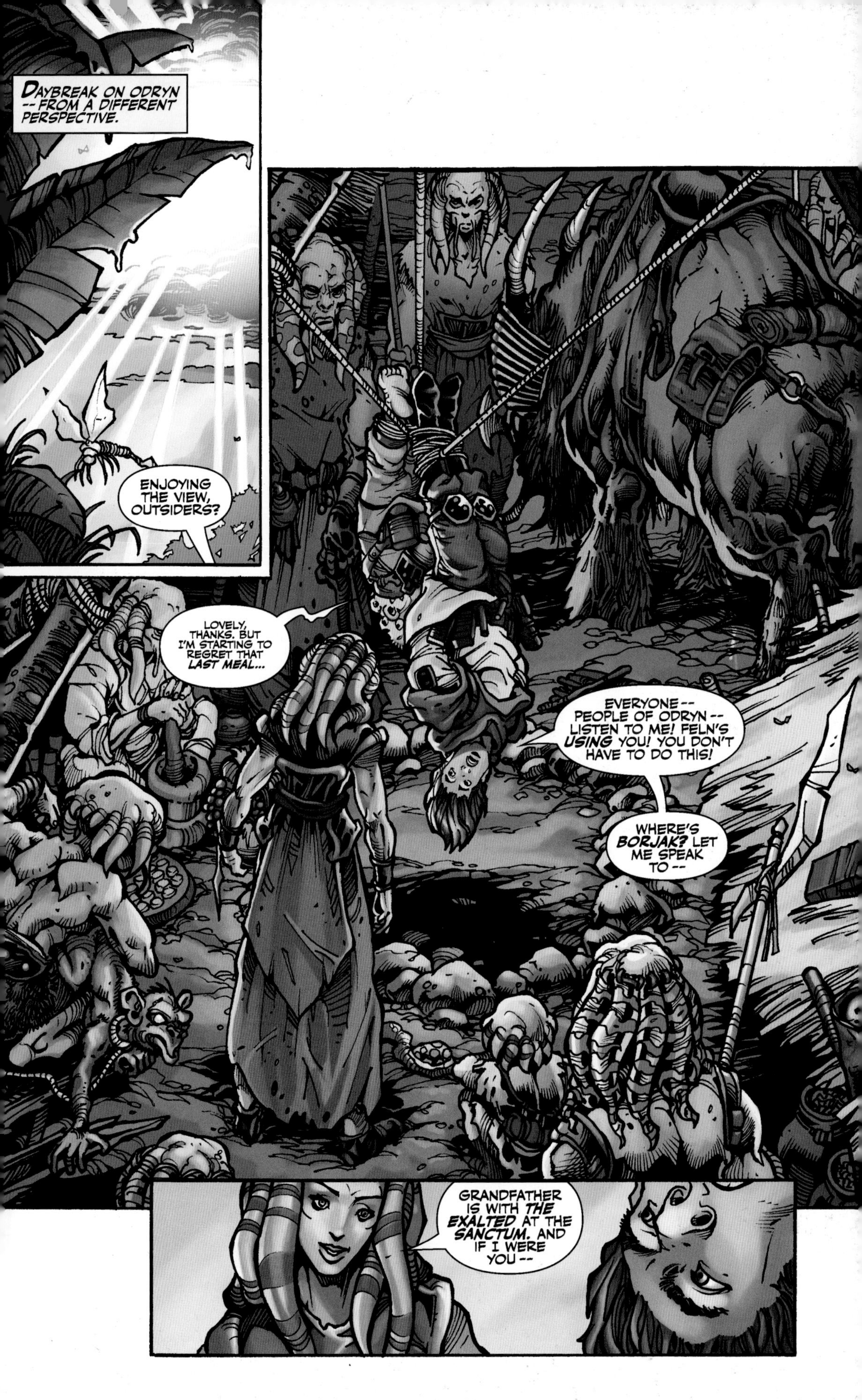
DAYBREAK ON ODRYN -- FROM A DIFFERENT PERSPECTIVE.
ENJOYING THE VIEW, OUTSIDERS?
LOVELY, THANKS. BUT I'M STARTING TO REGRET THAT LAST MEAL...
EVERYONE -- PEOPLE OF ODRYN -- LISTEN TO ME! FELN'S USING YOU! YOU DON'T HAVE TO DO THIS!
WHERE'S BORJAK? LET ME SPEAK TO --
GRANDFATHER IS WITH THE EXALTED AT THE SANCTUM. AND IF I WERE YOU --

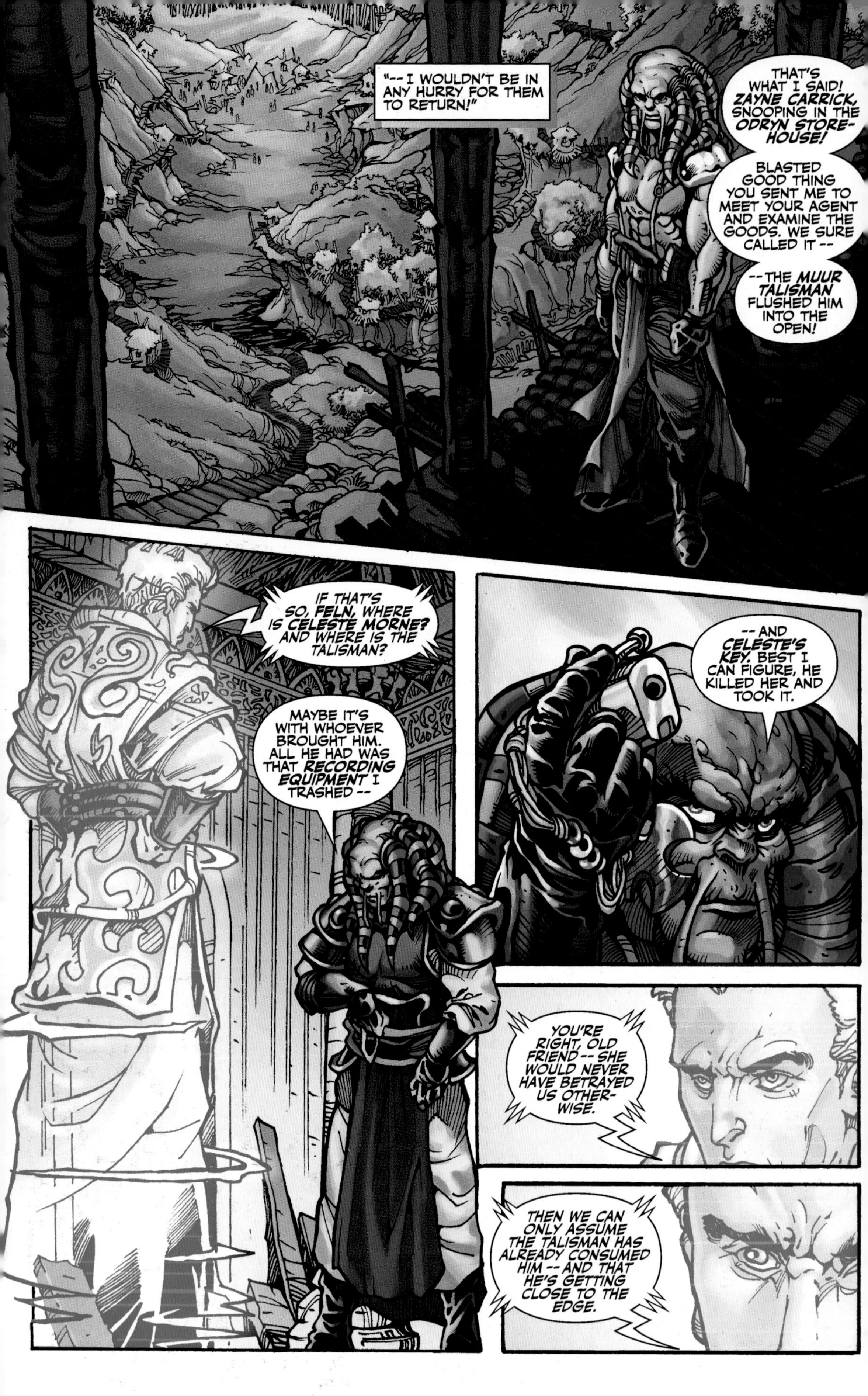
"-- I WOULDN'T BE IN ANY HURRY FOR THEM TO RETURN!"
THAT'S WHAT I SAID! ZAYNE CARRICK, SNOOPING IN THE ODRYN STORE-HOUSE!
BLASTED GOOD THING YOU SENT ME TO MEET YOUR AGENT AND EXAMINE THE GOODS. WE SURE CALLED IT --
-- THE MUUR TALISMAN FLUSHED HIM INTO THE OPEN!
IF THAT'S SO, FELN, WHERE IS CELESTE MORNE? AND WHERE IS THE TALISMAN?
MAYBE IT'S WITH WHOEVER BROUGHT HIM. ALL HE HAD WAS THAT RECORDING EQUIPMENT I TRASHED --
-- AND CELESTE'S KEY. BEST I CAN FIGURE, HE KILLED HER AND TOOK IT.
YOU'RE RIGHT, OLD FRIEND -- SHE WOULD NEVER HAVE BETRAYED US OTHER-WISE.
THEN WE CAN ONLY ASSUME THE TALISMAN HAS ALREADY CONSUMED HIM -- AND THAT HE'S GETTING CLOSE TO THE EDGE.

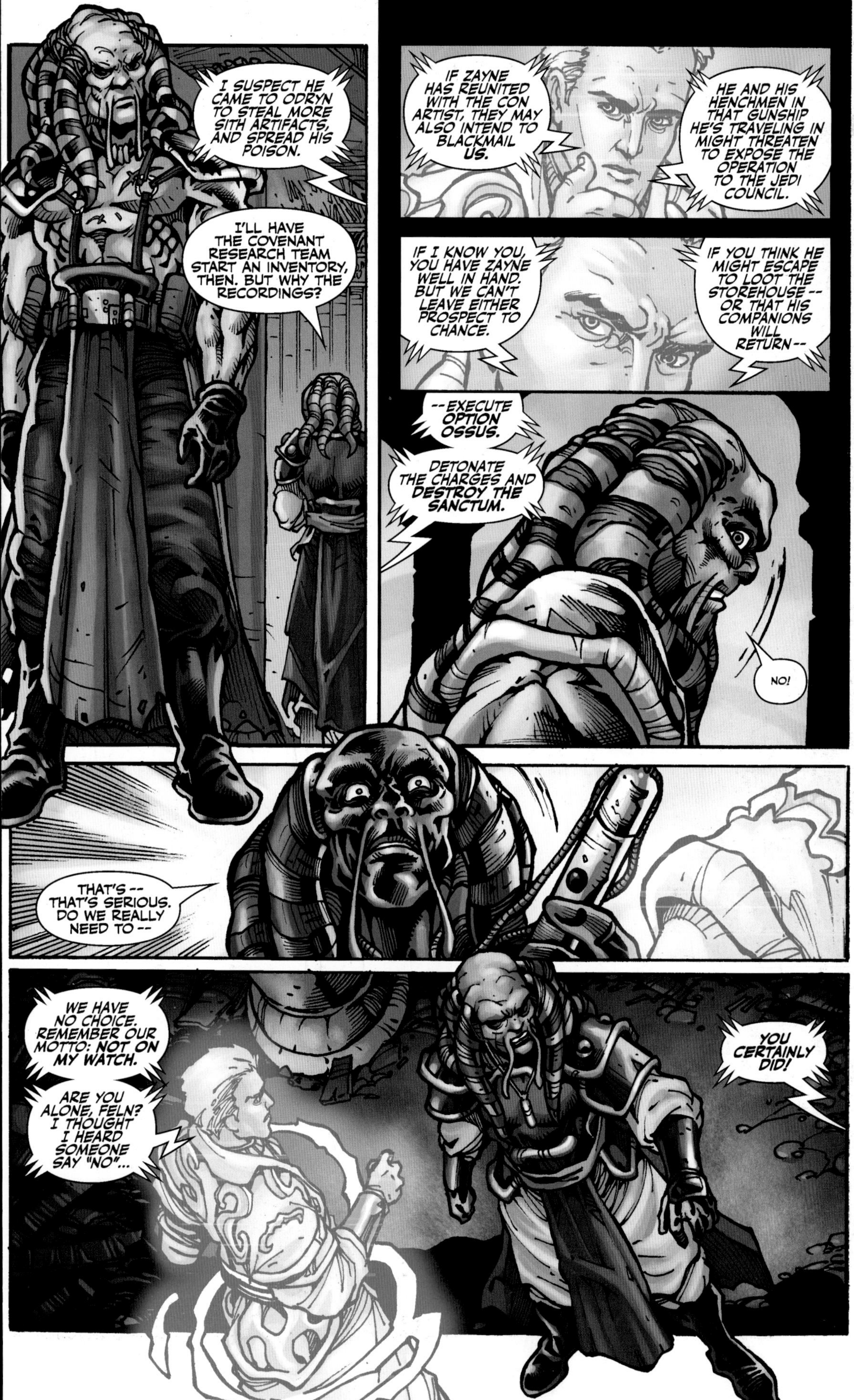
I SUSPECT HE CAME TO ODRYN TO STEAL MORE SITH ARTIFACTS, AND SPREAD HIS POISON.
I'LL HAVE THE COVENANT RESEARCH TEAM START AN INVENTORY, THEN. BUT WHY THE RECORDINGS?
IF ZAYNE HAS REUNITED WITH THE CON ARTIST, THEY MAY ALSO INTEND TO BLACKMAIL US.
HE AND HIS HENCHMEN IN THAT GUNSHIP HE'S TRAVELING IN MIGHT THREATEN TO EXPOSE THE OPERATION TO THE JEDI COUNCIL.
IF I KNOW YOU, YOU HAVE ZAYNE WELL IN HAND. BUT WE CAN'T LEAVE EITHER PROSPECT TO CHANCE.
IF YOU THINK HE MIGHT ESCAPE TO LOOT THE STOREHOUSE -- OR THAT HIS COMPANIONS WILL RETURN--
--EXECUTE OPTION OSSUS.
DETONATE THE CHARGES AND DESTROY THE SANCTUM.
NO!
THAT'S -- THAT'S SERIOUS. DO WE REALLY NEED TO --
WE HAVE NO CHOICE. REMEMBER OUR MOTTO: NOT ON MY WATCH.
ARE YOU ALONE, FELN? I THOUGHT I HEARD SOMEONE SAY "NO"...
YOU CERTAINLY DID!

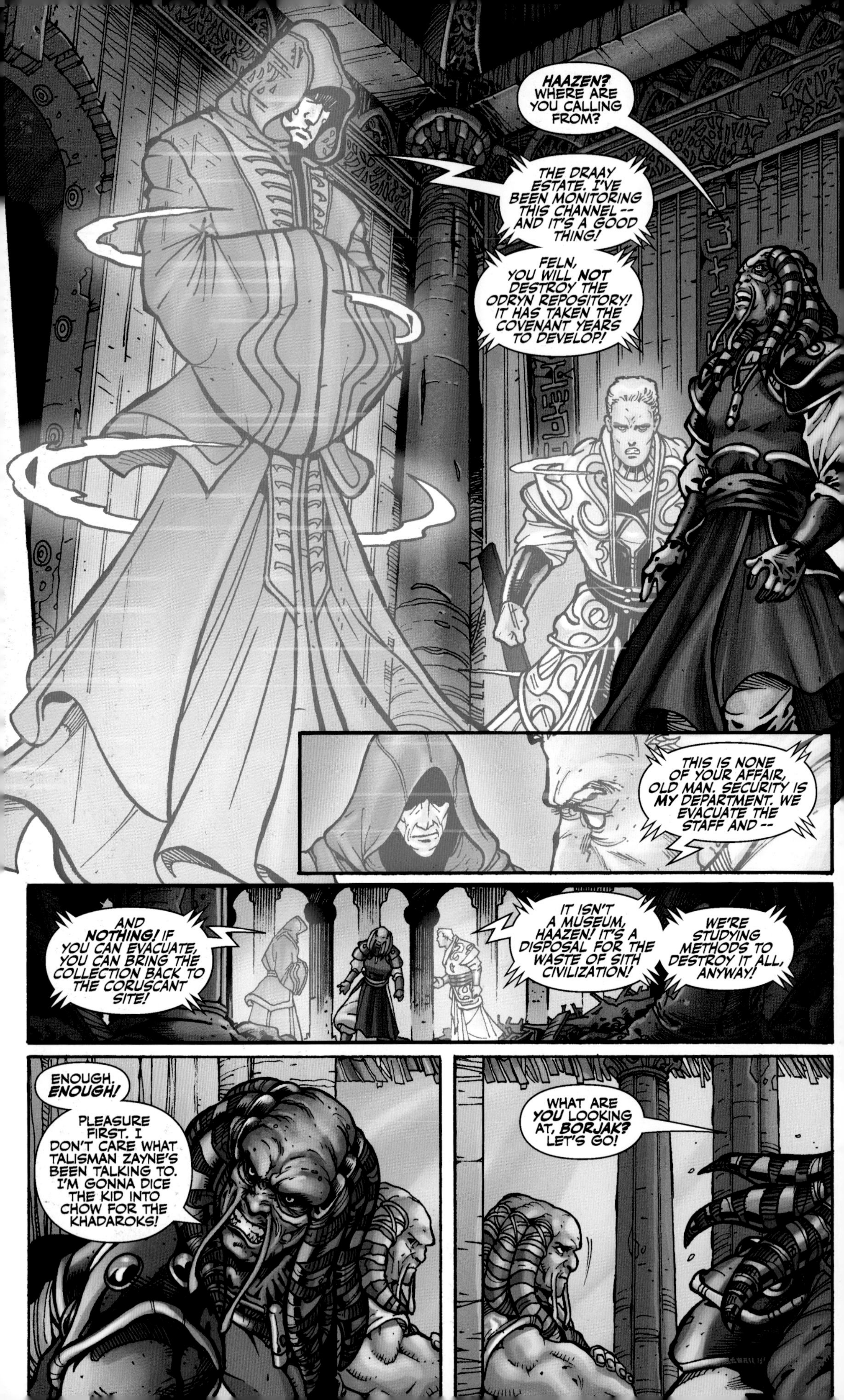
HAAZEN? WHERE ARE YOU CALLING FROM?
THE DRAAY ESTATE. I'VE BEEN MONITORING THIS CHANNEL -- AND IT'S A GOOD THING!
FELN, YOU WILL NOT DESTROY THE ODRYN REPOSITORY! IT HAS TAKEN THE COVENANT YEARS TO DEVELOP!
THIS IS NONE OF YOUR AFFAIR, OLD MAN. SECURITY IS MY DEPARTMENT. WE EVACUATE THE STAFF AND --
AND NOTHING! IF YOU CAN EVACUATE, YOU CAN BRING THE COLLECTION BACK TO THE CORUSCANT SITE!
IT ISN'T A MUSEUM, HAAZEN! IT'S A DISPOSAL FOR THE WASTE OF SITH CIVILIZATION!
WE'RE STUDYING METHODS TO DESTROY IT ALL, ANYWAY!
ENOUGH. ENOUGH!
PLEASURE FIRST. I DON'T CARE WHAT TALISMAN ZAYNE'S BEEN TALKING TO. I'M GONNA DICE THE KID INTO CHOW FOR THE KHADAROKS!
WHAT ARE YOU LOOKING AT, BORJAK? LET'S GO!

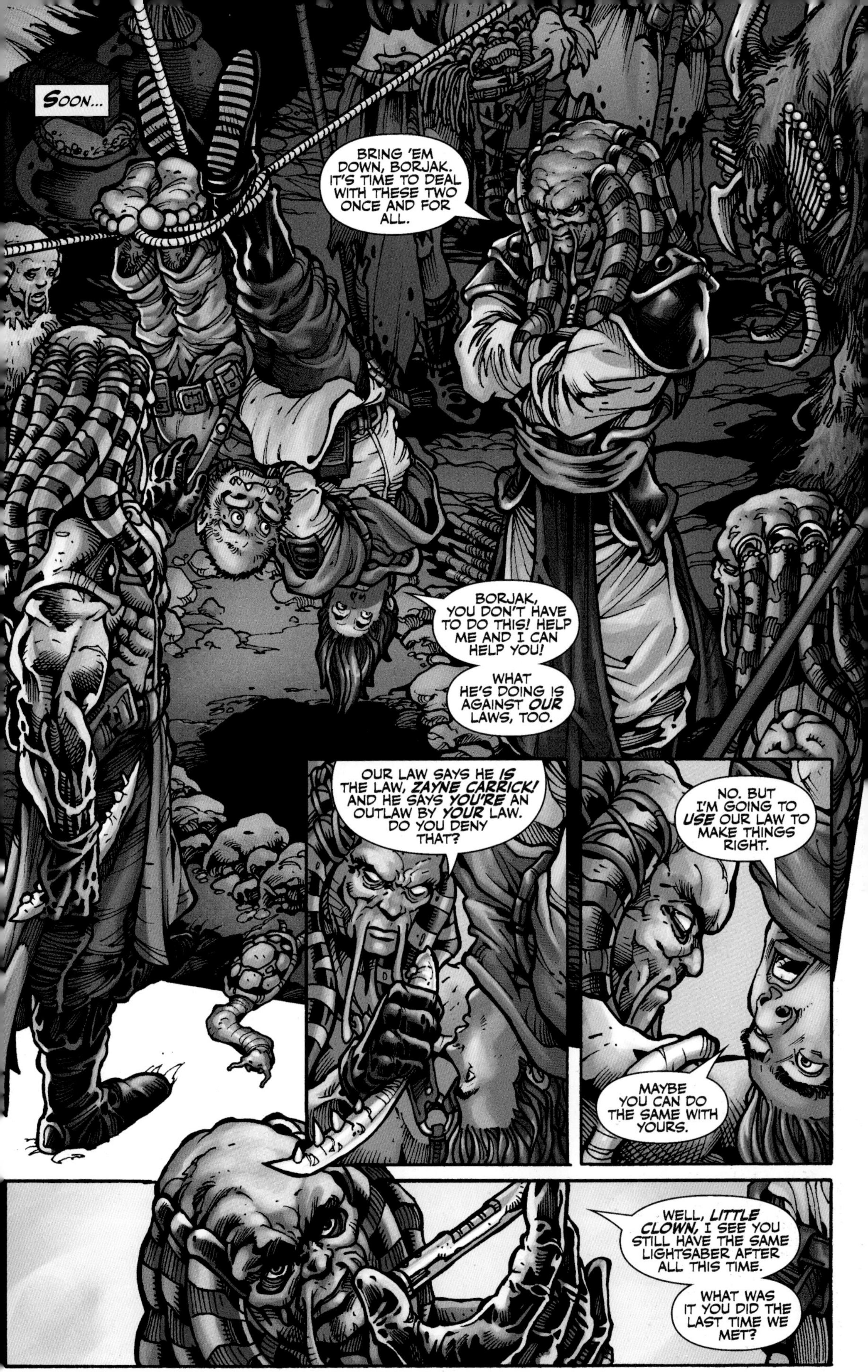
SOON...
BRING 'EM DOWN, BORJAK. IT'S TIME TO DEAL WITH THESE TWO ONCE AND FOR ALL.
BORJAK, YOU DON'T HAVE TO DO THIS! HELP ME AND I CAN HELP YOU!
WHAT HE'S DOING IS AGAINST OUR LAWS, TOO.
OUR LAW SAYS HE IS THE LAW, ZAYNE CARRICK! AND HE SAYS YOU'RE AN OUTLAW BY YOUR LAW. DO YOU DENY THAT?
NO. BUT I'M GOING TO USE OUR LAW TO MAKE THINGS RIGHT.
MAYBE YOU CAN DO THE SAME WITH YOURS.
WELL, LITTLE CLOWN, I SEE YOU STILL HAVE THE SAME LIGHTSABER AFTER ALL THIS TIME.
WHAT WAS IT YOU DID THE LAST TIME WE MET?

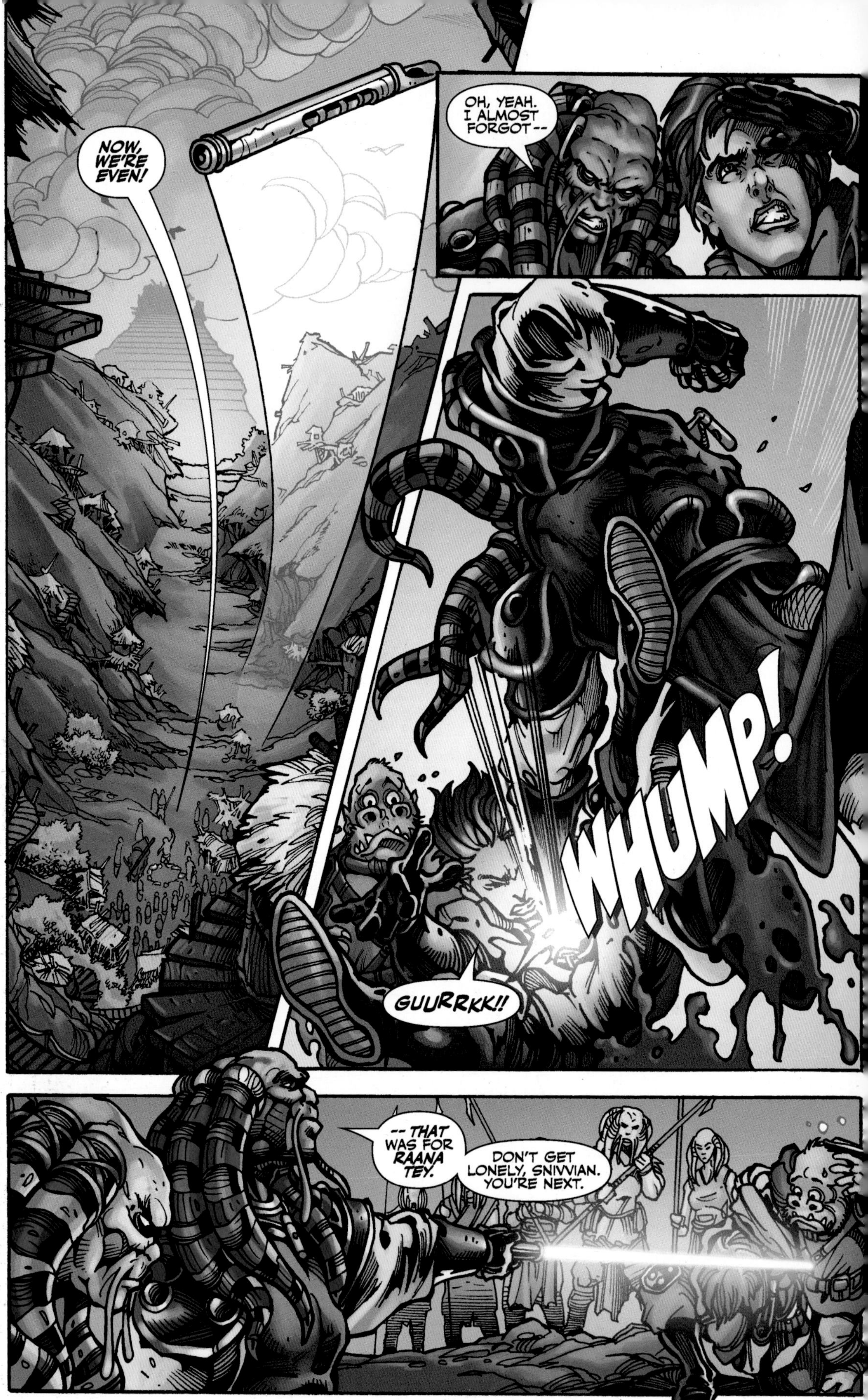
NOW, WE'RE EVEN!
OH, YEAH. I ALMOST FORGOT --
WHUMP!
GUURRKK!!
-- THAT WAS FOR RAANA TEY.
DON'T GET LONELY, SNIVVIAN. YOU'RE NEXT.

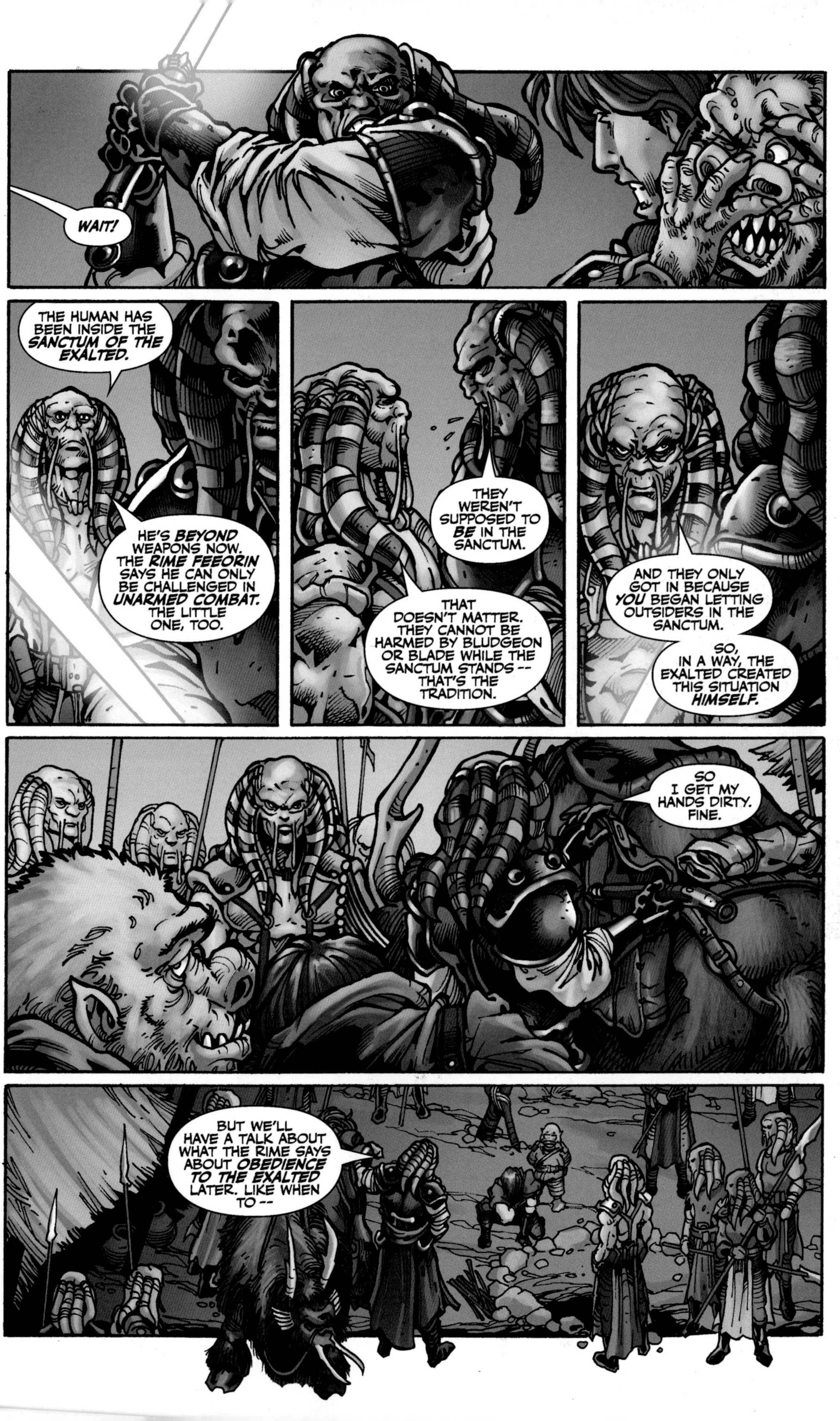
WAIT!
THE HUMAN HAS BEEN INSIDE THE SANCTUM OF THE EXALTED.
HE'S BEYOND WEAPONS NOW. THE RIME FEEORIN SAYS HE CAN ONLY BE CHALLENGED IN UNARMED COMBAT. THE LITTLE ONE, TOO.
THEY WEREN'T SUPPOSED TO BE IN THE SANCTUM.
THAT DOESN'T MATTER. THEY CANNOT BE HARMED BY BLUDGEON OR BLADE WHILE THE SANCTUM STANDS -- THAT'S THE TRADITION.
AND THEY ONLY GOT IN BECAUSE YOU BEGAN LETTING OUTSIDERS IN THE SANCTUM.
SO, IN A WAY, THE EXALTED CREATED THIS SITUATION HIMSELF.
SO I GET MY HANDS DIRTY. FINE.
BUT WE'LL HAVE A TALK ABOUT WHAT THE RIME SAYS ABOUT OBEDIENCE TO THE EXALTED LATER. LIKE WHEN TO --

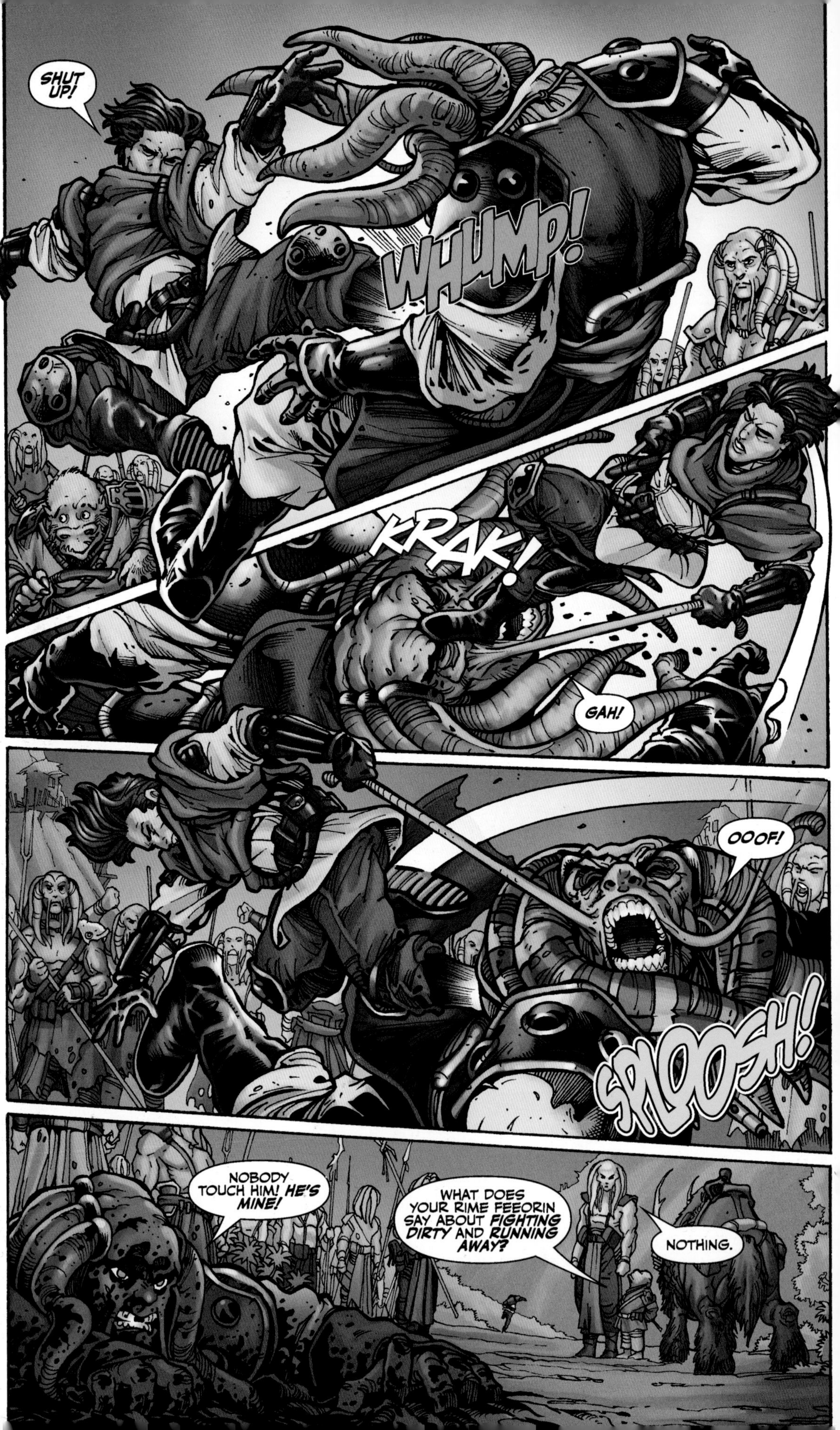
SHUT UP!
WHUMP!
KRAK!
GAH!
OOOF!
SPLOOSH!
NOBODY TOUCH HIM! HE'S MINE!
WHAT DOES YOUR RIME FEEORIN SAY ABOUT FIGHTING DIRTY AND RUNNING AWAY?
NOTHING.

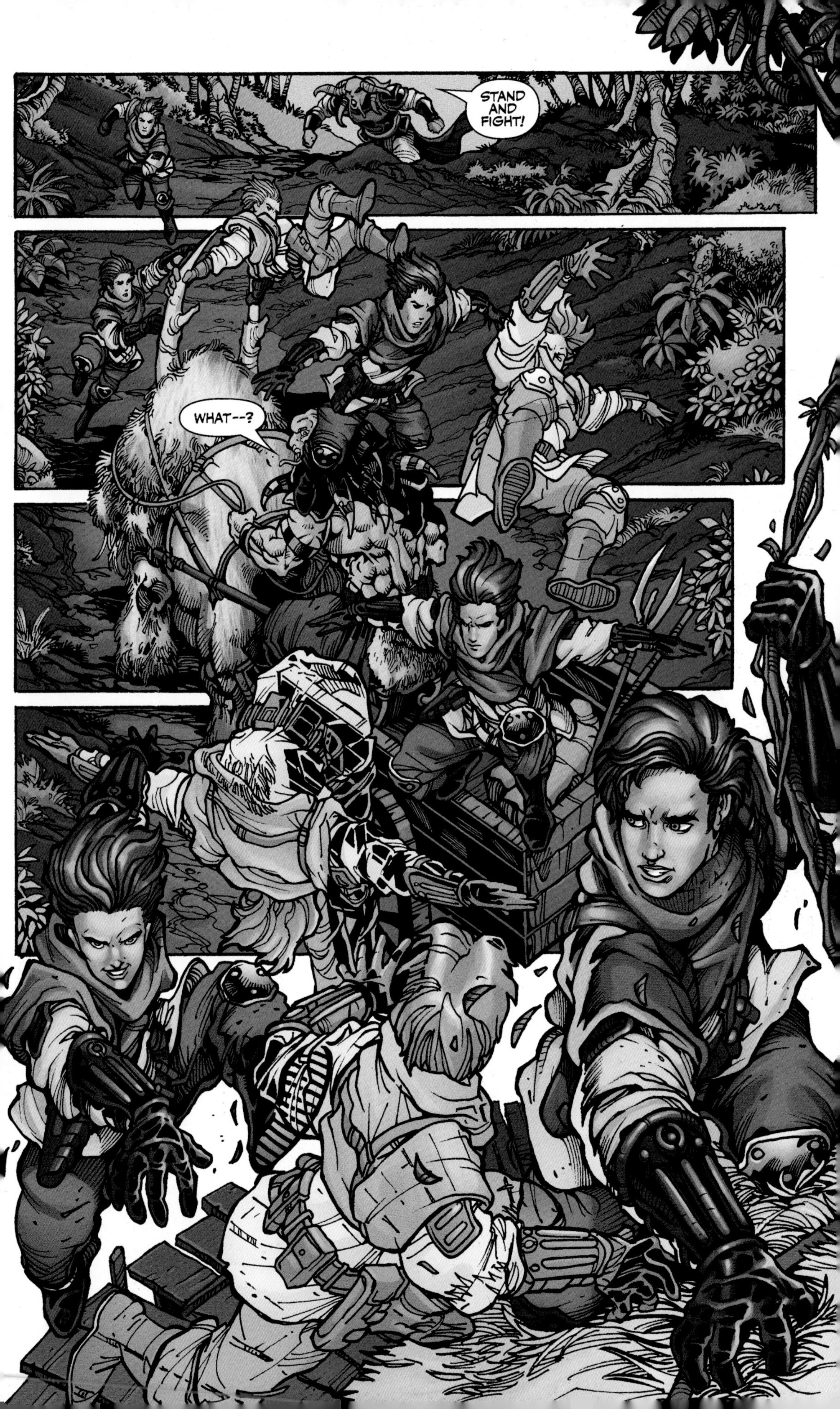
STAND AND FIGHT!
WHAT--?

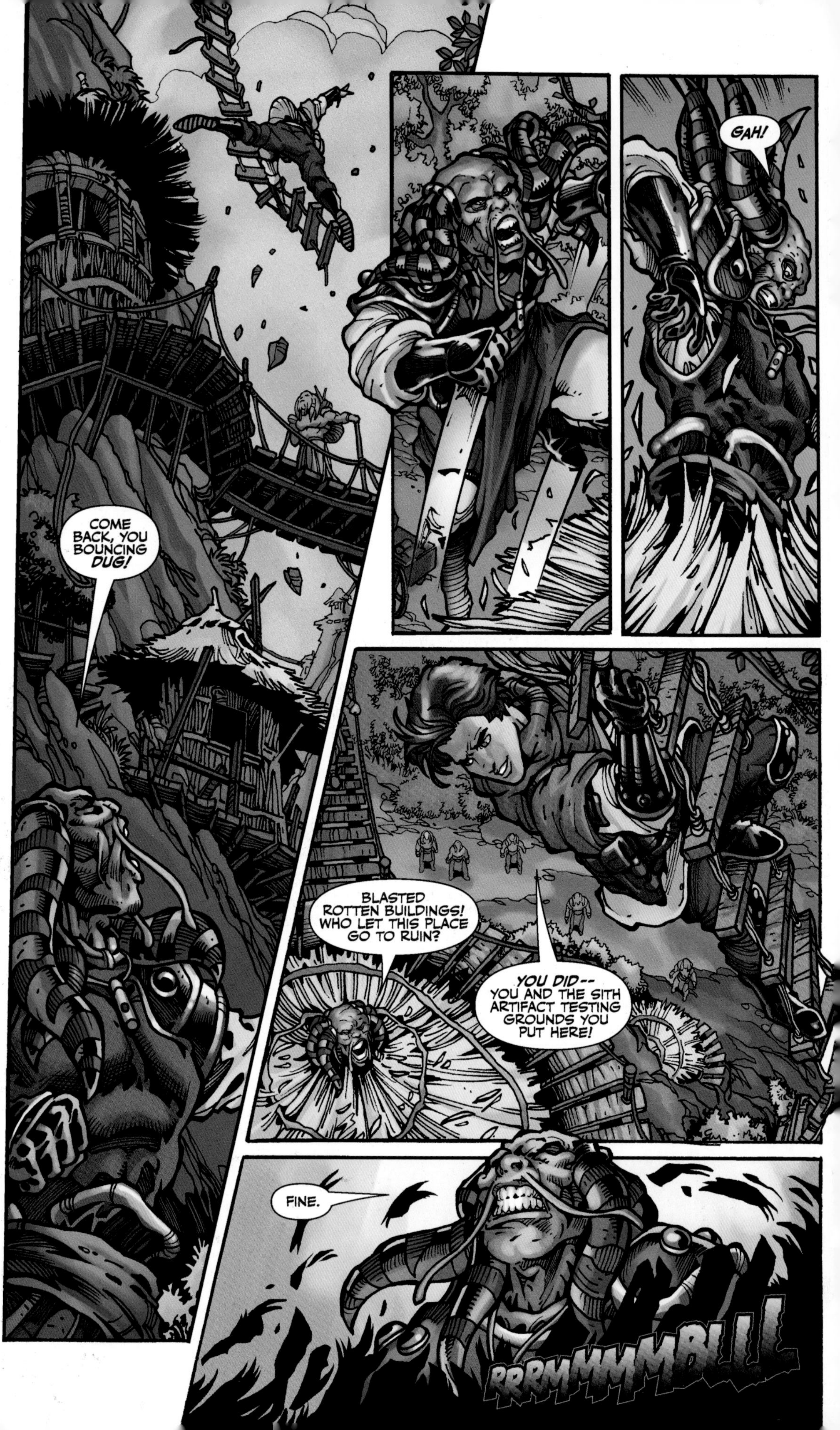
GAH!
COME BACK, YOU BOUNCING DUG!
BLASTED ROTTEN BUILDINGS! WHO LET THIS PLACE GO TO RUIN?
YOU DID-- YOU AND THE SITH ARTIFACT TESTING GROUNDS YOU PUT HERE!
FINE.
RRRMMMMBLLL

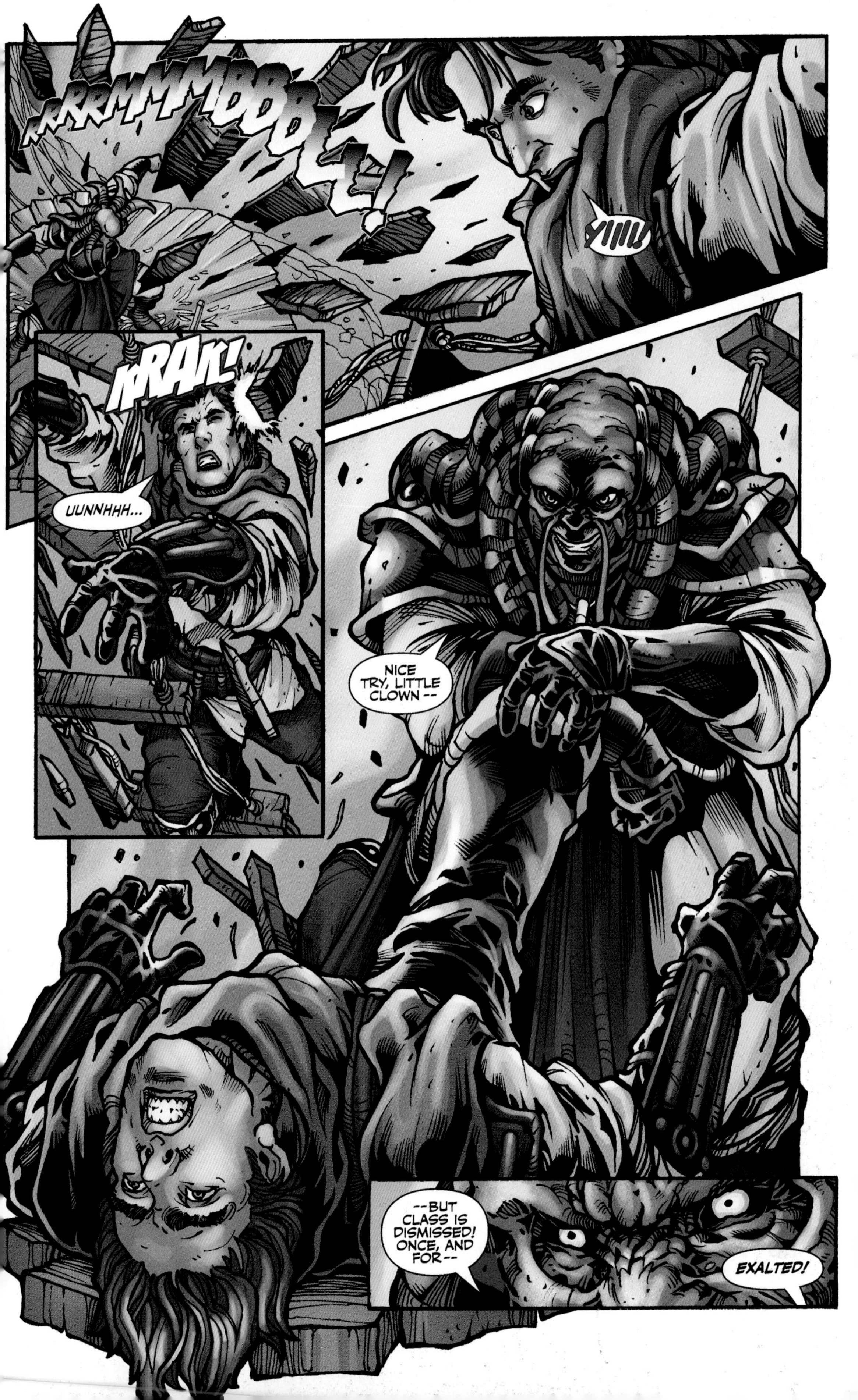
RRRMMMBBBLL!
YIII!
KRAK!
UUNNHHH...
NICE TRY, LITTLE CLOWN --
--BUT CLASS IS DISMISSED! ONCE, AND FOR--
EXALTED!

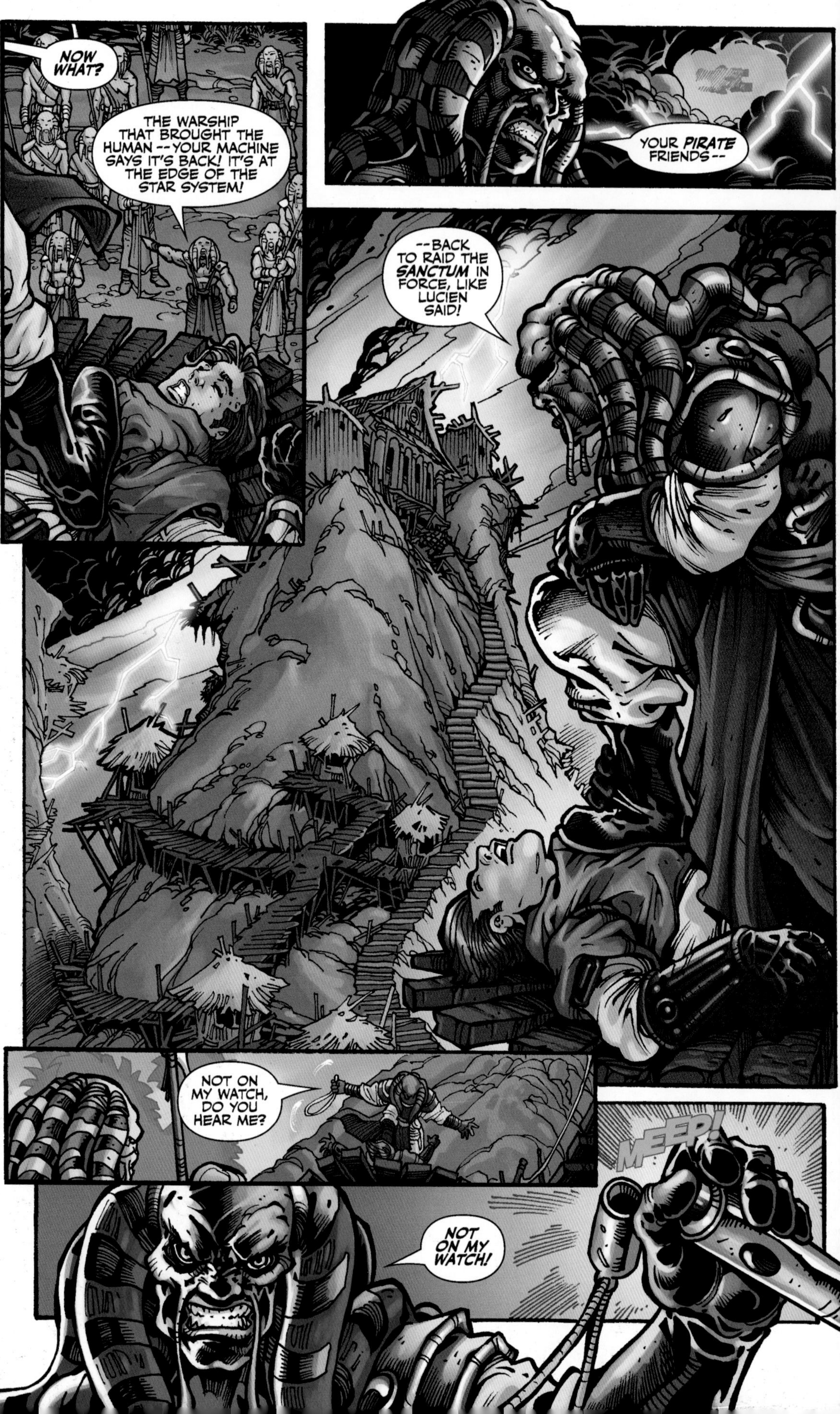
NOW WHAT?
THE WARSHIP THAT BROUGHT THE HUMAN--YOUR MACHINE SAYS IT'S BACK! IT'S AT THE EDGE OF THE STAR SYSTEM!
YOUR PIRATE FRIENDS--
--BACK TO RAID THE SANCTUM IN FORCE, LIKE LUCIEN SAID!
NOT ON MY WATCH, DO YOU HEAR ME?
MEEP!
NOT ON MY WATCH!

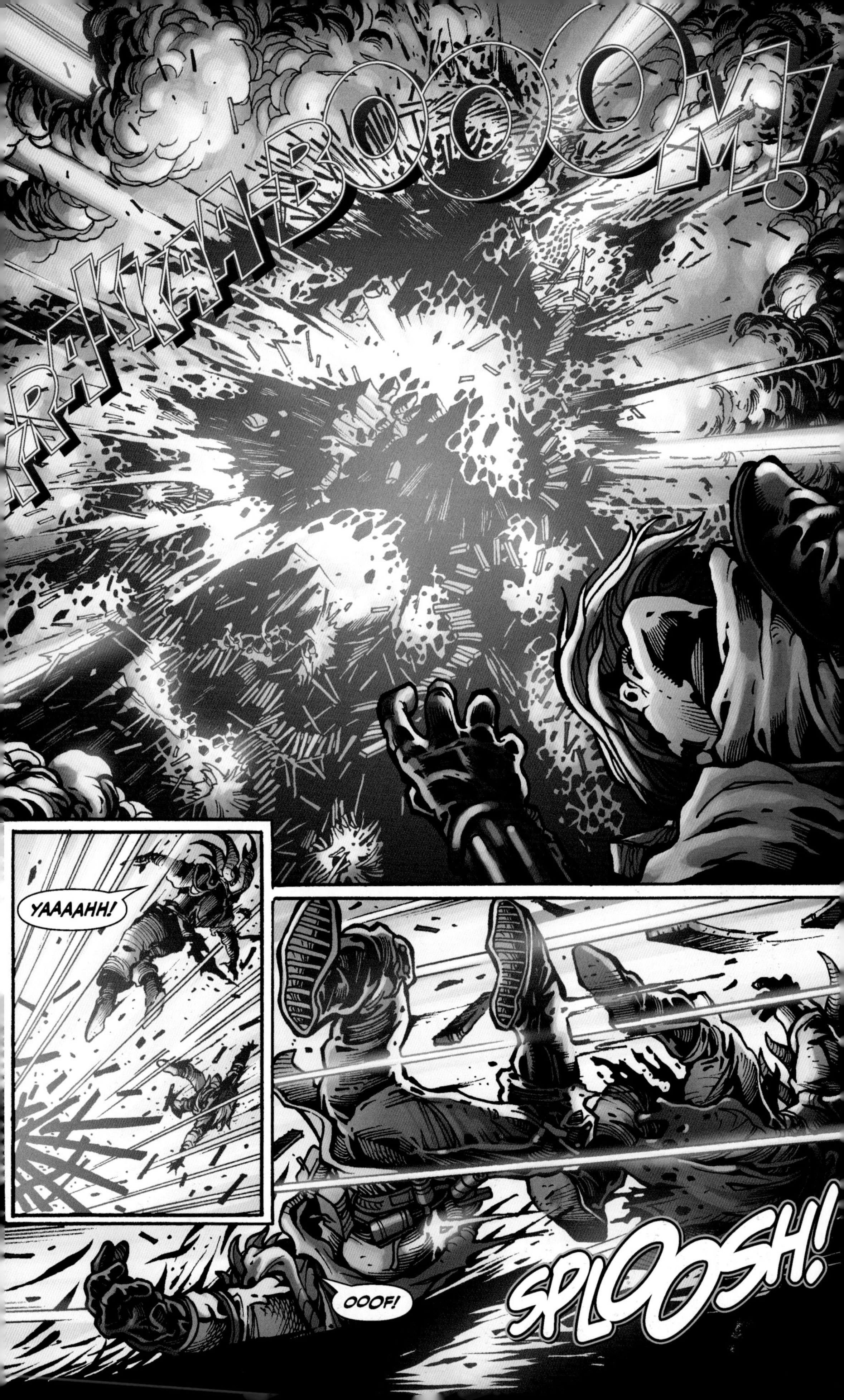
RAKKA-BOOOOM!!
YAAAAHH!
OOOF!
SPLOOSH!

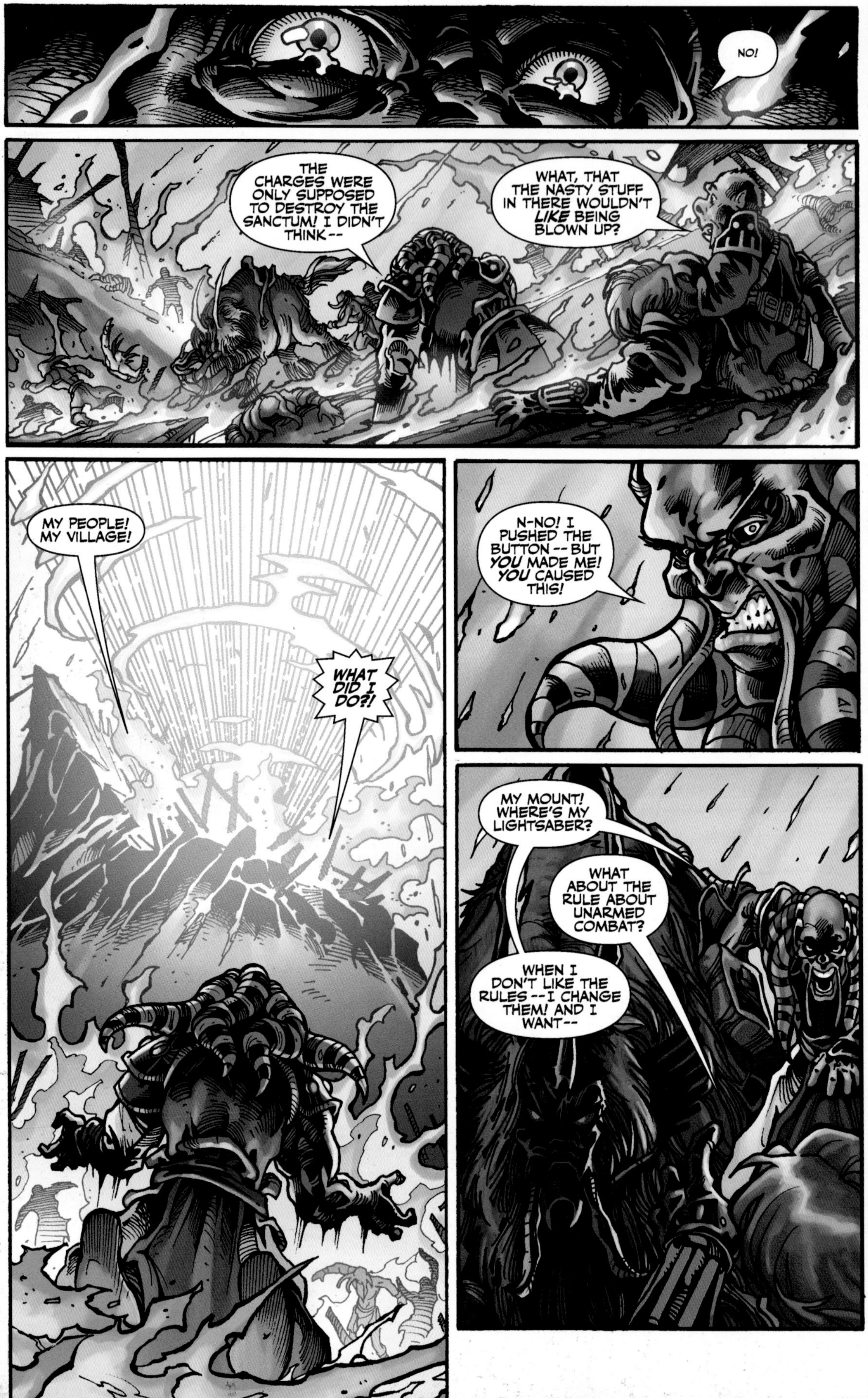
NO!
THE CHARGES WERE ONLY SUPPOSED TO DESTROY THE SANCTUM! I DIDN'T THINK--
WHAT, THAT THE NASTY STUFF IN THERE WOULDN'T *LIKE* BEING BLOWN UP?
MY PEOPLE! MY VILLAGE!
WHAT DID I DO?!
N-NO! I PUSHED THE BUTTON -- BUT *YOU* MADE ME! *YOU* CAUSED THIS!
MY MOUNT! WHERE'S MY LIGHTSABER?
WHAT ABOUT THE RULE ABOUT UNARMED COMBAT?
WHEN I DON'T LIKE THE RULES -- I CHANGE THEM! AND I WANT--

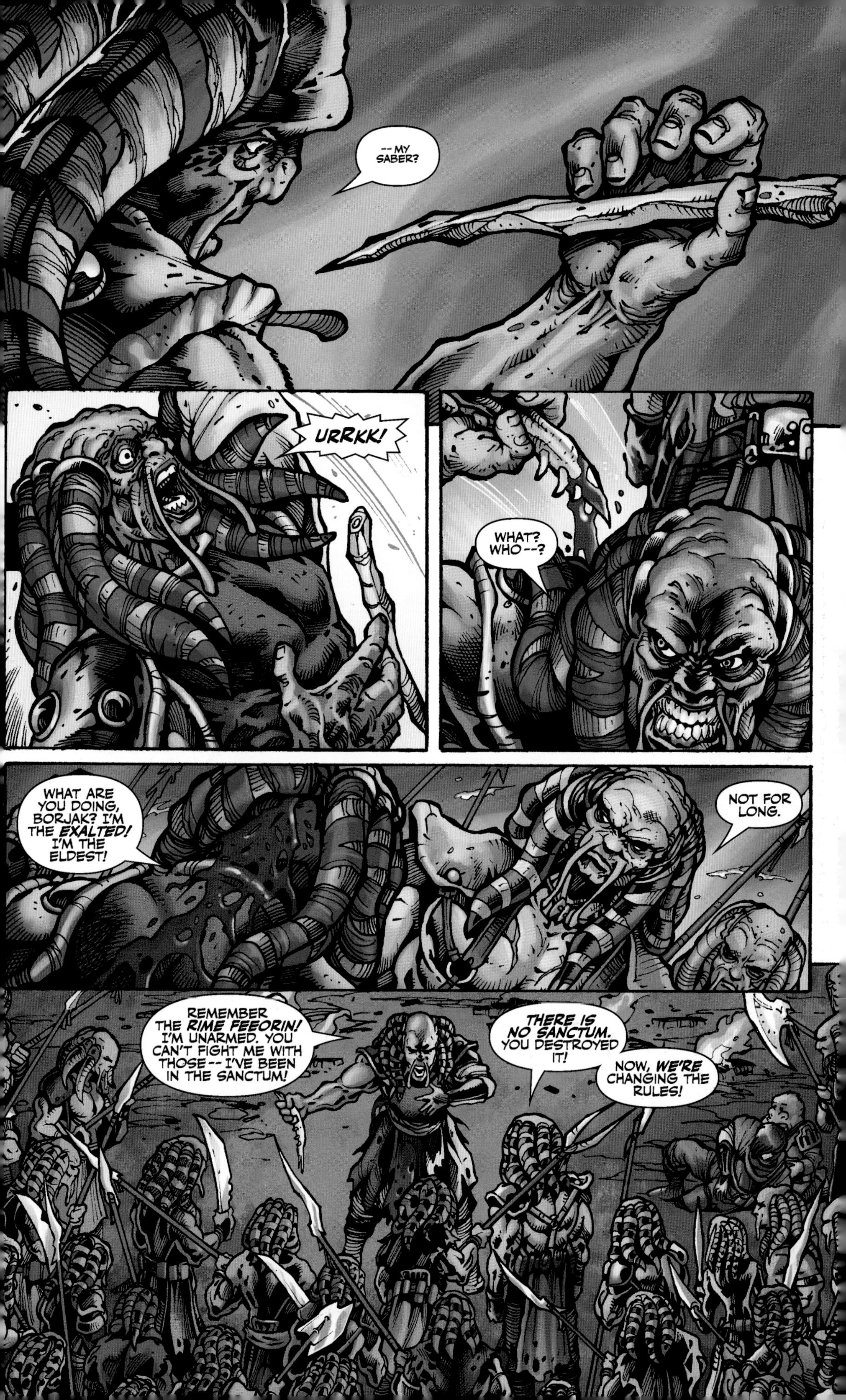

--MY SABER?
URRKK!
WHAT? WHO--?
WHAT ARE YOU DOING, BORJAK? I'M THE EXALTED! I'M THE ELDEST!
NOT FOR LONG.
REMEMBER THE RIME FEEORIN! I'M UNARMED. YOU CAN'T FIGHT ME WITH THOSE--I'VE BEEN IN THE SANCTUM!
THERE IS NO SANCTUM. YOU DESTROYED IT!
NOW, WE'RE CHANGING THE RULES!

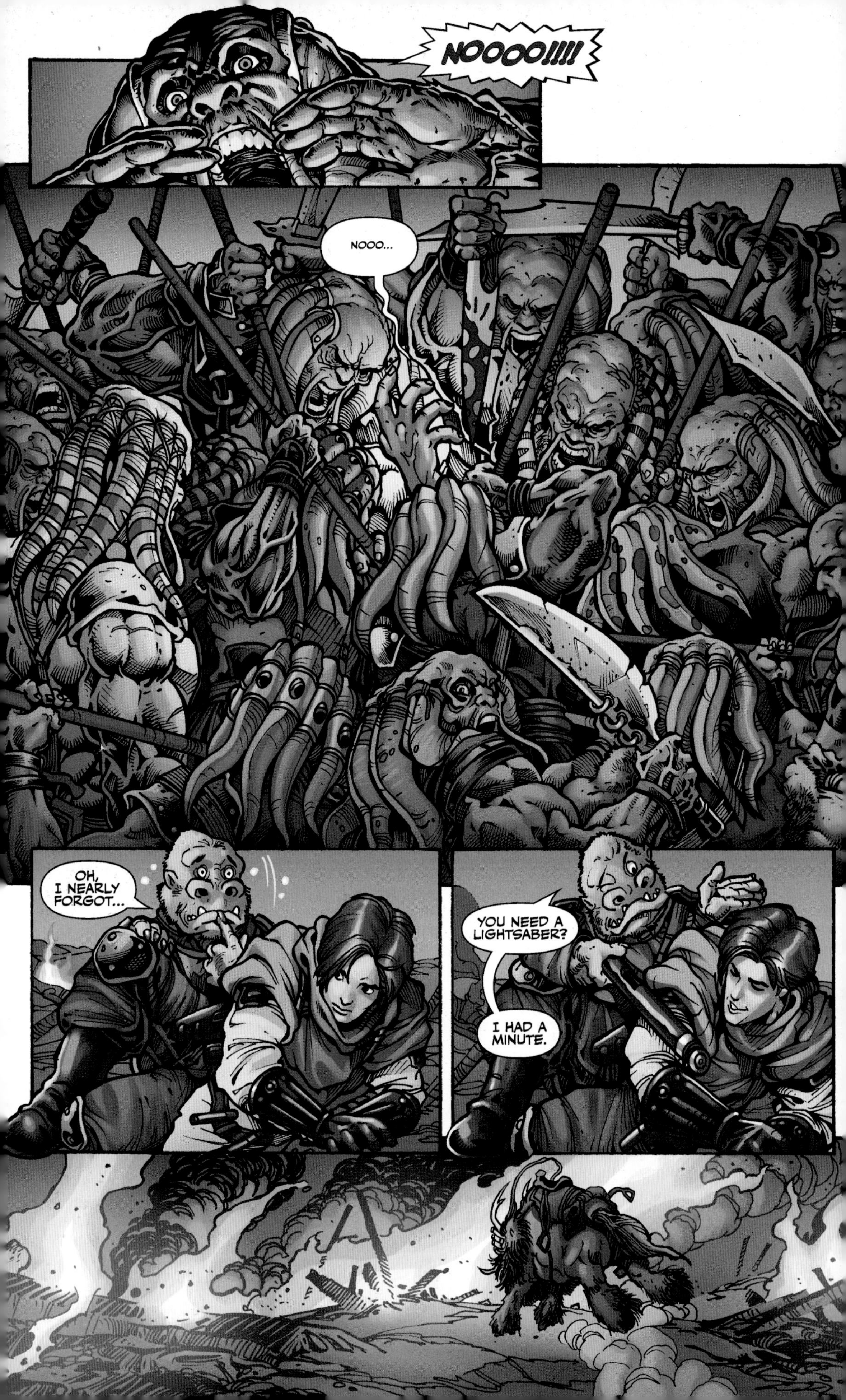
NOOOO!!!!
NOOO...
OH, I NEARLY FORGOT...
YOU NEED A LIGHTSABER?
I HAD A MINUTE.

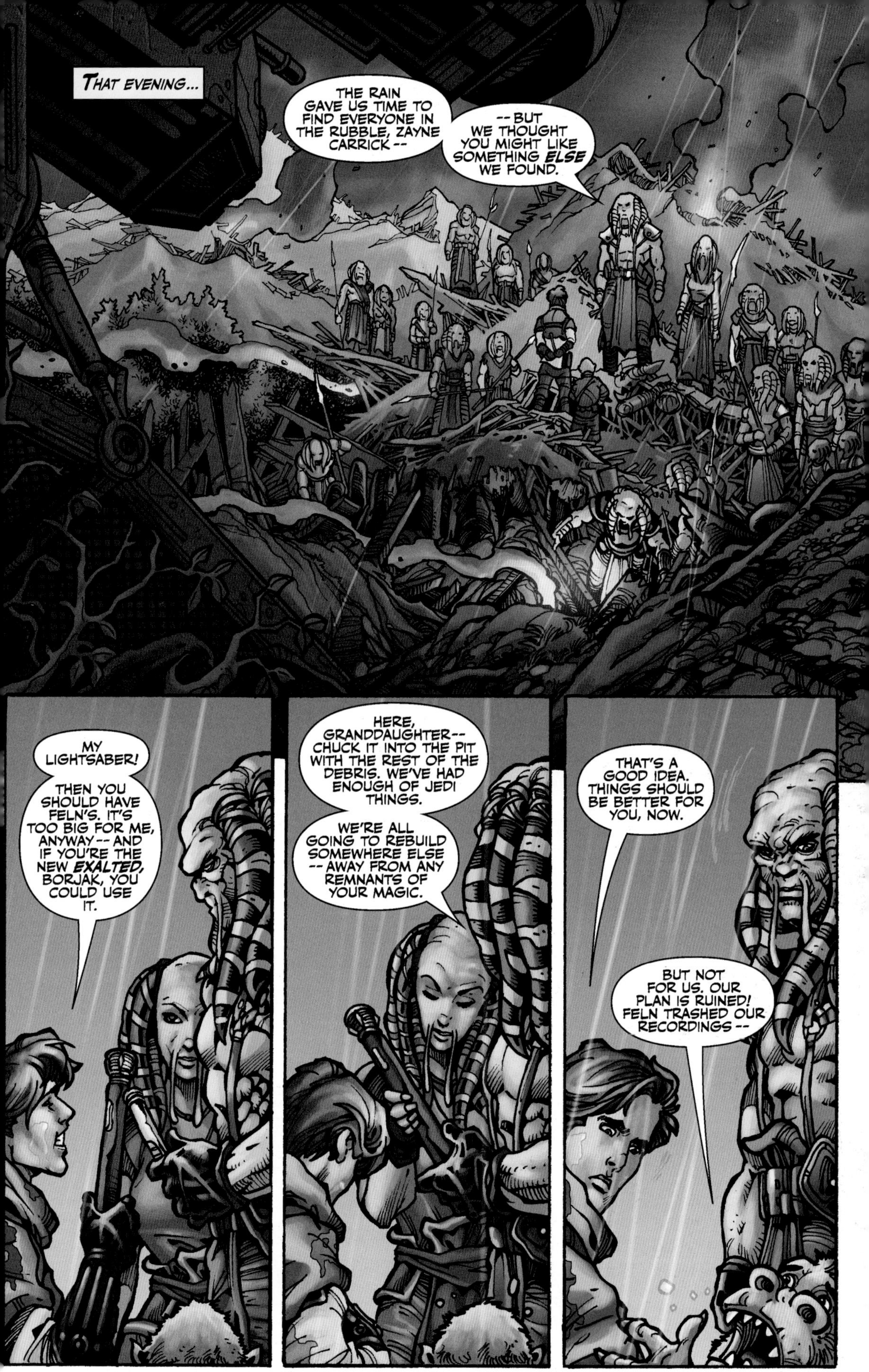
THAT EVENING...
THE RAIN GAVE US TIME TO FIND EVERYONE IN THE RUBBLE, ZAYNE CARRICK --
-- BUT WE THOUGHT YOU MIGHT LIKE SOMETHING ELSE WE FOUND.
MY LIGHTSABER!
THEN YOU SHOULD HAVE FELN'S. IT'S TOO BIG FOR ME, ANYWAY -- AND IF YOU'RE THE NEW EXALTED, BORJAK, YOU COULD USE IT.
HERE, GRANDDAUGHTER -- CHUCK IT INTO THE PIT WITH THE REST OF THE DEBRIS. WE'VE HAD ENOUGH OF JEDI THINGS.
WE'RE ALL GOING TO REBUILD SOMEWHERE ELSE -- AWAY FROM ANY REMNANTS OF YOUR MAGIC.
THAT'S A GOOD IDEA. THINGS SHOULD BE BETTER FOR YOU, NOW.
BUT NOT FOR US. OUR PLAN IS RUINED! FELN TRASHED OUR RECORDINGS --

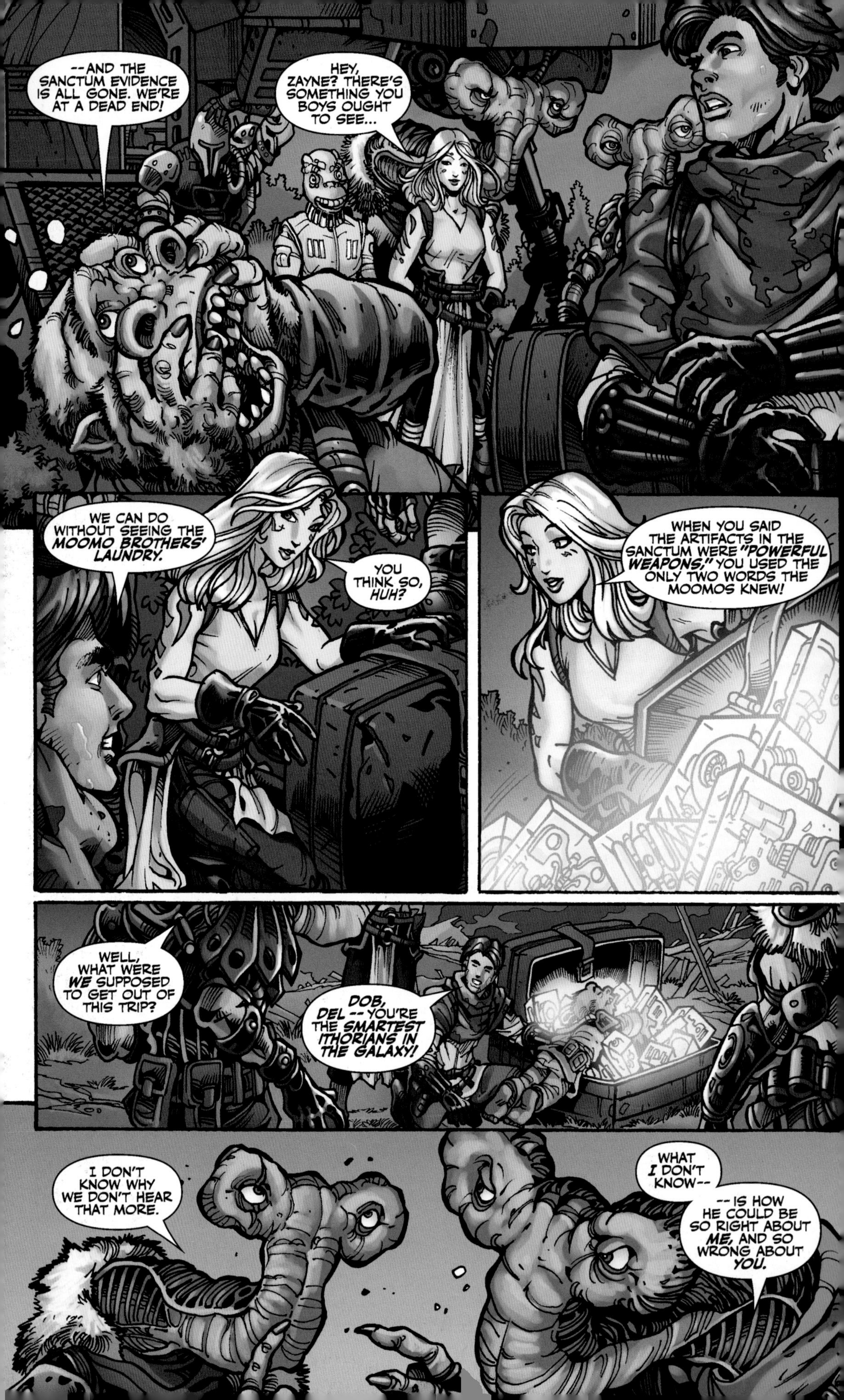
--AND THE SANCTUM EVIDENCE IS ALL GONE. WE'RE AT A DEAD END!
HEY, ZAYNE? THERE'S SOMETHING YOU BOYS OUGHT TO SEE...
WE CAN DO WITHOUT SEEING THE MOOMO BROTHERS' LAUNDRY.
YOU THINK SO, HUH?
WHEN YOU SAID THE ARTIFACTS IN THE SANCTUM WERE "POWERFUL WEAPONS," YOU USED THE ONLY TWO WORDS THE MOOMOS KNEW!
WELL, WHAT WERE WE SUPPOSED TO GET OUT OF THIS TRIP?
DOB, DEL--YOU'RE THE SMARTEST ITHORIANS IN THE GALAXY!
I DON'T KNOW WHY WE DON'T HEAR THAT MORE.
WHAT I DON'T KNOW--
--IS HOW HE COULD BE SO RIGHT ABOUT ME, AND SO WRONG ABOUT YOU.

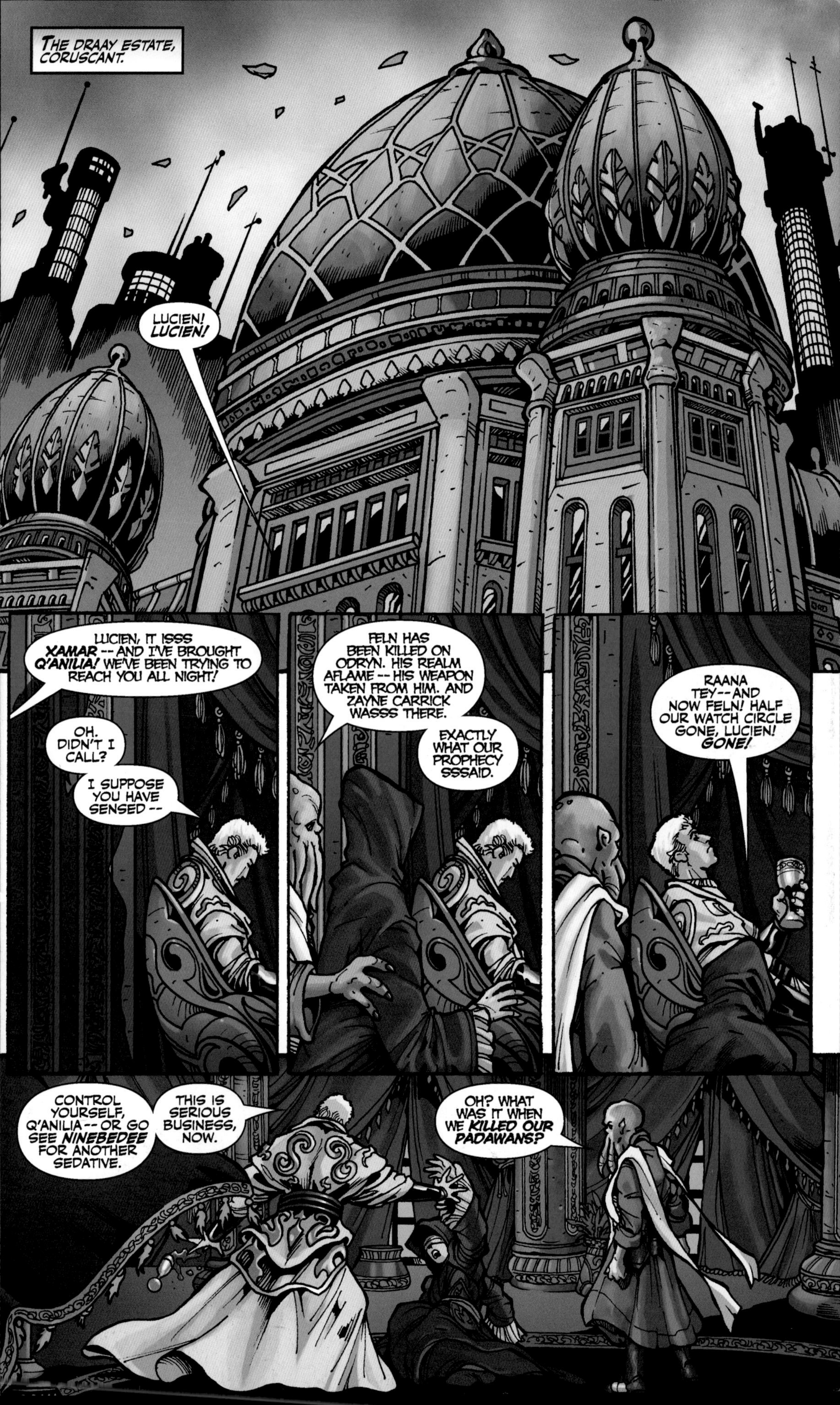

THE DRAAY ESTATE, CORUSCANT.
LUCIEN! LUCIEN!
LUCIEN, IT ISSS XAMAR -- AND I'VE BROUGHT Q'ANILIA! WE'VE BEEN TRYING TO REACH YOU ALL NIGHT!
OH. DIDN'T I CALL?
I SUPPOSE YOU HAVE SENSED --
FELN HAS BEEN KILLED ON ODRYN. HIS REALM AFLAME -- HIS WEAPON TAKEN FROM HIM. AND ZAYNE CARRICK WASSS THERE.
EXACTLY WHAT OUR PROPHECY SSSAID.
RAANA TEY -- AND NOW FELN! HALF OUR WATCH CIRCLE GONE, LUCIEN! GONE!
CONTROL YOURSELF, Q'ANILIA -- OR GO SEE NINEBEDEE FOR ANOTHER SEDATIVE.
THIS IS SERIOUS BUSINESS, NOW.
OH? WHAT WAS IT WHEN WE KILLED OUR PADAWANS?

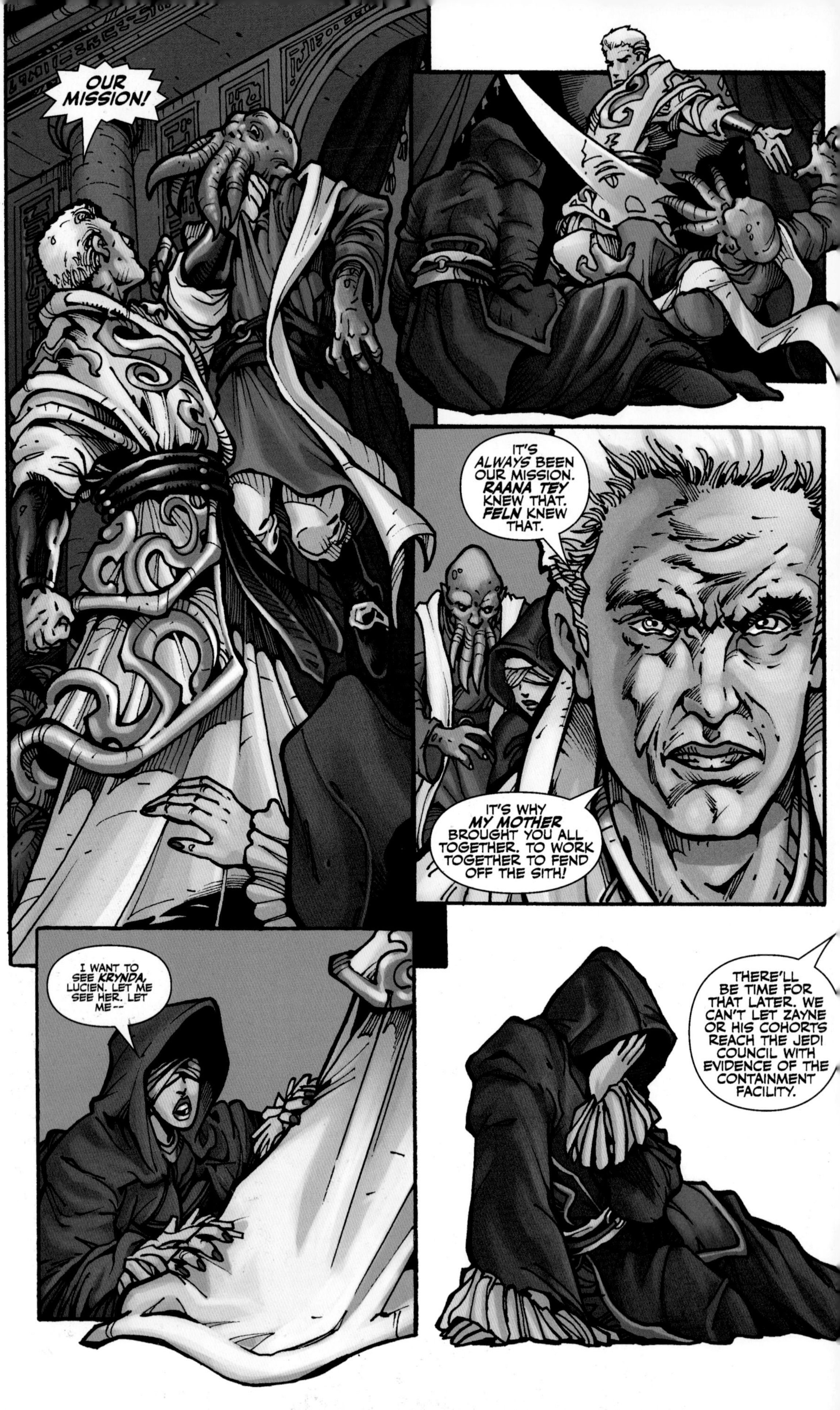
OUR MISSION!
IT'S ALWAYS BEEN OUR MISSION. RAANA TEY KNEW THAT. FELN KNEW THAT.
IT'S WHY MY MOTHER BROUGHT YOU ALL TOGETHER. TO WORK TOGETHER TO FEND OFF THE SITH!
I WANT TO SEE KRYNDA, LUCIEN. LET ME SEE HER. LET ME--
THERE'LL BE TIME FOR THAT LATER. WE CAN'T LET ZAYNE OR HIS COHORTS REACH THE JEDI COUNCIL WITH EVIDENCE OF THE CONTAINMENT FACILITY.

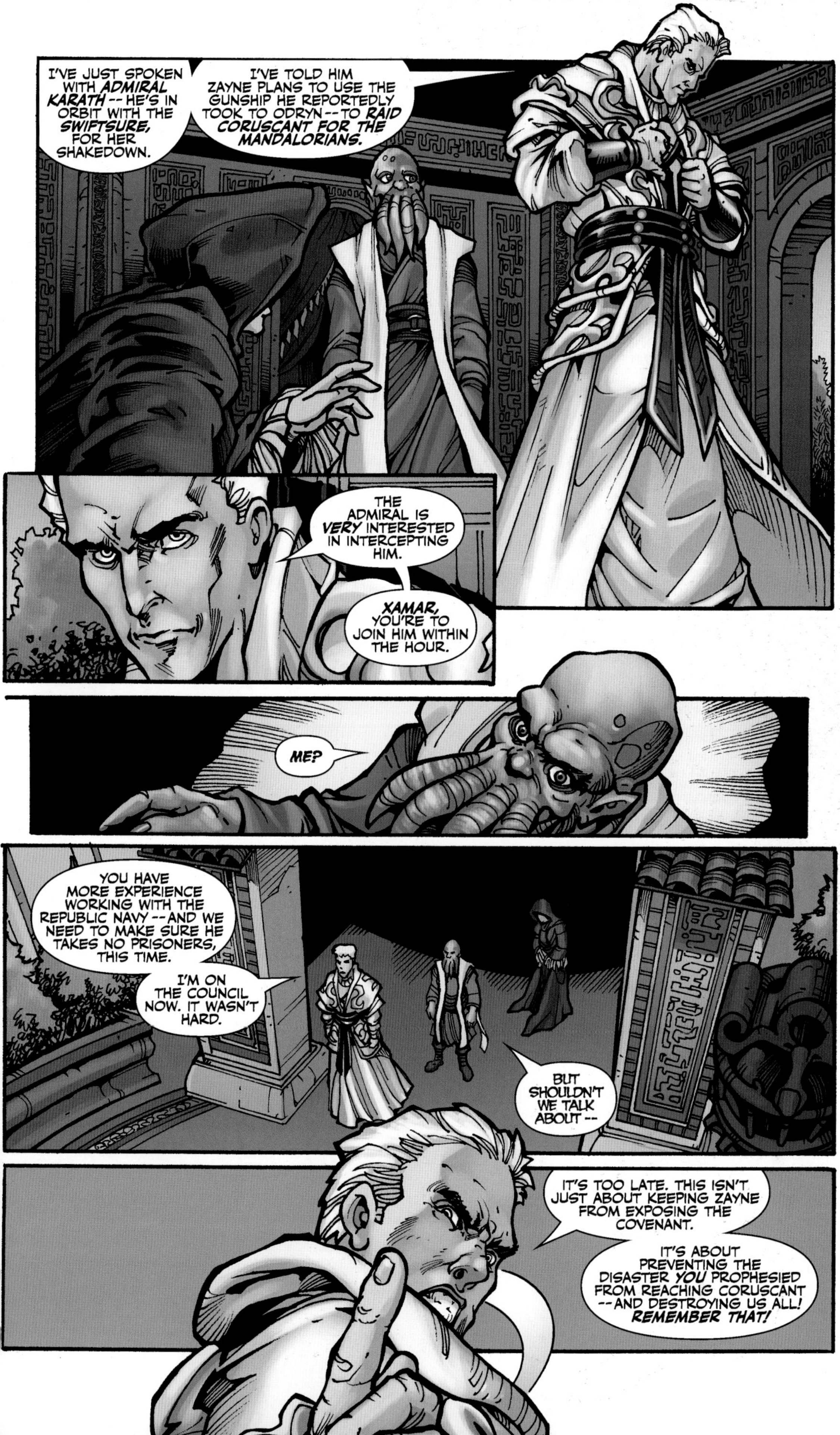
I'VE JUST SPOKEN WITH ADMIRAL KARATH -- HE'S IN ORBIT WITH THE SWIFTSURE, FOR HER SHAKEDOWN.
I'VE TOLD HIM ZAYNE PLANS TO USE THE GUNSHIP HE REPORTEDLY TOOK TO ODRYN -- TO RAID CORUSCANT FOR THE MANDALORIANS.
THE ADMIRAL IS VERY INTERESTED IN INTERCEPTING HIM.
XAMAR, YOU'RE TO JOIN HIM WITHIN THE HOUR.
ME?
YOU HAVE MORE EXPERIENCE WORKING WITH THE REPUBLIC NAVY -- AND WE NEED TO MAKE SURE HE TAKES NO PRISONERS, THIS TIME.
I'M ON THE COUNCIL NOW. IT WASN'T HARD.
BUT SHOULDN'T WE TALK ABOUT --
IT'S TOO LATE. THIS ISN'T JUST ABOUT KEEPING ZAYNE FROM EXPOSING THE COVENANT.
IT'S ABOUT PREVENTING THE DISASTER YOU PROPHESIED FROM REACHING CORUSCANT -- AND DESTROYING US ALL! REMEMBER THAT!

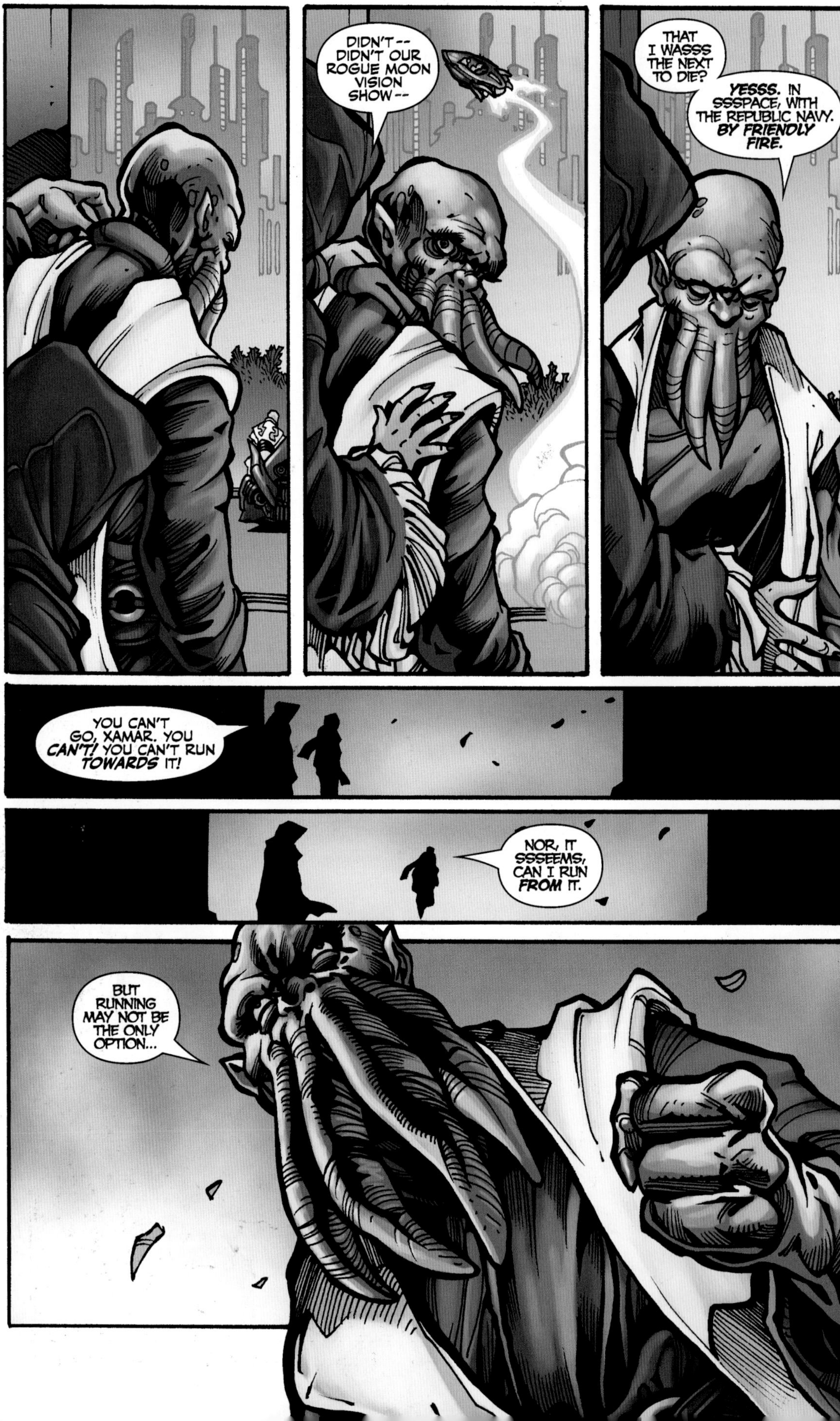
DIDN'T-- DIDN'T OUR ROGUE MOON VISION SHOW--
THAT I WASSS THE NEXT TO DIE?
YESSS. IN SSSPACE, WITH THE REPUBLIC NAVY. BY FRIENDLY FIRE.
YOU CAN'T GO, XAMAR. YOU CAN'T! YOU CAN'T RUN TOWARDS IT!
NOR, IT SSSEEMS, CAN I RUN FROM IT.
BUT RUNNING MAY NOT BE THE ONLY OPTION...

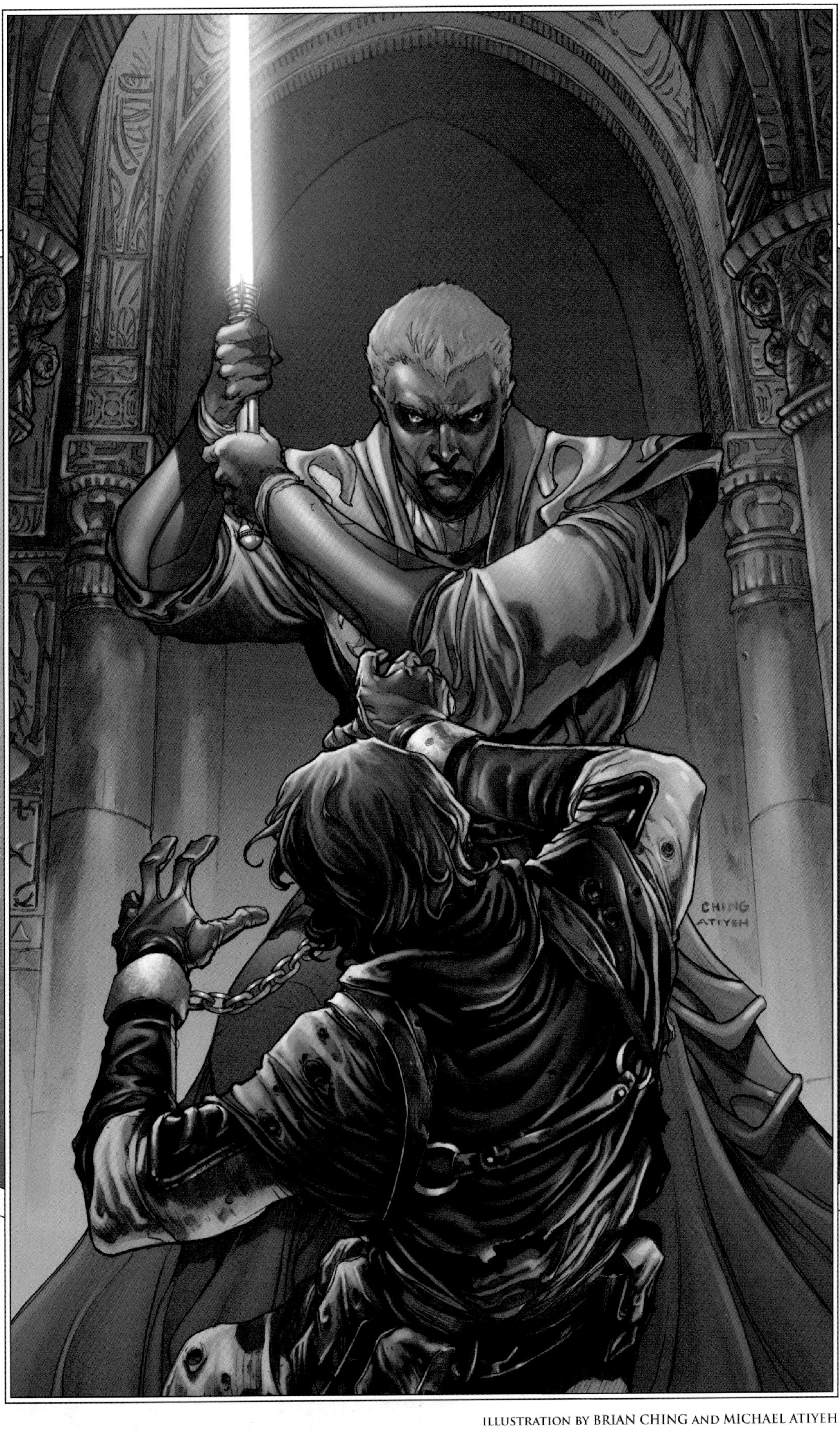
CHING
ATIYEH

ILLUSTRATION BY BRIAN CHING AND MICHAEL ATIYEH

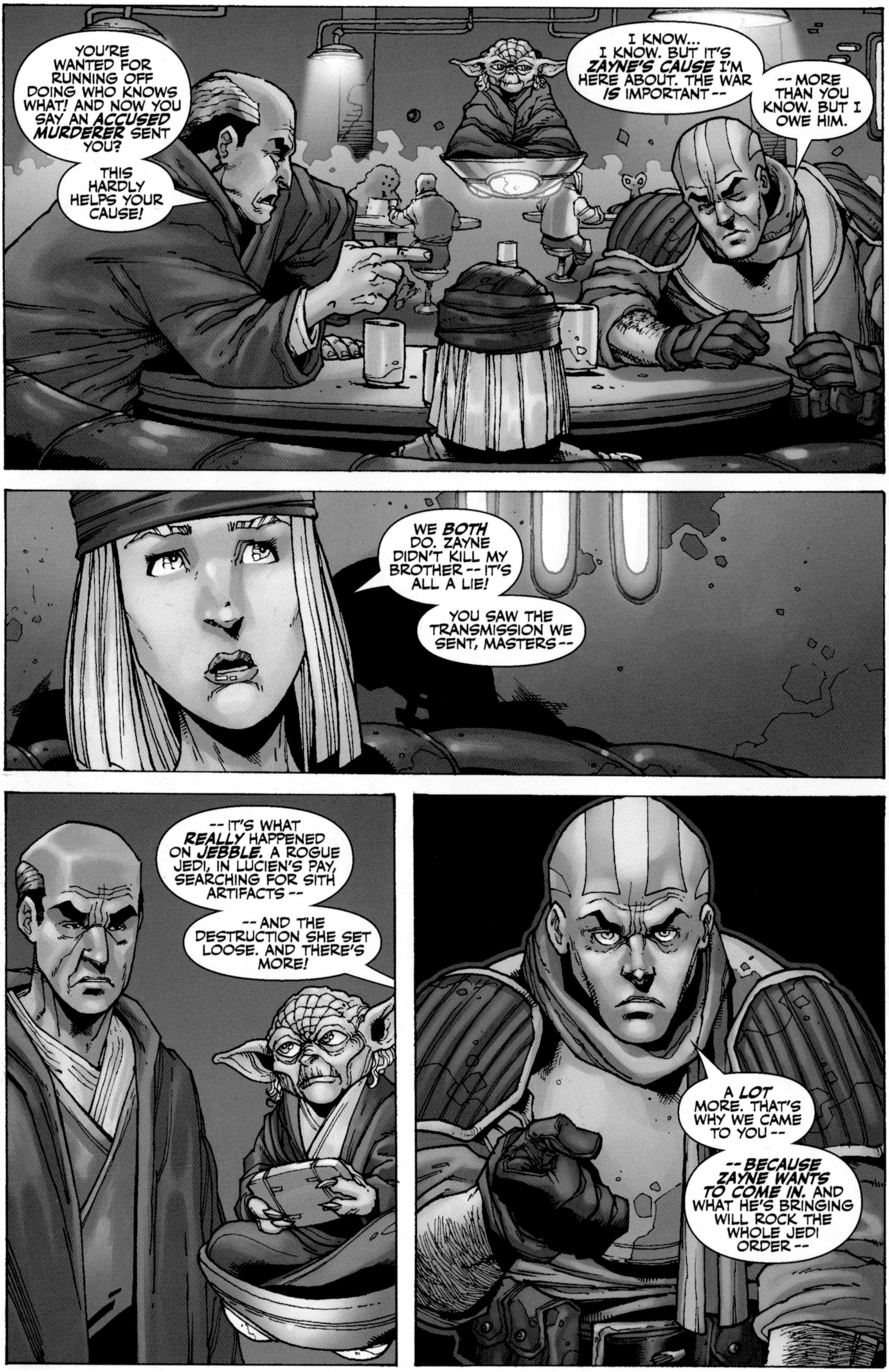
YOU'RE WANTED FOR RUNNING OFF DOING WHO KNOWS WHAT! AND NOW YOU SAY AN ACCUSED MURDERER SENT YOU?
THIS HARDLY HELPS YOUR CAUSE!
I KNOW... I KNOW. BUT IT'S ZAYNE'S CAUSE I'M HERE ABOUT. THE WAR IS IMPORTANT --
-- MORE THAN YOU KNOW. BUT I OWE HIM.
WE BOTH DO. ZAYNE DIDN'T KILL MY BROTHER -- IT'S ALL A LIE!
YOU SAW THE TRANSMISSION WE SENT, MASTERS --
-- IT'S WHAT REALLY HAPPENED ON JEBBLE. A ROGUE JEDI, IN LUCIEN'S PAY, SEARCHING FOR SITH ARTIFACTS --
-- AND THE DESTRUCTION SHE SET LOOSE. AND THERE'S MORE!
A LOT MORE. THAT'S WHY WE CAME TO YOU --
-- BECAUSE ZAYNE WANTS TO COME IN. AND WHAT HE'S BRINGING WILL ROCK THE WHOLE JEDI ORDER --

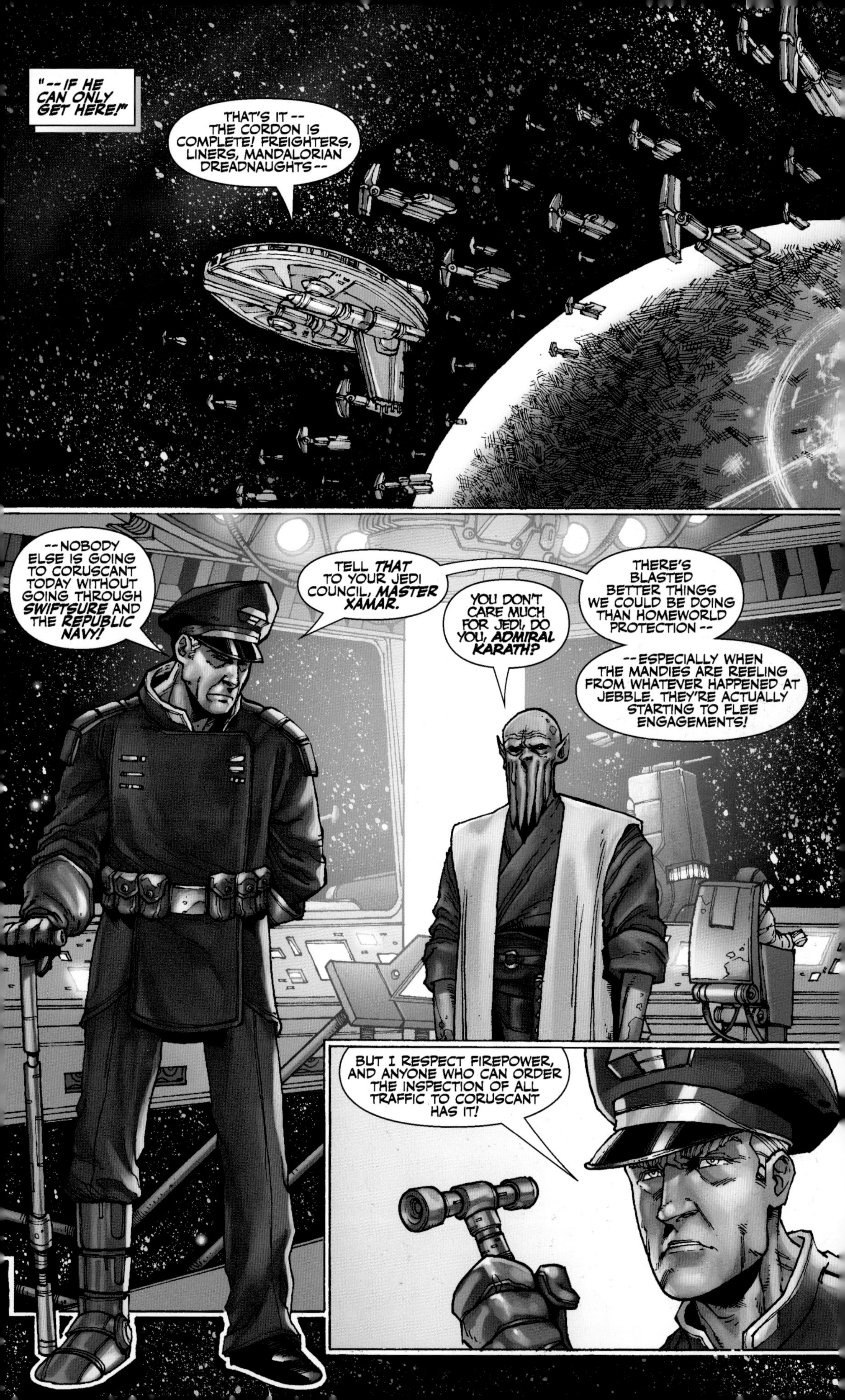
"--IF HE CAN ONLY GET HERE!"
THAT'S IT -- THE CORDON IS COMPLETE! FREIGHTERS, LINERS, MANDALORIAN DREADNAUGHTS--
--NOBODY ELSE IS GOING TO CORUSCANT TODAY WITHOUT GOING THROUGH SWIFTSURE AND THE REPUBLIC NAVY!
TELL THAT TO YOUR JEDI COUNCIL, MASTER XAMAR.
THERE'S BLASTED BETTER THINGS WE COULD BE DOING THAN HOMEWORLD PROTECTION --
YOU DON'T CARE MUCH FOR JEDI, DO YOU, ADMIRAL KARATH?
--ESPECIALLY WHEN THE MANDIES ARE REELING FROM WHATEVER HAPPENED AT JEBBLE. THEY'RE ACTUALLY STARTING TO FLEE ENGAGEMENTS!
BUT I RESPECT FIREPOWER, AND ANYONE WHO CAN ORDER THE INSPECTION OF ALL TRAFFIC TO CORUSCANT HAS IT!

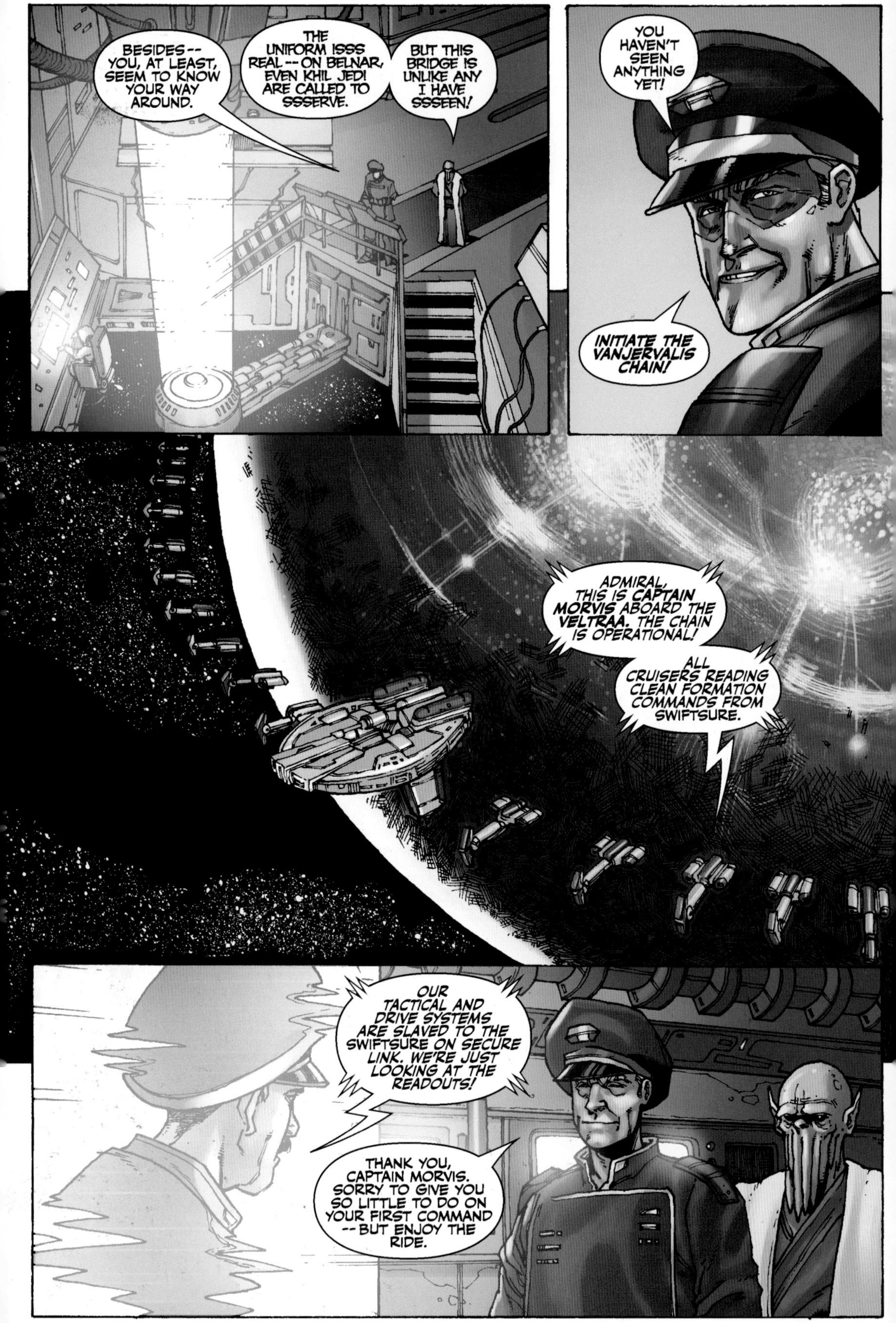
BESIDES-- YOU, AT LEAST, SEEM TO KNOW YOUR WAY AROUND.
THE UNIFORM ISSS REAL--ON BELNAR, EVEN KHIL JEDI ARE CALLED TO SSSERVE.
BUT THIS BRIDGE IS UNLIKE ANY I HAVE SSSEEN!
YOU HAVEN'T SEEN ANYTHING YET!
INITIATE THE VANJERVALIS CHAIN!
ADMIRAL, THIS IS CAPTAIN MORVIS ABOARD THE VELTRAA. THE CHAIN IS OPERATIONAL!
ALL CRUISERS READING CLEAN FORMATION COMMANDS FROM SWIFTSURE.
OUR TACTICAL AND DRIVE SYSTEMS ARE SLAVED TO THE SWIFTSURE ON SECURE LINK. WE'RE JUST LOOKING AT THE READOUTS!
THANK YOU, CAPTAIN MORVIS. SORRY TO GIVE YOU SO LITTLE TO DO ON YOUR FIRST COMMAND --BUT ENJOY THE RIDE.

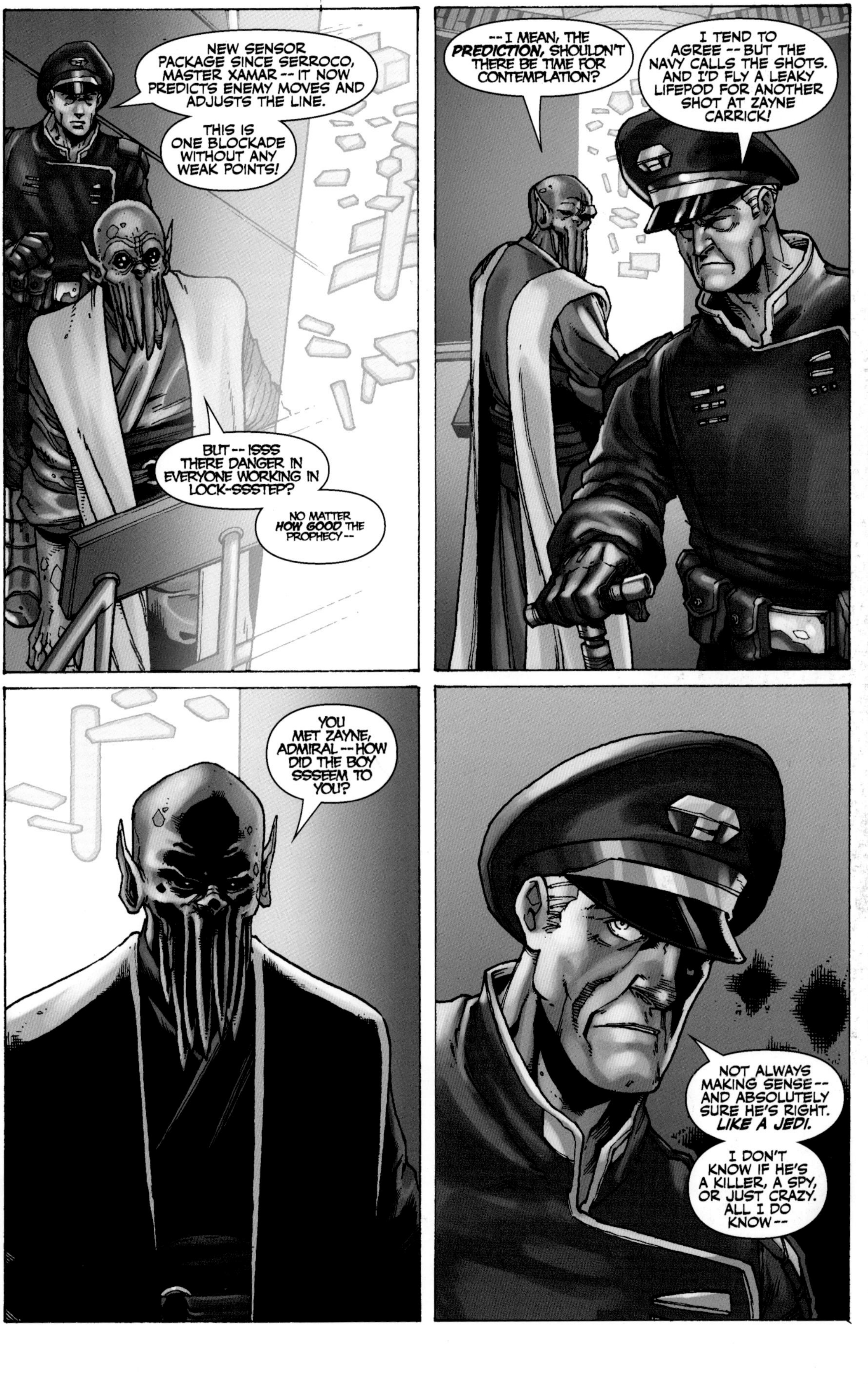

NEW SENSOR PACKAGE SINCE SERROCO, MASTER XAMAR -- IT NOW PREDICTS ENEMY MOVES AND ADJUSTS THE LINE.
THIS IS ONE BLOCKADE WITHOUT ANY WEAK POINTS!
BUT -- ISSS THERE DANGER IN EVERYONE WORKING IN LOCK-SSSTEP?
NO MATTER **HOW GOOD** THE PROPHECY --
-- I MEAN, THE **PREDICTION,** SHOULDN'T THERE BE TIME FOR CONTEMPLATION?
I TEND TO AGREE -- BUT THE NAVY CALLS THE SHOTS. AND I'D FLY A LEAKY LIFEPOD FOR ANOTHER SHOT AT ZAYNE CARRICK!
YOU MET ZAYNE, ADMIRAL -- HOW DID THE BOY SSSEEM TO YOU?
NOT ALWAYS MAKING SENSE -- AND ABSOLUTELY SURE HE'S RIGHT. **LIKE A JEDI.**
I DON'T KNOW IF HE'S A KILLER, A SPY, OR JUST CRAZY. ALL I DO KNOW --

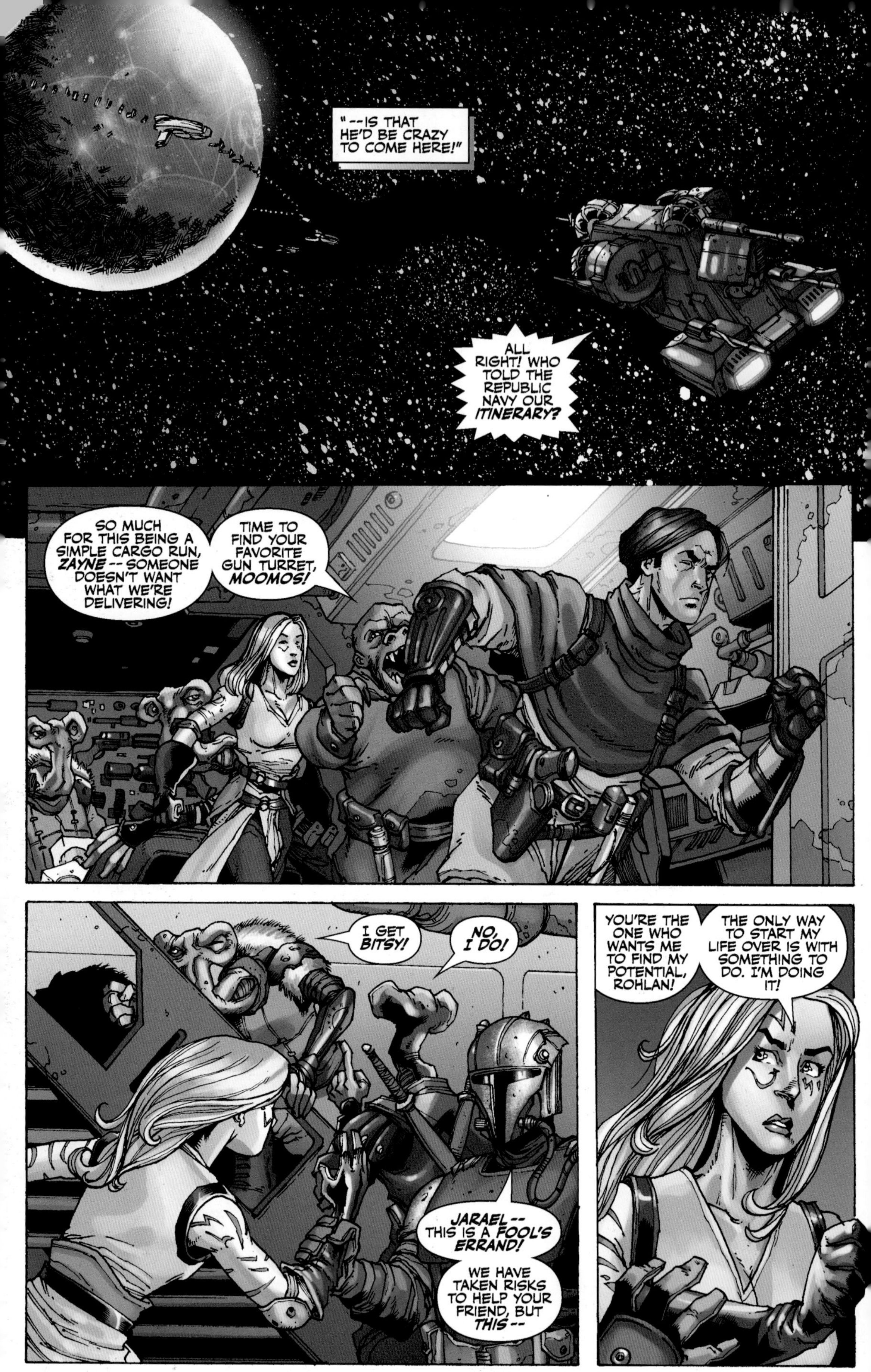
"--IS THAT HE'D BE CRAZY TO COME HERE!"
ALL RIGHT! WHO TOLD THE REPUBLIC NAVY OUR ITINERARY?
SO MUCH FOR THIS BEING A SIMPLE CARGO RUN, ZAYNE -- SOMEONE DOESN'T WANT WHAT WE'RE DELIVERING!
TIME TO FIND YOUR FAVORITE GUN TURRET, MOOMOS!
I GET BITSY!
NO, I DO!
JARAEL -- THIS IS A FOOL'S ERRAND!
WE HAVE TAKEN RISKS TO HELP YOUR FRIEND, BUT THIS --
YOU'RE THE ONE WHO WANTS ME TO FIND MY POTENTIAL, ROHLAN!
THE ONLY WAY TO START MY LIFE OVER IS WITH SOMETHING TO DO. I'M DOING IT!

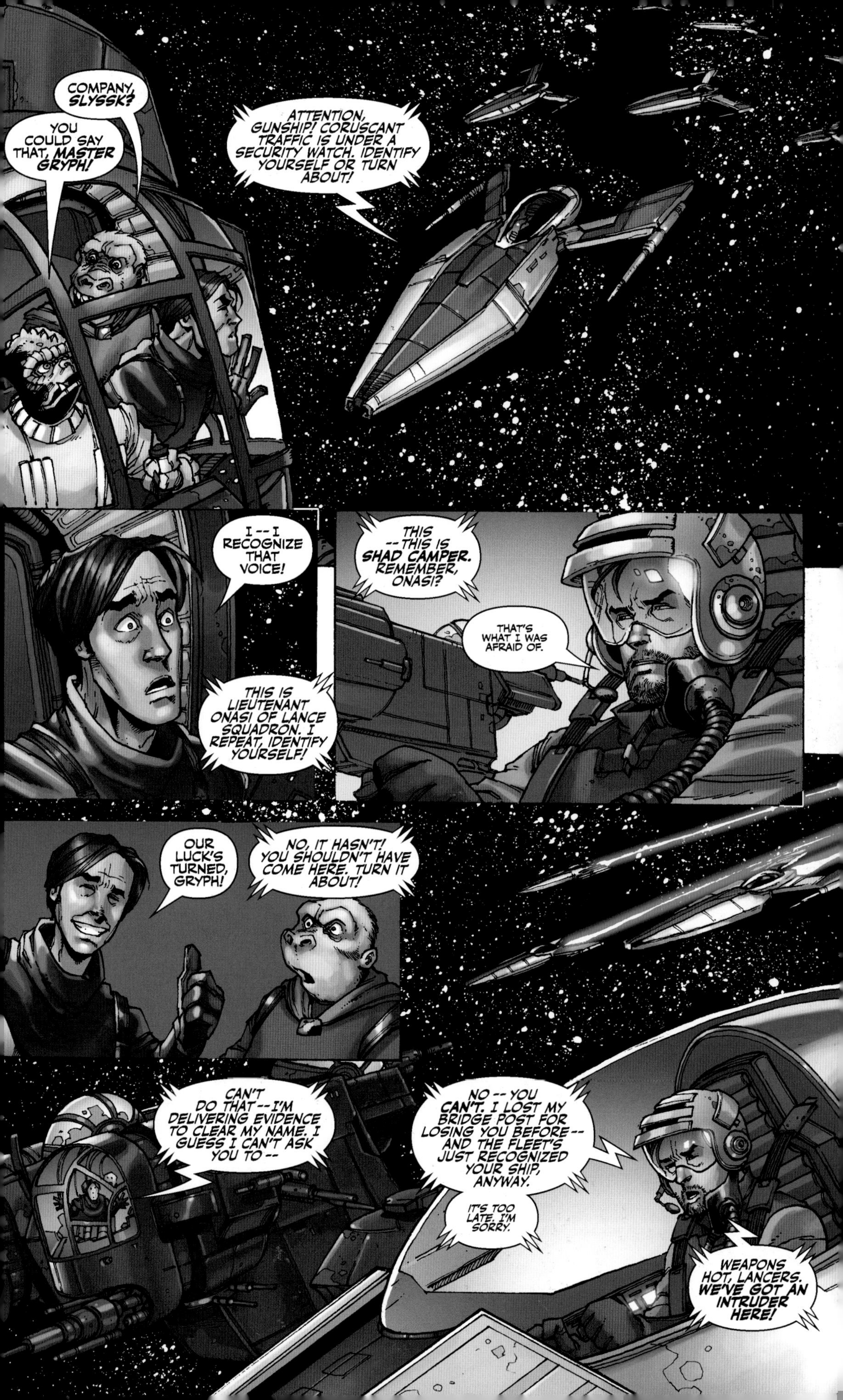
COMPANY, SLYSSK?
YOU COULD SAY THAT, MASTER GRYPH!
ATTENTION, GUNSHIP! CORUSCANT TRAFFIC IS UNDER A SECURITY WATCH. IDENTIFY YOURSELF OR TURN ABOUT!
I -- I RECOGNIZE THAT VOICE!
THIS IS LIEUTENANT ONASI OF LANCE SQUADRON. I REPEAT, IDENTIFY YOURSELF!
THIS --THIS IS SHAD CAMPER. REMEMBER, ONASI?
THAT'S WHAT I WAS AFRAID OF.
OUR LUCK'S TURNED, GRYPH!
NO, IT HASN'T! YOU SHOULDN'T HAVE COME HERE. TURN IT ABOUT!
CAN'T DO THAT -- I'M DELIVERING EVIDENCE TO CLEAR MY NAME. I GUESS I CAN'T ASK YOU TO --
NO -- YOU CAN'T. I LOST MY BRIDGE POST FOR LOSING YOU BEFORE -- AND THE FLEET'S JUST RECOGNIZED YOUR SHIP, ANYWAY.
IT'S TOO LATE. I'M SORRY.
WEAPONS HOT, LANCERS. WE'VE GOT AN INTRUDER HERE!

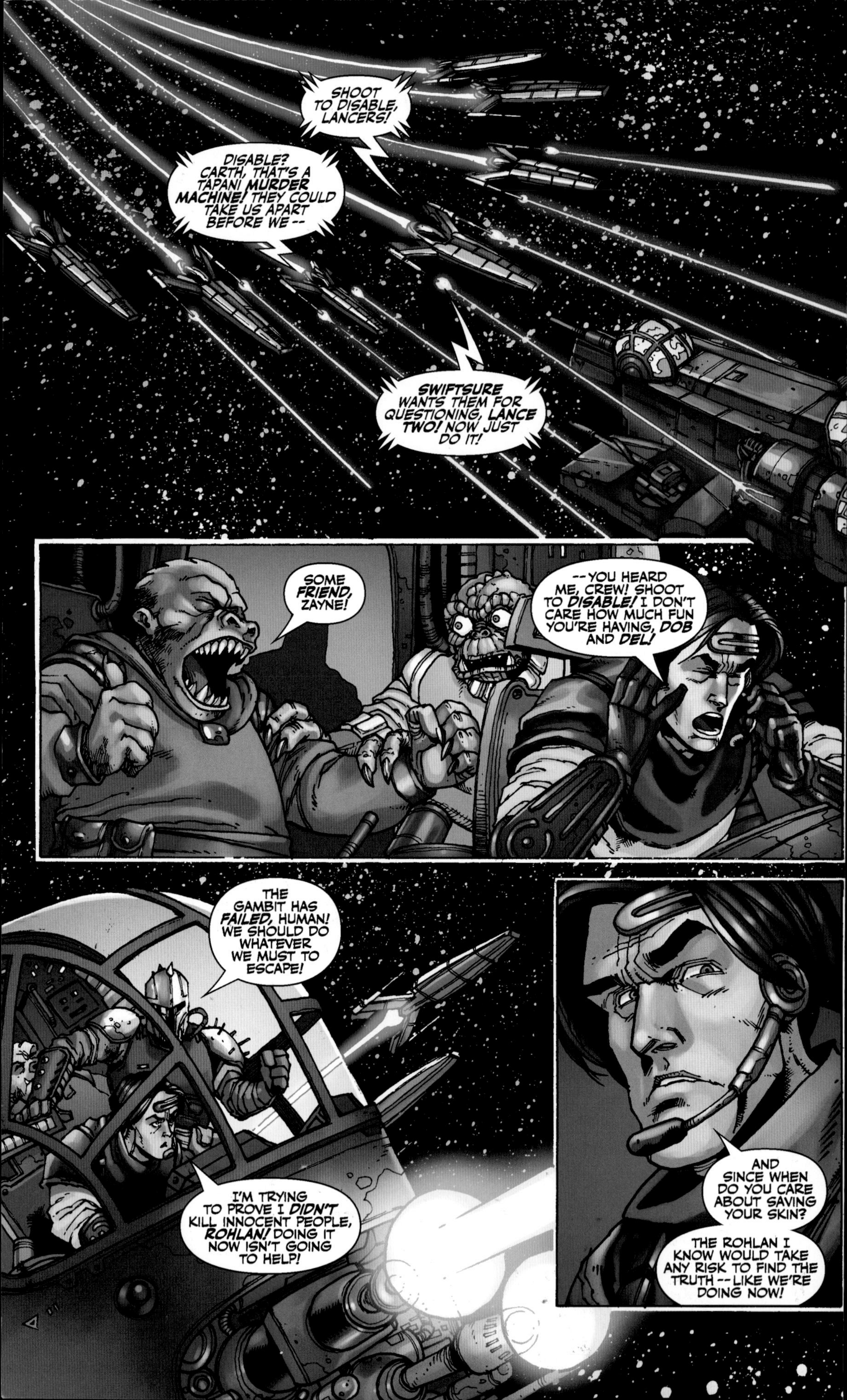
SHOOT TO DISABLE, LANCERS!
DISABLE? CARTH, THAT'S A TAPANI MURDER MACHINE! THEY COULD TAKE US APART BEFORE WE --
SWIFTSURE WANTS THEM FOR QUESTIONING, LANCE TWO! NOW JUST DO IT!
SOME FRIEND, ZAYNE!
--YOU HEARD ME, CREW! SHOOT TO DISABLE! I DON'T CARE HOW MUCH FUN YOU'RE HAVING, DOB AND DEL!
THE GAMBIT HAS FAILED, HUMAN! WE SHOULD DO WHATEVER WE MUST TO ESCAPE!
I'M TRYING TO PROVE I DIDN'T KILL INNOCENT PEOPLE, ROHLAN! DOING IT NOW ISN'T GOING TO HELP!
AND SINCE WHEN DO YOU CARE ABOUT SAVING YOUR SKIN?
THE ROHLAN I KNOW WOULD TAKE ANY RISK TO FIND THE TRUTH -- LIKE WE'RE DOING NOW!

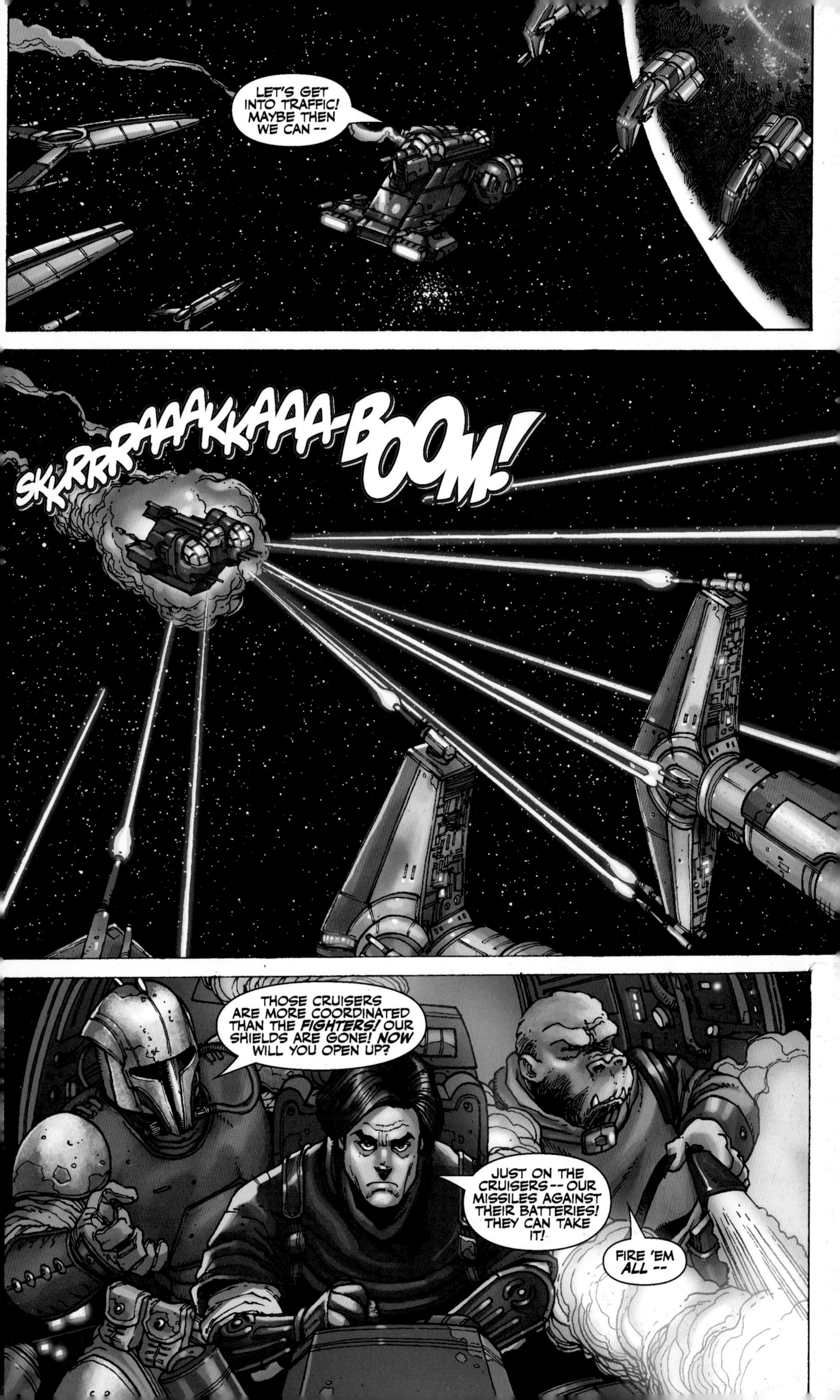
LET'S GET INTO TRAFFIC! MAYBE THEN WE CAN --
SKKRRRAAAKKAAA-BOOM!
THOSE CRUISERS ARE MORE COORDINATED THAN THE FIGHTERS! OUR SHIELDS ARE GONE! NOW WILL YOU OPEN UP?
JUST ON THE CRUISERS -- OUR MISSILES AGAINST THEIR BATTERIES! THEY CAN TAKE IT!
FIRE 'EM ALL --

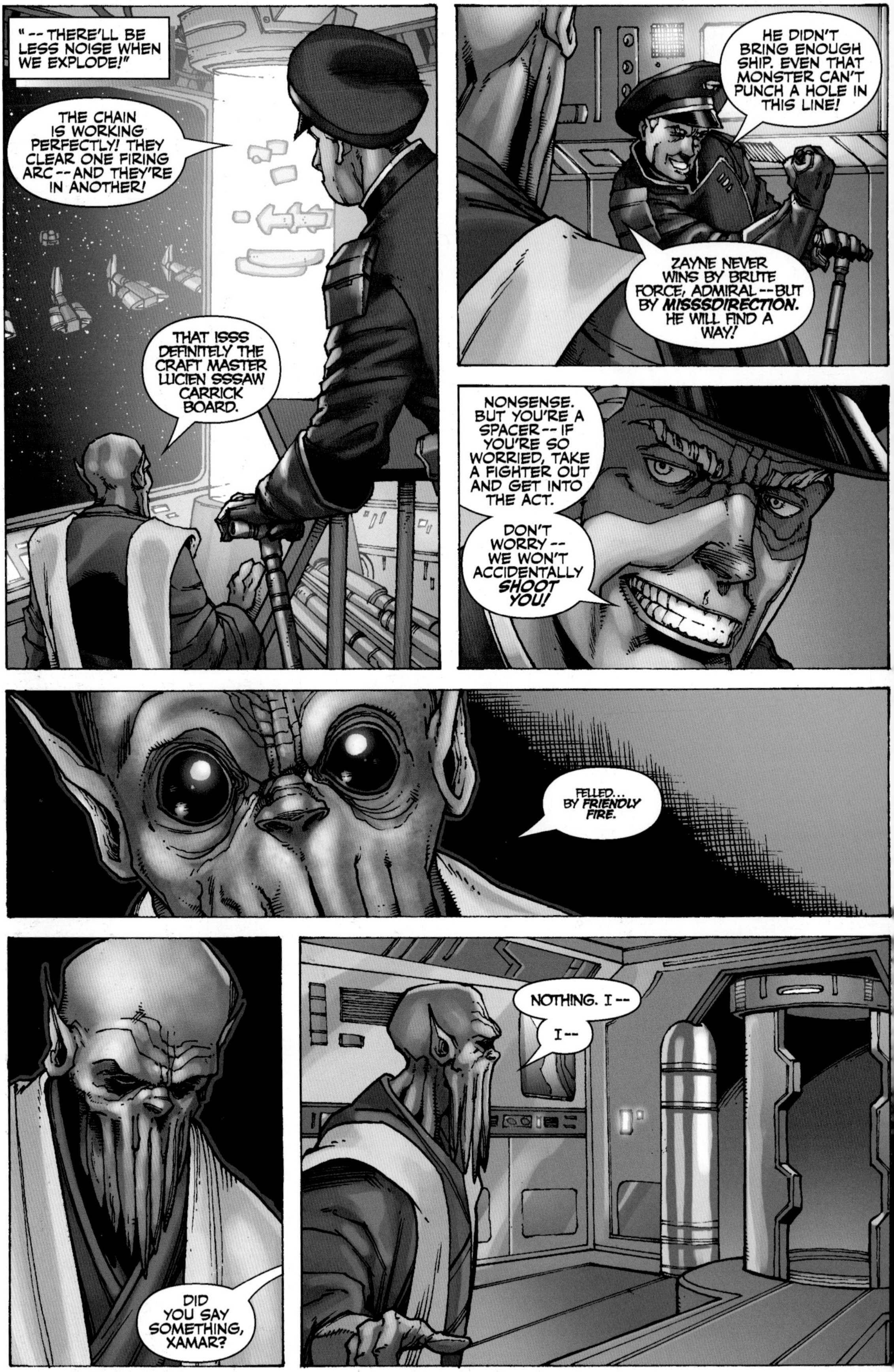
"--THERE'LL BE LESS NOISE WHEN WE EXPLODE!"
THE CHAIN IS WORKING PERFECTLY! THEY CLEAR ONE FIRING ARC--AND THEY'RE IN ANOTHER!
THAT ISSS DEFINITELY THE CRAFT MASTER LUCIEN SSSAW CARRICK BOARD.
HE DIDN'T BRING ENOUGH SHIP. EVEN THAT MONSTER CAN'T PUNCH A HOLE IN THIS LINE!
ZAYNE NEVER WINS BY BRUTE FORCE, ADMIRAL--BUT BY MISSSDIRECTION. HE WILL FIND A WAY!
NONSENSE. BUT YOU'RE A SPACER--IF YOU'RE SO WORRIED, TAKE A FIGHTER OUT AND GET INTO THE ACT.
DON'T WORRY--WE WON'T ACCIDENTALLY SHOOT YOU!
FELLED... BY FRIENDLY FIRE.
DID YOU SAY SOMETHING, XAMAR?
NOTHING. I--
I--

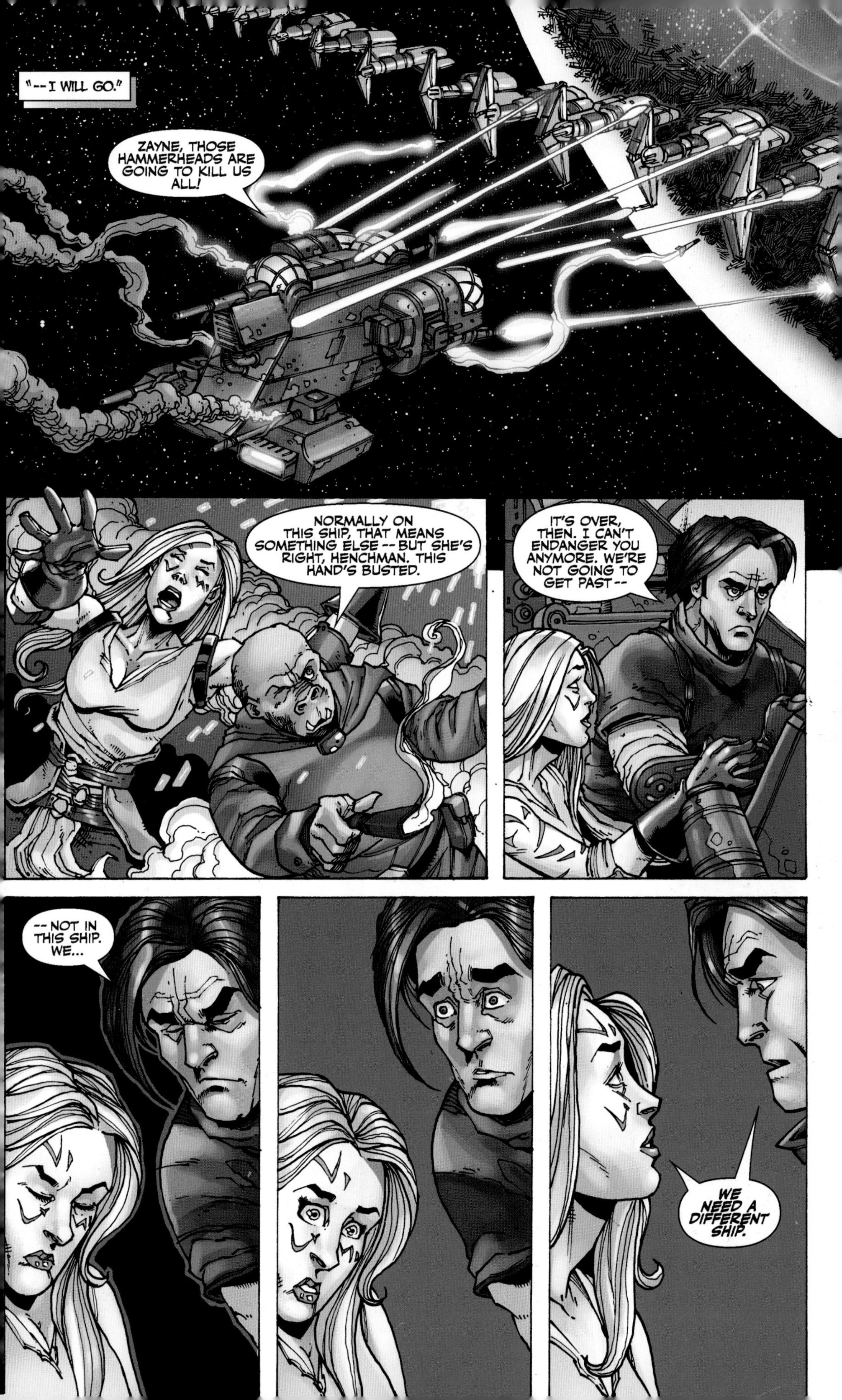

"--I WILL GO."
ZAYNE, THOSE HAMMERHEADS ARE GOING TO KILL US ALL!
NORMALLY ON THIS SHIP, THAT MEANS SOMETHING ELSE--BUT SHE'S RIGHT, HENCHMAN. THIS HAND'S BUSTED.
IT'S OVER, THEN. I CAN'T ENDANGER YOU ANYMORE. WE'RE NOT GOING TO GET PAST--
--NOT IN THIS SHIP. WE...
WE NEED A DIFFERENT SHIP.

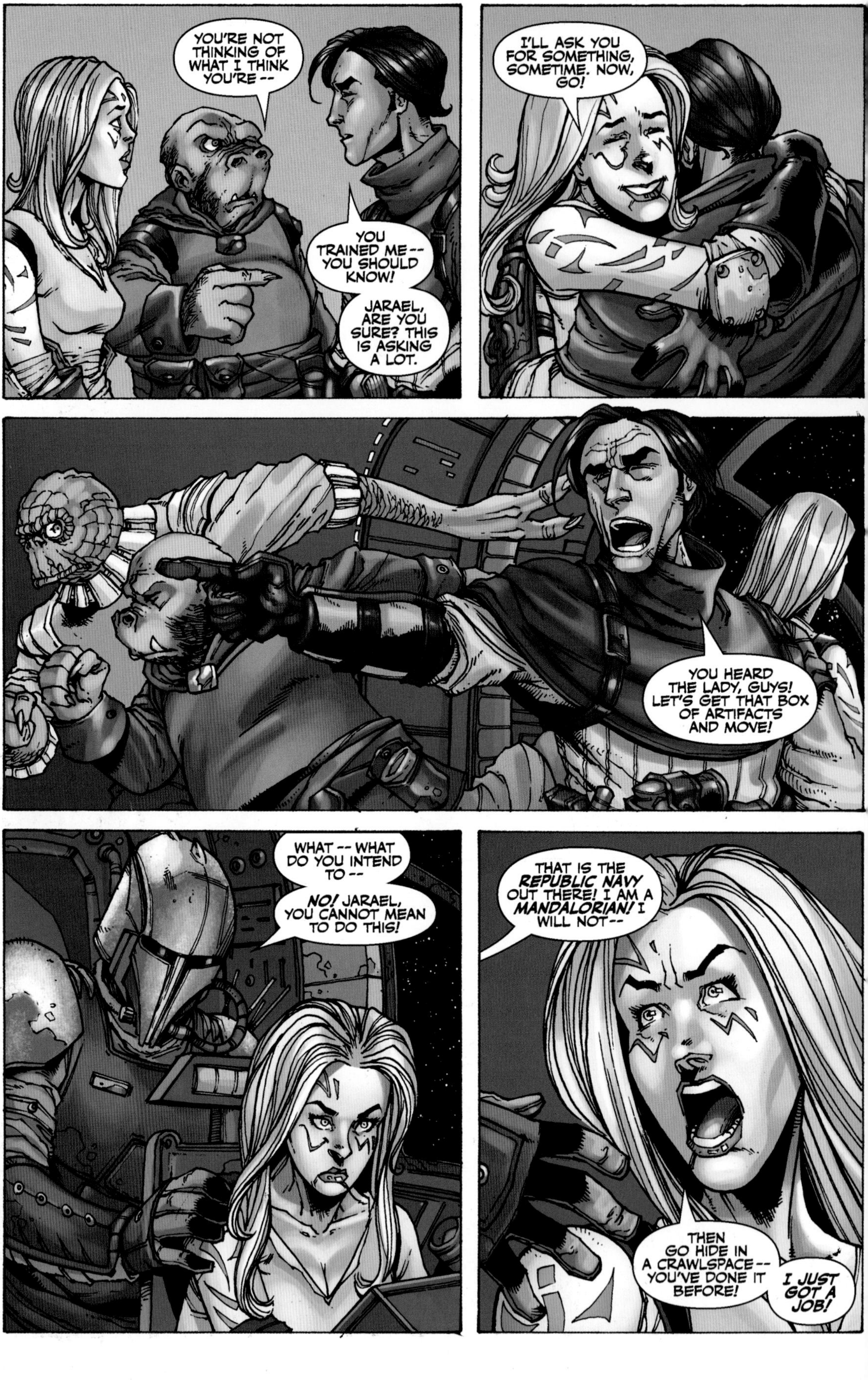
YOU'RE NOT THINKING OF WHAT I THINK YOU'RE --
YOU TRAINED ME -- YOU SHOULD KNOW!
JARAEL, ARE YOU SURE? THIS IS ASKING A LOT.
I'LL ASK YOU FOR SOMETHING, SOMETIME. NOW, GO!
YOU HEARD THE LADY, GUYS! LET'S GET THAT BOX OF ARTIFACTS AND MOVE!
WHAT -- WHAT DO YOU INTEND TO --
NO! JARAEL, YOU CANNOT MEAN TO DO THIS!
THAT IS THE REPUBLIC NAVY OUT THERE! I AM A MANDALORIAN! I WILL NOT--
THEN GO HIDE IN A CRAWLSPACE -- YOU'VE DONE IT BEFORE!
I JUST GOT A JOB!

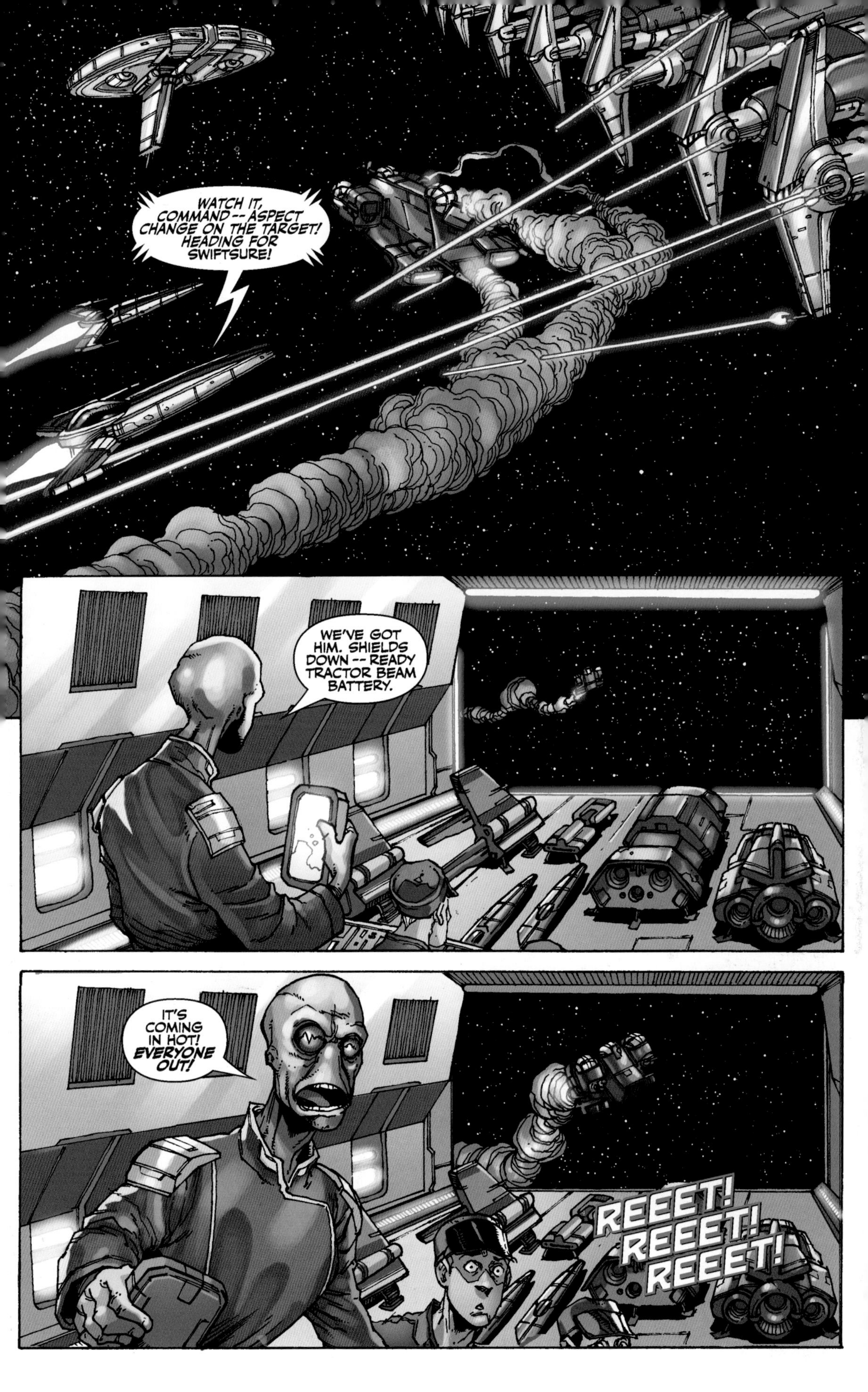
WATCH IT, COMMAND-- ASPECT CHANGE ON THE TARGET! HEADING FOR SWIFTSURE!
WE'VE GOT HIM. SHIELDS DOWN -- READY TRACTOR BEAM BATTERY.
IT'S COMING IN HOT! EVERYONE OUT!
REEET! REEET! REEET!

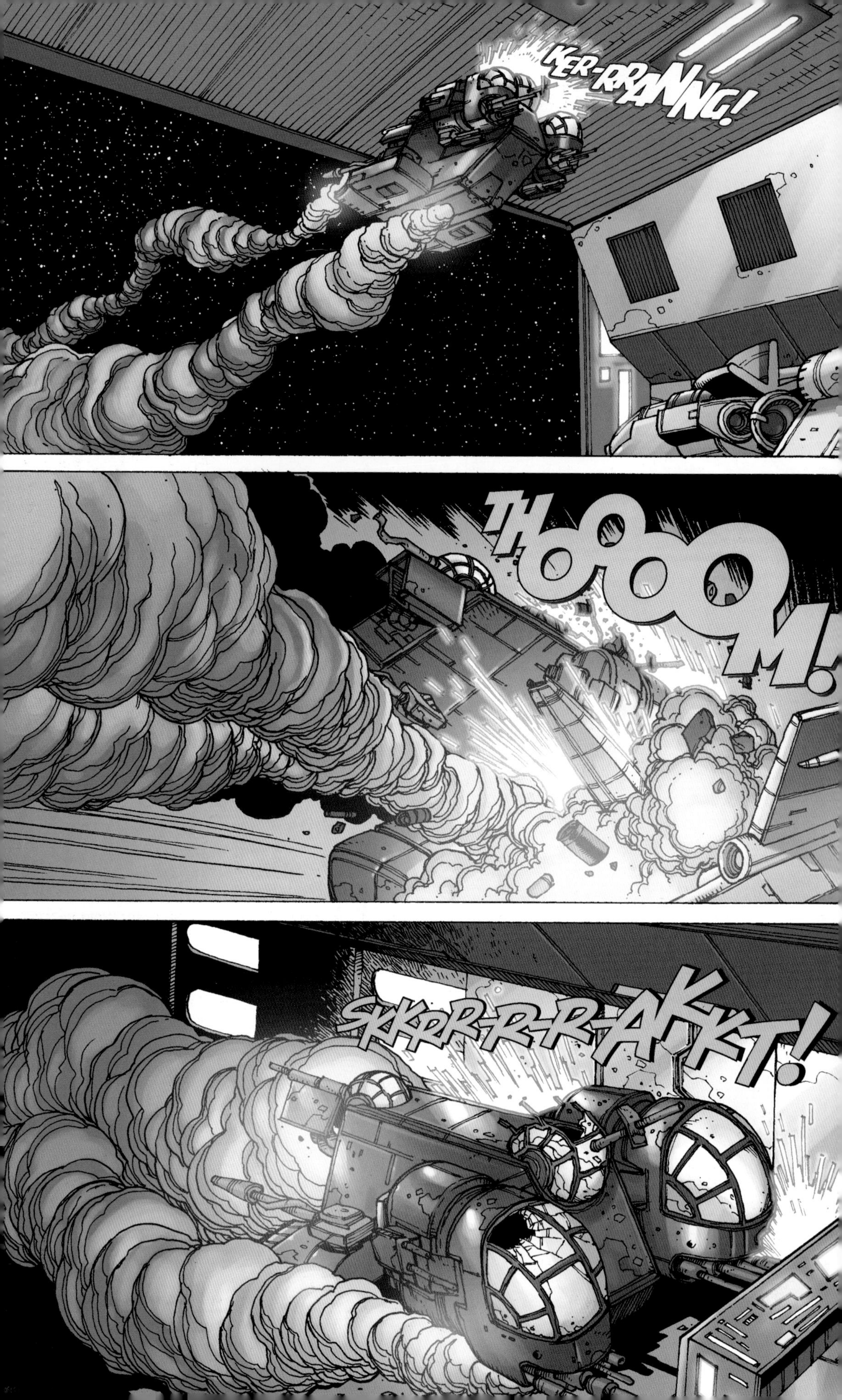
KER-RRANNG!
THOOOOM!
SKKRR-R-R-AKKT!

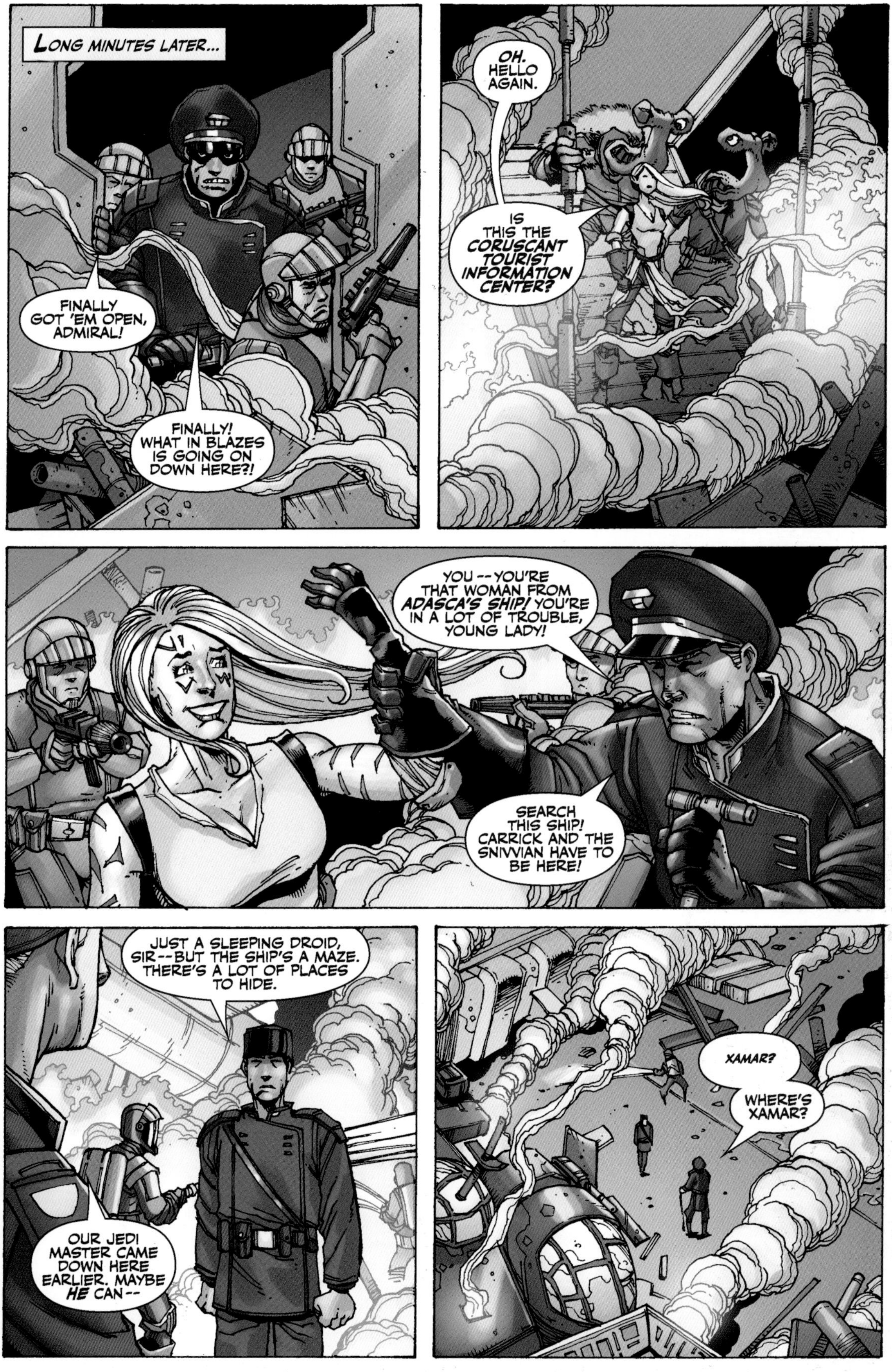
LONG MINUTES LATER...
FINALLY GOT 'EM OPEN, ADMIRAL!
FINALLY! WHAT IN BLAZES IS GOING ON DOWN HERE?!
OH. HELLO AGAIN.
IS THIS THE CORUSCANT TOURIST INFORMATION CENTER?
YOU--YOU'RE THAT WOMAN FROM ADASCA'S SHIP! YOU'RE IN A LOT OF TROUBLE, YOUNG LADY!
SEARCH THIS SHIP! CARRICK AND THE SNIVVIAN HAVE TO BE HERE!
JUST A SLEEPING DROID, SIR--BUT THE SHIP'S A MAZE. THERE'S A LOT OF PLACES TO HIDE.
OUR JEDI MASTER CAME DOWN HERE EARLIER. MAYBE HE CAN--
XAMAR?
WHERE'S XAMAR?

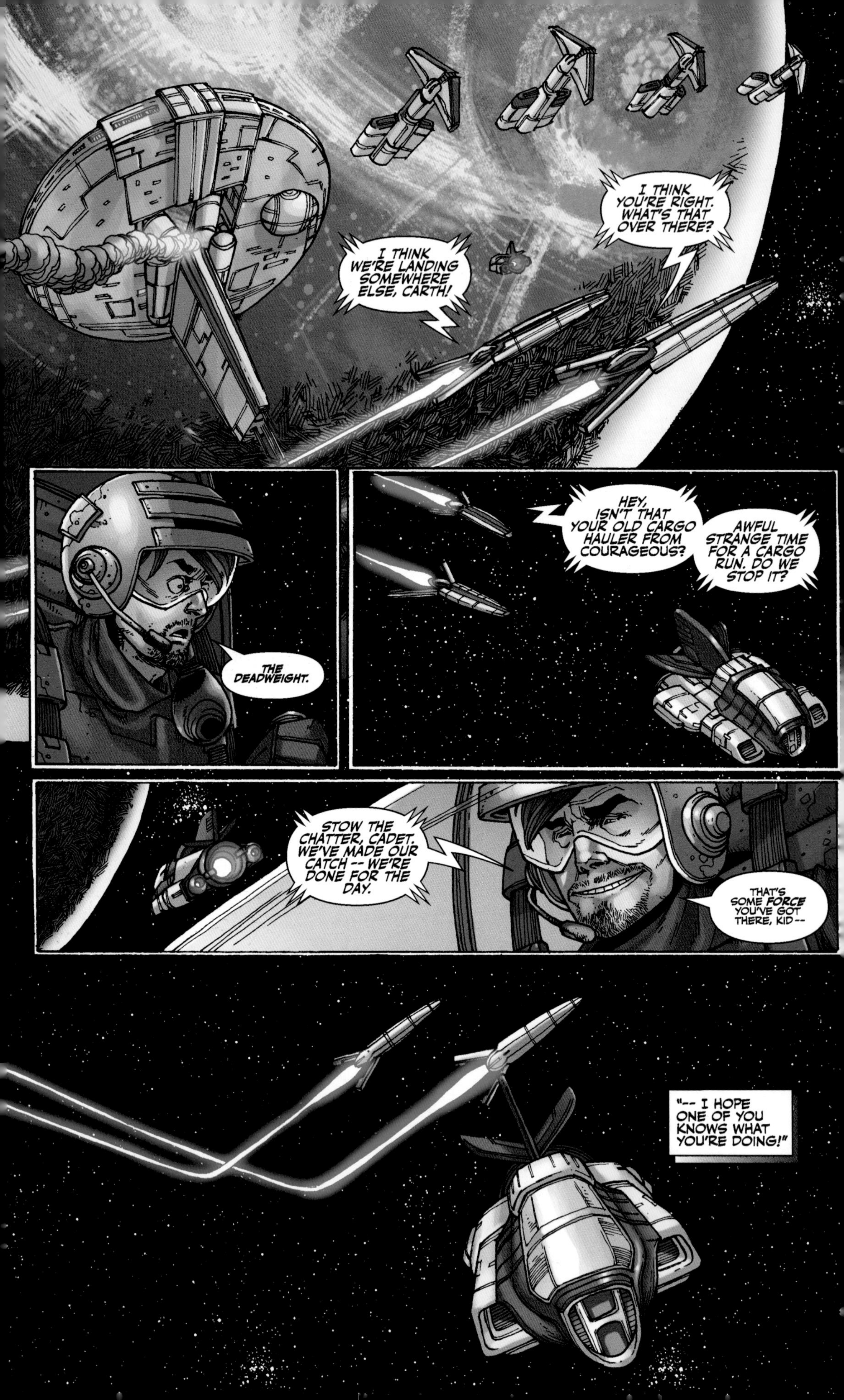
I THINK WE'RE LANDING SOMEWHERE ELSE, CARTH!
I THINK YOU'RE RIGHT. WHAT'S THAT OVER THERE?
THE DEADWEIGHT.
HEY, ISN'T THAT YOUR OLD CARGO HAULER FROM COURAGEOUS?
AWFUL STRANGE TIME FOR A CARGO RUN. DO WE STOP IT?
STOW THE CHATTER, CADET. WE'VE MADE OUR CATCH -- WE'RE DONE FOR THE DAY.
THAT'S SOME FORCE YOU'VE GOT THERE, KID--
"-- I HOPE ONE OF YOU KNOWS WHAT YOU'RE DOING!"

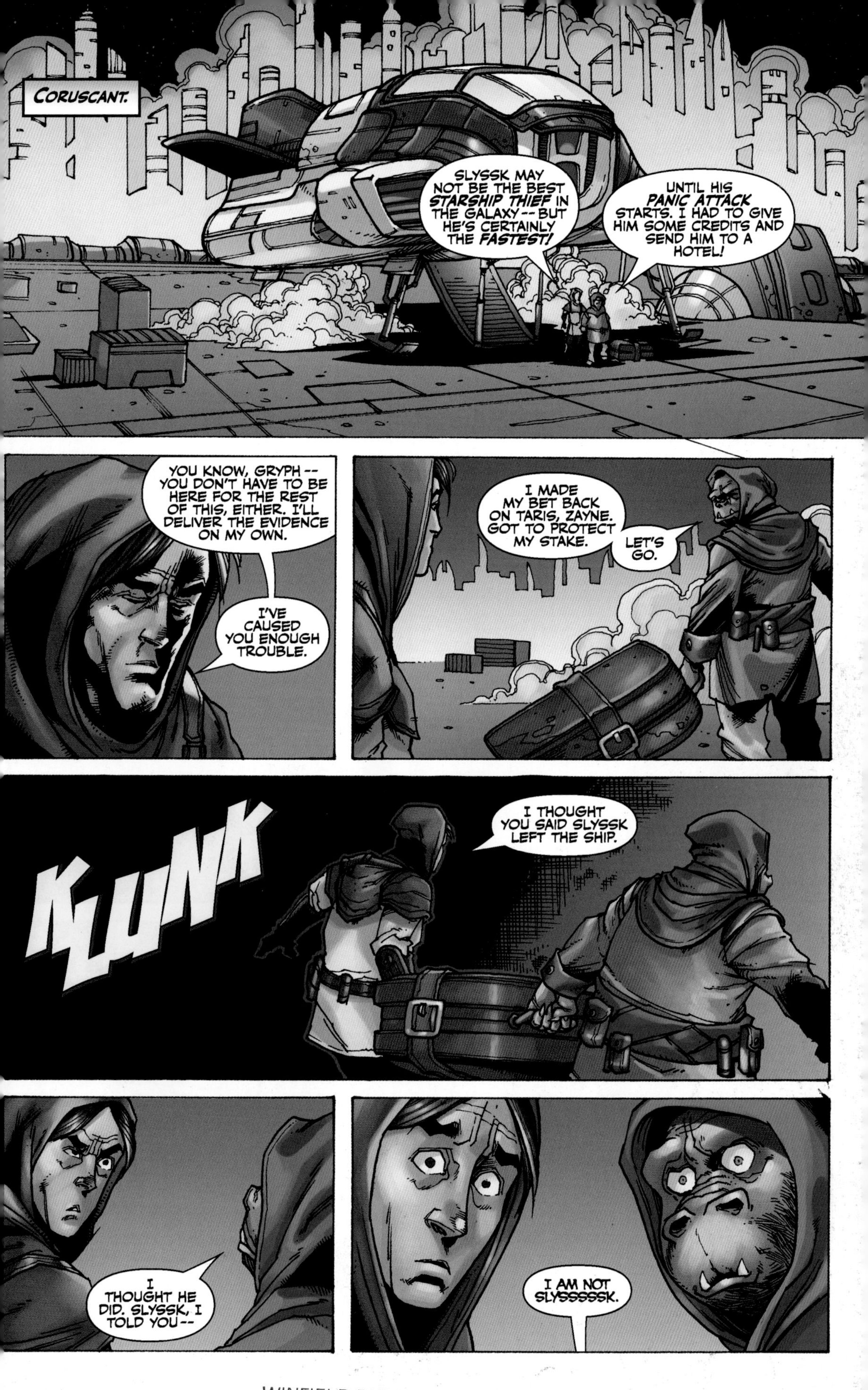

CORUSCANT.
SLYSSK MAY NOT BE THE BEST STARSHIP THIEF IN THE GALAXY -- BUT HE'S CERTAINLY THE FASTEST!
UNTIL HIS PANIC ATTACK STARTS. I HAD TO GIVE HIM SOME CREDITS AND SEND HIM TO A HOTEL!
YOU KNOW, GRYPH -- YOU DON'T HAVE TO BE HERE FOR THE REST OF THIS, EITHER. I'LL DELIVER THE EVIDENCE ON MY OWN.
I'VE CAUSED YOU ENOUGH TROUBLE.
I MADE MY BET BACK ON TARIS, ZAYNE. GOT TO PROTECT MY STAKE.
LET'S GO.
KLUNK
I THOUGHT YOU SAID SLYSSK LEFT THE SHIP.
I THOUGHT HE DID. SLYSSK, I TOLD YOU --
I AM NOT SLYSSSSSK.

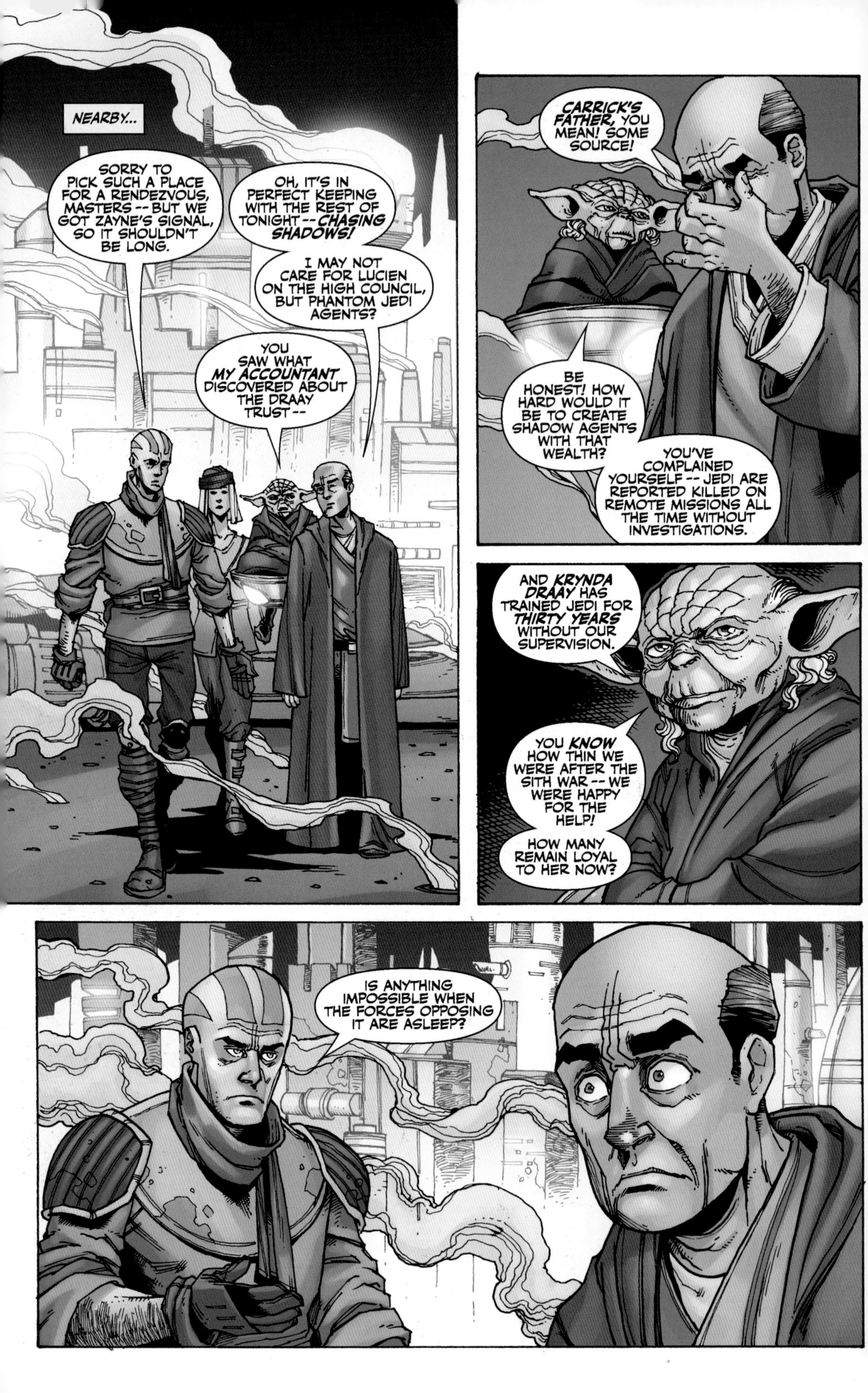
NEARBY...
SORRY TO PICK SUCH A PLACE FOR A RENDEZVOUS, MASTERS -- BUT WE GOT ZAYNE'S SIGNAL, SO IT SHOULDN'T BE LONG.
OH, IT'S IN PERFECT KEEPING WITH THE REST OF TONIGHT -- CHASING SHADOWS!
I MAY NOT CARE FOR LUCIEN ON THE HIGH COUNCIL, BUT PHANTOM JEDI AGENTS?
YOU SAW WHAT MY ACCOUNTANT DISCOVERED ABOUT THE DRAAY TRUST --
CARRICK'S FATHER, YOU MEAN! SOME SOURCE!
BE HONEST! HOW HARD WOULD IT BE TO CREATE SHADOW AGENTS WITH THAT WEALTH?
YOU'VE COMPLAINED YOURSELF -- JEDI ARE REPORTED KILLED ON REMOTE MISSIONS ALL THE TIME WITHOUT INVESTIGATIONS.
AND KRYNDA DRAAY HAS TRAINED JEDI FOR THIRTY YEARS WITHOUT OUR SUPERVISION.
YOU KNOW HOW THIN WE WERE AFTER THE SITH WAR -- WE WERE HAPPY FOR THE HELP!
HOW MANY REMAIN LOYAL TO HER NOW?
IS ANYTHING IMPOSSIBLE WHEN THE FORCES OPPOSING IT ARE ASLEEP?

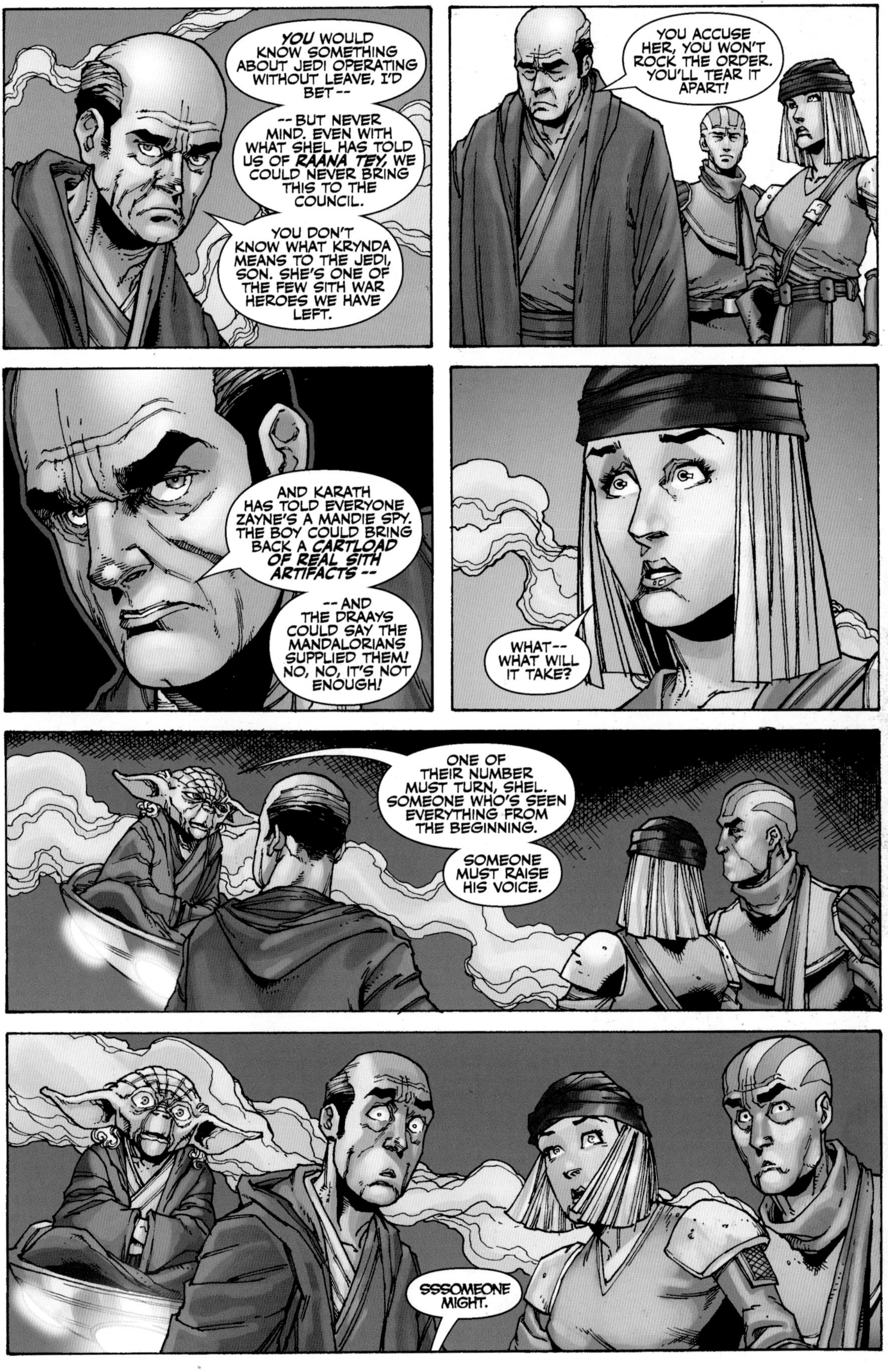
YOU WOULD KNOW SOMETHING ABOUT JEDI OPERATING WITHOUT LEAVE, I'D BET--
--BUT NEVER MIND. EVEN WITH WHAT SHEL HAS TOLD US OF ***RAANA TEY,*** WE COULD NEVER BRING THIS TO THE COUNCIL.
YOU DON'T KNOW WHAT KRYNDA MEANS TO THE JEDI, SON. SHE'S ONE OF THE FEW SITH WAR HEROES WE HAVE LEFT.
YOU ACCUSE HER, YOU WON'T ROCK THE ORDER. YOU'LL TEAR IT APART!
AND KARATH HAS TOLD EVERYONE ZAYNE'S A MANDIE SPY. THE BOY COULD BRING BACK A ***CARTLOAD OF REAL SITH ARTIFACTS--***
--AND THE DRAAYS COULD SAY THE MANDALORIANS SUPPLIED THEM! NO, NO, IT'S NOT ENOUGH!
WHAT-- WHAT WILL IT TAKE?
ONE OF THEIR NUMBER MUST TURN, SHEL. SOMEONE WHO'S SEEN EVERYTHING FROM THE BEGINNING.
SOMEONE MUST RAISE HIS VOICE.
SSSOMEONE MIGHT.

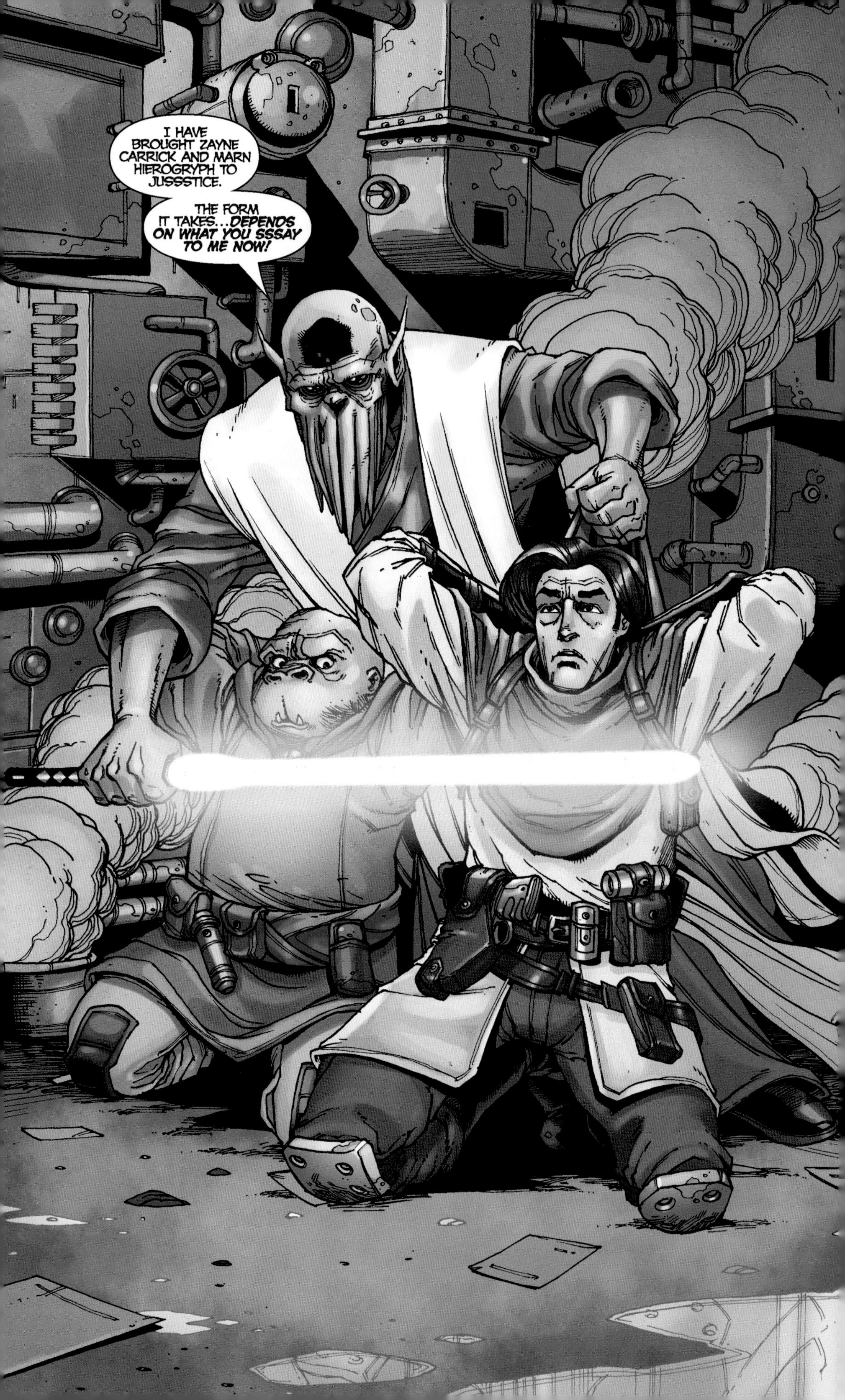
I HAVE BROUGHT ZAYNE CARRICK AND MARN HIEROGRYPH TO JUSSSTICE.
THE FORM IT TAKES...*DEPENDS ON WHAT YOU SSSAY TO ME NOW!*

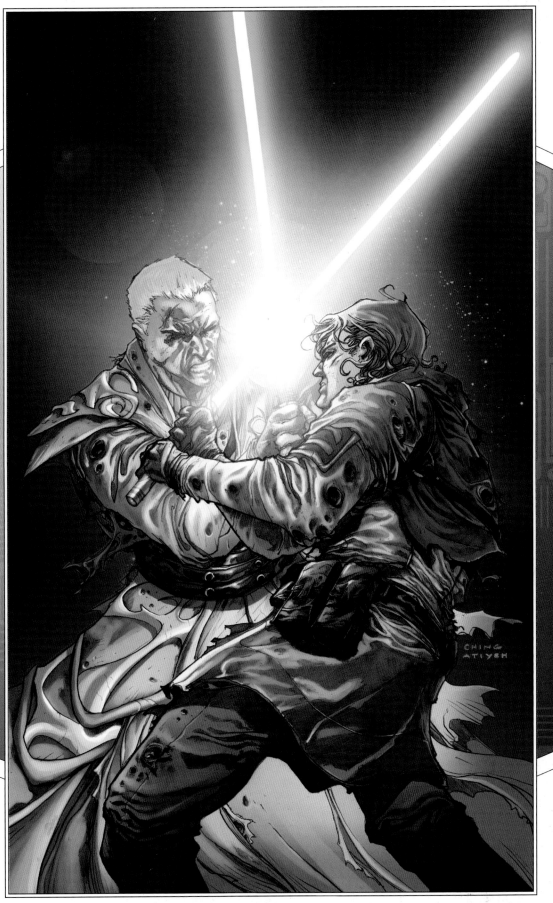

ILLUSTRATION BY BRIAN CHING AND MICHAEL ATIYEH

VINDICATION

art by Brian Ching (pages 77–98 and 121–164)
pencils by Bong Dazo and inks by Joe Pimentel (pages 99–120)

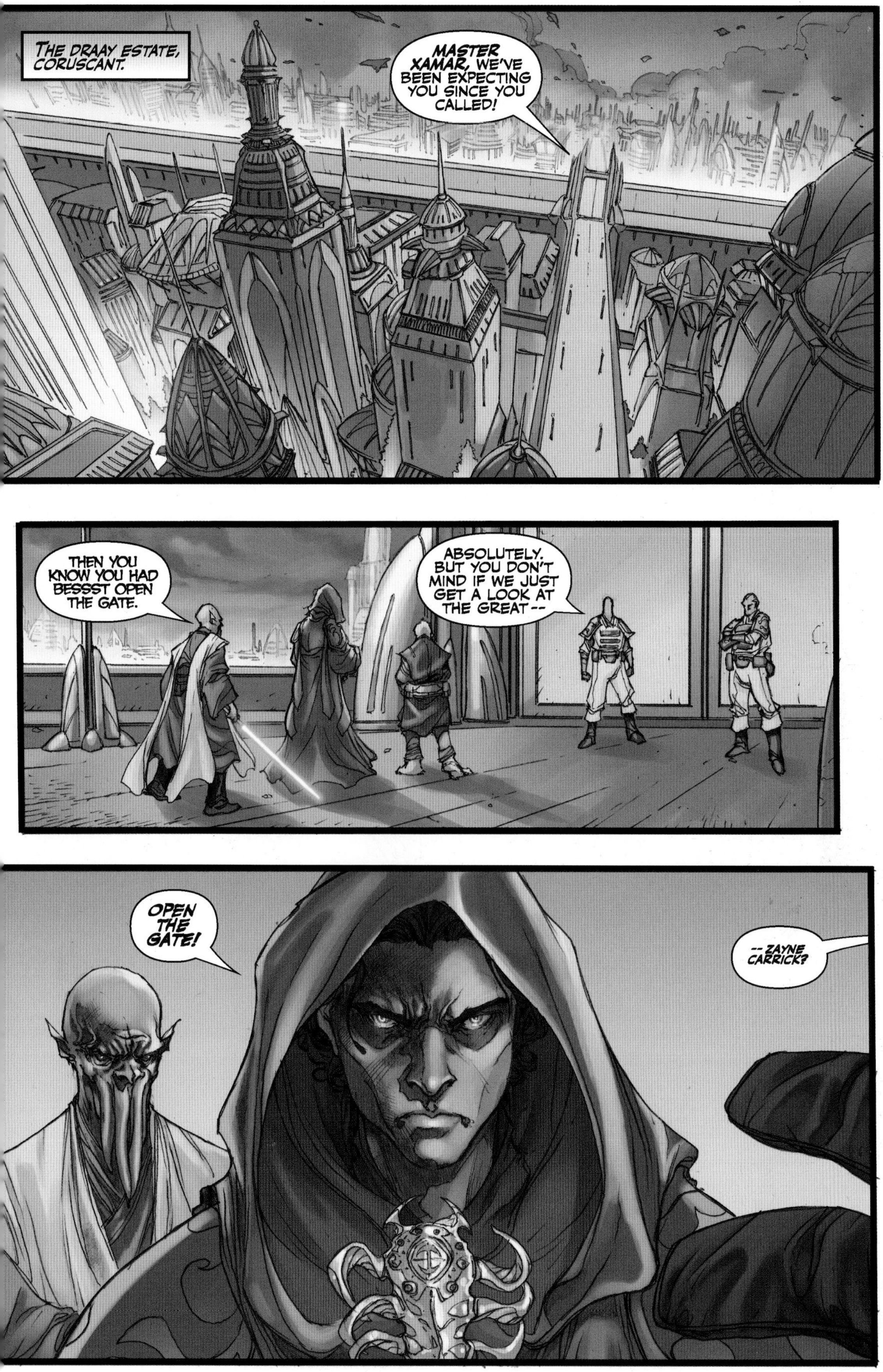
THE DRAAY ESTATE, CORUSCANT.
MASTER XAMAR, WE'VE BEEN EXPECTING YOU SINCE YOU CALLED!
THEN YOU KNOW YOU HAD BESSST OPEN THE GATE.
ABSOLUTELY. BUT YOU DON'T MIND IF WE JUST GET A LOOK AT THE GREAT --
OPEN THE GATE!
-- ZAYNE CARRICK?

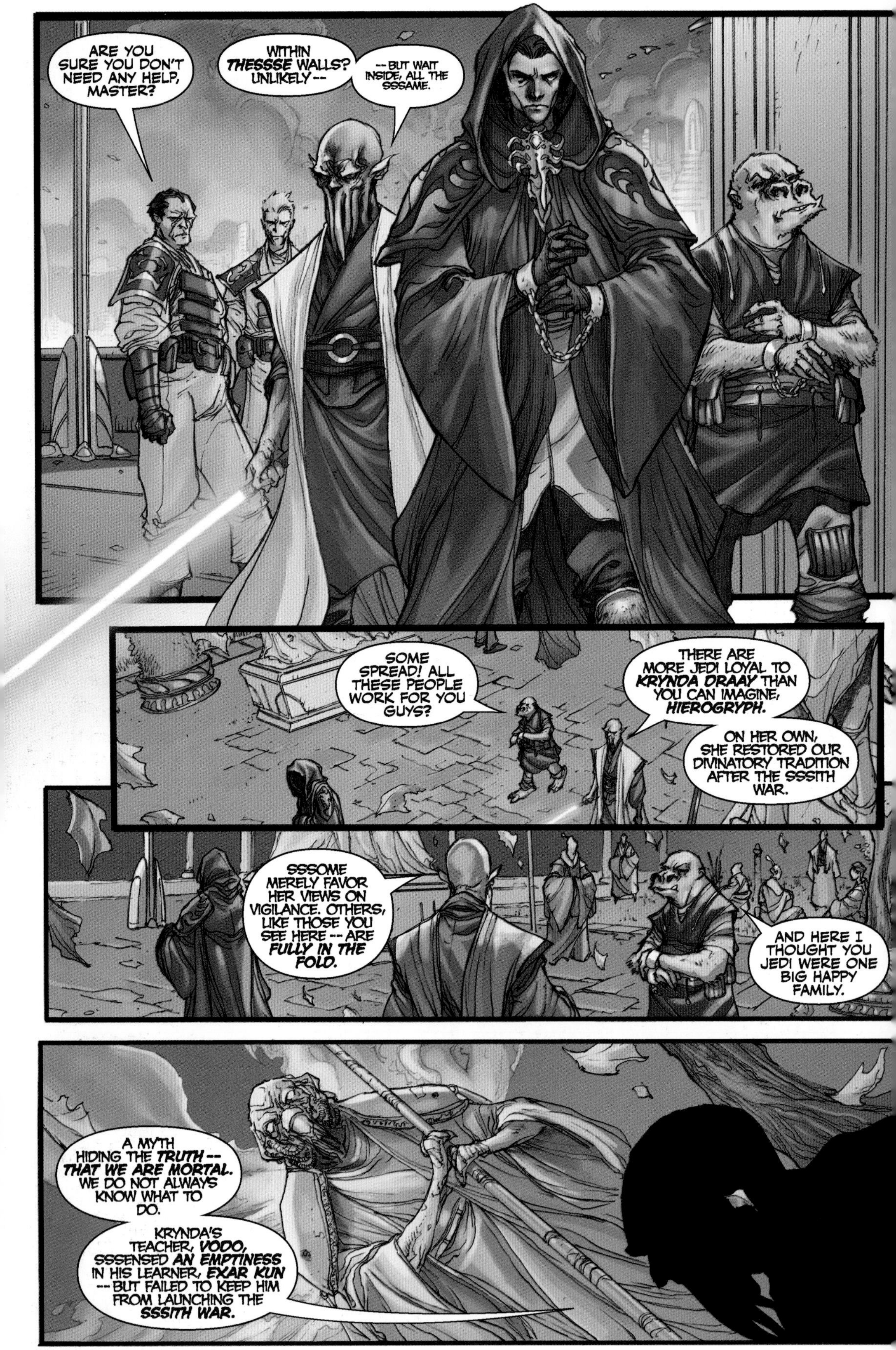

ARE YOU SURE YOU DON'T NEED ANY HELP, MASTER?
WITHIN THESSSE WALLS? UNLIKELY--
--BUT WAIT INSIDE, ALL THE SSSAME.
SOME SPREAD! ALL THESE PEOPLE WORK FOR YOU GUYS?
THERE ARE MORE JEDI LOYAL TO KRYNDA DRAAY THAN YOU CAN IMAGINE, HIEROGRYPH.
ON HER OWN, SHE RESTORED OUR DIVINATORY TRADITION AFTER THE SSSITH WAR.
SSSOME MERELY FAVOR HER VIEWS ON VIGILANCE. OTHERS, LIKE THOSE YOU SEE HERE--ARE FULLY IN THE FOLD.
AND HERE I THOUGHT YOU JEDI WERE ONE BIG HAPPY FAMILY.
A MYTH HIDING THE TRUTH--THAT WE ARE MORTAL. WE DO NOT ALWAYS KNOW WHAT TO DO.
KRYNDA'S TEACHER, VODO, SSSENSED AN EMPTINESS IN HIS LEARNER, EXAR KUN--BUT FAILED TO KEEP HIM FROM LAUNCHING THE SSSITH WAR.

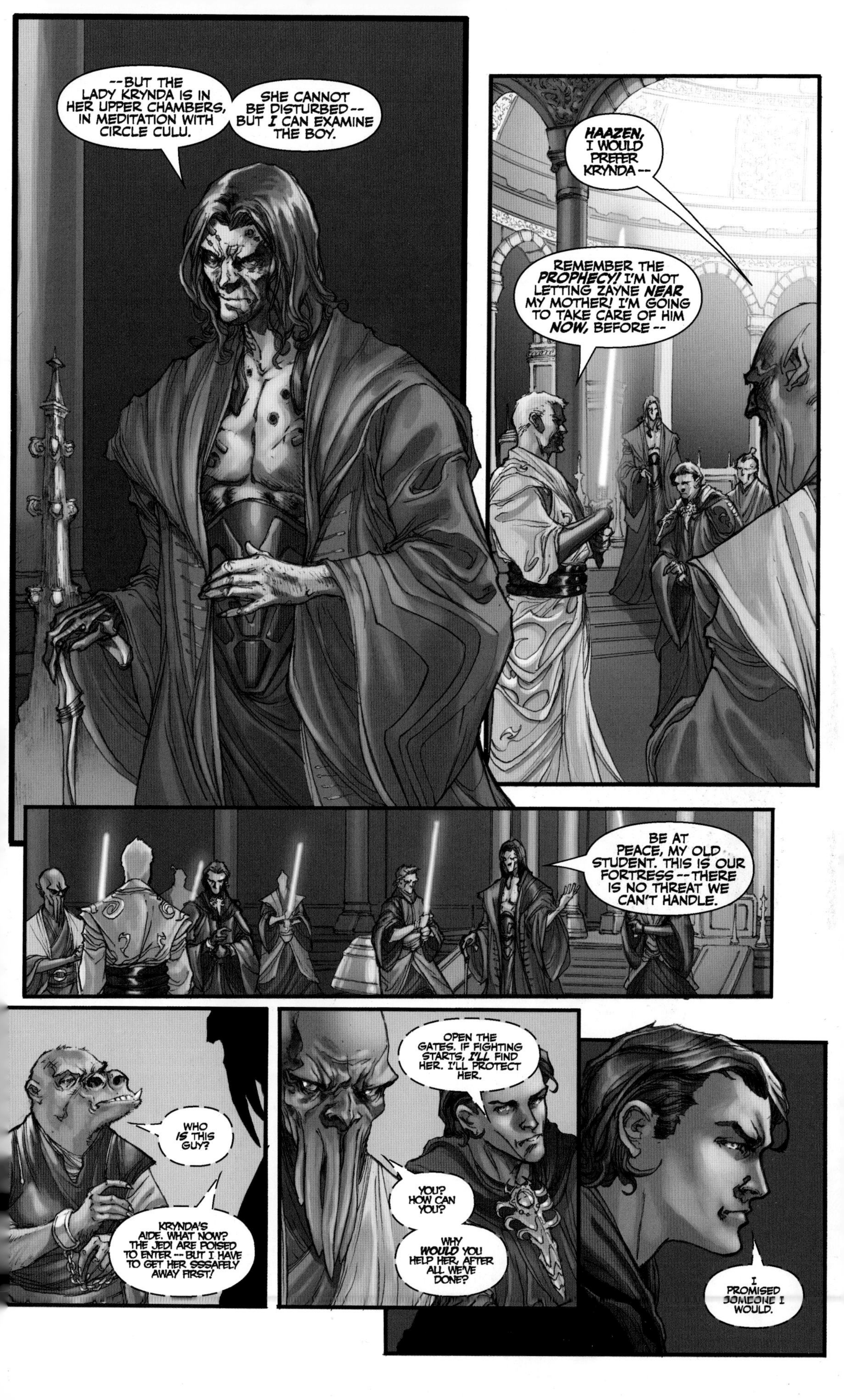
--BUT THE LADY KRYNDA IS IN HER UPPER CHAMBERS, IN MEDITATION WITH CIRCLE CULU.
SHE CANNOT BE DISTURBED-- BUT I CAN EXAMINE THE BOY.
HAAZEN, I WOULD PREFER KRYNDA--
REMEMBER THE PROPHECY! I'M NOT LETTING ZAYNE NEAR MY MOTHER! I'M GOING TO TAKE CARE OF HIM NOW, BEFORE--
BE AT PEACE, MY OLD STUDENT. THIS IS OUR FORTRESS--THERE IS NO THREAT WE CAN'T HANDLE.
WHO IS THIS GUY?
KRYNDA'S AIDE. WHAT NOW? THE JEDI ARE POISED TO ENTER--BUT I HAVE TO GET HER SSSAFELY AWAY FIRST!
OPEN THE GATES. IF FIGHTING STARTS, I'LL FIND HER. I'LL PROTECT HER.
YOU? HOW CAN YOU?
WHY WOULD YOU HELP HER, AFTER ALL WE'VE DONE?
I PROMISED SOMEONE I WOULD.

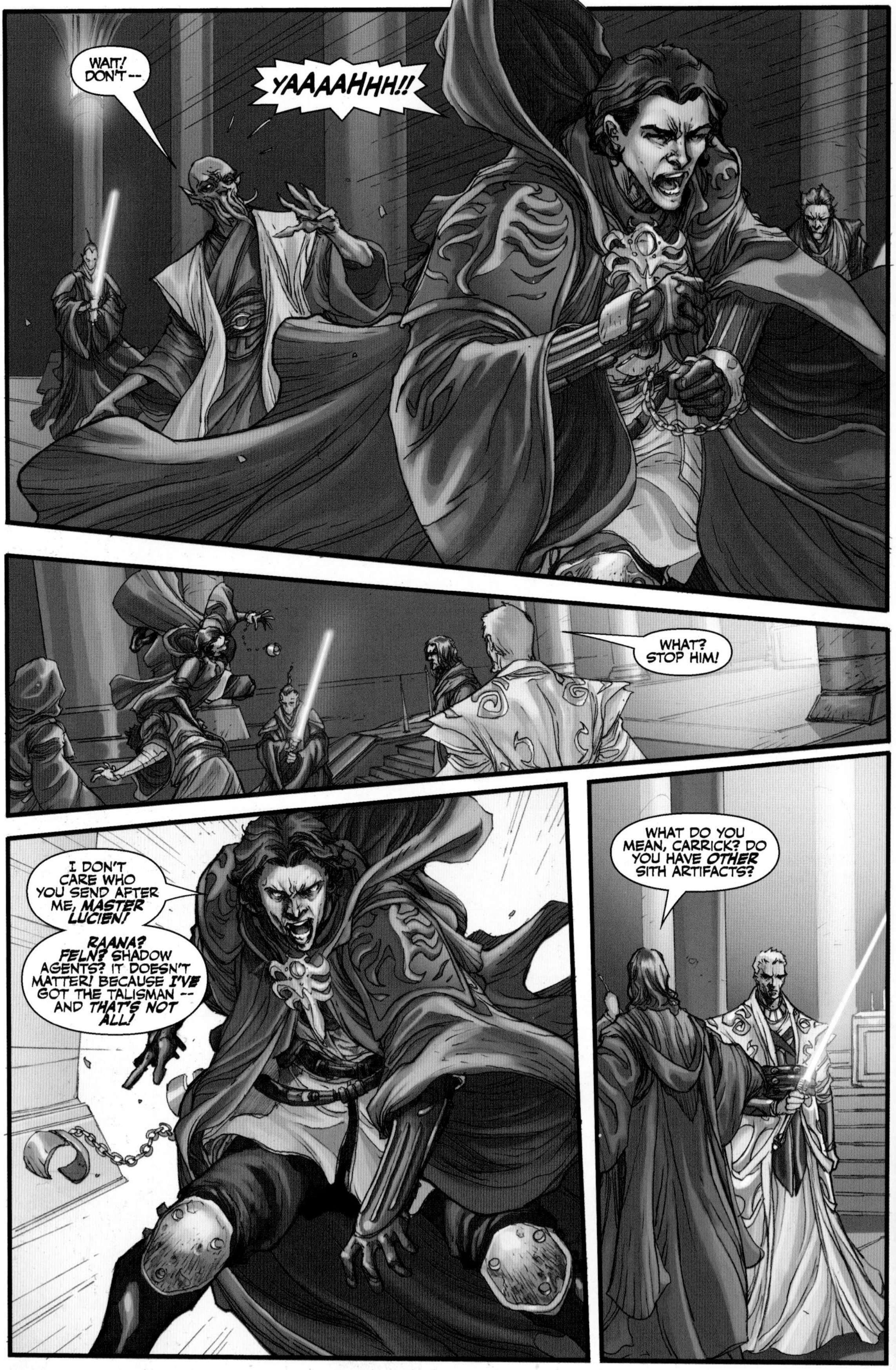
WAIT! DON'T --
YAAAAHHH!!
WHAT? STOP HIM!
I DON'T CARE WHO YOU SEND AFTER ME, MASTER LUCIEN!
RAANA? FELN? SHADOW AGENTS? IT DOESN'T MATTER! BECAUSE I'VE GOT THE TALISMAN -- AND THAT'S NOT ALL!
WHAT DO YOU MEAN, CARRICK? DO YOU HAVE OTHER SITH ARTIFACTS?

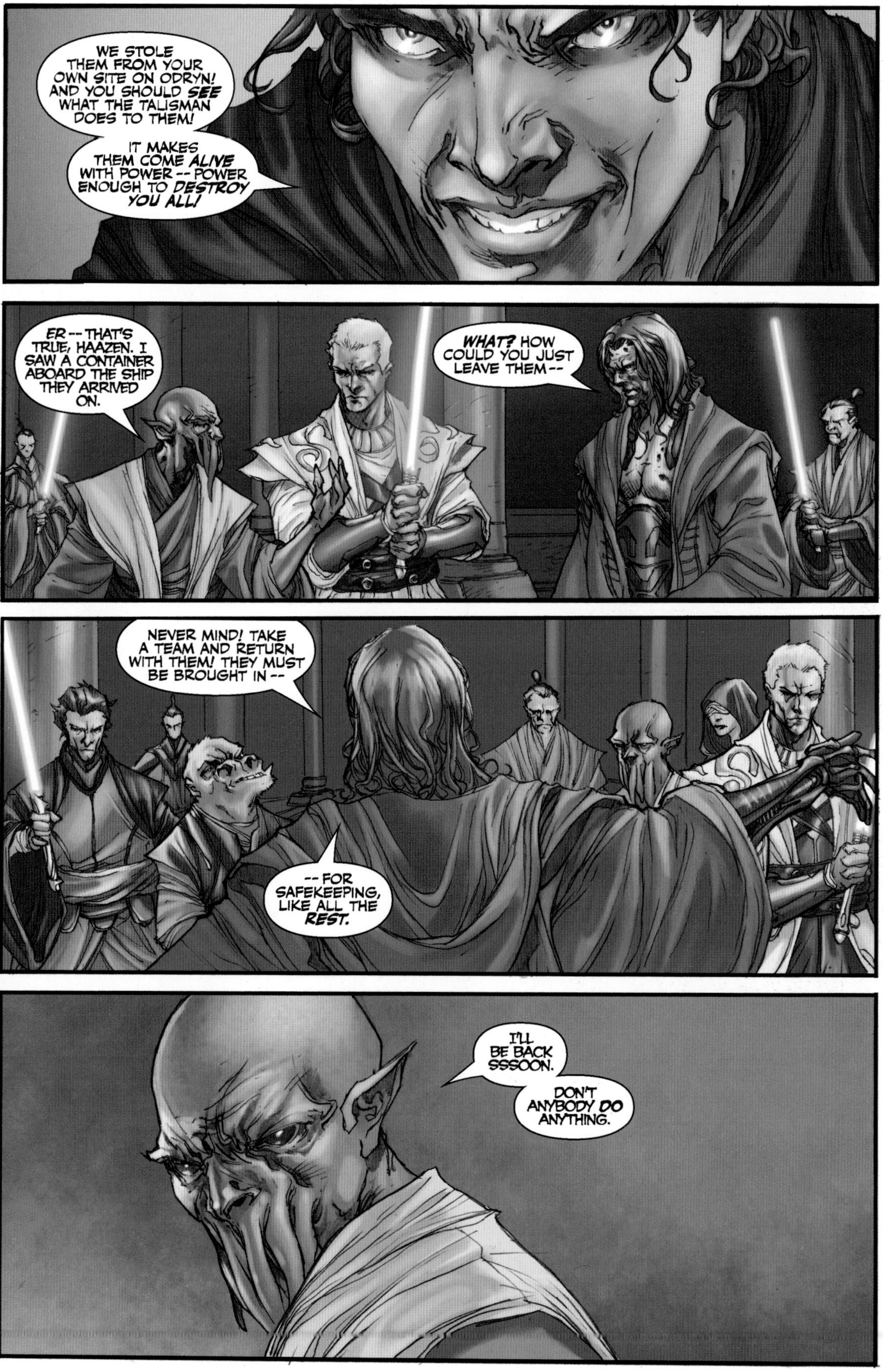

WE STOLE THEM FROM YOUR OWN SITE ON ODRYN! AND YOU SHOULD SEE WHAT THE TALISMAN DOES TO THEM!
IT MAKES THEM COME ALIVE WITH POWER -- POWER ENOUGH TO DESTROY YOU ALL!
ER -- THAT'S TRUE, HAAZEN. I SAW A CONTAINER ABOARD THE SHIP THEY ARRIVED ON.
WHAT? HOW COULD YOU JUST LEAVE THEM --
NEVER MIND! TAKE A TEAM AND RETURN WITH THEM! THEY MUST BE BROUGHT IN --
-- FOR SAFEKEEPING, LIKE ALL THE REST.
I'LL BE BACK SSSOON.
DON'T ANYBODY DO ANYTHING.

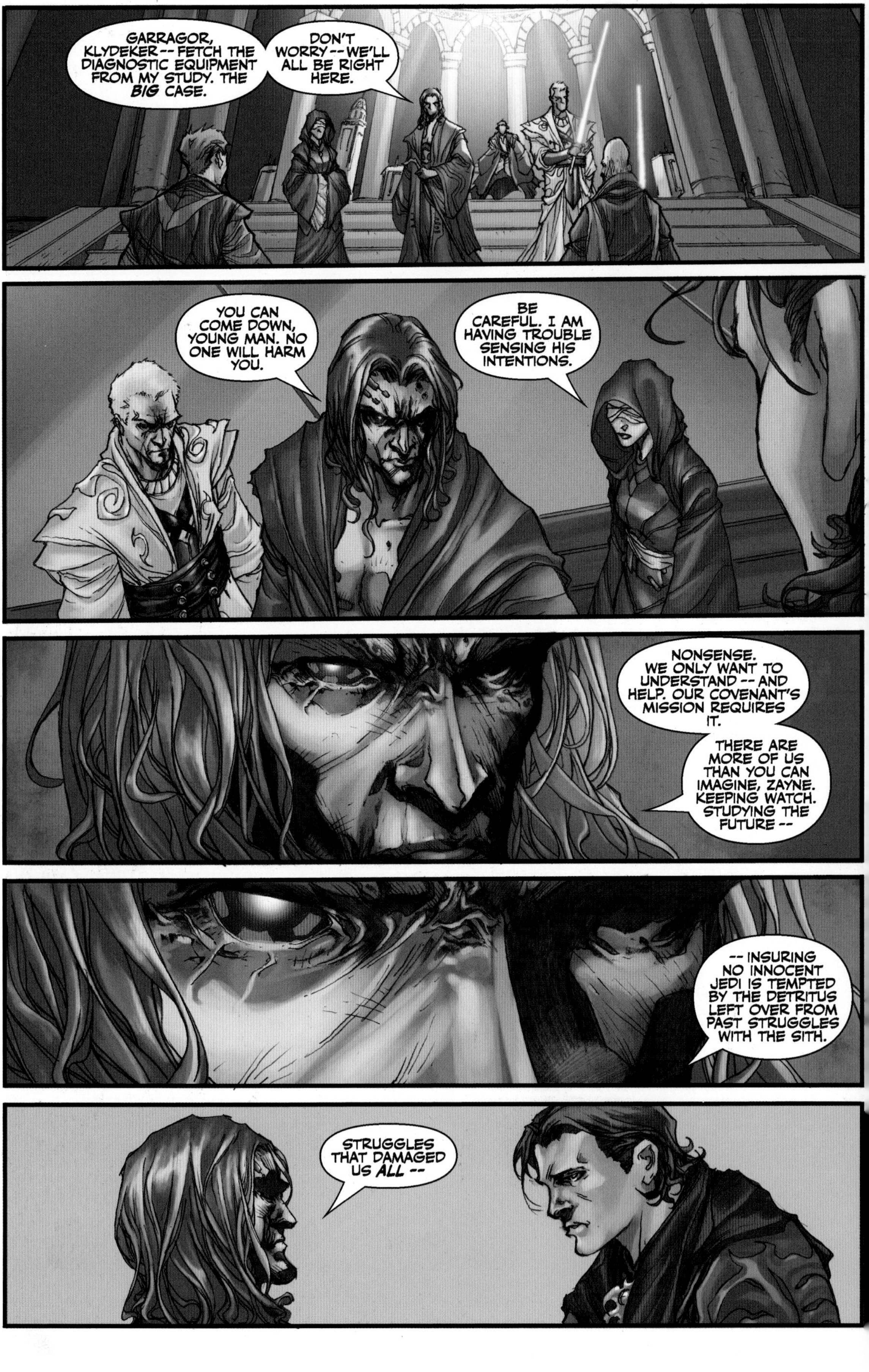
GARRAGOR, KLYDEKER -- FETCH THE DIAGNOSTIC EQUIPMENT FROM MY STUDY. THE *BIG* CASE.
DON'T WORRY -- WE'LL ALL BE RIGHT HERE.
YOU CAN COME DOWN, YOUNG MAN. NO ONE WILL HARM YOU.
BE CAREFUL. I AM HAVING TROUBLE SENSING HIS INTENTIONS.
NONSENSE. WE ONLY WANT TO UNDERSTAND -- AND HELP. OUR COVENANT'S MISSION REQUIRES IT.
THERE ARE MORE OF US THAN YOU CAN IMAGINE, ZAYNE. KEEPING WATCH. STUDYING THE FUTURE --
-- INSURING NO INNOCENT JEDI IS TEMPTED BY THE DETRITUS LEFT OVER FROM PAST STRUGGLES WITH THE SITH.
STRUGGLES THAT DAMAGED US *ALL* --

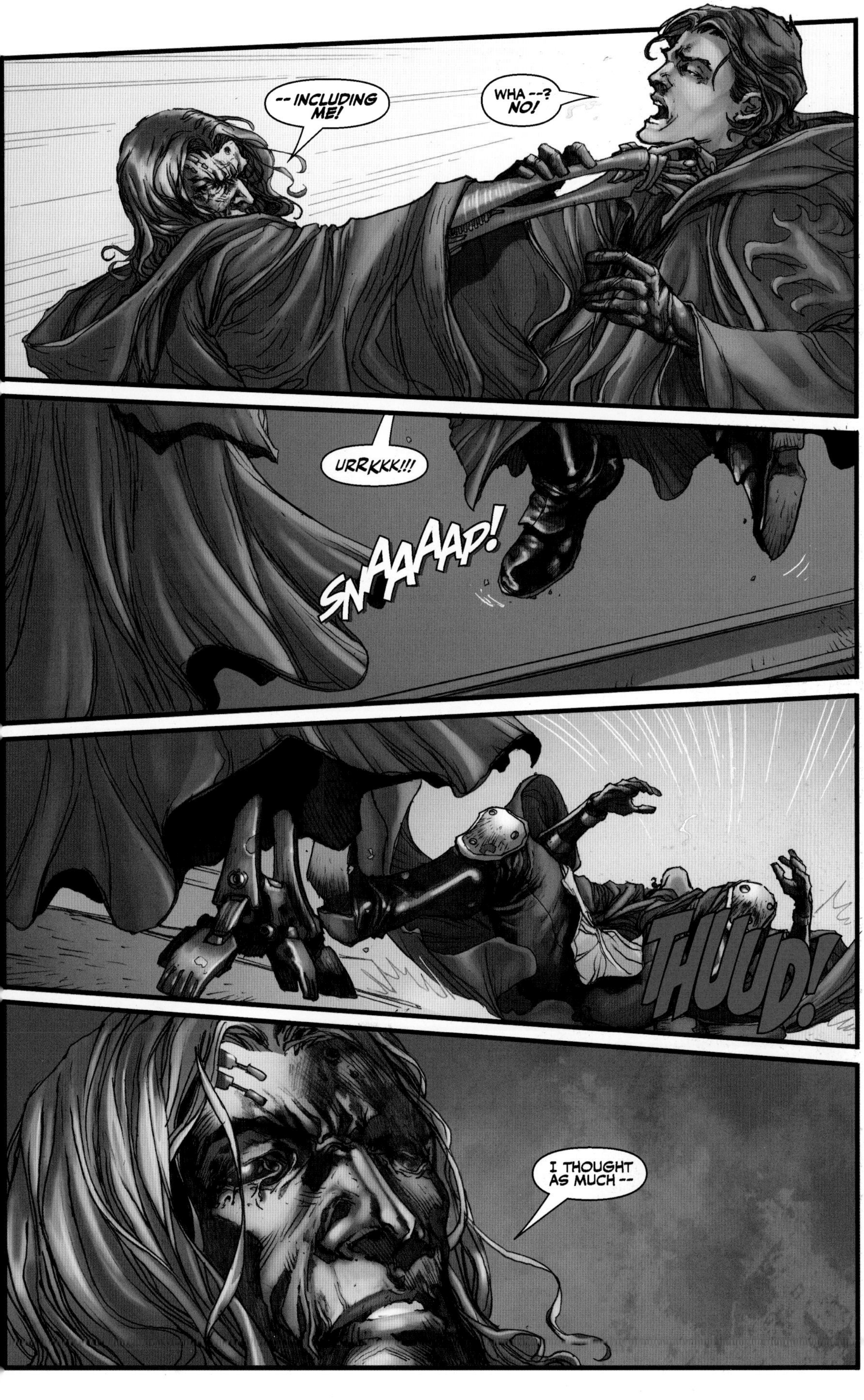
-- INCLUDING ME!
WHA --? NO!
URRKKK!!!
SNAAAAP!
THUUD!
I THOUGHT AS MUCH --

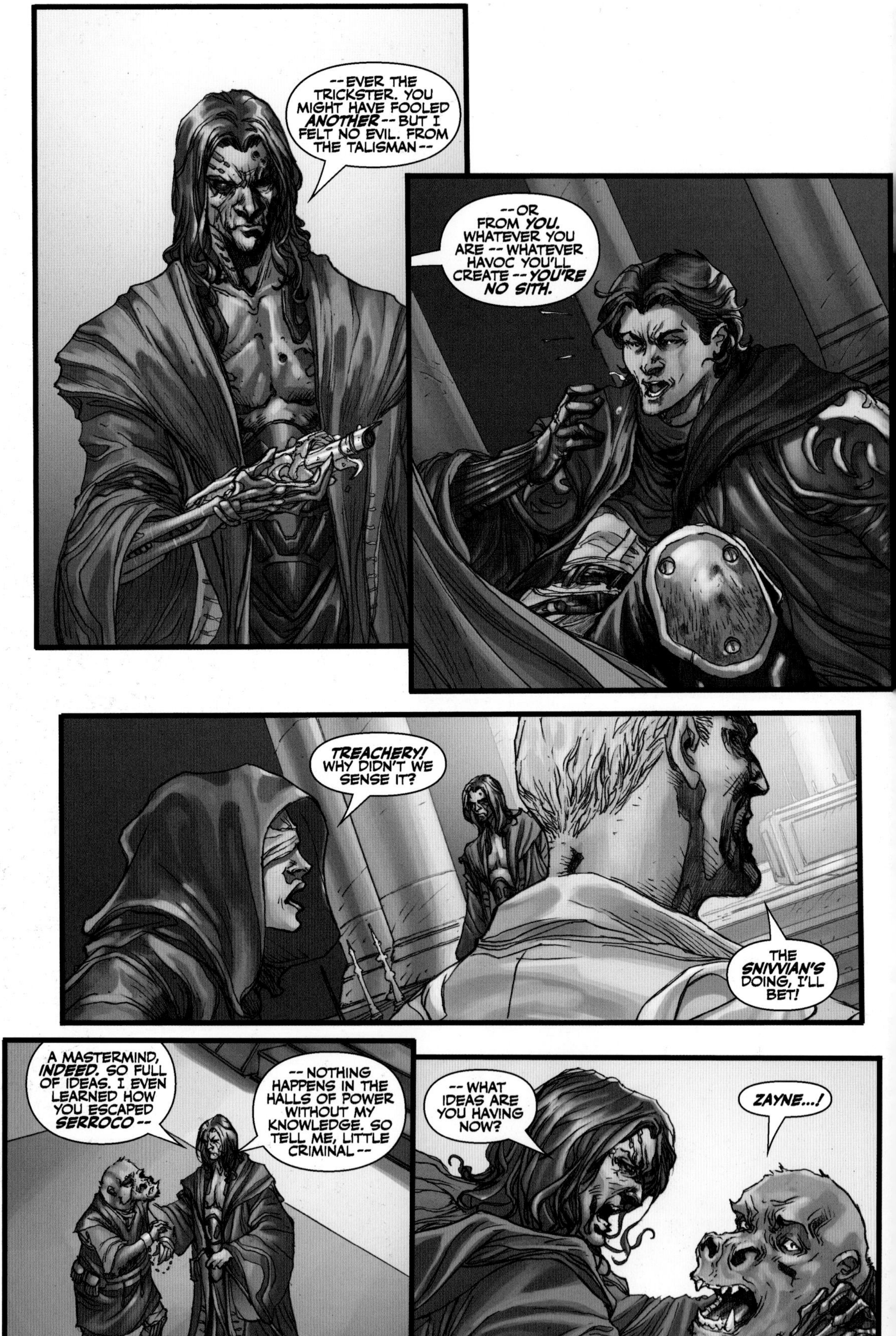
--EVER THE TRICKSTER. YOU MIGHT HAVE FOOLED ANOTHER--BUT I FELT NO EVIL. FROM THE TALISMAN--
--OR FROM YOU. WHATEVER YOU ARE--WHATEVER HAVOC YOU'LL CREATE--YOU'RE NO SITH.
TREACHERY! WHY DIDN'T WE SENSE IT?
THE SNIVVIAN'S DOING, I'LL BET!
A MASTERMIND, INDEED. SO FULL OF IDEAS. I EVEN LEARNED HOW YOU ESCAPED SERROCO--
--NOTHING HAPPENS IN THE HALLS OF POWER WITHOUT MY KNOWLEDGE. SO TELL ME, LITTLE CRIMINAL--
--WHAT IDEAS ARE YOU HAVING NOW?
ZAYNE...!

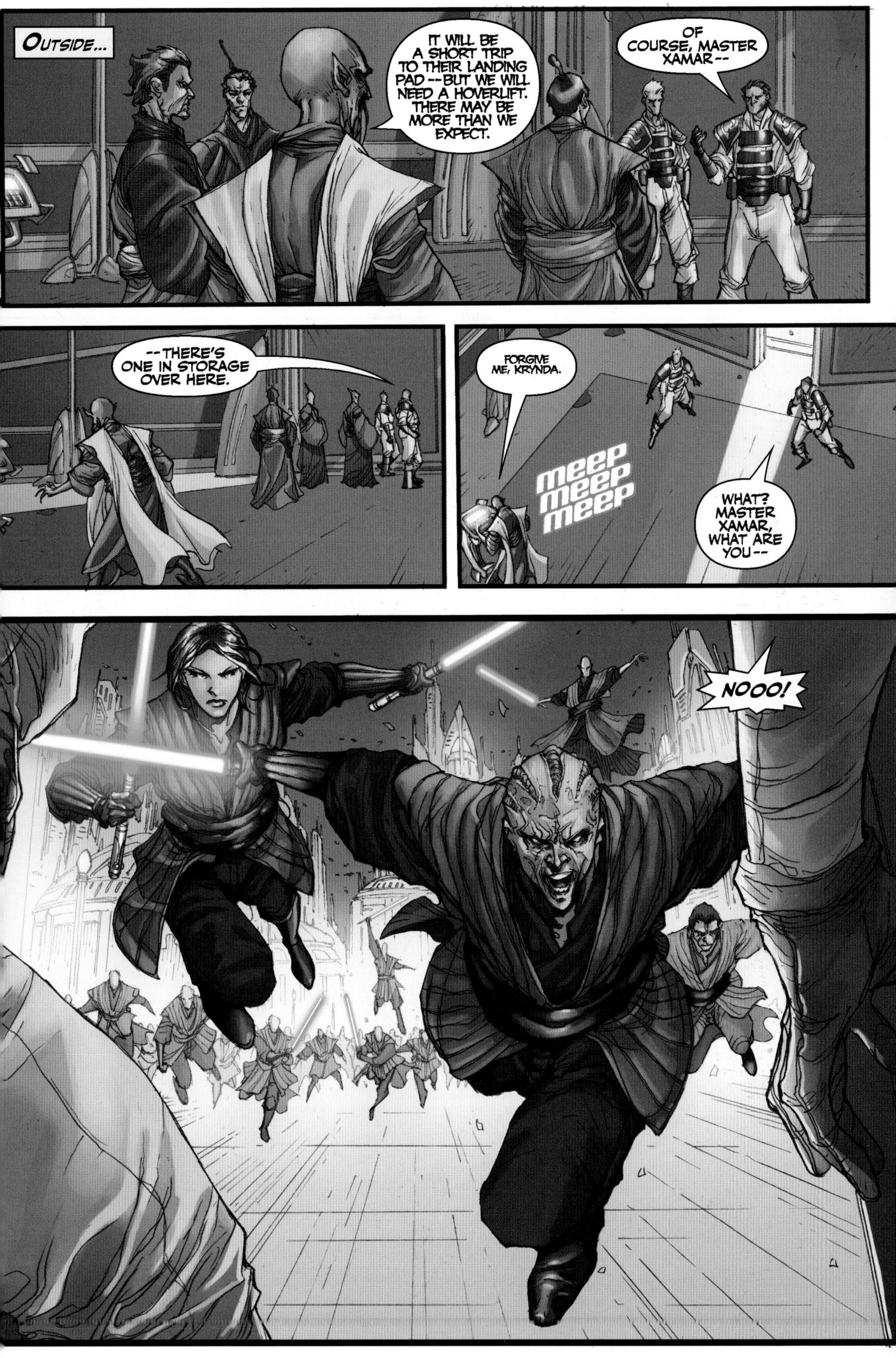
OUTSIDE...
IT WILL BE A SHORT TRIP TO THEIR LANDING PAD -- BUT WE WILL NEED A HOVERLIFT. THERE MAY BE MORE THAN WE EXPECT.
OF COURSE, MASTER XAMAR --
-- THERE'S ONE IN STORAGE OVER HERE.
FORGIVE ME, KRYNDA.
meep meep meep
WHAT? MASTER XAMAR, WHAT ARE YOU --
NOOO!

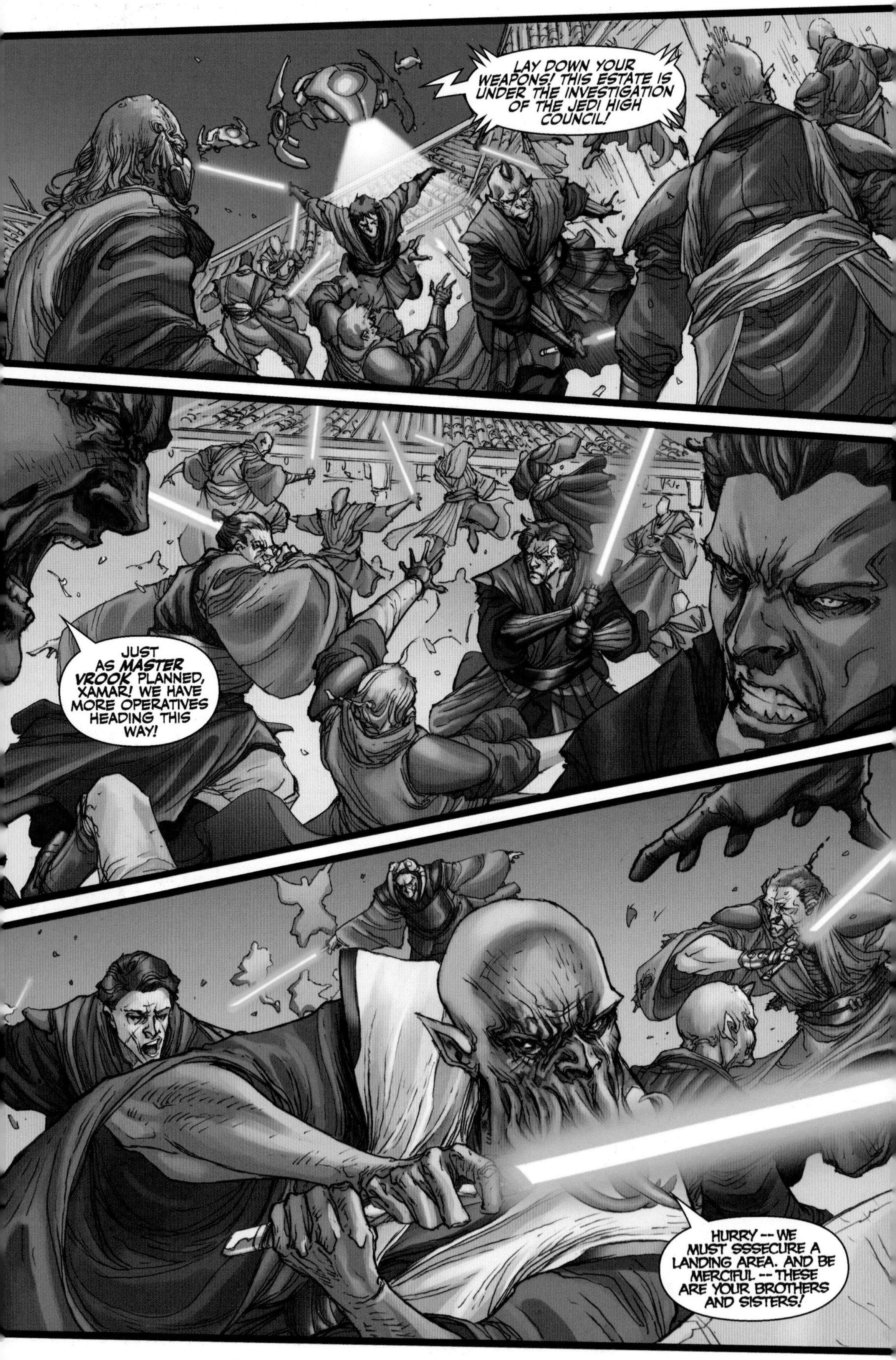

LAY DOWN YOUR WEAPONS! THIS ESTATE IS UNDER THE INVESTIGATION OF THE JEDI HIGH COUNCIL!
JUST AS MASTER VROOK PLANNED, XAMAR! WE HAVE MORE OPERATIVES HEADING THIS WAY!
HURRY -- WE MUST SSSECURE A LANDING AREA. AND BE MERCIFUL -- THESE ARE YOUR BROTHERS AND SISTERS!

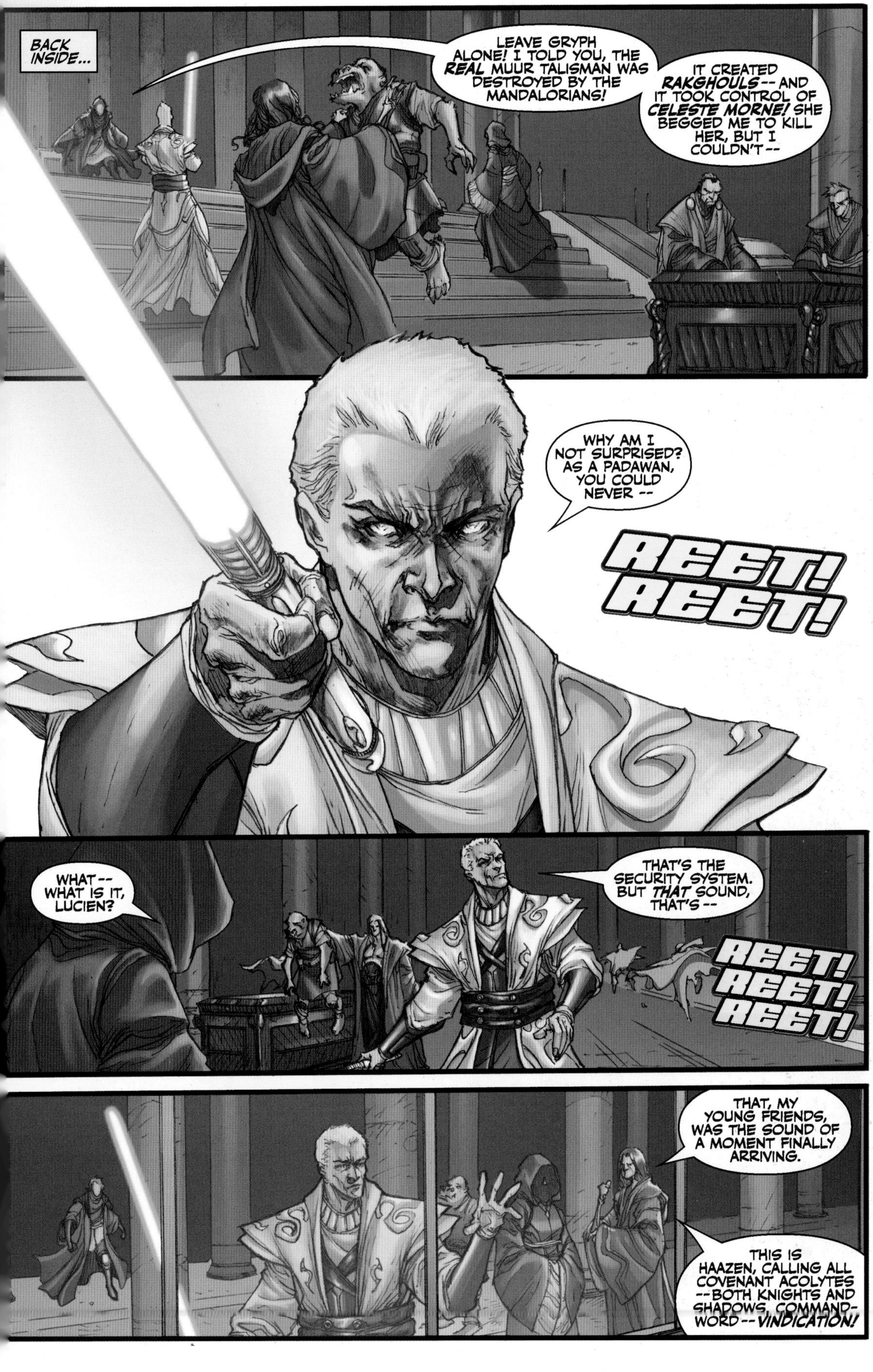
BACK INSIDE...
LEAVE GRYPH ALONE! I TOLD YOU, THE *REAL* MUUR TALISMAN WAS DESTROYED BY THE MANDALORIANS!
IT CREATED *RAKGHOULS*-- AND IT TOOK CONTROL OF *CELESTE MORNE!* SHE BEGGED ME TO KILL HER, BUT I COULDN'T--
WHY AM I NOT SURPRISED? AS A PADAWAN, YOU COULD NEVER --
REET! REET!
WHAT-- WHAT IS IT, LUCIEN?
THAT'S THE SECURITY SYSTEM. BUT *THAT* SOUND, THAT'S--
REET! REET! REET!
THAT, MY YOUNG FRIENDS, WAS THE SOUND OF A MOMENT FINALLY ARRIVING.
THIS IS HAAZEN, CALLING ALL COVENANT ACOLYTES --BOTH KNIGHTS AND SHADOWS, COMMAND-WORD-- *VINDICATION!*

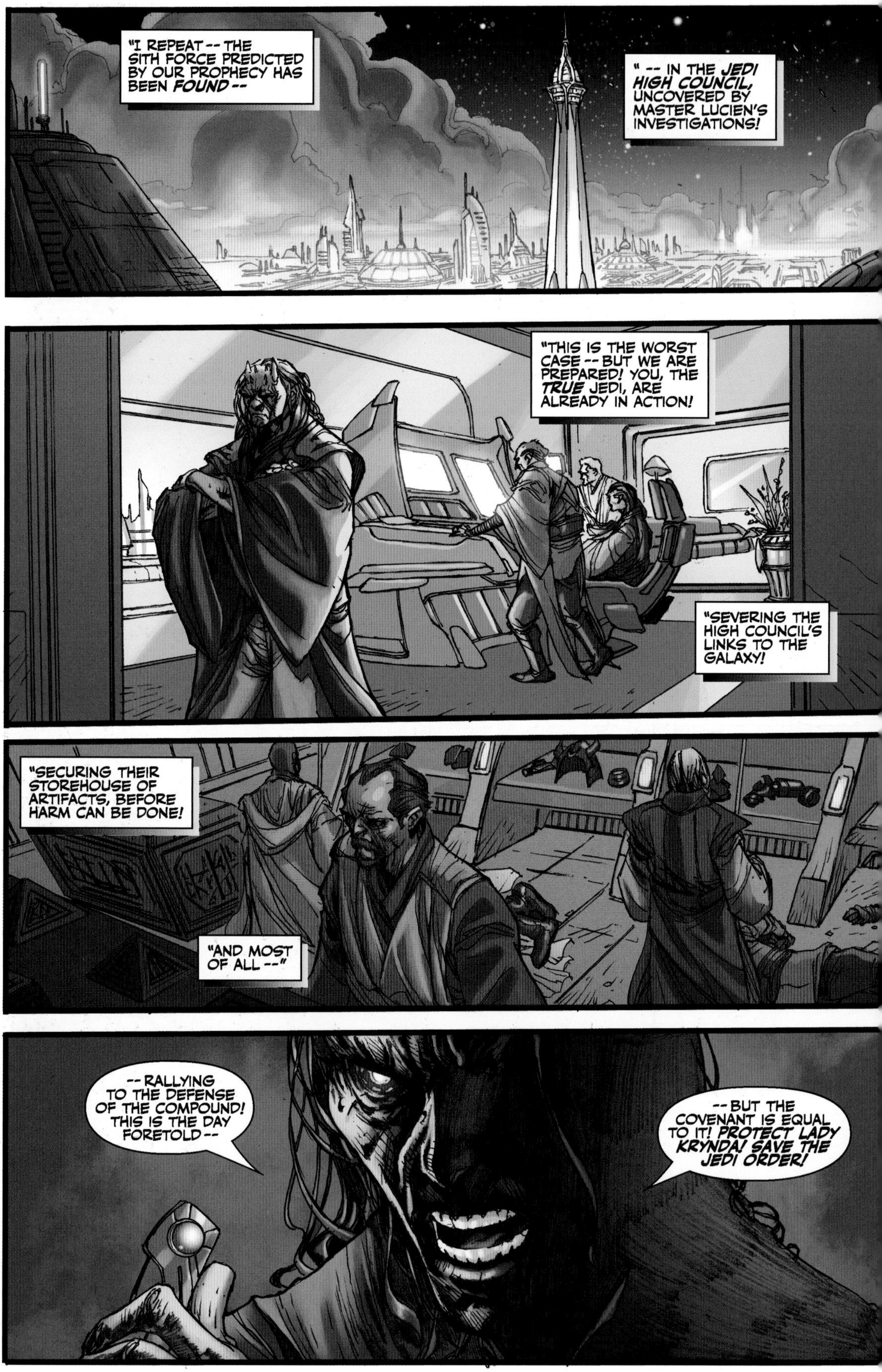
"I REPEAT -- THE SITH FORCE PREDICTED BY OUR PROPHECY HAS BEEN *FOUND* --
" -- IN THE *JEDI HIGH COUNCIL,* UNCOVERED BY MASTER LUCIEN'S INVESTIGATIONS!
"THIS IS THE WORST CASE -- BUT WE ARE PREPARED! YOU, THE *TRUE* JEDI, ARE ALREADY IN ACTION!
"SEVERING THE HIGH COUNCIL'S LINKS TO THE GALAXY!
"SECURING THEIR STOREHOUSE OF ARTIFACTS, BEFORE HARM CAN BE DONE!
"AND MOST OF ALL --"
-- RALLYING TO THE DEFENSE OF THE COMPOUND! THIS IS THE DAY FORETOLD --
-- BUT THE COVENANT IS EQUAL TO IT! *PROTECT LADY KRYNDA! SAVE THE JEDI ORDER!*

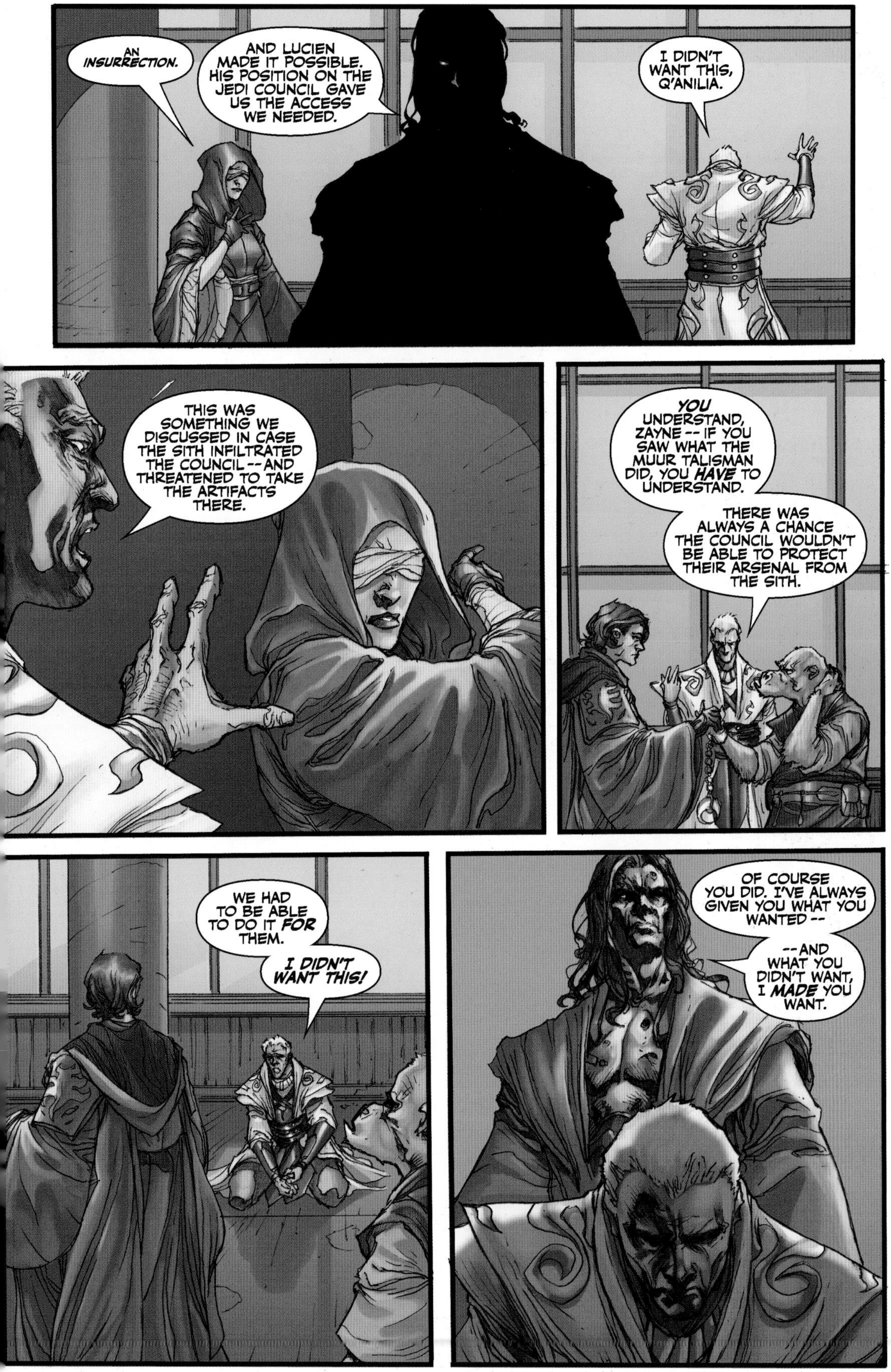
AN INSURRECTION.
AND LUCIEN MADE IT POSSIBLE. HIS POSITION ON THE JEDI COUNCIL GAVE US THE ACCESS WE NEEDED.
I DIDN'T WANT THIS, Q'ANILIA.
THIS WAS SOMETHING WE DISCUSSED IN CASE THE SITH INFILTRATED THE COUNCIL -- AND THREATENED TO TAKE THE ARTIFACTS THERE.
YOU UNDERSTAND, ZAYNE -- IF YOU SAW WHAT THE MUUR TALISMAN DID, YOU HAVE TO UNDERSTAND.
THERE WAS ALWAYS A CHANCE THE COUNCIL WOULDN'T BE ABLE TO PROTECT THEIR ARSENAL FROM THE SITH.
WE HAD TO BE ABLE TO DO IT FOR THEM.
I DIDN'T WANT THIS!
OF COURSE YOU DID. I'VE ALWAYS GIVEN YOU WHAT YOU WANTED --
-- AND WHAT YOU DIDN'T WANT, I MADE YOU WANT.

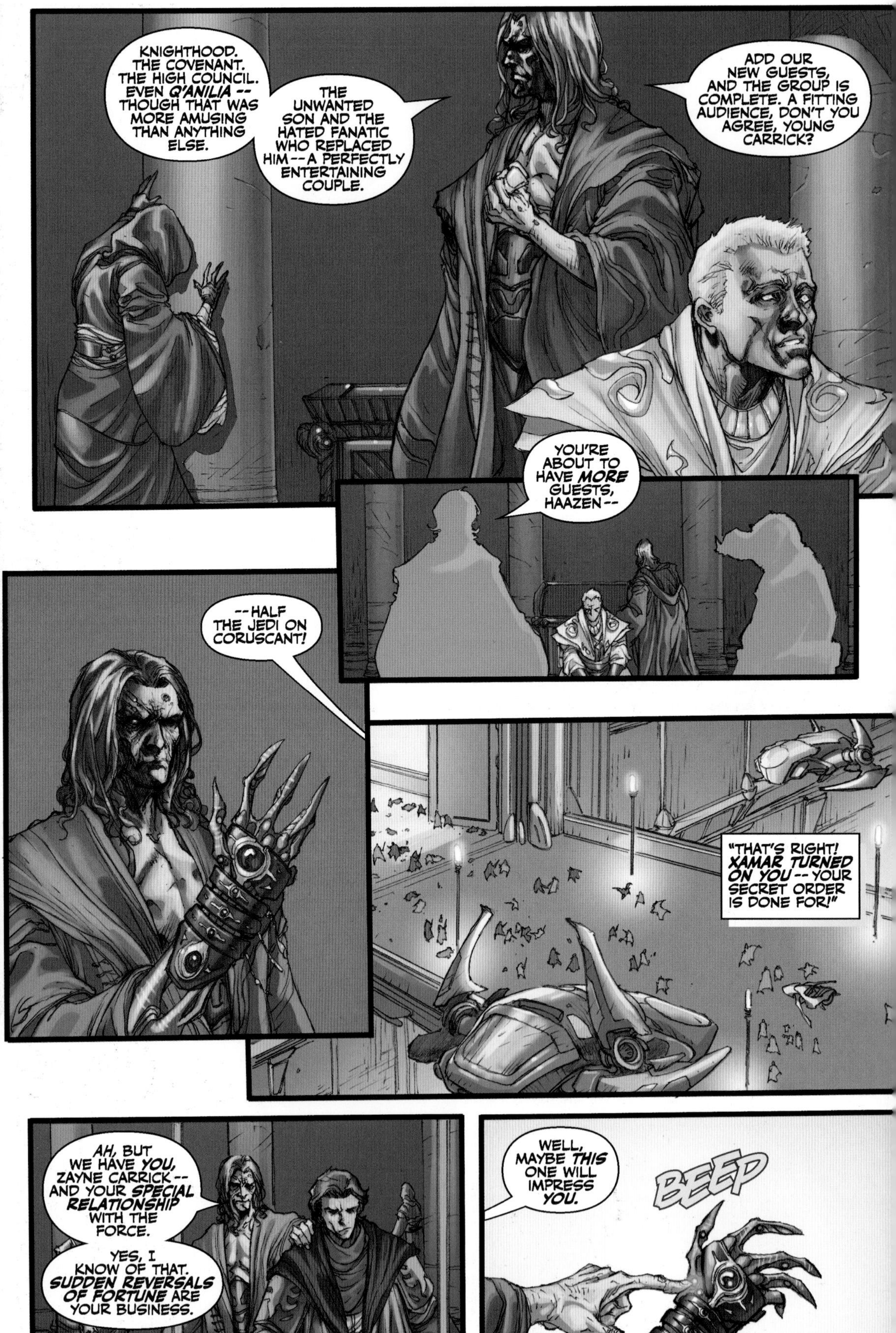
KNIGHTHOOD. THE COVENANT. THE HIGH COUNCIL. EVEN Q'ANILIA -- THOUGH THAT WAS MORE AMUSING THAN ANYTHING ELSE.
THE UNWANTED SON AND THE HATED FANATIC WHO REPLACED HIM -- A PERFECTLY ENTERTAINING COUPLE.
ADD OUR NEW GUESTS, AND THE GROUP IS COMPLETE. A FITTING AUDIENCE, DON'T YOU AGREE, YOUNG CARRICK?
YOU'RE ABOUT TO HAVE MORE GUESTS, HAAZEN --
-- HALF THE JEDI ON CORUSCANT!
"THAT'S RIGHT! XAMAR TURNED ON YOU -- YOUR SECRET ORDER IS DONE FOR!"
AH, BUT WE HAVE YOU, ZAYNE CARRICK -- AND YOUR SPECIAL RELATIONSHIP WITH THE FORCE.
YES, I KNOW OF THAT. SUDDEN REVERSALS OF FORTUNE ARE YOUR BUSINESS.
WELL, MAYBE THIS ONE WILL IMPRESS YOU.
BEEP

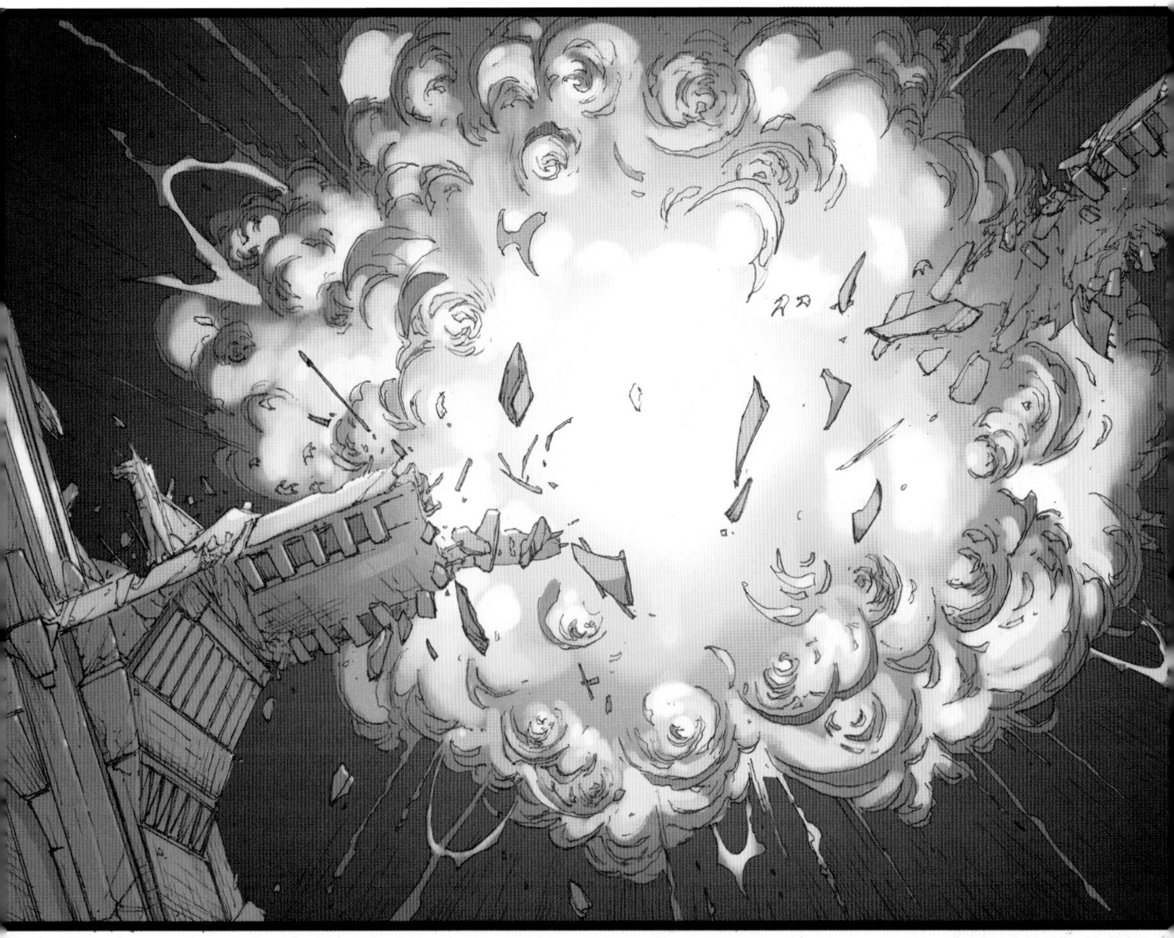

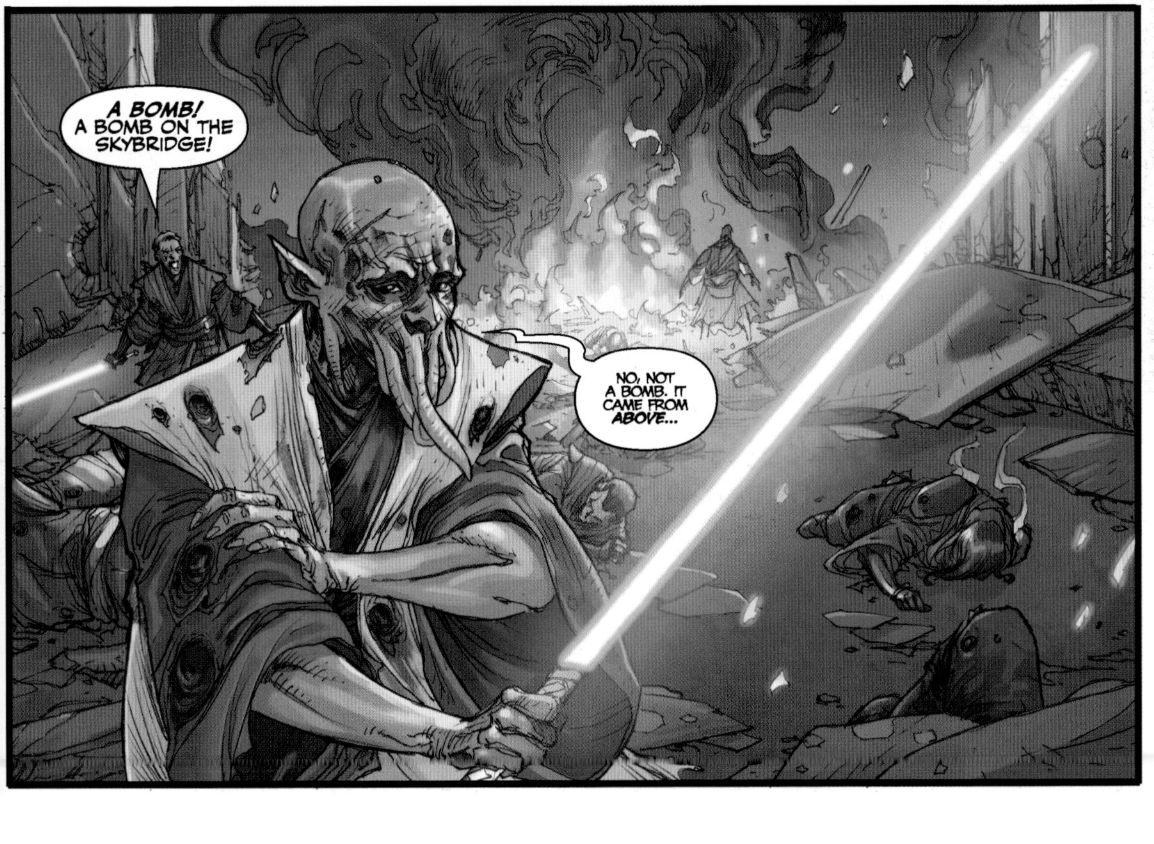

A BOMB! A BOMB ON THE SKYBRIDGE!
NO, NOT A BOMB. IT CAME FROM *ABOVE...*

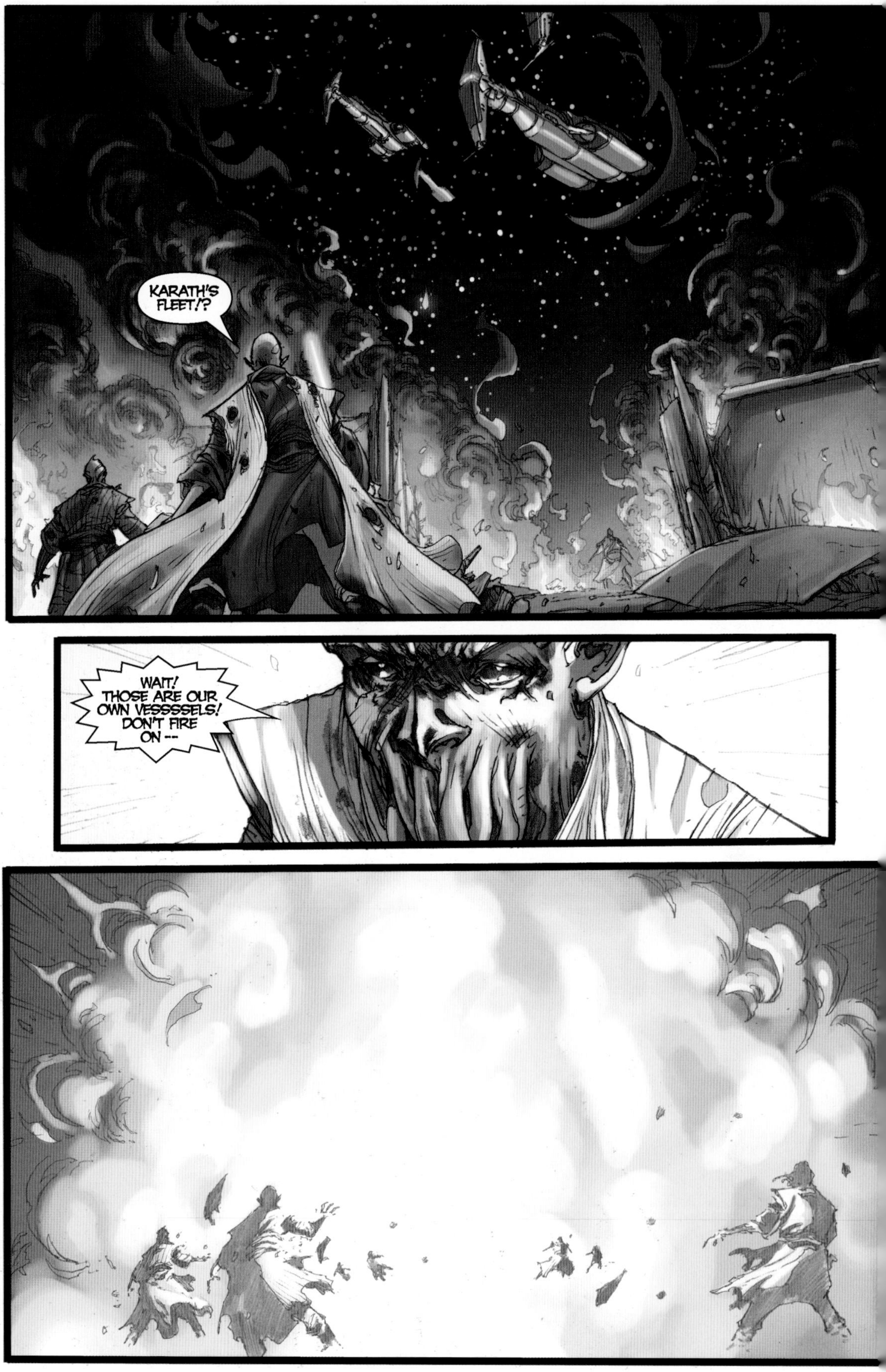
KARATH'S FLEET!?
WAIT! THOSE ARE OUR OWN VESSSSELS! DON'T FIRE ON --

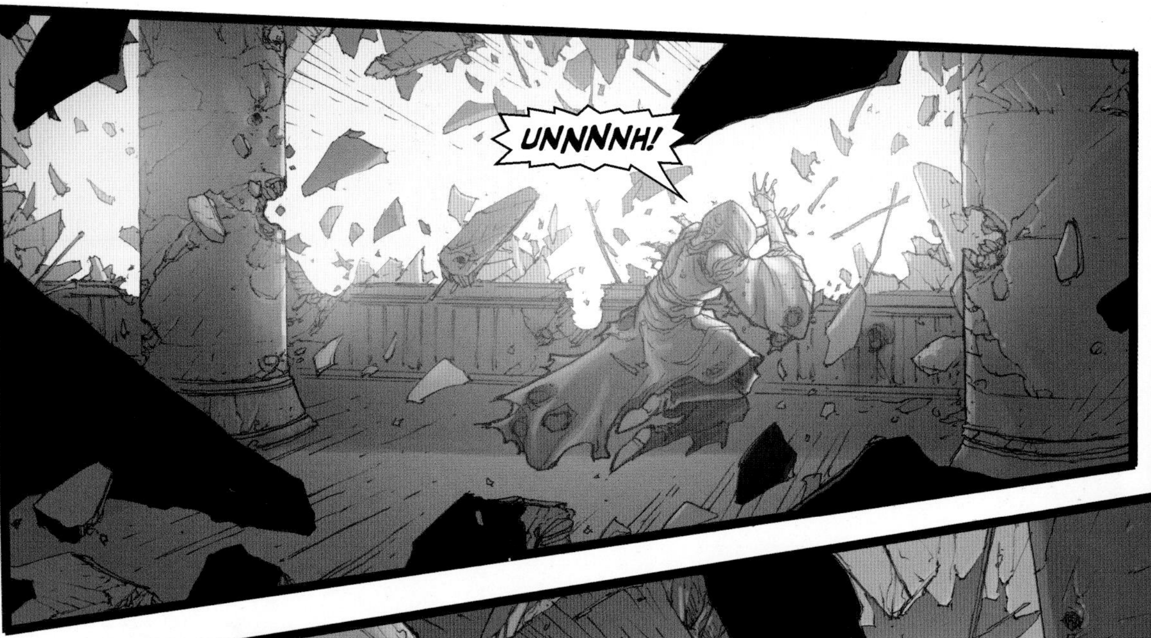
UNNNNH!

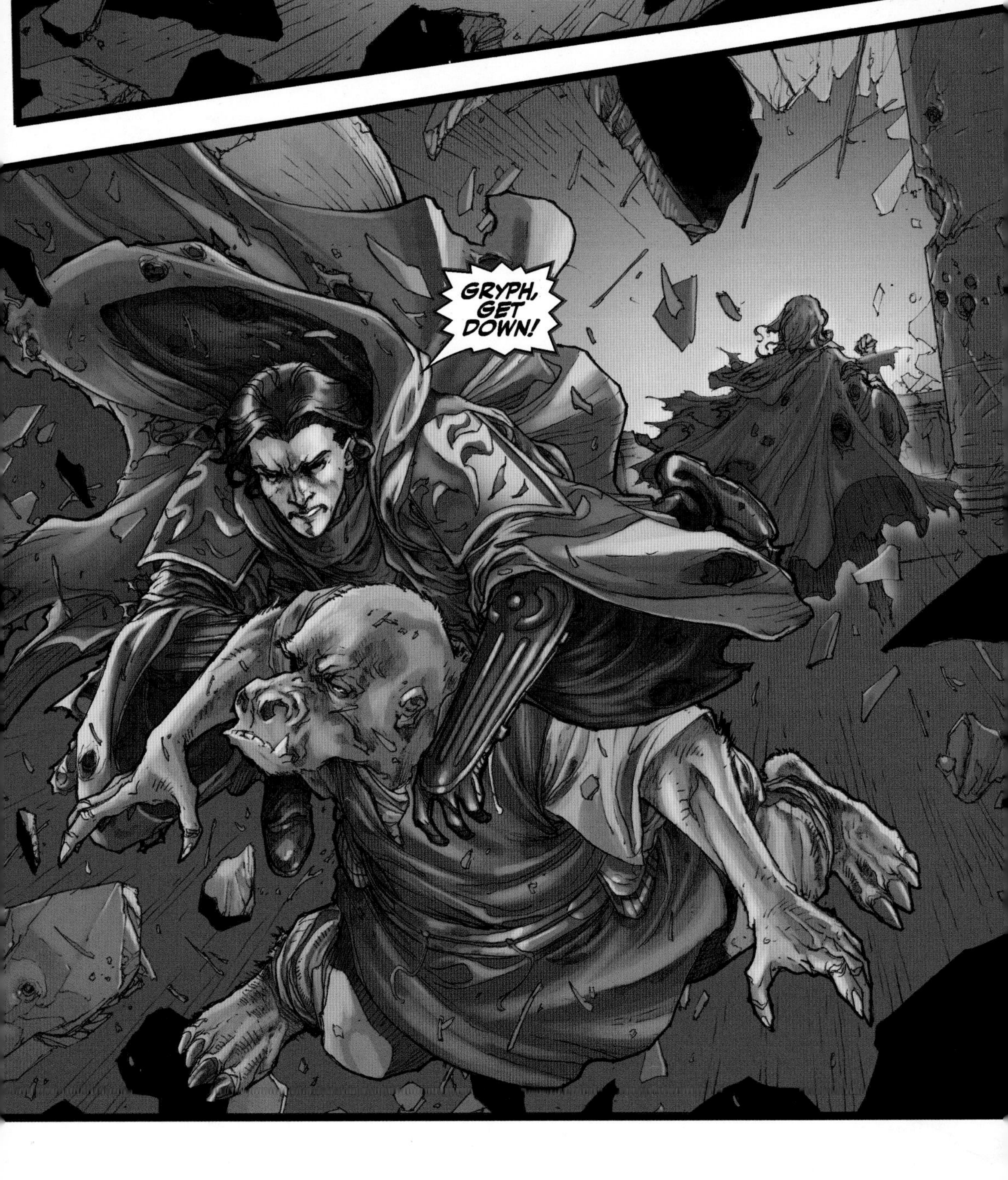
GRYPH, GET DOWN!

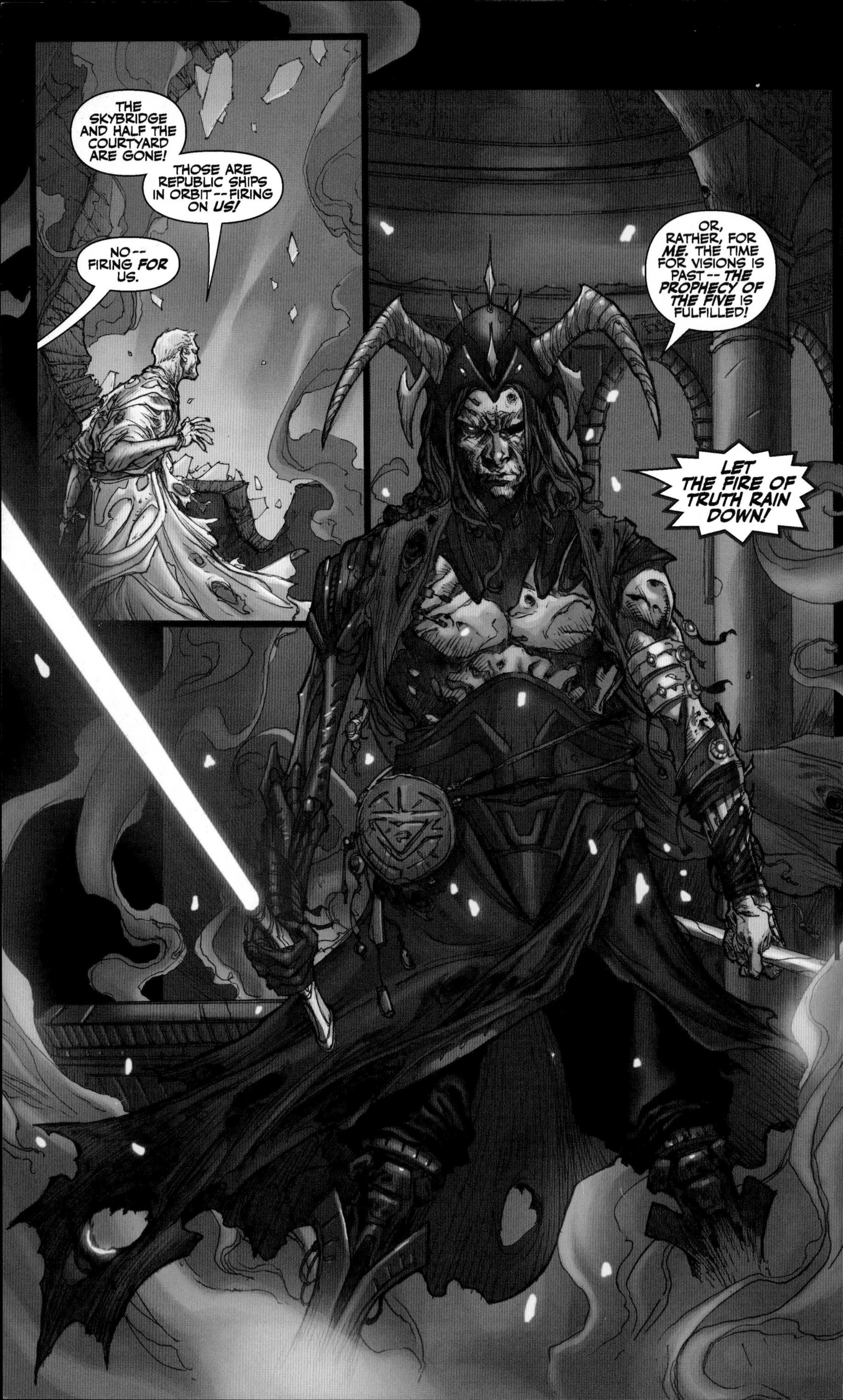
THE SKYBRIDGE AND HALF THE COURTYARD ARE GONE!
THOSE ARE REPUBLIC SHIPS IN ORBIT--FIRING ON *US!*
NO--FIRING *FOR* US.
OR, RATHER, FOR *ME.* THE TIME FOR VISIONS IS PAST--*THE PROPHECY OF THE FIVE* IS FULFILLED!
LET THE FIRE OF TRUTH RAIN DOWN!

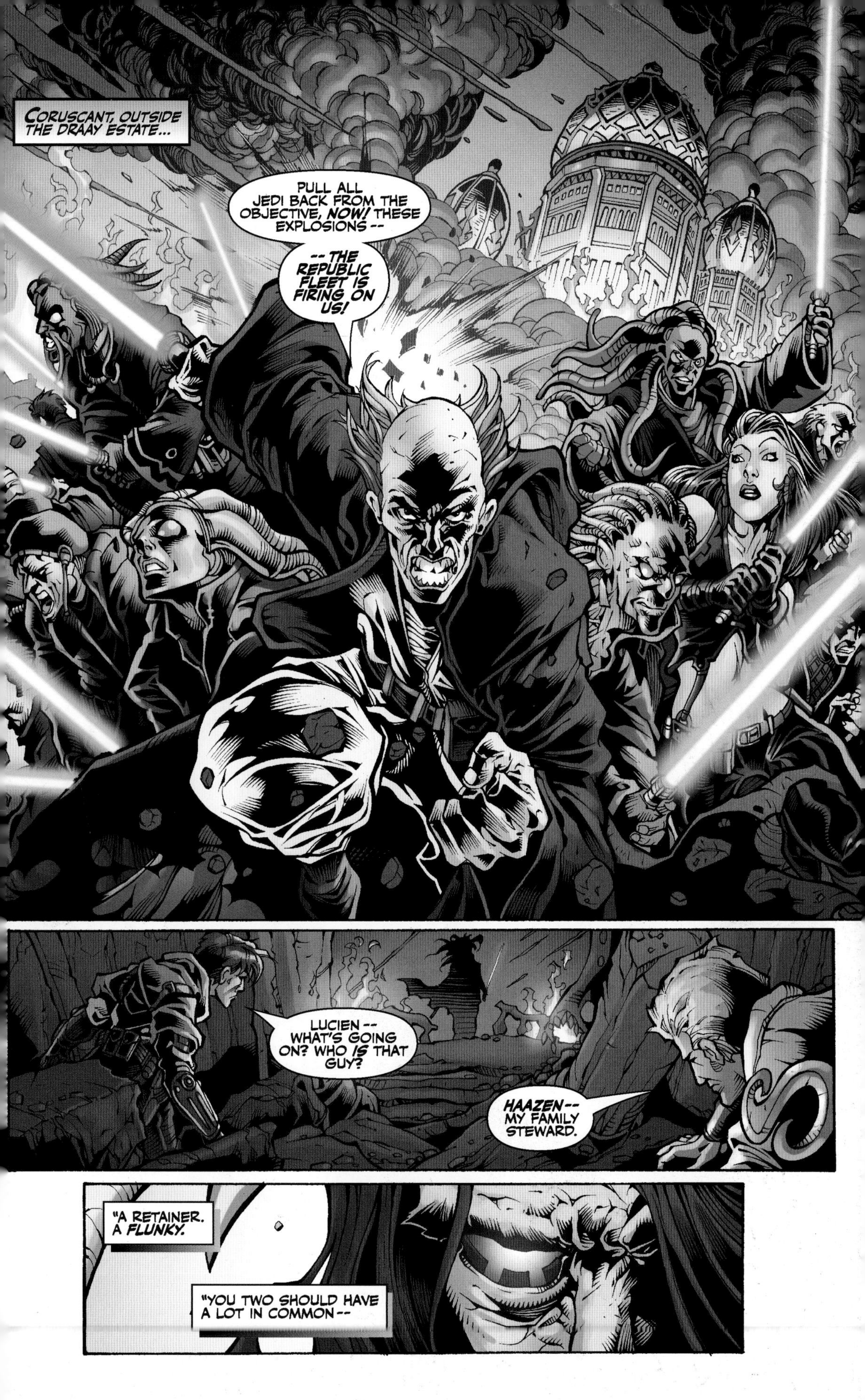
Coruscant, outside the Draay Estate...
Pull all Jedi back from the objective, now! These explosions --
-- The Republic fleet is firing on us!
Lucien -- what's going on? Who is that guy?
Haazen -- my family steward.
"A retainer. A flunky.
"You two should have a lot in common --

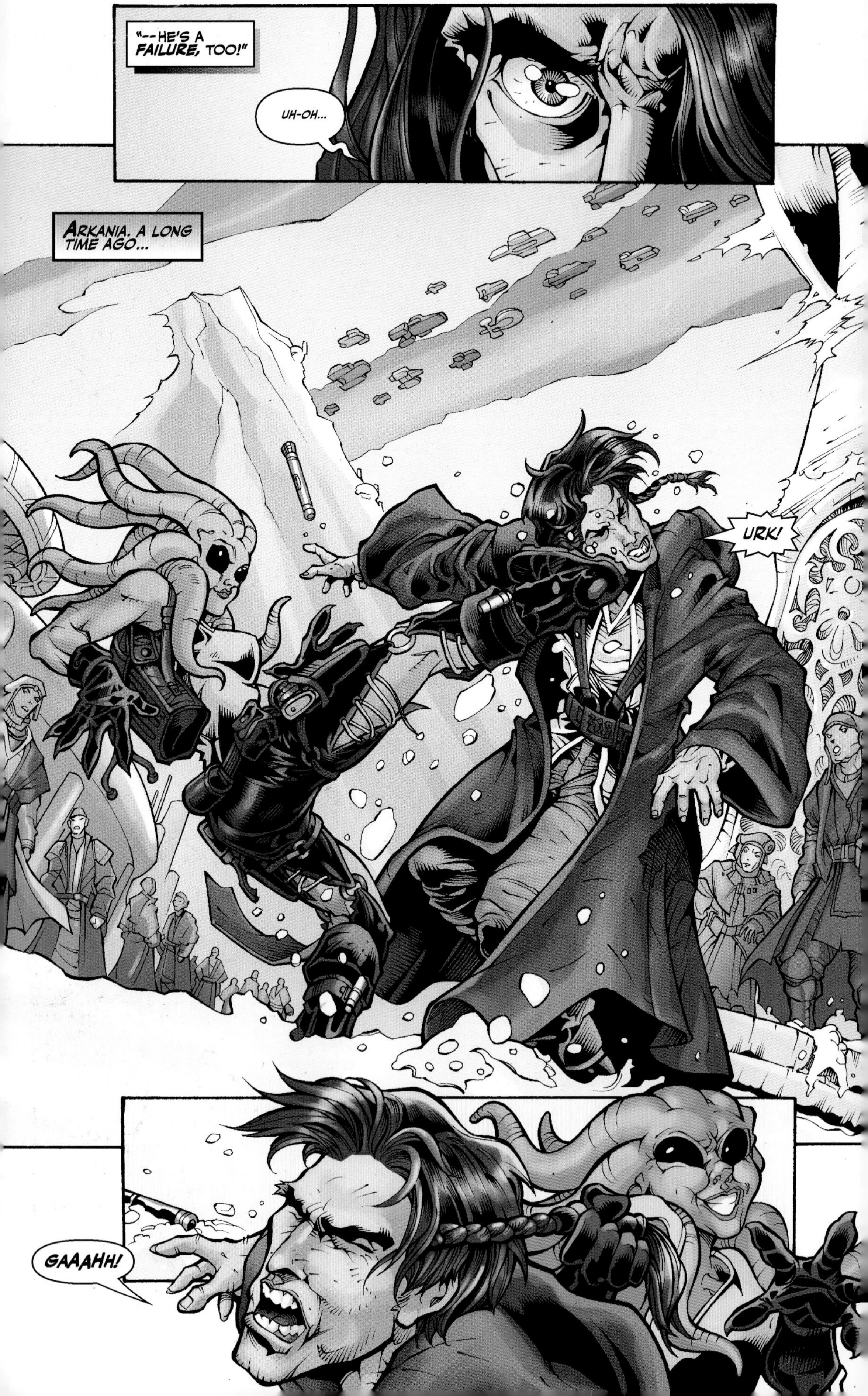
"--HE'S A FAILURE, TOO!"
UH-OH...
ARKANIA. A LONG TIME AGO...
URK!
GAAAHH!

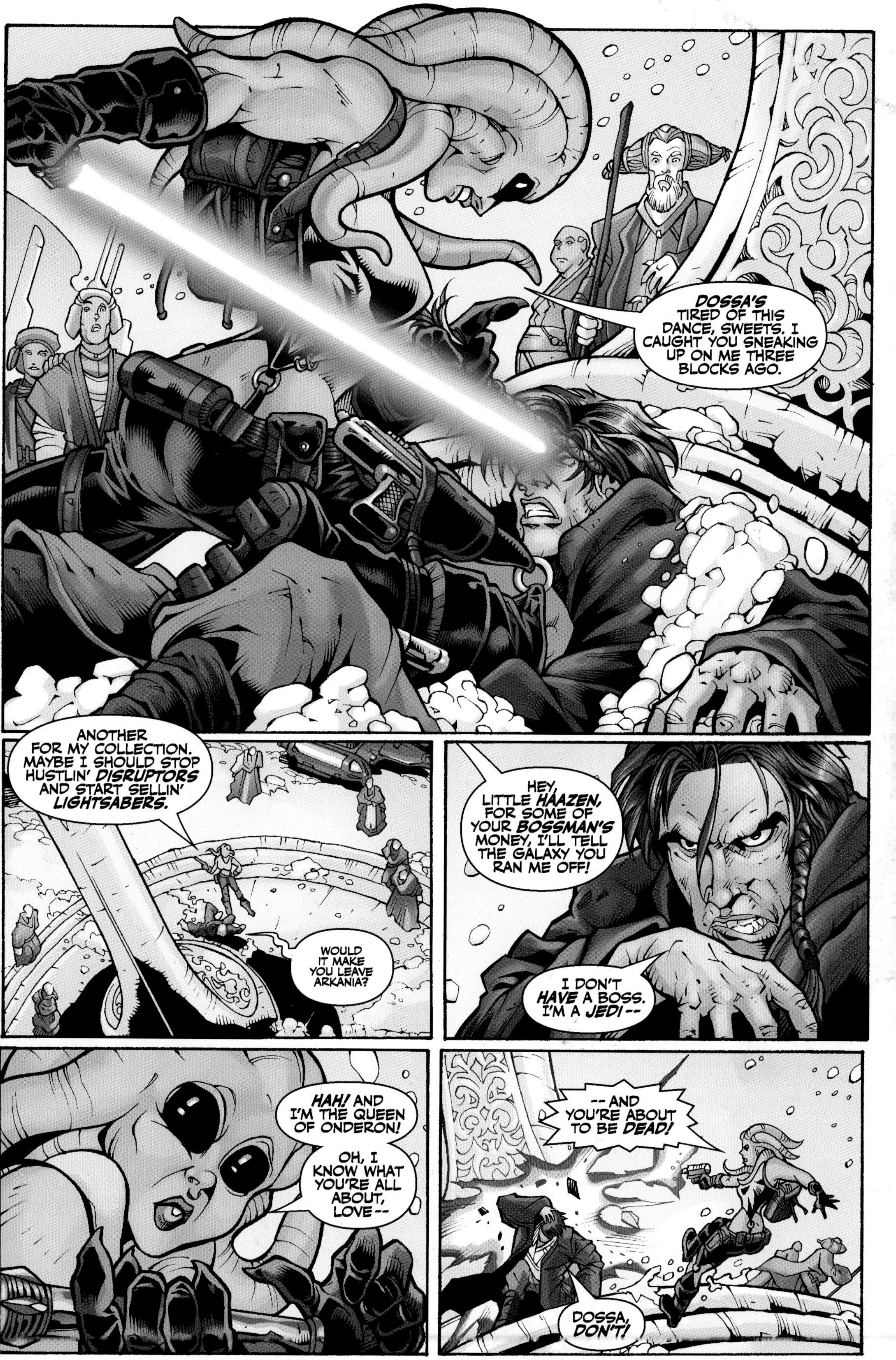
DOSSA'S TIRED OF THIS DANCE, SWEETS. I CAUGHT YOU SNEAKING UP ON ME THREE BLOCKS AGO.
ANOTHER FOR MY COLLECTION. MAYBE I SHOULD STOP HUSTLIN' DISRUPTORS AND START SELLIN' LIGHTSABERS.
WOULD IT MAKE YOU LEAVE ARKANIA?
HEY, LITTLE HAAZEN, FOR SOME OF YOUR BOSSMAN'S MONEY, I'LL TELL THE GALAXY YOU RAN ME OFF!
I DON'T HAVE A BOSS. I'M A JEDI --
HAH! AND I'M THE QUEEN OF ONDERON!
OH, I KNOW WHAT YOU'RE ALL ABOUT, LOVE --
-- AND YOU'RE ABOUT TO BE DEAD!
DOSSA, DON'T!

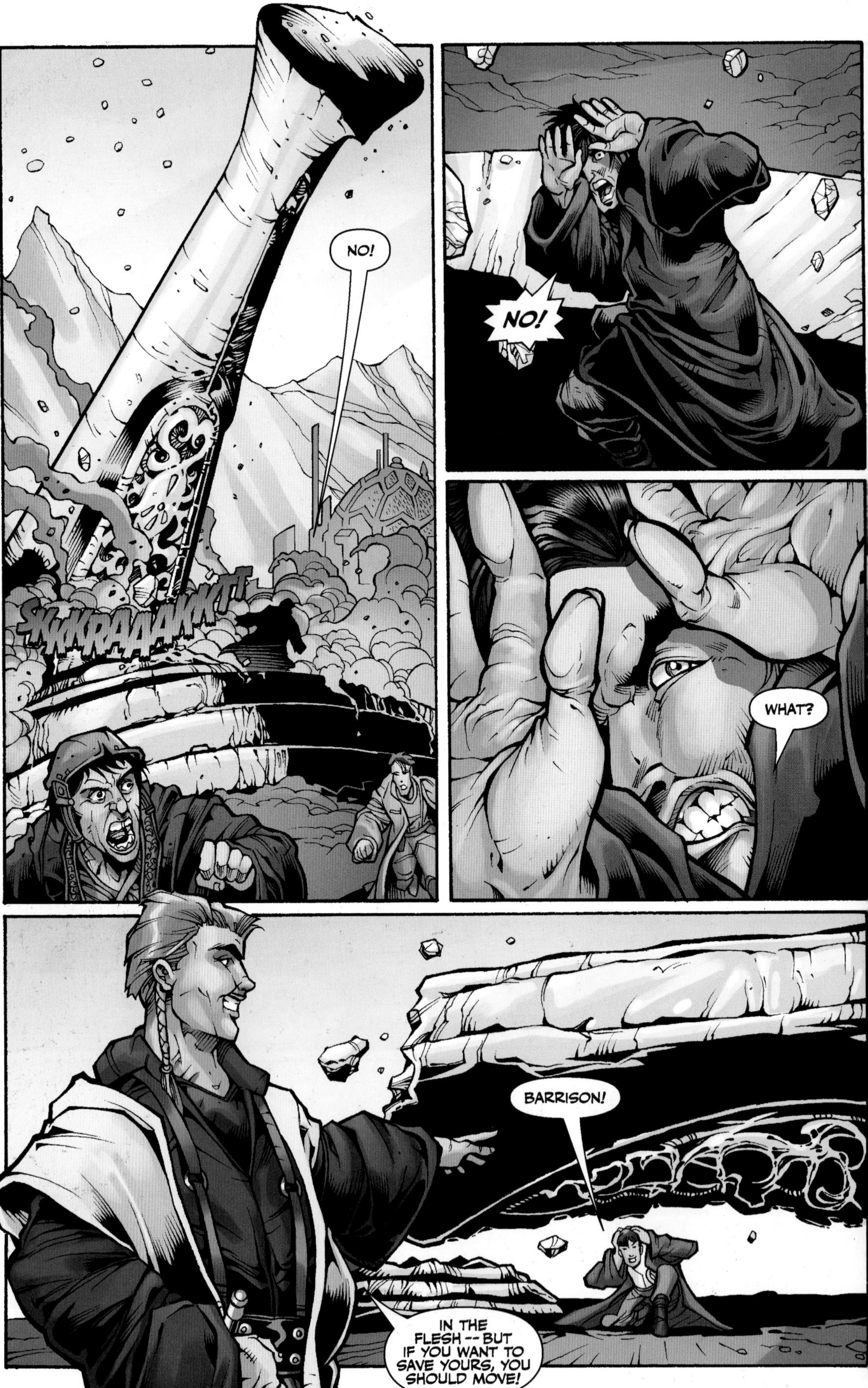
NO!
SKKKRAAAAKKKT!
NO!
WHAT?
BARRISON!
IN THE FLESH -- BUT IF YOU WANT TO SAVE YOURS, YOU SHOULD MOVE!

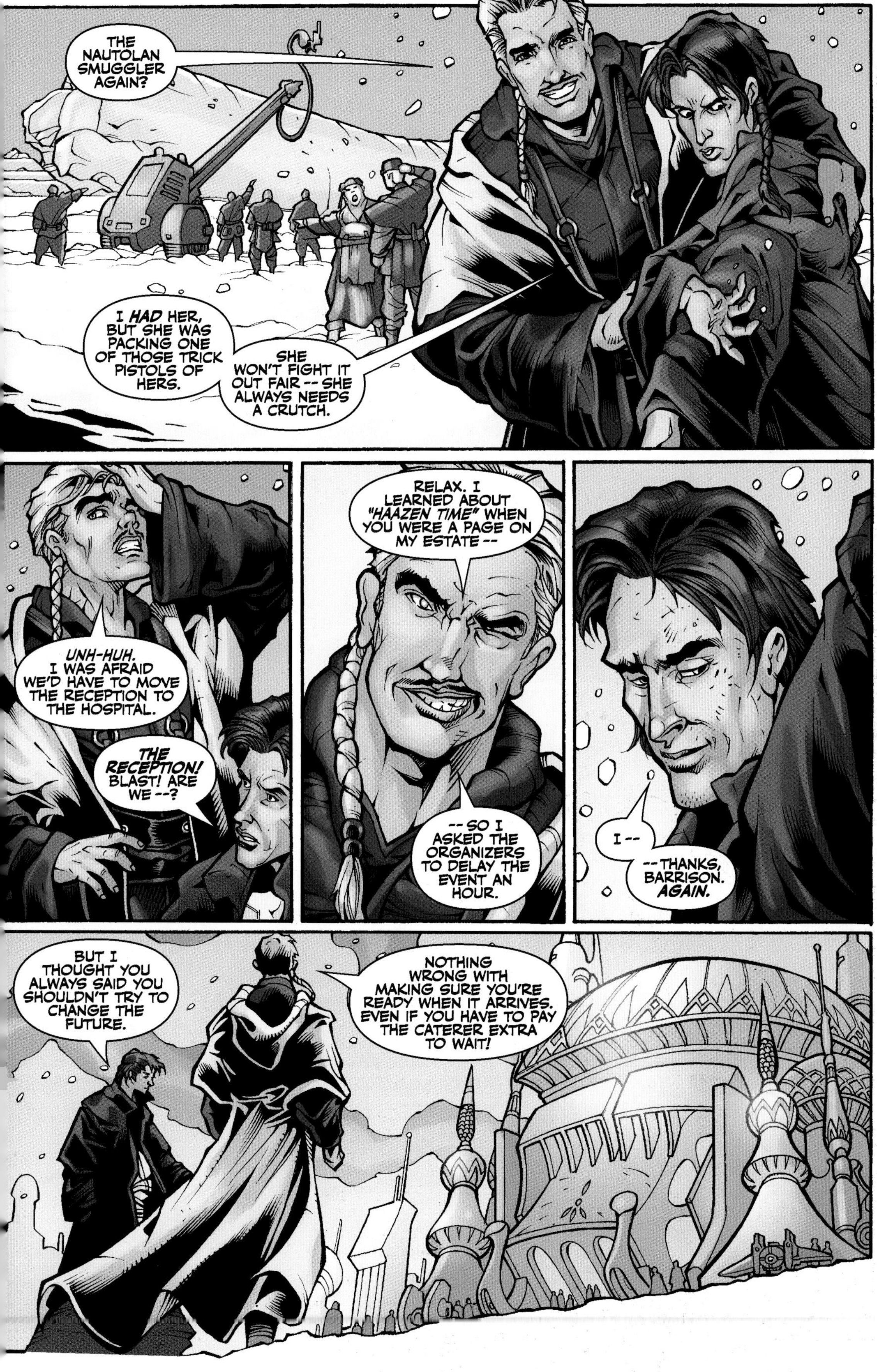

THE NAUTOLAN SMUGGLER AGAIN?
I *HAD* HER, BUT SHE WAS PACKING ONE OF THOSE TRICK PISTOLS OF HERS.
SHE WON'T FIGHT IT OUT FAIR -- SHE ALWAYS NEEDS A CRUTCH.
UNH-HUH. I WAS AFRAID WE'D HAVE TO MOVE THE RECEPTION TO THE HOSPITAL.
THE RECEPTION! BLAST! ARE WE --?
RELAX. I LEARNED ABOUT *"HAAZEN TIME"* WHEN YOU WERE A PAGE ON MY ESTATE --
-- SO I ASKED THE ORGANIZERS TO DELAY THE EVENT AN HOUR.
I --
-- THANKS, BARRISON. *AGAIN.*
BUT I THOUGHT YOU ALWAYS SAID YOU SHOULDN'T TRY TO CHANGE THE FUTURE.
NOTHING WRONG WITH MAKING SURE YOU'RE READY WHEN IT ARRIVES. EVEN IF YOU HAVE TO PAY THE CATERER EXTRA TO WAIT!

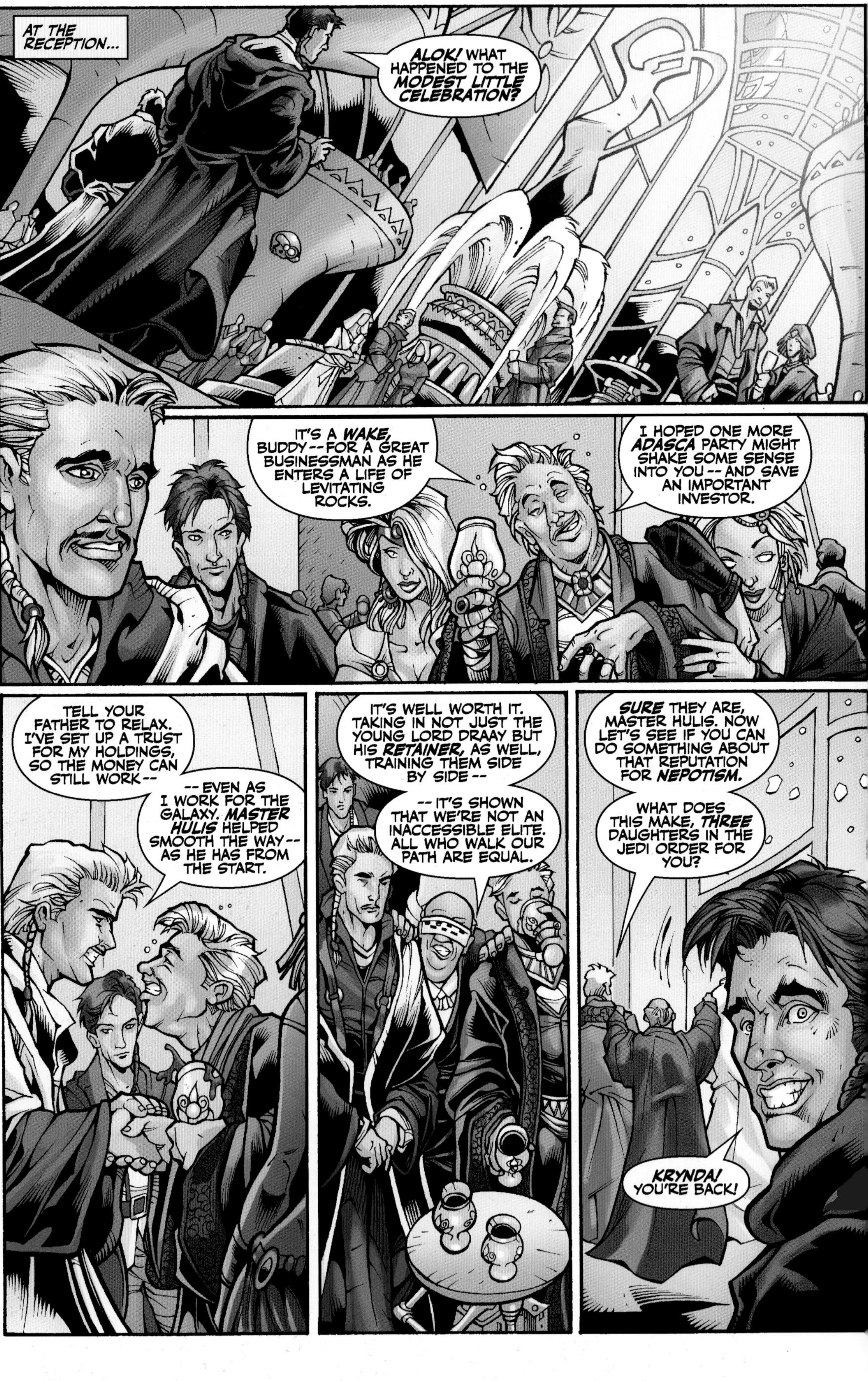

AT THE RECEPTION...
ALOK! WHAT HAPPENED TO THE MODEST LITTLE CELEBRATION?
IT'S A WAKE, BUDDY--FOR A GREAT BUSINESSMAN AS HE ENTERS A LIFE OF LEVITATING ROCKS.
I HOPED ONE MORE ADASCA PARTY MIGHT SHAKE SOME SENSE INTO YOU--AND SAVE AN IMPORTANT INVESTOR.
TELL YOUR FATHER TO RELAX. I'VE SET UP A TRUST FOR MY HOLDINGS, SO THE MONEY CAN STILL WORK--
--EVEN AS I WORK FOR THE GALAXY. MASTER HULIS HELPED SMOOTH THE WAY--AS HE HAS FROM THE START.
IT'S WELL WORTH IT. TAKING IN NOT JUST THE YOUNG LORD DRAAY BUT HIS RETAINER, AS WELL, TRAINING THEM SIDE BY SIDE--
--IT'S SHOWN THAT WE'RE NOT AN INACCESSIBLE ELITE. ALL WHO WALK OUR PATH ARE EQUAL.
SURE THEY ARE, MASTER HULIS. NOW LET'S SEE IF YOU CAN DO SOMETHING ABOUT THAT REPUTATION FOR NEPOTISM.
WHAT DOES THIS MAKE, THREE DAUGHTERS IN THE JEDI ORDER FOR YOU?
KRYNDA! YOU'RE BACK!

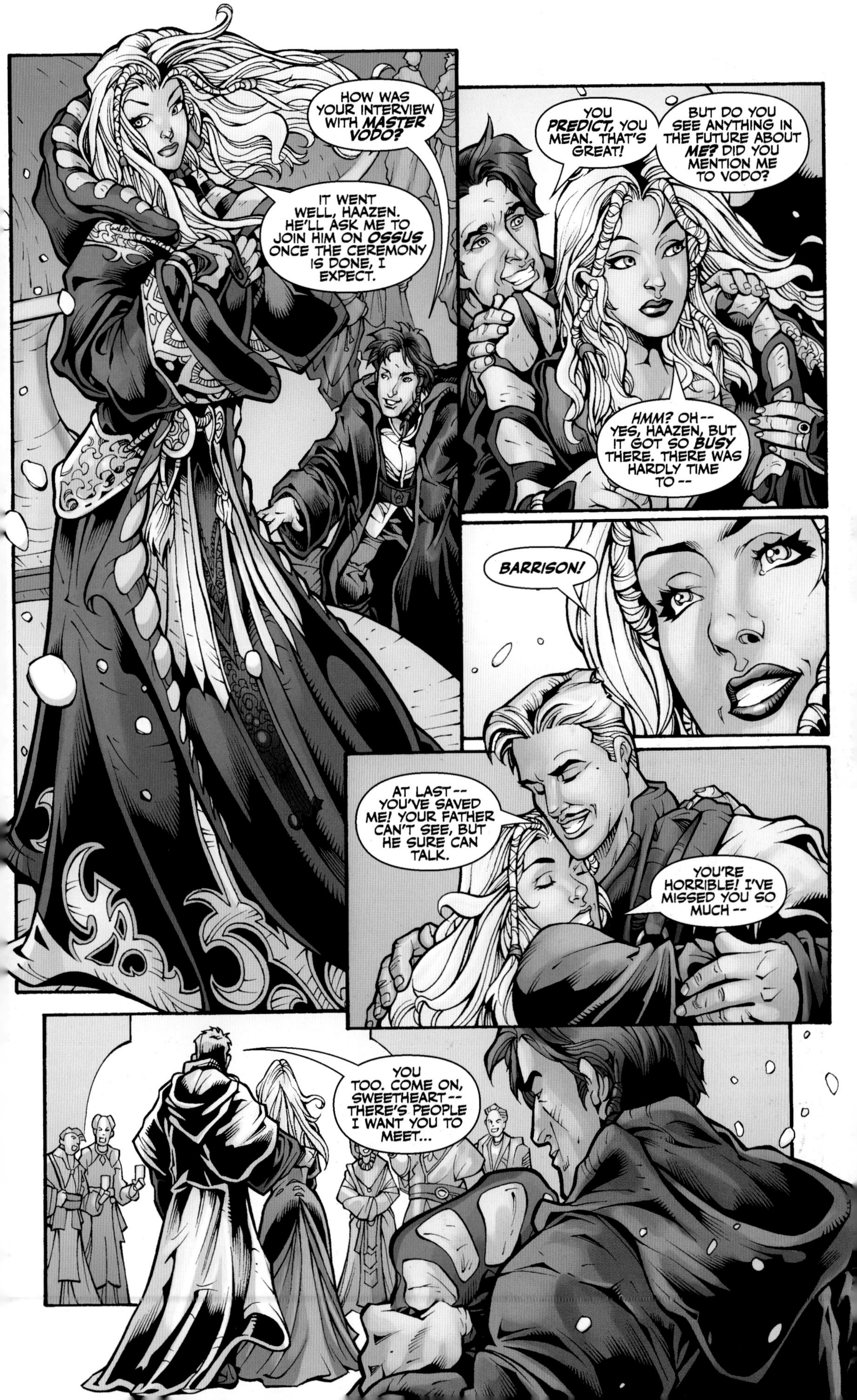
HOW WAS YOUR INTERVIEW WITH MASTER VODO?
IT WENT WELL, HAAZEN. HE'LL ASK ME TO JOIN HIM ON OSSUS ONCE THE CEREMONY IS DONE, I EXPECT.
YOU PREDICT, YOU MEAN. THAT'S GREAT!
BUT DO YOU SEE ANYTHING IN THE FUTURE ABOUT ME? DID YOU MENTION ME TO VODO?
HMM? OH -- YES, HAAZEN, BUT IT GOT SO BUSY THERE. THERE WAS HARDLY TIME TO --
BARRISON!
AT LAST -- YOU'VE SAVED ME! YOUR FATHER CAN'T SEE, BUT HE SURE CAN TALK.
YOU'RE HORRIBLE! I'VE MISSED YOU SO MUCH --
YOU TOO. COME ON, SWEETHEART -- THERE'S PEOPLE I WANT YOU TO MEET...

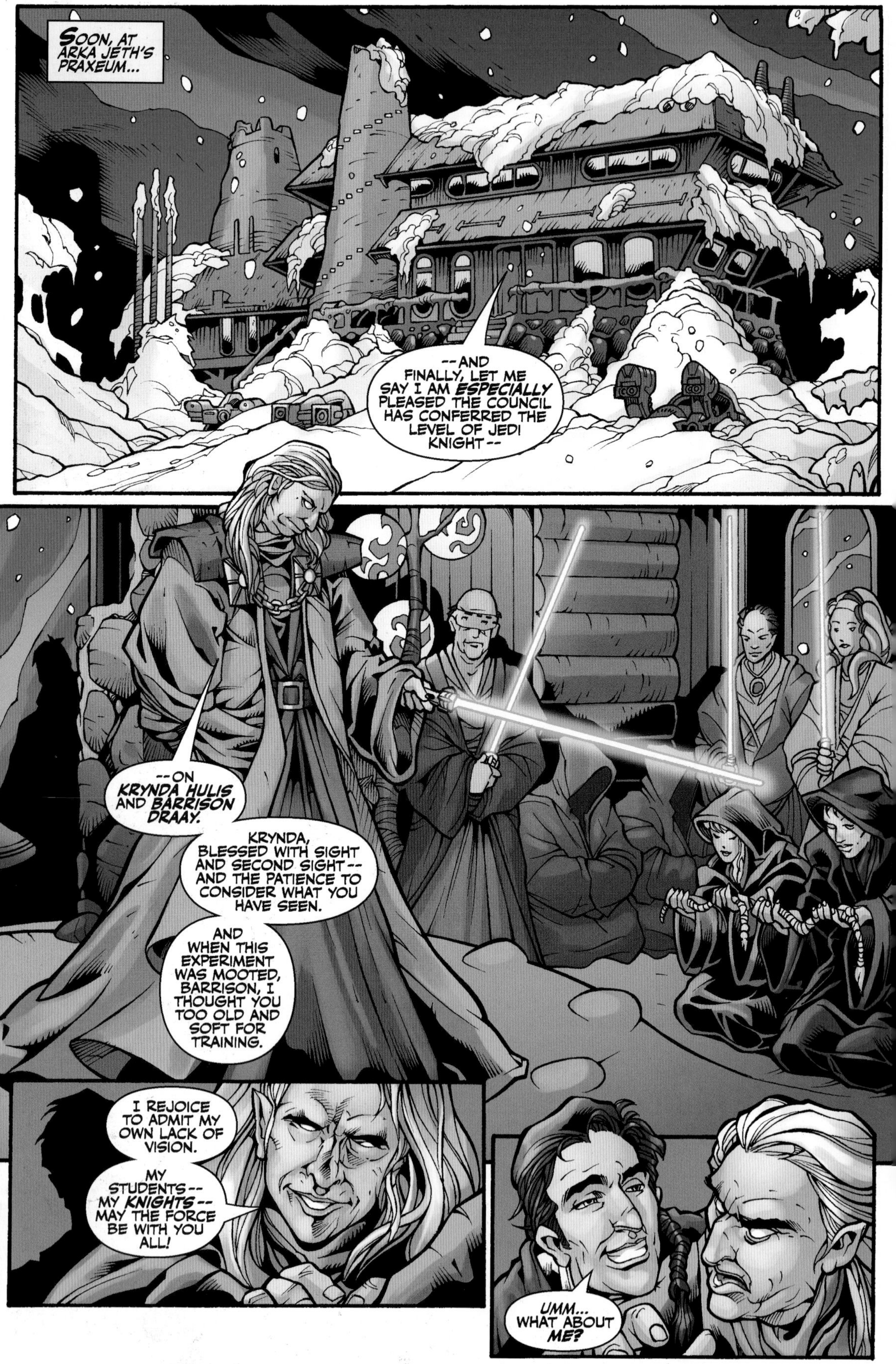
SOON, AT ARKA JETH'S PRAXEUM...
--AND FINALLY, LET ME SAY I AM *ESPECIALLY* PLEASED THE COUNCIL HAS CONFERRED THE LEVEL OF JEDI KNIGHT--
--ON *KRYNDA HULIS* AND *BARRISON DRAAY.*
KRYNDA, BLESSED WITH SIGHT AND SECOND SIGHT-- AND THE PATIENCE TO CONSIDER WHAT YOU HAVE SEEN.
AND WHEN THIS EXPERIMENT WAS MOOTED, BARRISON, I THOUGHT YOU TOO OLD AND SOFT FOR TRAINING.
I REJOICE TO ADMIT MY OWN LACK OF VISION.
MY STUDENTS-- MY *KNIGHTS*-- MAY THE FORCE BE WITH YOU ALL!
UMM... WHAT ABOUT *ME?*

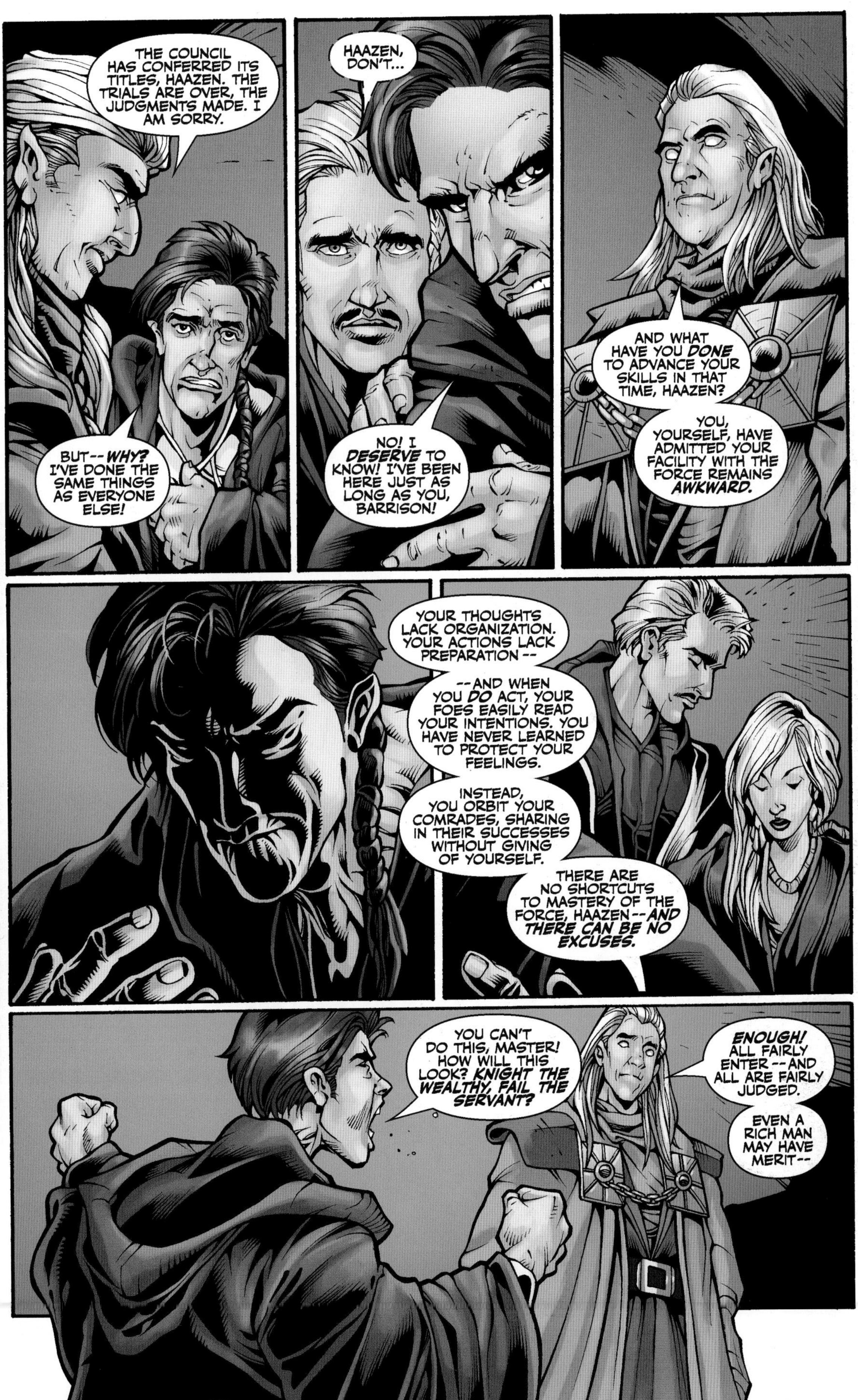
THE COUNCIL HAS CONFERRED ITS TITLES, HAAZEN. THE TRIALS ARE OVER, THE JUDGMENTS MADE. I AM SORRY.
BUT--*WHY?* I'VE DONE THE SAME THINGS AS EVERYONE ELSE!
HAAZEN, DON'T...
NO! I *DESERVE* TO KNOW! I'VE BEEN HERE JUST AS LONG AS YOU, BARRISON!
AND WHAT HAVE YOU *DONE* TO ADVANCE YOUR SKILLS IN THAT TIME, HAAZEN?
YOU, YOURSELF, HAVE ADMITTED YOUR FACILITY WITH THE FORCE REMAINS *AWKWARD.*
YOUR THOUGHTS LACK ORGANIZATION. YOUR ACTIONS LACK PREPARATION--
--AND WHEN YOU *DO* ACT, YOUR FOES EASILY READ YOUR INTENTIONS. YOU HAVE NEVER LEARNED TO PROTECT YOUR FEELINGS.
INSTEAD, YOU ORBIT YOUR COMRADES, SHARING IN THEIR SUCCESSES WITHOUT GIVING OF YOURSELF.
THERE ARE NO SHORTCUTS TO MASTERY OF THE FORCE, HAAZEN--*AND THERE CAN BE NO EXCUSES.*
YOU CAN'T DO THIS, MASTER! HOW WILL THIS LOOK? *KNIGHT THE WEALTHY, FAIL THE SERVANT?*
ENOUGH! ALL FAIRLY ENTER--AND ALL ARE FAIRLY JUDGED.
EVEN A RICH MAN MAY HAVE MERIT--

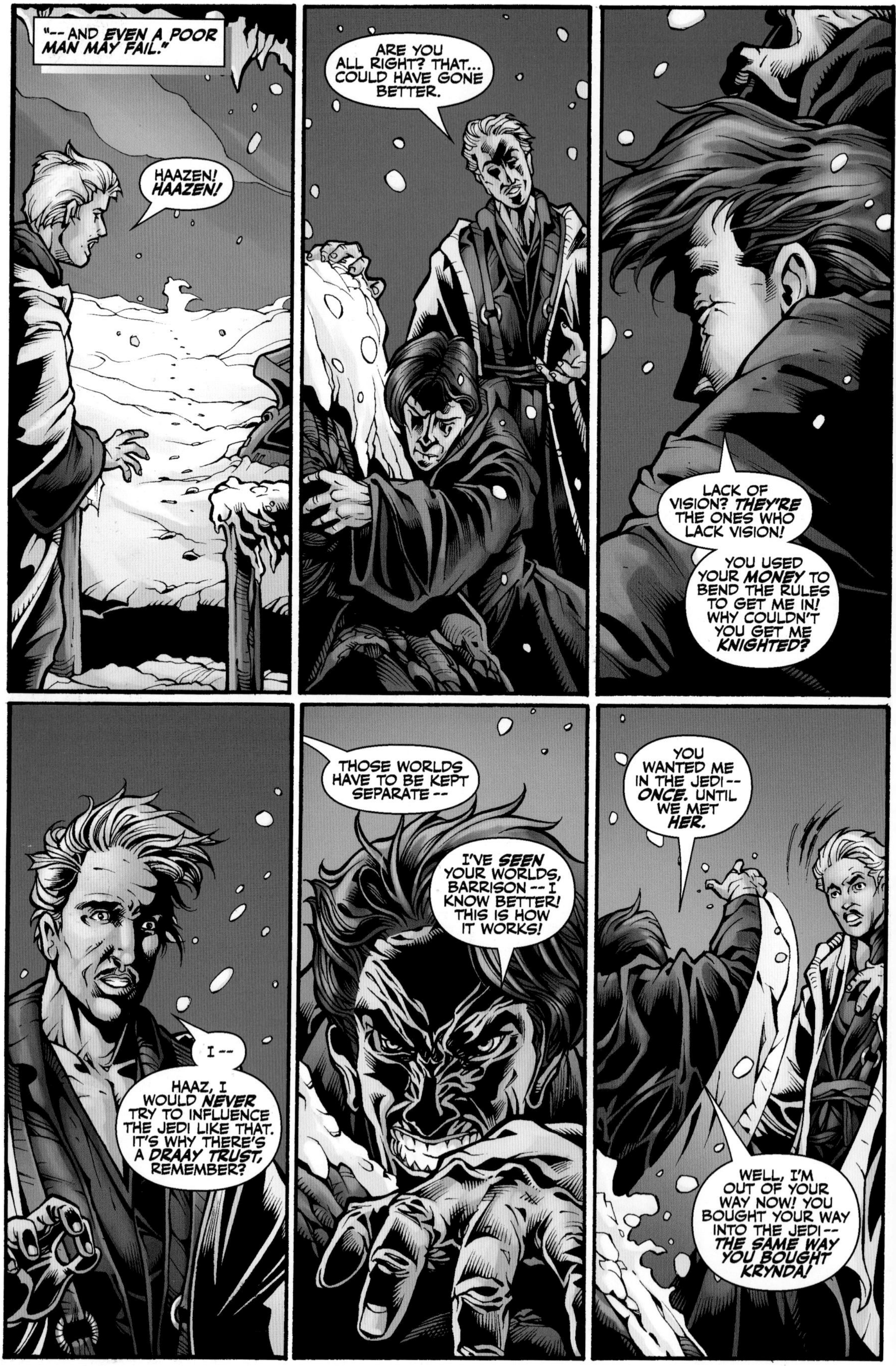
"-- AND EVEN A POOR MAN MAY FAIL."
HAAZEN! HAAZEN!
ARE YOU ALL RIGHT? THAT... COULD HAVE GONE BETTER.
LACK OF VISION? THEY'RE THE ONES WHO LACK VISION!
YOU USED YOUR MONEY TO BEND THE RULES TO GET ME IN! WHY COULDN'T YOU GET ME KNIGHTED?
I --
HAAZ, I WOULD NEVER TRY TO INFLUENCE THE JEDI LIKE THAT. IT'S WHY THERE'S A DRAAY TRUST, REMEMBER?
THOSE WORLDS HAVE TO BE KEPT SEPARATE --
I'VE SEEN YOUR WORLDS, BARRISON -- I KNOW BETTER! THIS IS HOW IT WORKS!
YOU WANTED ME IN THE JEDI -- ONCE. UNTIL WE MET HER.
WELL, I'M OUT OF YOUR WAY NOW! YOU BOUGHT YOUR WAY INTO THE JEDI -- THE SAME WAY YOU BOUGHT KRYNDA!

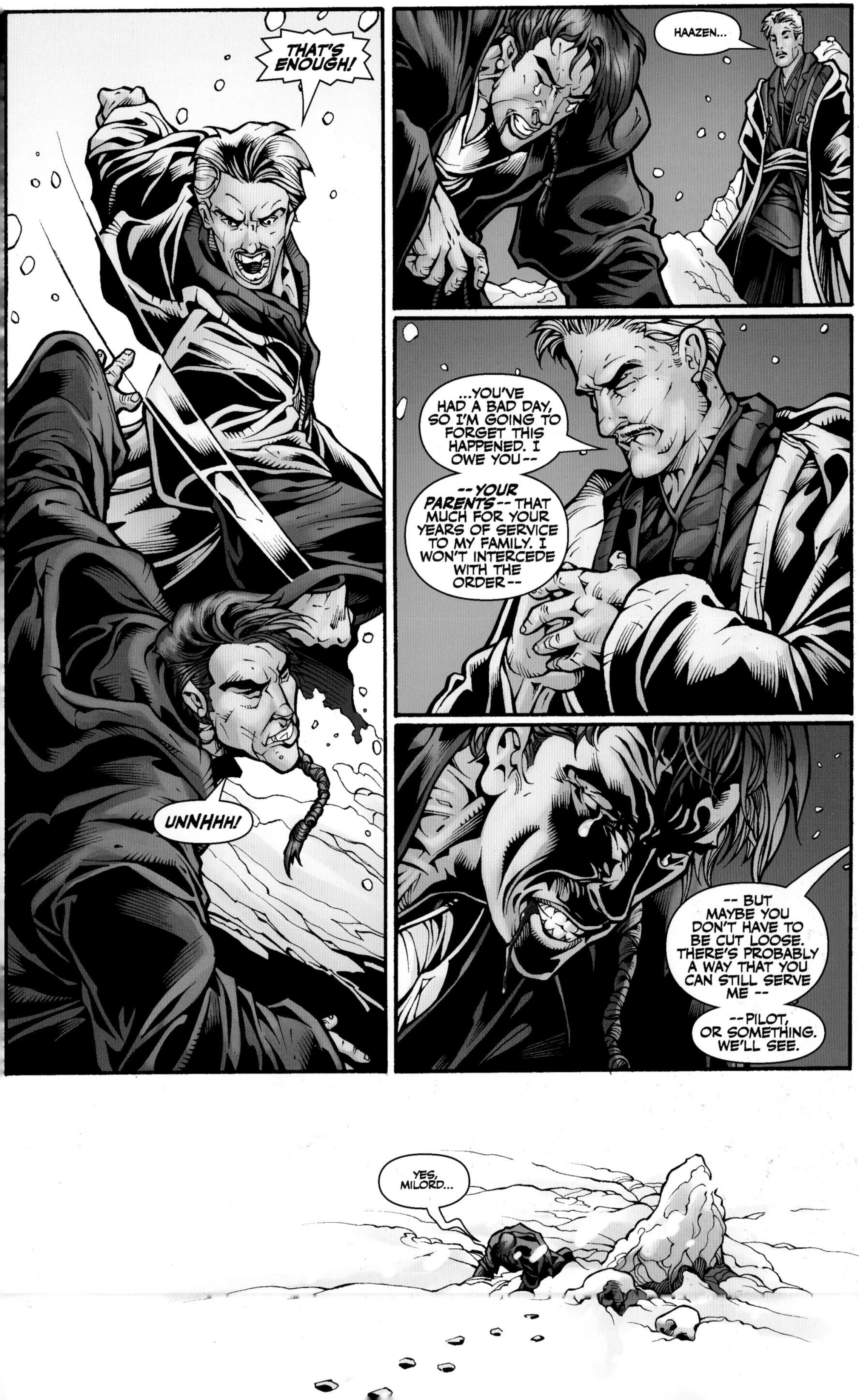
THAT'S ENOUGH!
UNNHHH!
HAAZEN...
...YOU'VE HAD A BAD DAY, SO I'M GOING TO FORGET THIS HAPPENED. I OWE YOU--
--YOUR PARENTS-- THAT MUCH FOR YOUR YEARS OF SERVICE TO MY FAMILY. I WON'T INTERCEDE WITH THE ORDER--
-- BUT MAYBE YOU DON'T HAVE TO BE CUT LOOSE. THERE'S PROBABLY A WAY THAT YOU CAN STILL SERVE ME --
--PILOT, OR SOMETHING. WE'LL SEE.
YES, MILORD...

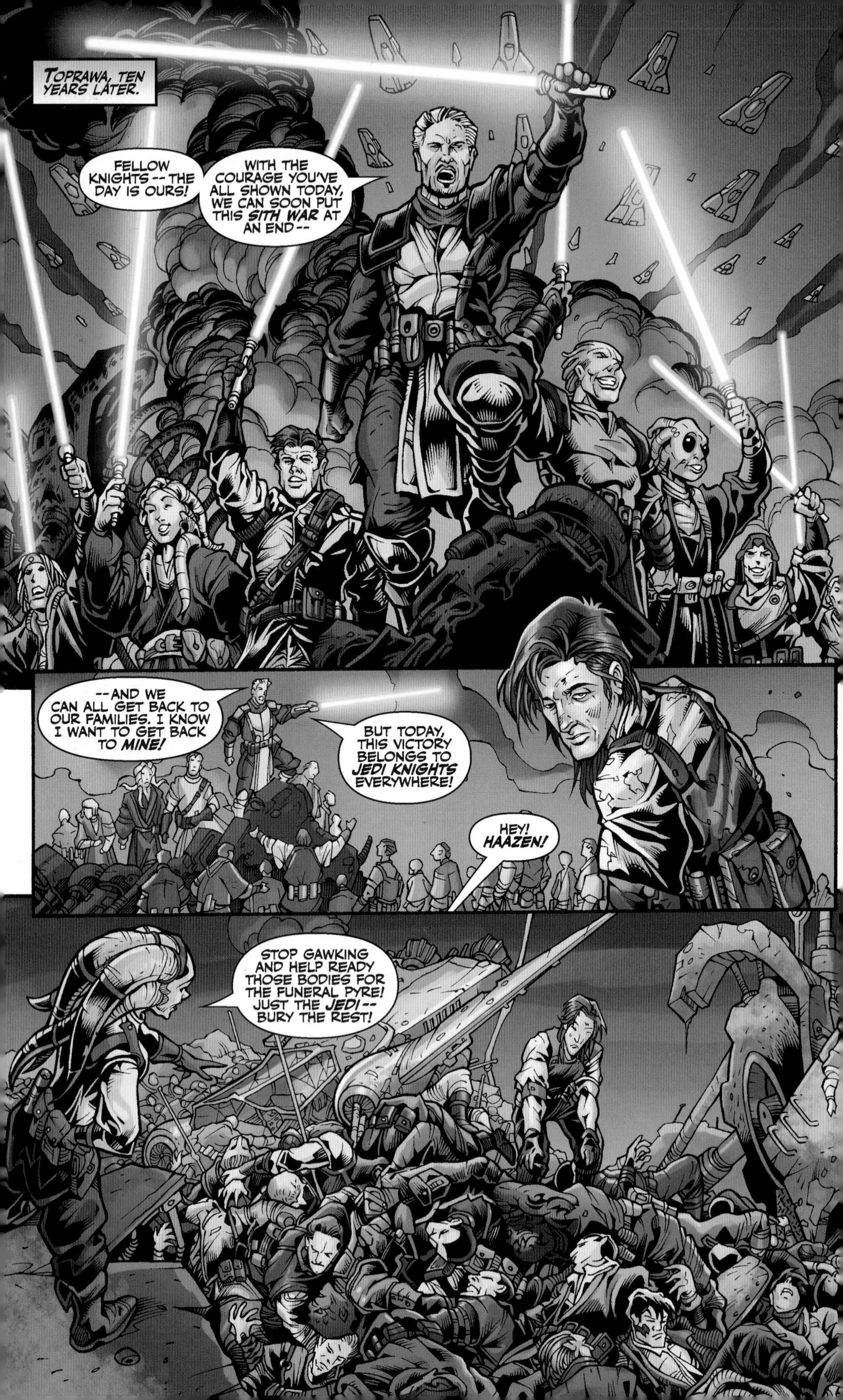
TOPRAWA, TEN YEARS LATER.
FELLOW KNIGHTS -- THE DAY IS OURS!
WITH THE COURAGE YOU'VE ALL SHOWN TODAY, WE CAN SOON PUT THIS SITH WAR AT AN END--
--AND WE CAN ALL GET BACK TO OUR FAMILIES. I KNOW I WANT TO GET BACK TO MINE!
BUT TODAY, THIS VICTORY BELONGS TO JEDI KNIGHTS EVERYWHERE!
HEY! HAAZEN!
STOP GAWKING AND HELP READY THOSE BODIES FOR THE FUNERAL PYRE! JUST THE JEDI-- BURY THE REST!

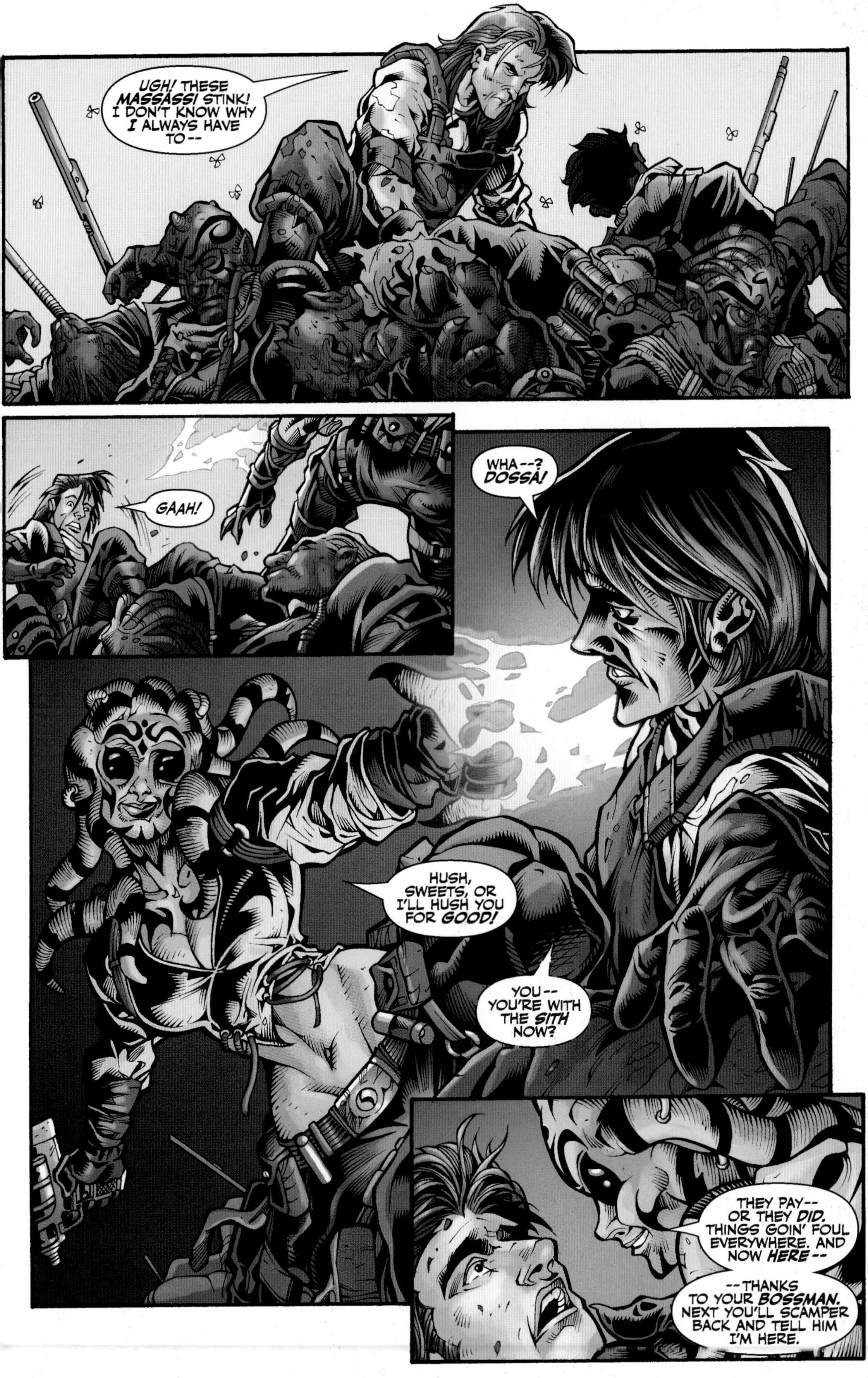
UGH! THESE MASSASSI STINK! I DON'T KNOW WHY I ALWAYS HAVE TO--
GAAH!
WHA--? DOSSA!
HUSH, SWEETS, OR I'LL HUSH YOU FOR GOOD!
YOU-- YOU'RE WITH THE SITH NOW?
THEY PAY-- OR THEY DID. THINGS GOIN' FOUL EVERYWHERE. AND NOW HERE--
--THANKS TO YOUR BOSSMAN. NEXT YOU'LL SCAMPER BACK AND TELL HIM I'M HERE.

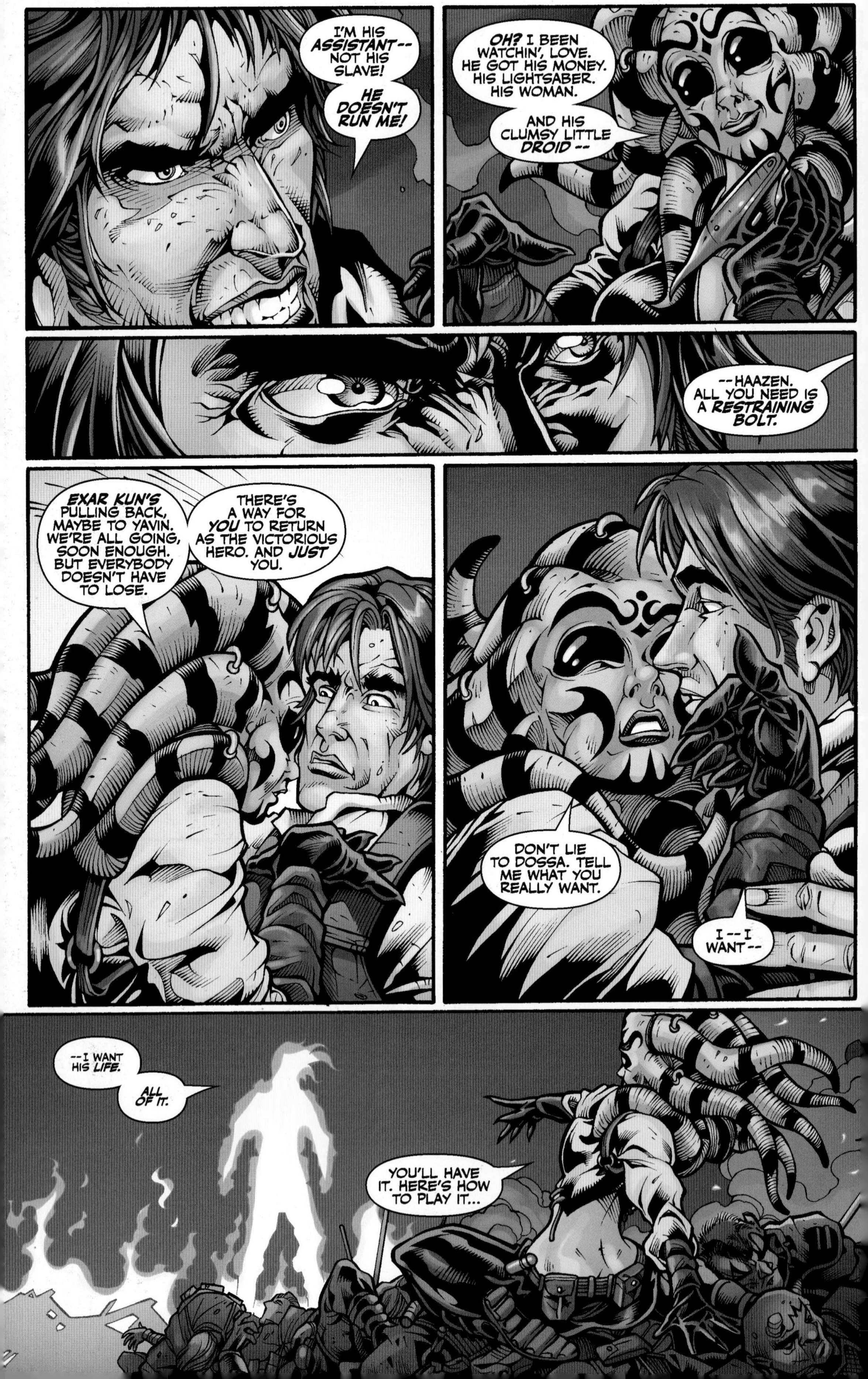
I'M HIS *ASSISTANT* -- NOT HIS SLAVE!
HE DOESN'T RUN ME!
OH? I BEEN WATCHIN', LOVE. HE GOT HIS MONEY. HIS LIGHTSABER. HIS WOMAN.
AND HIS CLUMSY LITTLE *DROID* --
--HAAZEN. ALL YOU NEED IS A *RESTRAINING BOLT.*
EXAR KUN'S PULLING BACK, MAYBE TO YAVIN. WE'RE ALL GOING, SOON ENOUGH. BUT EVERYBODY DOESN'T HAVE TO LOSE.
THERE'S A WAY FOR *YOU* TO RETURN AS THE VICTORIOUS HERO. AND *JUST* YOU.
DON'T LIE TO DOSSA. TELL ME WHAT YOU REALLY WANT.
I -- I WANT --
--I WANT HIS *LIFE.*
ALL OF IT.
YOU'LL HAVE IT. HERE'S HOW TO PLAY IT...

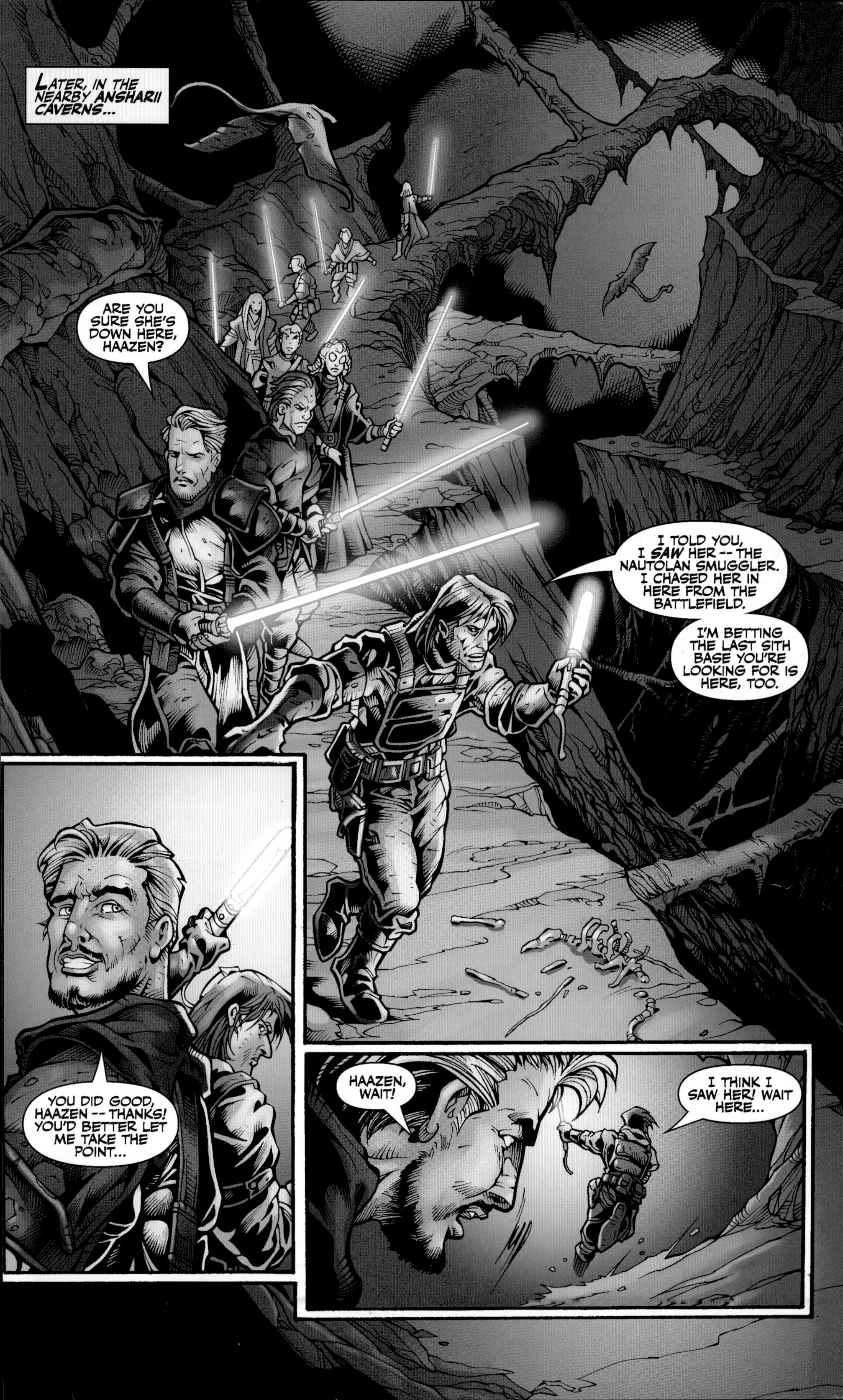
LATER, IN THE NEARBY ANSHARII CAVERNS...
ARE YOU SURE SHE'S DOWN HERE, HAAZEN?
I TOLD YOU, I SAW HER -- THE NAUTOLAN SMUGGLER. I CHASED HER IN HERE FROM THE BATTLEFIELD.
I'M BETTING THE LAST SITH BASE YOU'RE LOOKING FOR IS HERE, TOO.
YOU DID GOOD, HAAZEN -- THANKS! YOU'D BETTER LET ME TAKE THE POINT...
HAAZEN, WAIT!
I THINK I SAW HER! WAIT HERE...

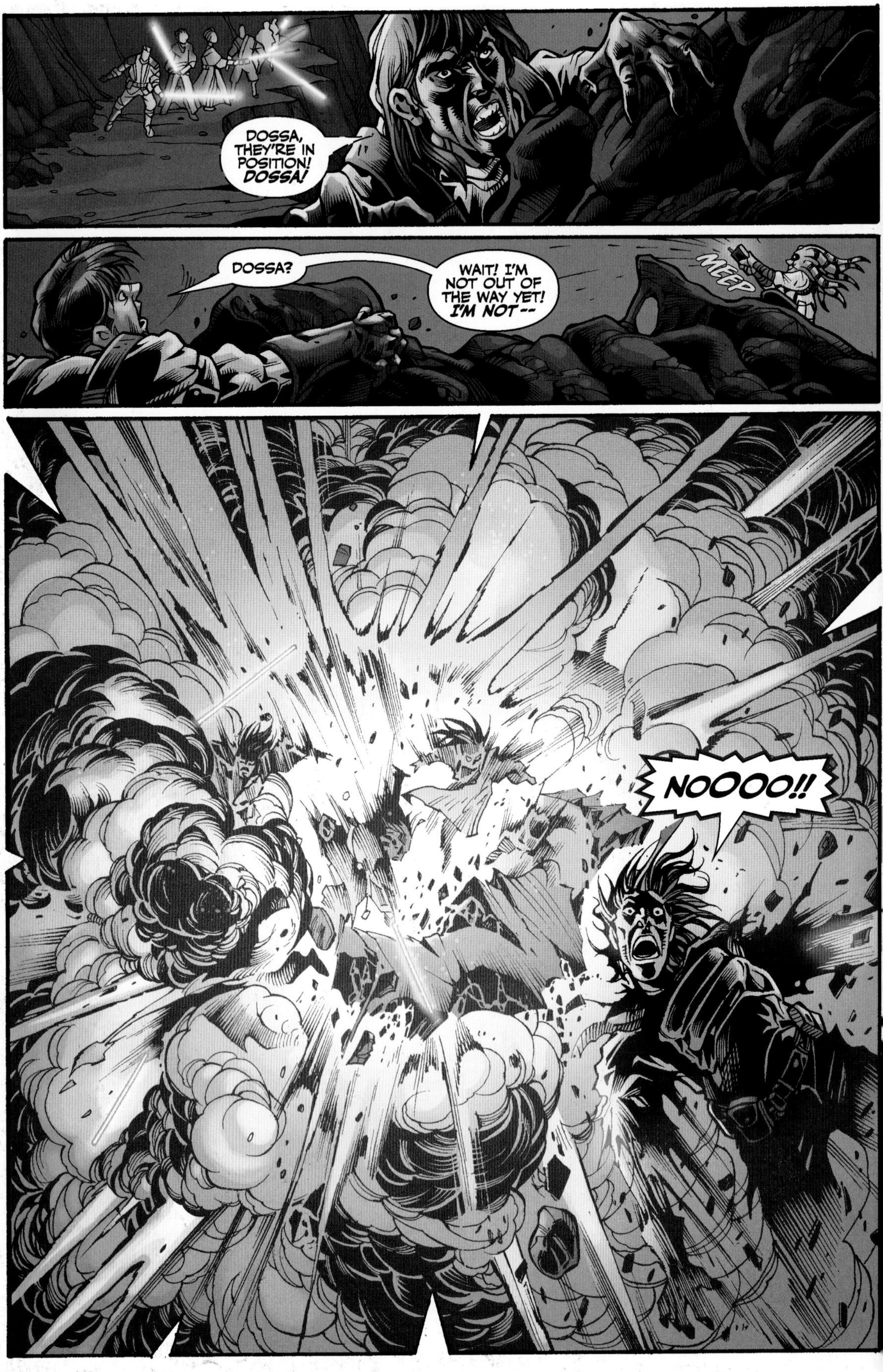
DOSSA, THEY'RE IN POSITION! DOSSA!
DOSSA?
WAIT! I'M NOT OUT OF THE WAY YET! I'M NOT --
MEEP
NOOOO!!

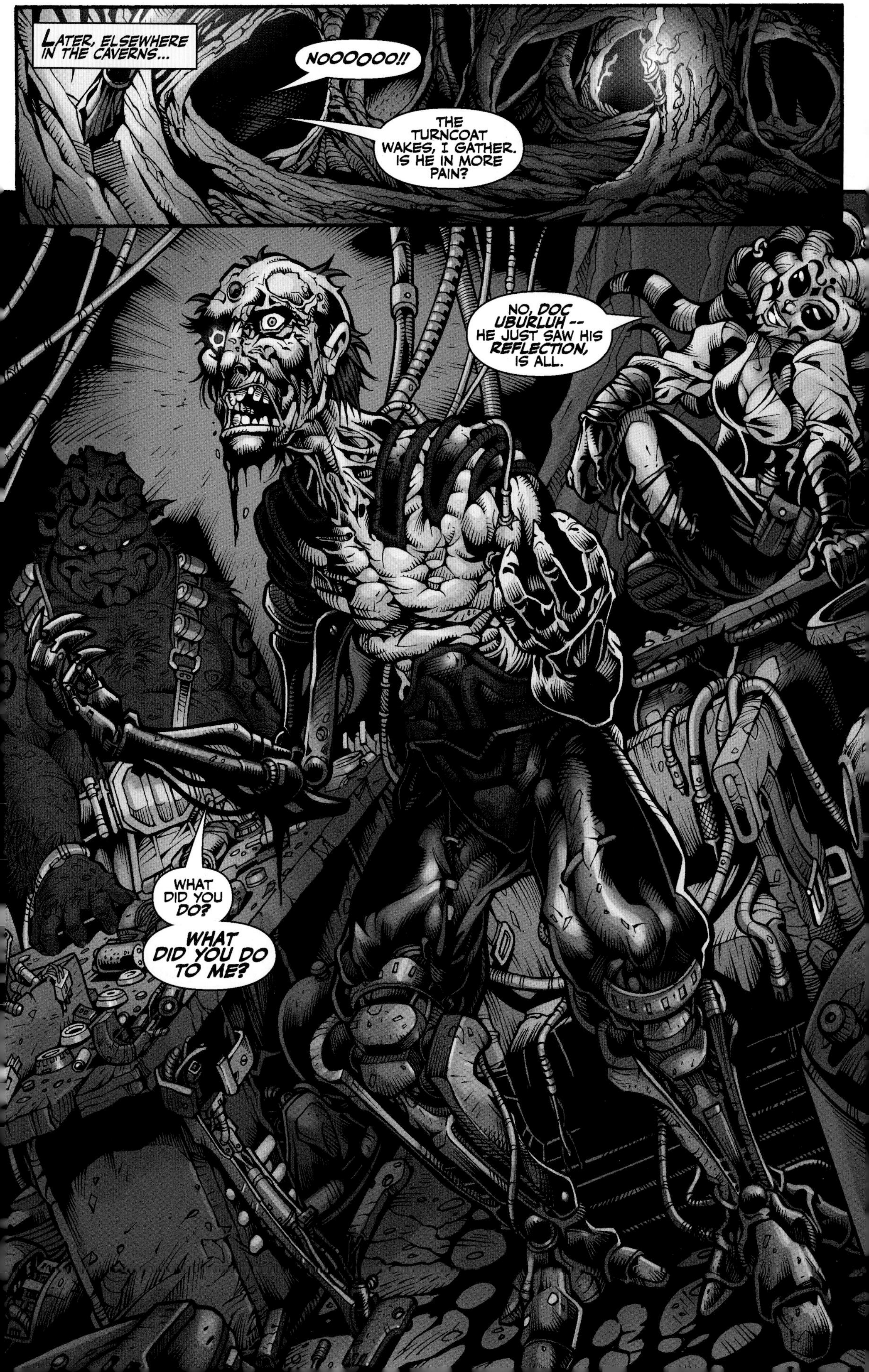
LATER, ELSEWHERE IN THE CAVERNS...
NOOOOOO!!
THE TURNCOAT WAKES, I GATHER. IS HE IN MORE PAIN?
NO, DOC UBURLUH -- HE JUST SAW HIS REFLECTION, IS ALL.
WHAT DID YOU DO?
WHAT DID YOU DO TO ME?

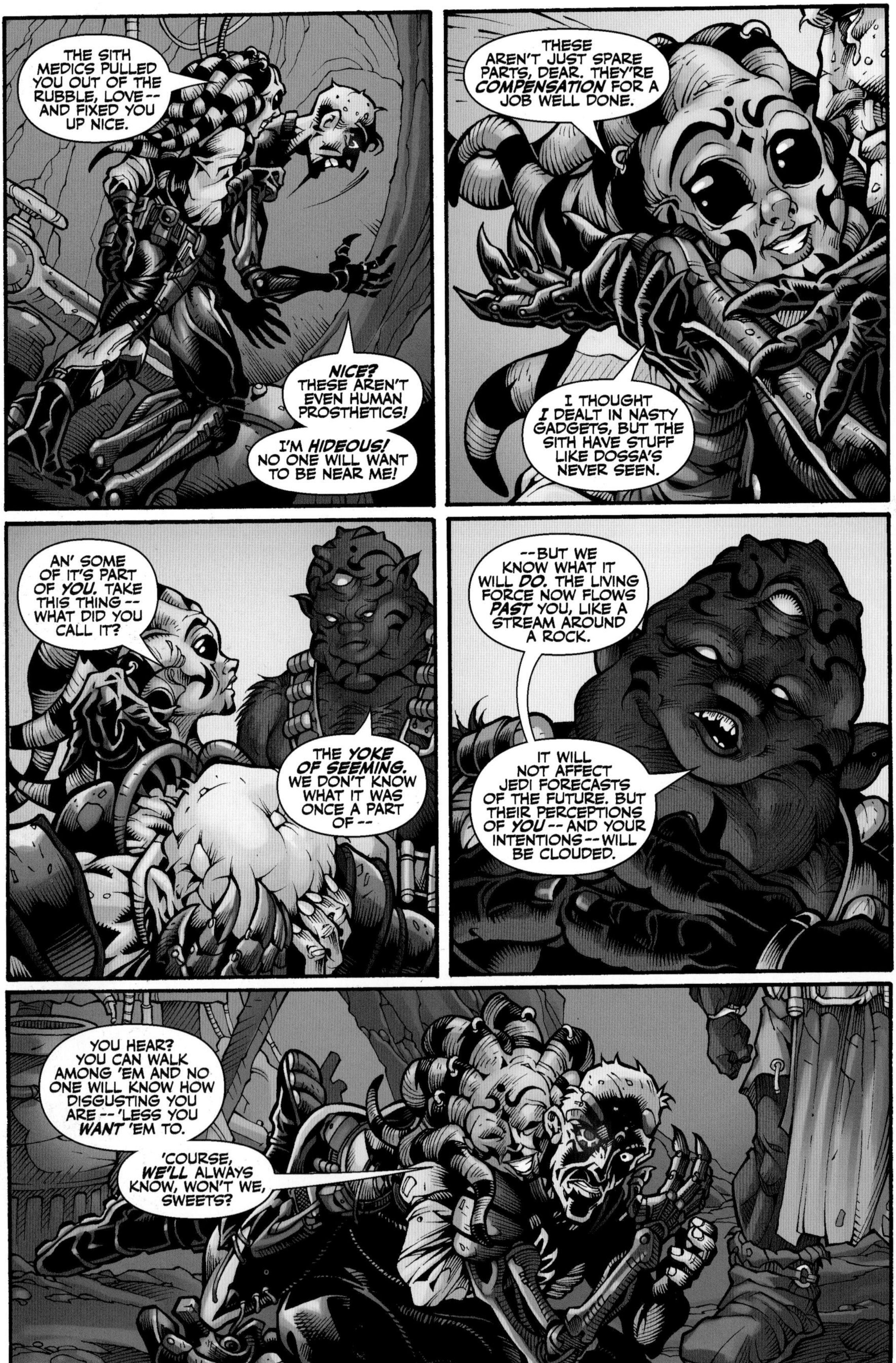

THE SITH MEDICS PULLED YOU OUT OF THE RUBBLE, LOVE-- AND FIXED YOU UP NICE.
NICE? THESE AREN'T EVEN HUMAN PROSTHETICS!
I'M HIDEOUS! NO ONE WILL WANT TO BE NEAR ME!
THESE AREN'T JUST SPARE PARTS, DEAR. THEY'RE COMPENSATION FOR A JOB WELL DONE.
I THOUGHT I DEALT IN NASTY GADGETS, BUT THE SITH HAVE STUFF LIKE DOSSA'S NEVER SEEN.
AN' SOME OF IT'S PART OF YOU. TAKE THIS THING-- WHAT DID YOU CALL IT?
THE YOKE OF SEEMING. WE DON'T KNOW WHAT IT WAS ONCE A PART OF--
--BUT WE KNOW WHAT IT WILL DO. THE LIVING FORCE NOW FLOWS PAST YOU, LIKE A STREAM AROUND A ROCK.
IT WILL NOT AFFECT JEDI FORECASTS OF THE FUTURE. BUT THEIR PERCEPTIONS OF YOU--AND YOUR INTENTIONS--WILL BE CLOUDED.
YOU HEAR? YOU CAN WALK AMONG 'EM AND NO ONE WILL KNOW HOW DISGUSTING YOU ARE--'LESS YOU WANT 'EM TO.
'COURSE, WE'LL ALWAYS KNOW, WON'T WE, SWEETS?

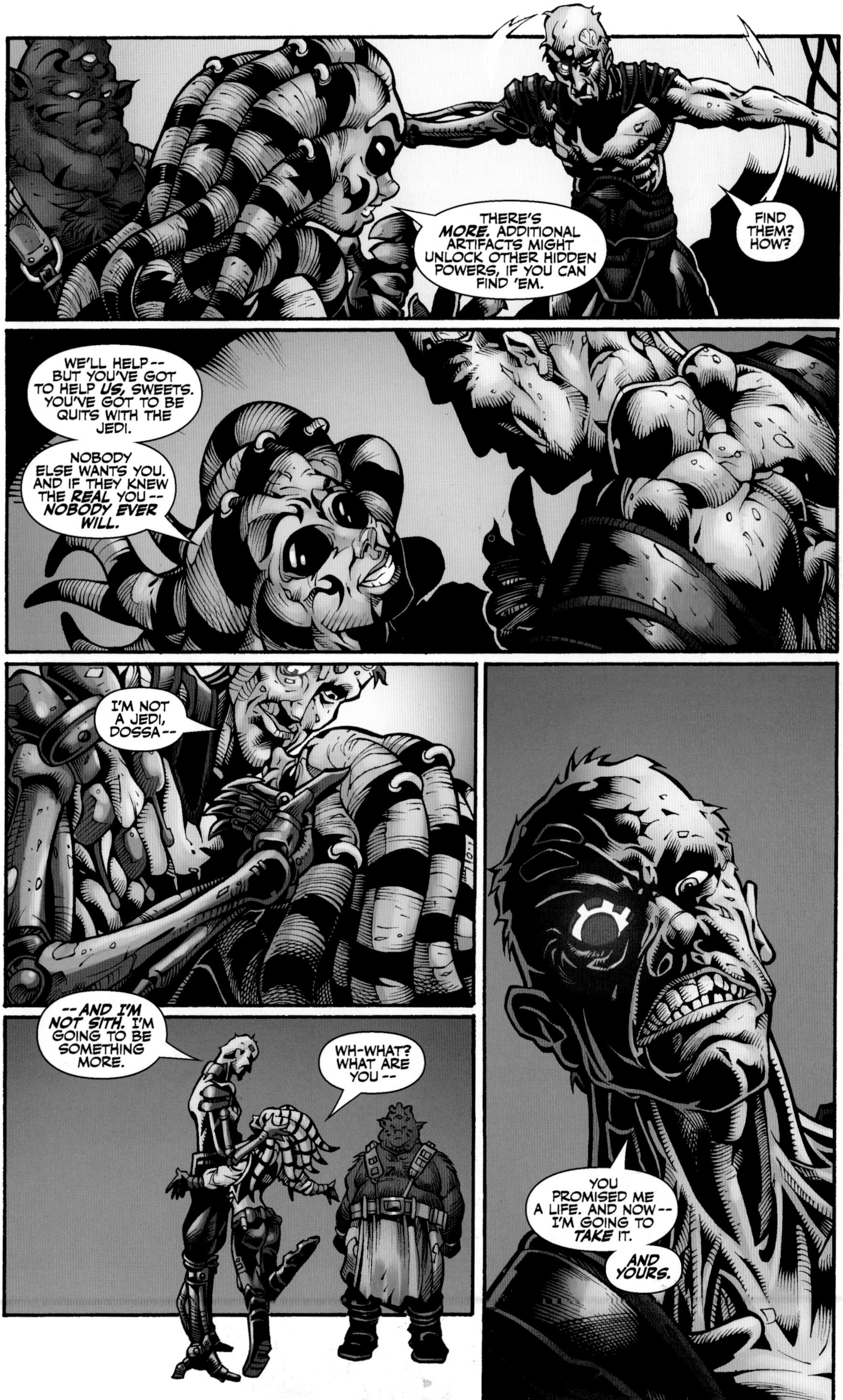
THERE'S MORE. ADDITIONAL ARTIFACTS MIGHT UNLOCK OTHER HIDDEN POWERS, IF YOU CAN FIND 'EM.
FIND THEM? HOW?
WE'LL HELP-- BUT YOU'VE GOT TO HELP US, SWEETS. YOU'VE GOT TO BE QUITS WITH THE JEDI.
NOBODY ELSE WANTS YOU. AND IF THEY KNEW THE REAL YOU-- NOBODY EVER WILL.
I'M NOT A JEDI, DOSSA--
--AND I'M NOT SITH. I'M GOING TO BE SOMETHING MORE.
WH-WHAT? WHAT ARE YOU --
YOU PROMISED ME A LIFE. AND NOW-- I'M GOING TO TAKE IT.
AND YOURS.

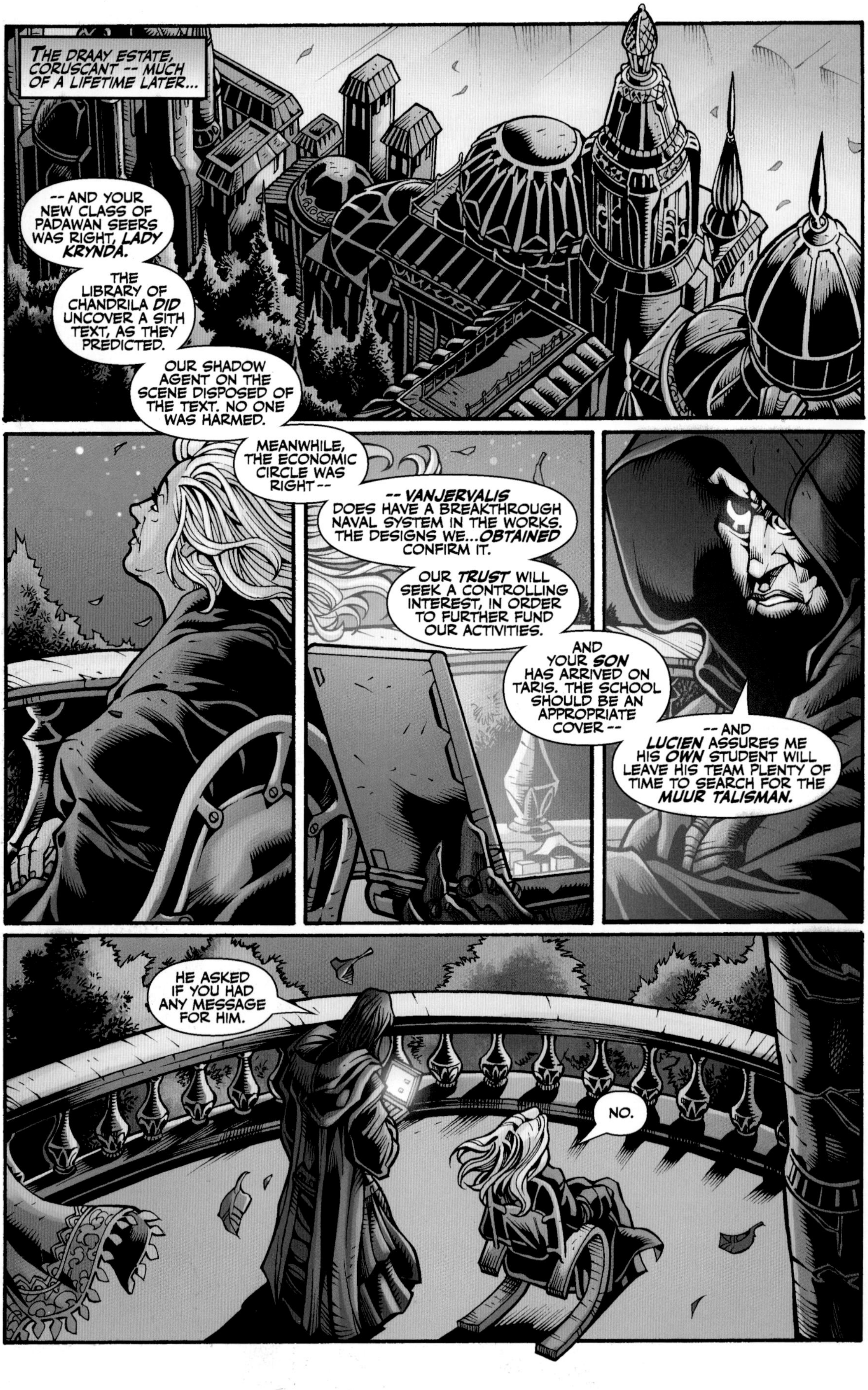

THE DRAAY ESTATE, CORUSCANT -- MUCH OF A LIFETIME LATER...
-- AND YOUR NEW CLASS OF PADAWAN SEERS WAS RIGHT, LADY KRYNDA.
THE LIBRARY OF CHANDRILA DID UNCOVER A SITH TEXT, AS THEY PREDICTED.
OUR SHADOW AGENT ON THE SCENE DISPOSED OF THE TEXT. NO ONE WAS HARMED.
MEANWHILE, THE ECONOMIC CIRCLE WAS RIGHT --
-- VANJERVALIS DOES HAVE A BREAKTHROUGH NAVAL SYSTEM IN THE WORKS. THE DESIGNS WE...OBTAINED CONFIRM IT.
OUR TRUST WILL SEEK A CONTROLLING INTEREST, IN ORDER TO FURTHER FUND OUR ACTIVITIES.
AND YOUR SON HAS ARRIVED ON TARIS. THE SCHOOL SHOULD BE AN APPROPRIATE COVER --
-- AND LUCIEN ASSURES ME HIS OWN STUDENT WILL LEAVE HIS TEAM PLENTY OF TIME TO SEARCH FOR THE MUUR TALISMAN.
HE ASKED IF YOU HAD ANY MESSAGE FOR HIM.
NO.

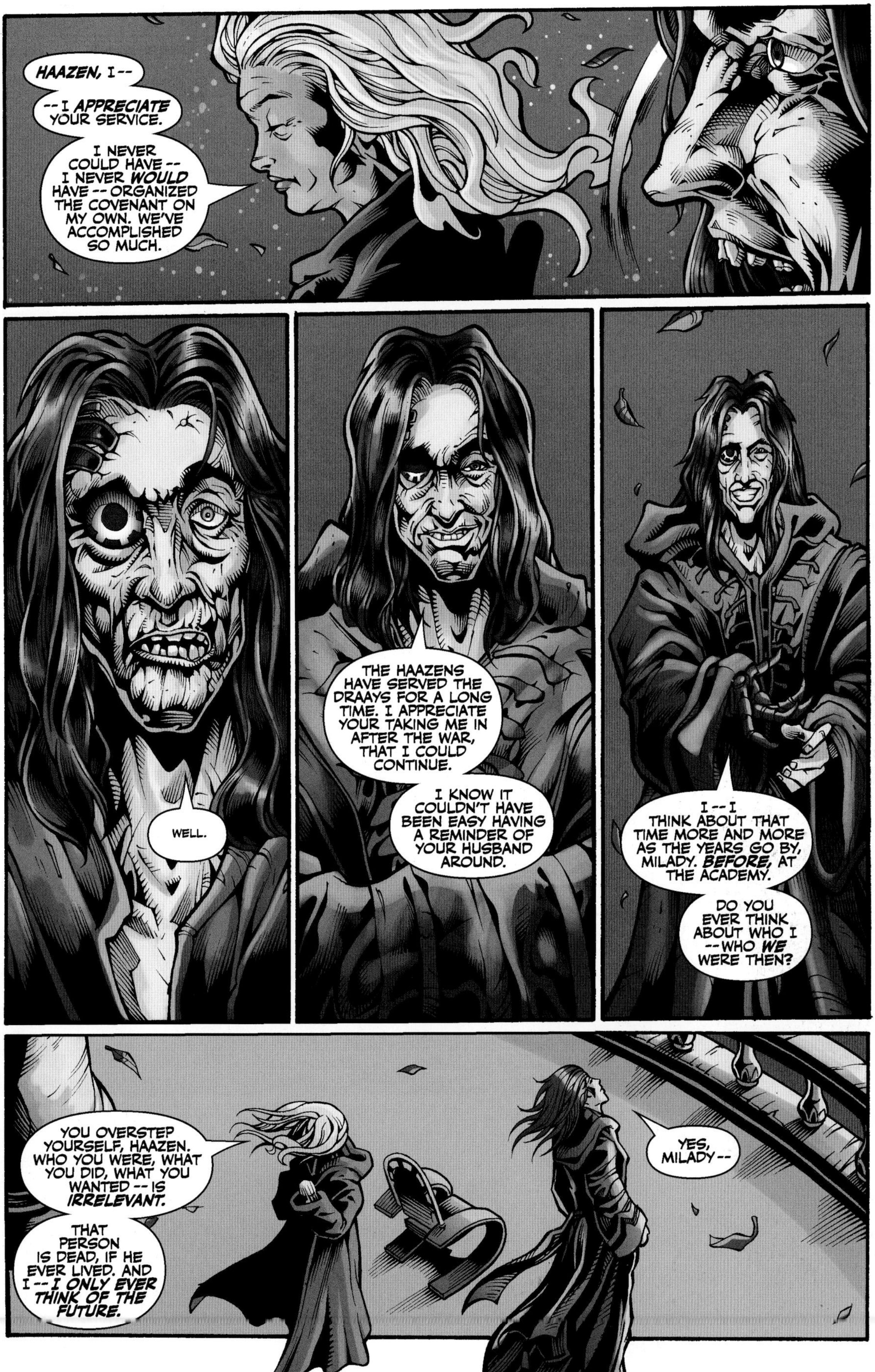
HAAZEN, I--
--I APPRECIATE YOUR SERVICE.
I NEVER COULD HAVE -- I NEVER WOULD HAVE -- ORGANIZED THE COVENANT ON MY OWN. WE'VE ACCOMPLISHED SO MUCH.
WELL.
THE HAAZENS HAVE SERVED THE DRAAYS FOR A LONG TIME. I APPRECIATE YOUR TAKING ME IN AFTER THE WAR, THAT I COULD CONTINUE.
I KNOW IT COULDN'T HAVE BEEN EASY HAVING A REMINDER OF YOUR HUSBAND AROUND.
I--I THINK ABOUT THAT TIME MORE AND MORE AS THE YEARS GO BY, MILADY. BEFORE, AT THE ACADEMY.
DO YOU EVER THINK ABOUT WHO I --WHO WE WERE THEN?
YOU OVERSTEP YOURSELF, HAAZEN. WHO YOU WERE, WHAT YOU DID, WHAT YOU WANTED -- IS IRRELEVANT.
THAT PERSON IS DEAD, IF HE EVER LIVED. AND I -- I ONLY EVER THINK OF THE FUTURE.
YES, MILADY--

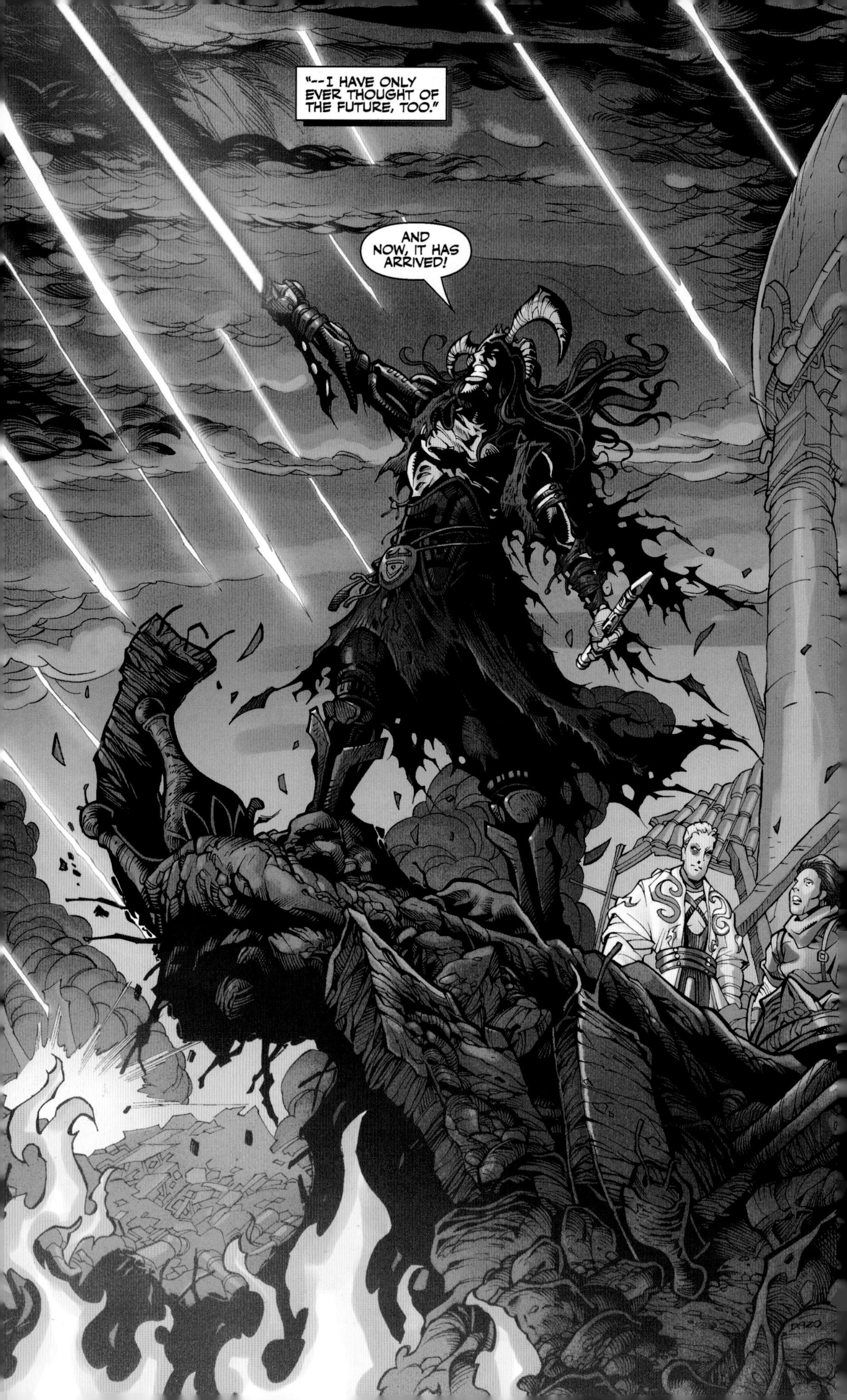
"--I HAVE ONLY EVER THOUGHT OF THE FUTURE, TOO."
AND NOW, IT HAS ARRIVED!

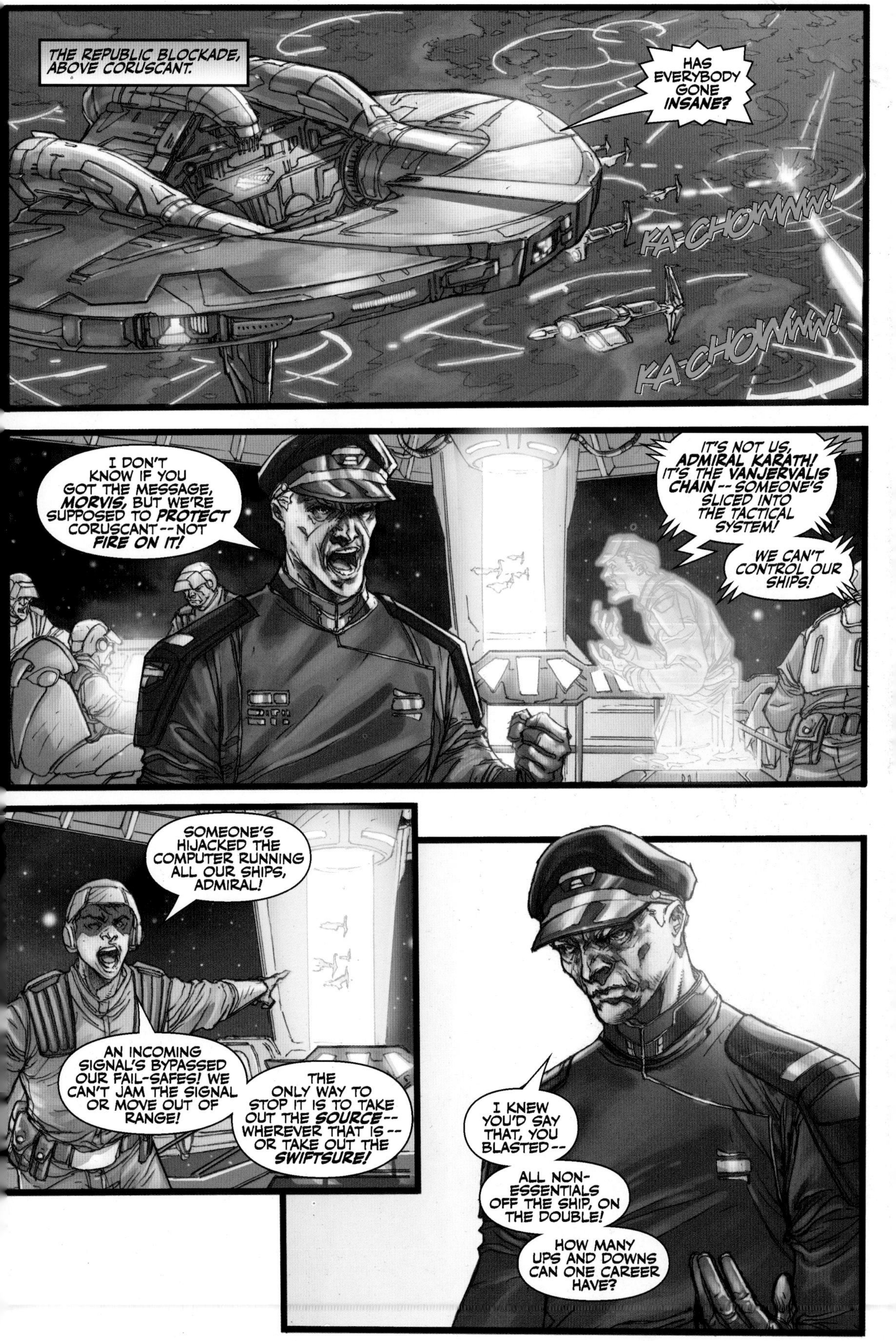
THE REPUBLIC BLOCKADE, ABOVE CORUSCANT.
HAS EVERYBODY GONE INSANE?
KA-CHOWWW!
KA-CHOWWW!
I DON'T KNOW IF YOU GOT THE MESSAGE, MORVIS, BUT WE'RE SUPPOSED TO PROTECT CORUSCANT--NOT FIRE ON IT!
IT'S NOT US, ADMIRAL KARATH! IT'S THE VANJERVALIS CHAIN--SOMEONE'S SLICED INTO THE TACTICAL SYSTEM!
WE CAN'T CONTROL OUR SHIPS!
SOMEONE'S HIJACKED THE COMPUTER RUNNING ALL OUR SHIPS, ADMIRAL!
AN INCOMING SIGNAL'S BYPASSED OUR FAIL-SAFES! WE CAN'T JAM THE SIGNAL OR MOVE OUT OF RANGE!
THE ONLY WAY TO STOP IT IS TO TAKE OUT THE SOURCE--WHEREVER THAT IS--OR TAKE OUT THE SWIFTSURE!
I KNEW YOU'D SAY THAT, YOU BLASTED--
ALL NON-ESSENTIALS OFF THE SHIP, ON THE DOUBLE!
HOW MANY UPS AND DOWNS CAN ONE CAREER HAVE?

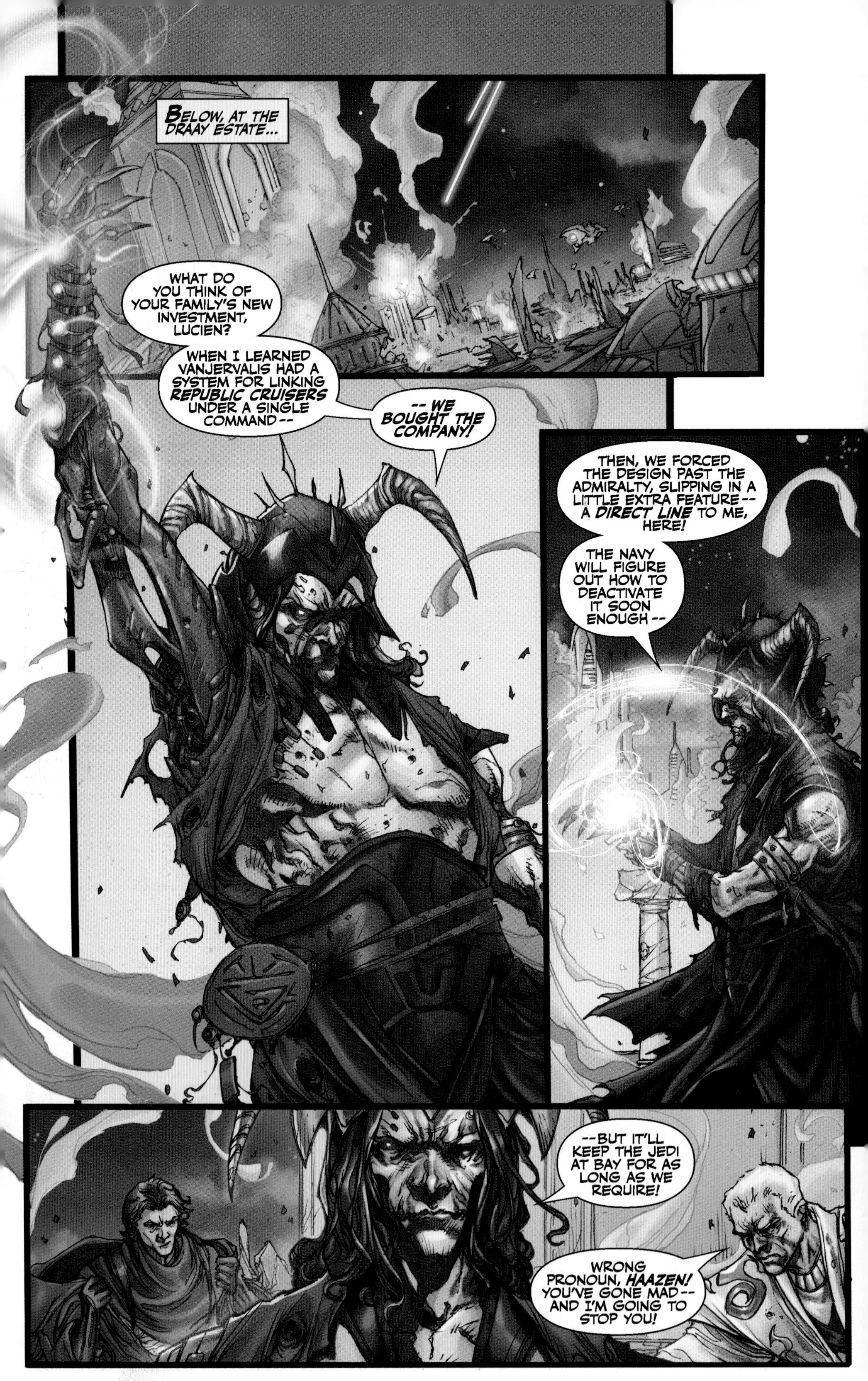
BELOW, AT THE DRAAY ESTATE...
WHAT DO YOU THINK OF YOUR FAMILY'S NEW INVESTMENT, LUCIEN?
WHEN I LEARNED VANJERVALIS HAD A SYSTEM FOR LINKING *REPUBLIC CRUISERS* UNDER A SINGLE COMMAND--
-- WE BOUGHT THE COMPANY!
THEN, WE FORCED THE DESIGN PAST THE ADMIRALTY, SLIPPING IN A LITTLE EXTRA FEATURE-- A *DIRECT LINE* TO ME, HERE!
THE NAVY WILL FIGURE OUT HOW TO DEACTIVATE IT SOON ENOUGH--
--BUT IT'LL KEEP THE JEDI AT BAY FOR AS LONG AS WE REQUIRE!
WRONG PRONOUN, *HAAZEN!* YOU'VE GONE MAD-- AND I'M GOING TO STOP YOU!

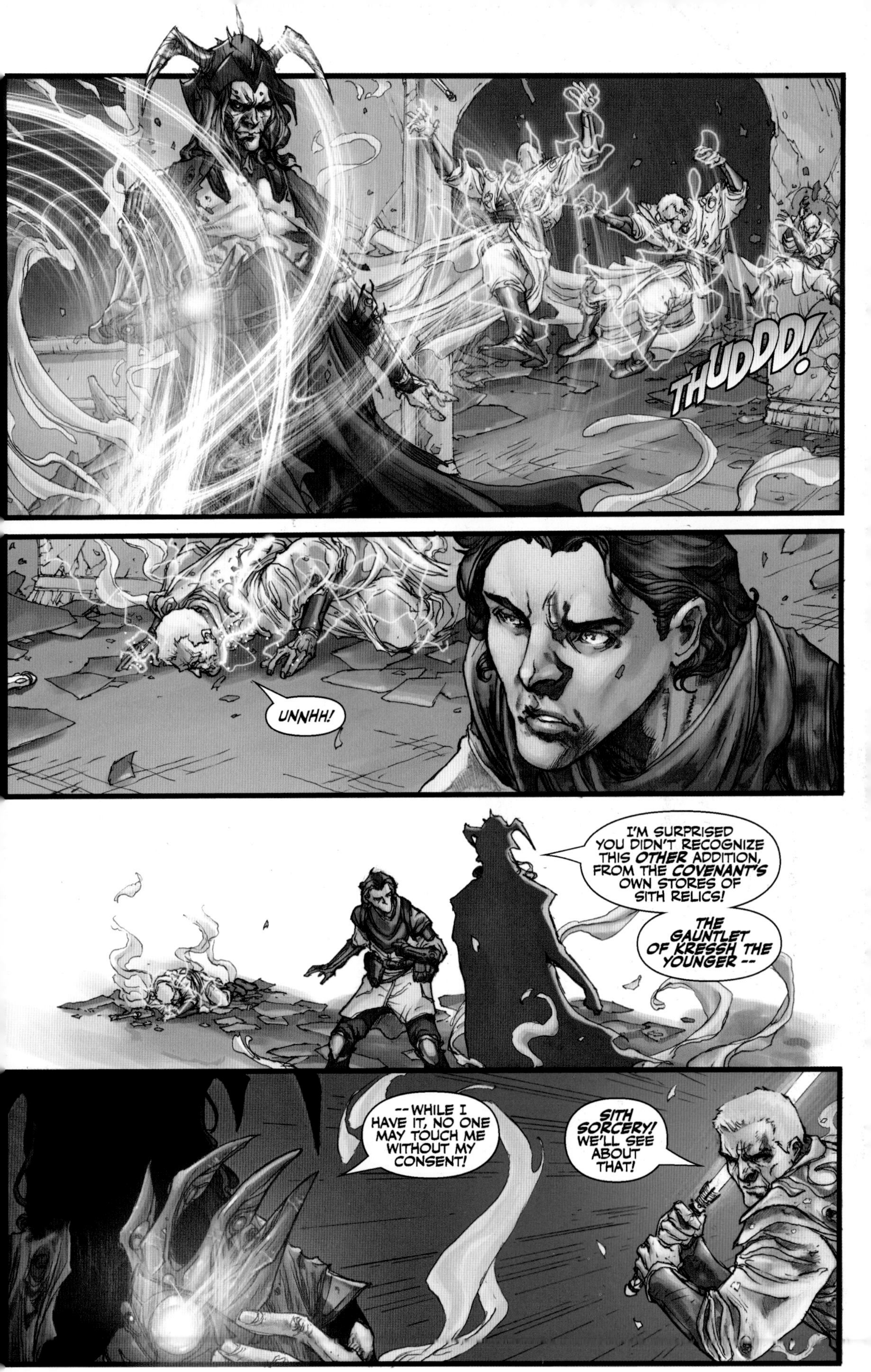
THUDDD!
UNNHH!
I'M SURPRISED YOU DIDN'T RECOGNIZE THIS OTHER ADDITION, FROM THE COVENANT'S OWN STORES OF SITH RELICS!
THE GAUNTLET OF KRESSH THE YOUNGER --
-- WHILE I HAVE IT, NO ONE MAY TOUCH ME WITHOUT MY CONSENT!
SITH SORCERY! WE'LL SEE ABOUT THAT!

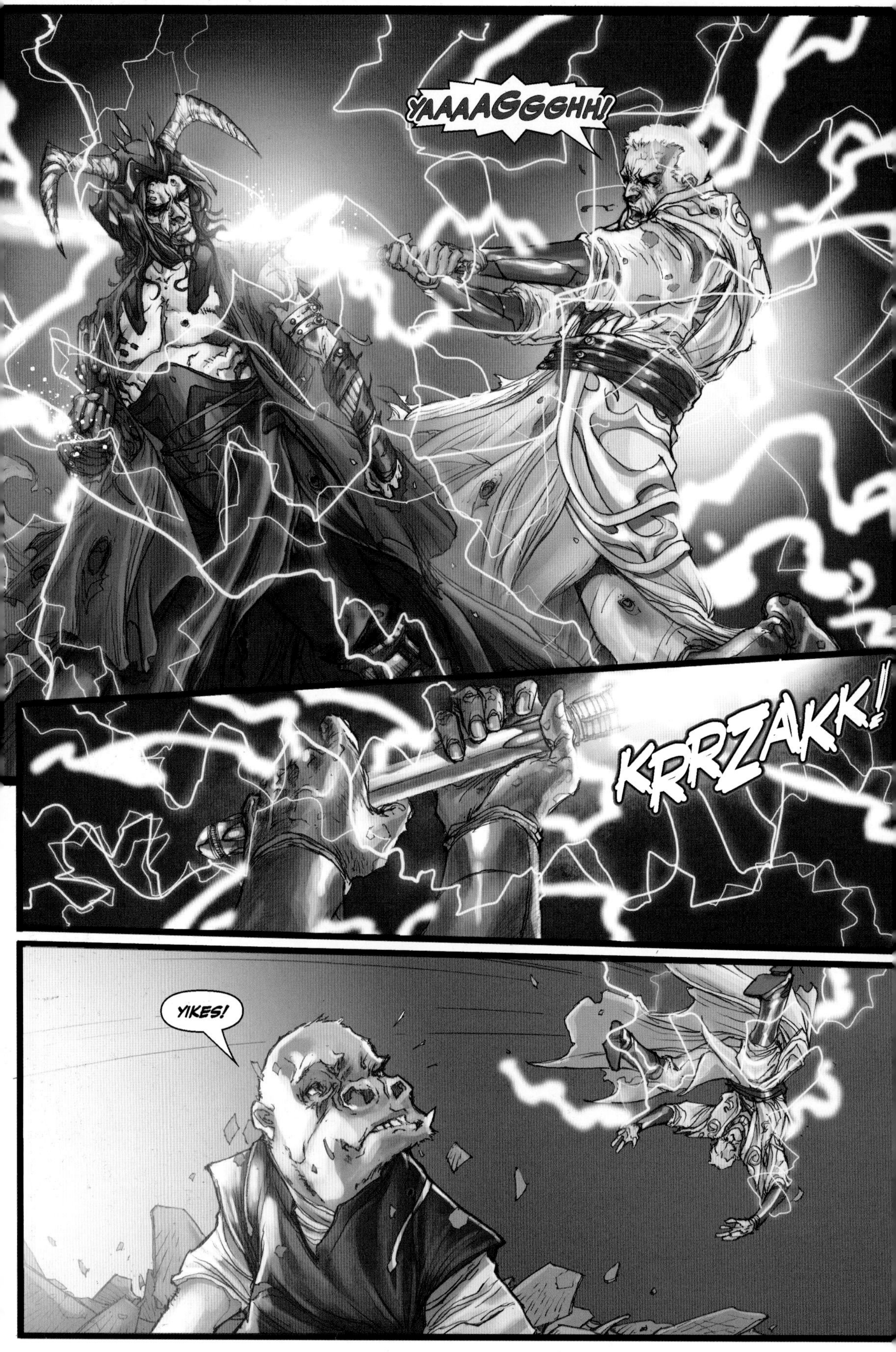
YAAAAGGGHH!
KRRZAKK!
YIKES!

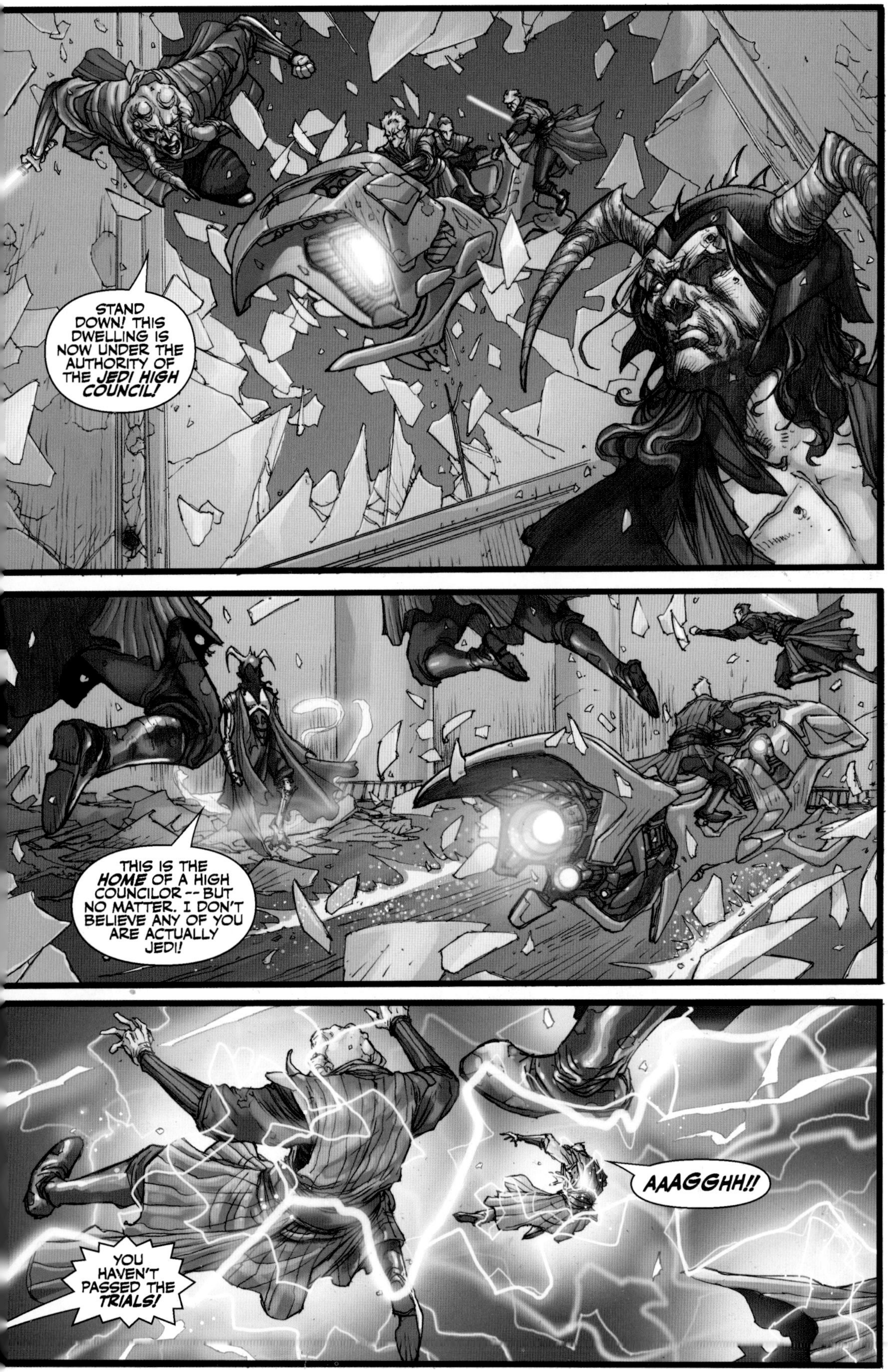
STAND DOWN! THIS DWELLING IS NOW UNDER THE AUTHORITY OF THE JEDI HIGH COUNCIL!
THIS IS THE HOME OF A HIGH COUNCILOR -- BUT NO MATTER. I DON'T BELIEVE ANY OF YOU ARE ACTUALLY JEDI!
AAAGGHH!!
YOU HAVEN'T PASSED THE TRIALS!

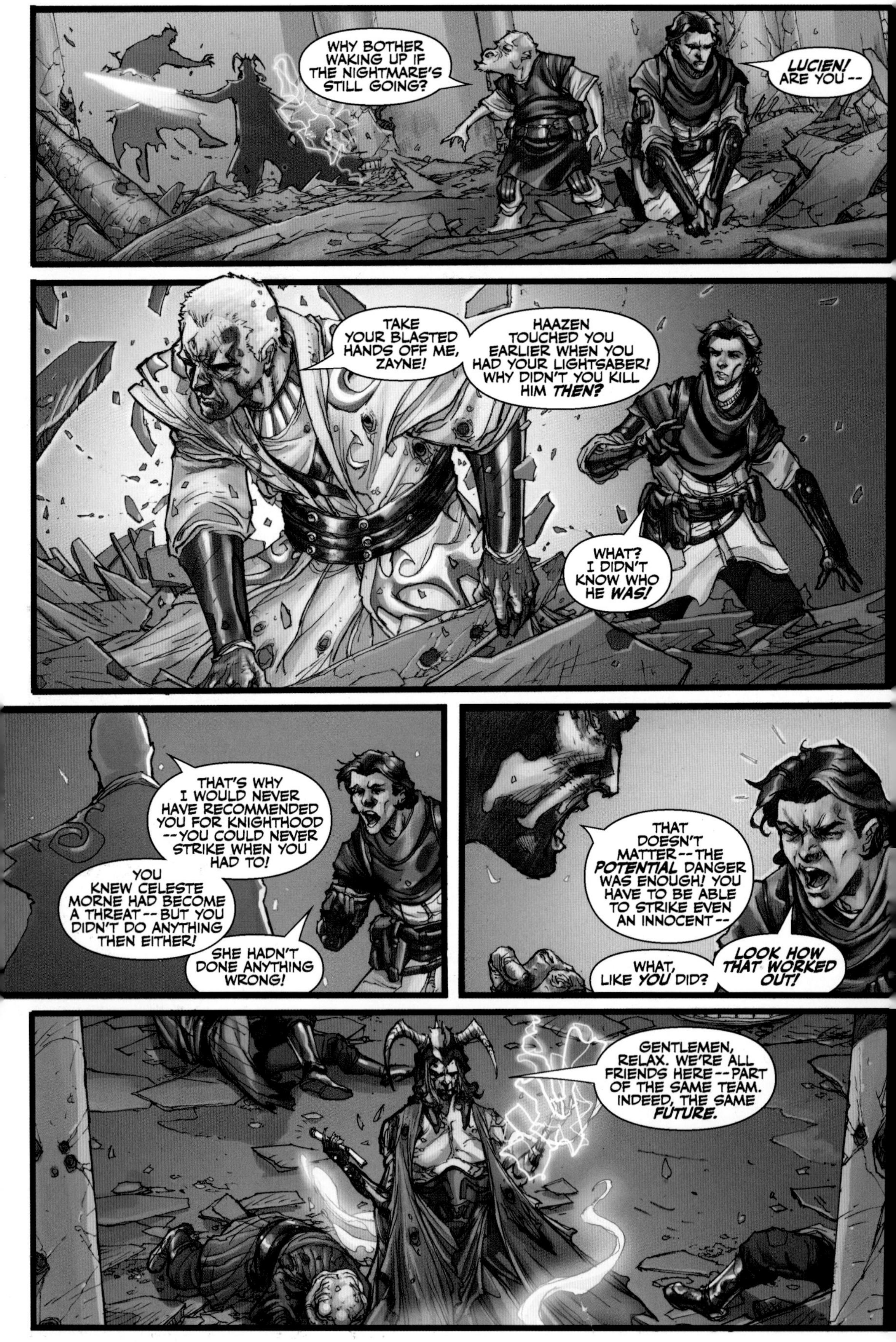
WHY BOTHER WAKING UP IF THE NIGHTMARE'S STILL GOING?
LUCIEN! ARE YOU --
TAKE YOUR BLASTED HANDS OFF ME, ZAYNE!
HAAZEN TOUCHED YOU EARLIER WHEN YOU HAD YOUR LIGHTSABER! WHY DIDN'T YOU KILL HIM THEN?
WHAT? I DIDN'T KNOW WHO HE WAS!
THAT'S WHY I WOULD NEVER HAVE RECOMMENDED YOU FOR KNIGHTHOOD --YOU COULD NEVER STRIKE WHEN YOU HAD TO!
YOU KNEW CELESTE MORNE HAD BECOME A THREAT -- BUT YOU DIDN'T DO ANYTHING THEN EITHER!
SHE HADN'T DONE ANYTHING WRONG!
THAT DOESN'T MATTER -- THE POTENTIAL DANGER WAS ENOUGH! YOU HAVE TO BE ABLE TO STRIKE EVEN AN INNOCENT --
WHAT, LIKE YOU DID?
LOOK HOW THAT WORKED OUT!
GENTLEMEN, RELAX. WE'RE ALL FRIENDS HERE -- PART OF THE SAME TEAM. INDEED, THE SAME FUTURE.

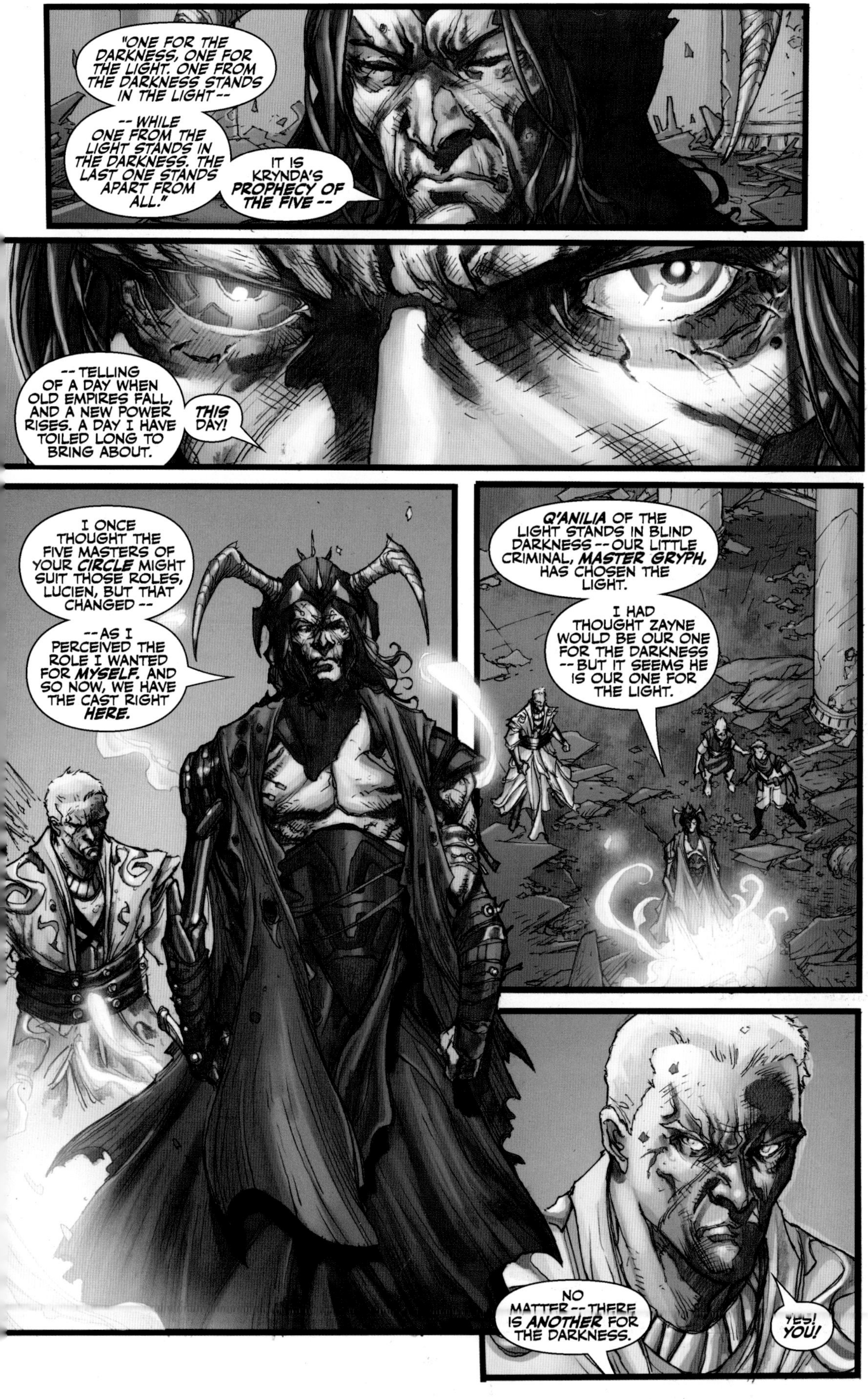

"ONE FOR THE DARKNESS, ONE FOR THE LIGHT. ONE FROM THE DARKNESS STANDS IN THE LIGHT --
-- WHILE ONE FROM THE LIGHT STANDS IN THE DARKNESS. THE LAST ONE STANDS APART FROM ALL."
IT IS KRYNDA'S PROPHECY OF THE FIVE --
-- TELLING OF A DAY WHEN OLD EMPIRES FALL, AND A NEW POWER RISES. A DAY I HAVE TOILED LONG TO BRING ABOUT.
THIS DAY!
I ONCE THOUGHT THE FIVE MASTERS OF YOUR CIRCLE MIGHT SUIT THOSE ROLES, LUCIEN, BUT THAT CHANGED --
-- AS I PERCEIVED THE ROLE I WANTED FOR MYSELF. AND SO NOW, WE HAVE THE CAST RIGHT HERE.
Q'ANILIA OF THE LIGHT STANDS IN BLIND DARKNESS -- OUR LITTLE CRIMINAL, MASTER GRYPH, HAS CHOSEN THE LIGHT.
I HAD THOUGHT ZAYNE WOULD BE OUR ONE FOR THE DARKNESS -- BUT IT SEEMS HE IS OUR ONE FOR THE LIGHT.
NO MATTER -- THERE IS ANOTHER FOR THE DARKNESS.
YES! YOU!

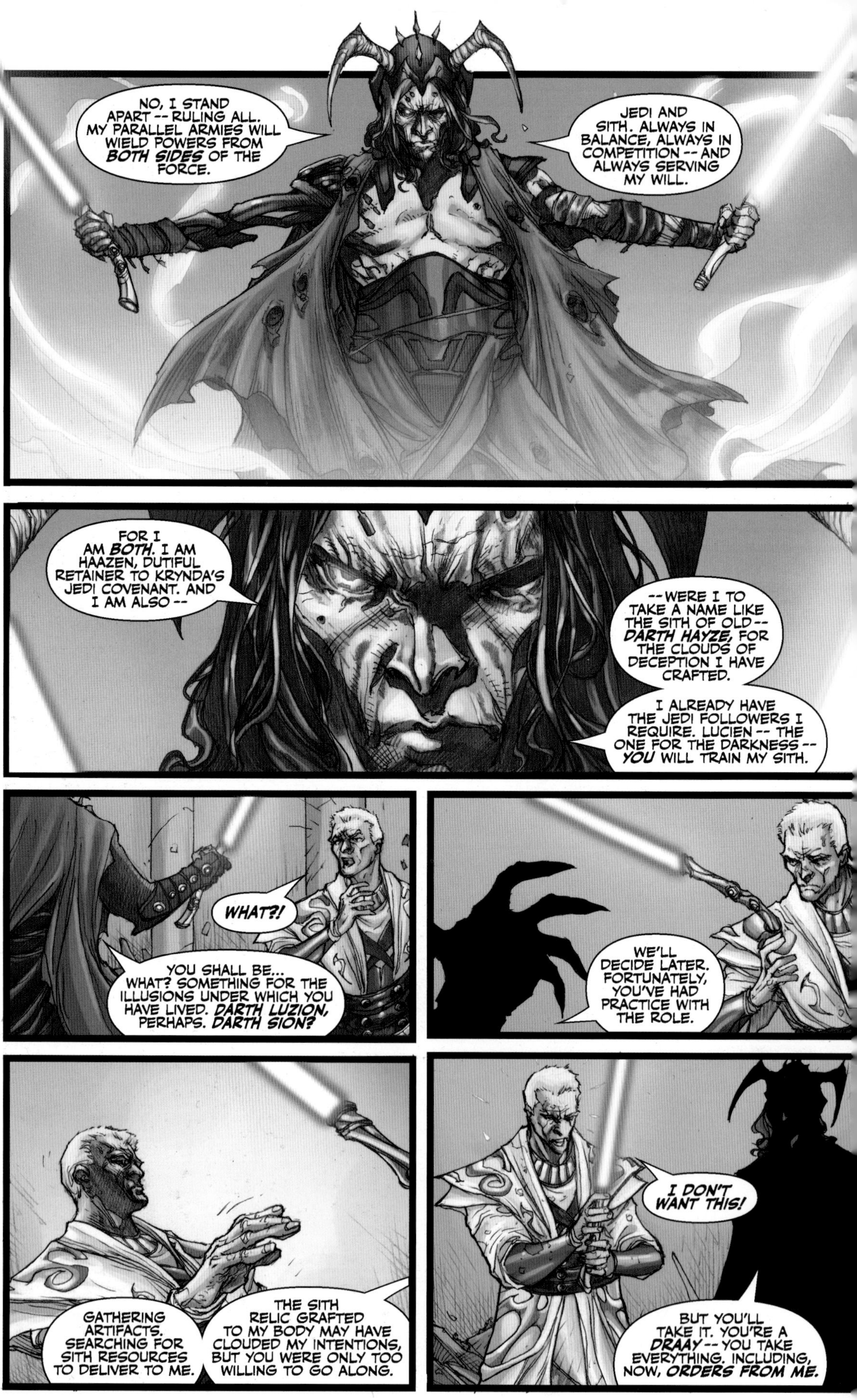

NO, I STAND APART -- RULING ALL. MY PARALLEL ARMIES WILL WIELD POWERS FROM *BOTH SIDES* OF THE FORCE.
JEDI AND SITH. ALWAYS IN BALANCE, ALWAYS IN COMPETITION -- AND ALWAYS SERVING MY WILL.
FOR I AM *BOTH*. I AM HAAZEN, DUTIFUL RETAINER TO KRYNDA'S JEDI COVENANT. AND I AM ALSO --
--WERE I TO TAKE A NAME LIKE THE SITH OF OLD -- *DARTH HAYZE*, FOR THE CLOUDS OF DECEPTION I HAVE CRAFTED.
I ALREADY HAVE THE JEDI FOLLOWERS I REQUIRE. LUCIEN -- THE ONE FOR THE DARKNESS -- *YOU* WILL TRAIN MY SITH.
WHAT?!
YOU SHALL BE... WHAT? SOMETHING FOR THE ILLUSIONS UNDER WHICH YOU HAVE LIVED. *DARTH LUZION*, PERHAPS. *DARTH SION?*
WE'LL DECIDE LATER. FORTUNATELY, YOU'VE HAD PRACTICE WITH THE ROLE.
GATHERING ARTIFACTS. SEARCHING FOR SITH RESOURCES TO DELIVER TO ME.
THE SITH RELIC GRAFTED TO MY BODY MAY HAVE CLOUDED MY INTENTIONS, BUT YOU WERE ONLY TOO WILLING TO GO ALONG.
I DON'T WANT THIS!
BUT YOU'LL TAKE IT. YOU'RE A *DRAAY* -- YOU TAKE EVERYTHING. INCLUDING, NOW, *ORDERS FROM ME.*

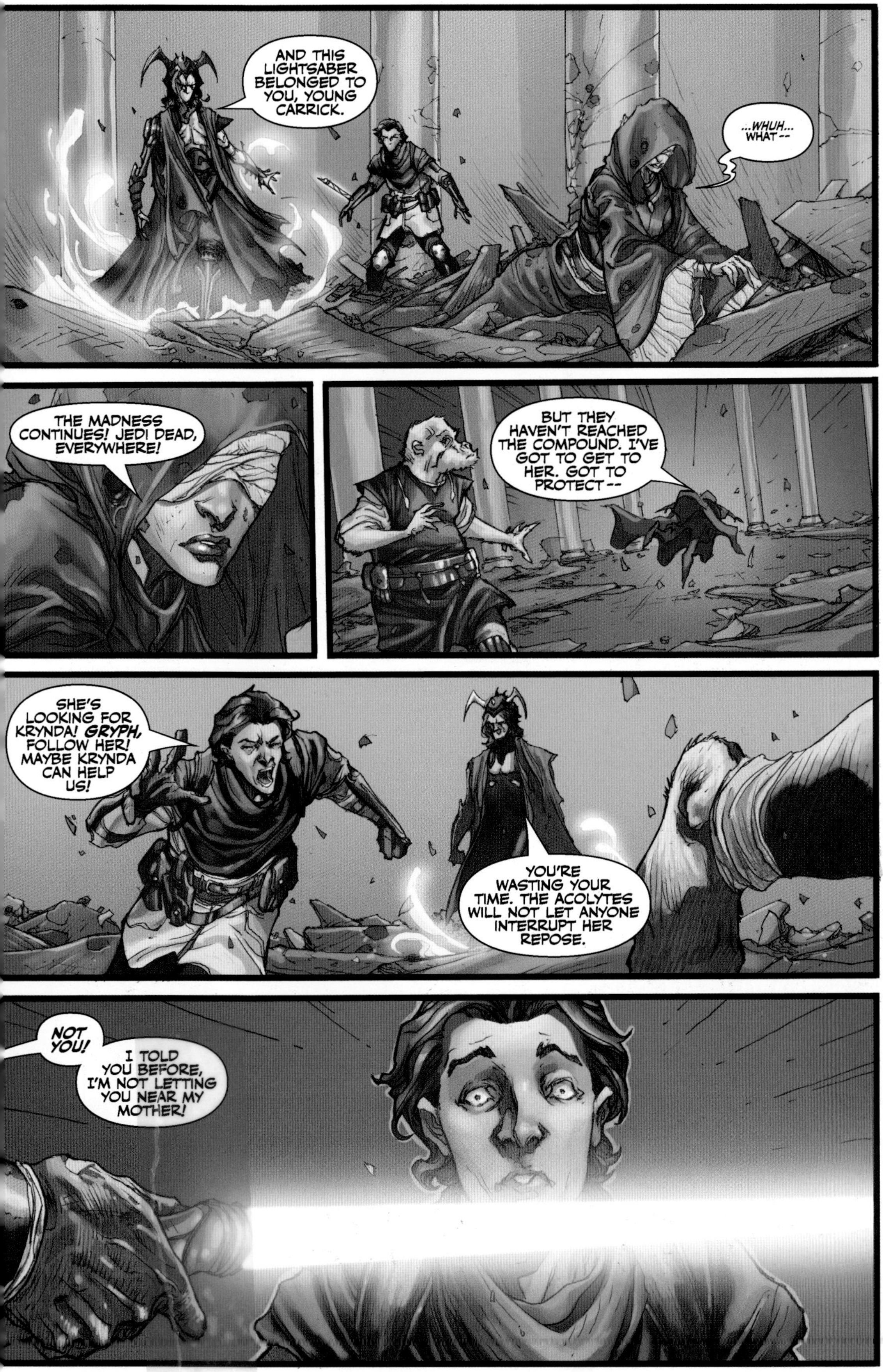

AND THIS LIGHTSABER BELONGED TO YOU, YOUNG CARRICK.
...WHUH... WHAT--
THE MADNESS CONTINUES! JEDI DEAD, EVERYWHERE!
BUT THEY HAVEN'T REACHED THE COMPOUND. I'VE GOT TO GET TO HER. GOT TO PROTECT--
SHE'S LOOKING FOR KRYNDA! GRYPH, FOLLOW HER! MAYBE KRYNDA CAN HELP US!
YOU'RE WASTING YOUR TIME. THE ACOLYTES WILL NOT LET ANYONE INTERRUPT HER REPOSE.
NOT YOU!
I TOLD YOU BEFORE, I'M NOT LETTING YOU NEAR MY MOTHER!

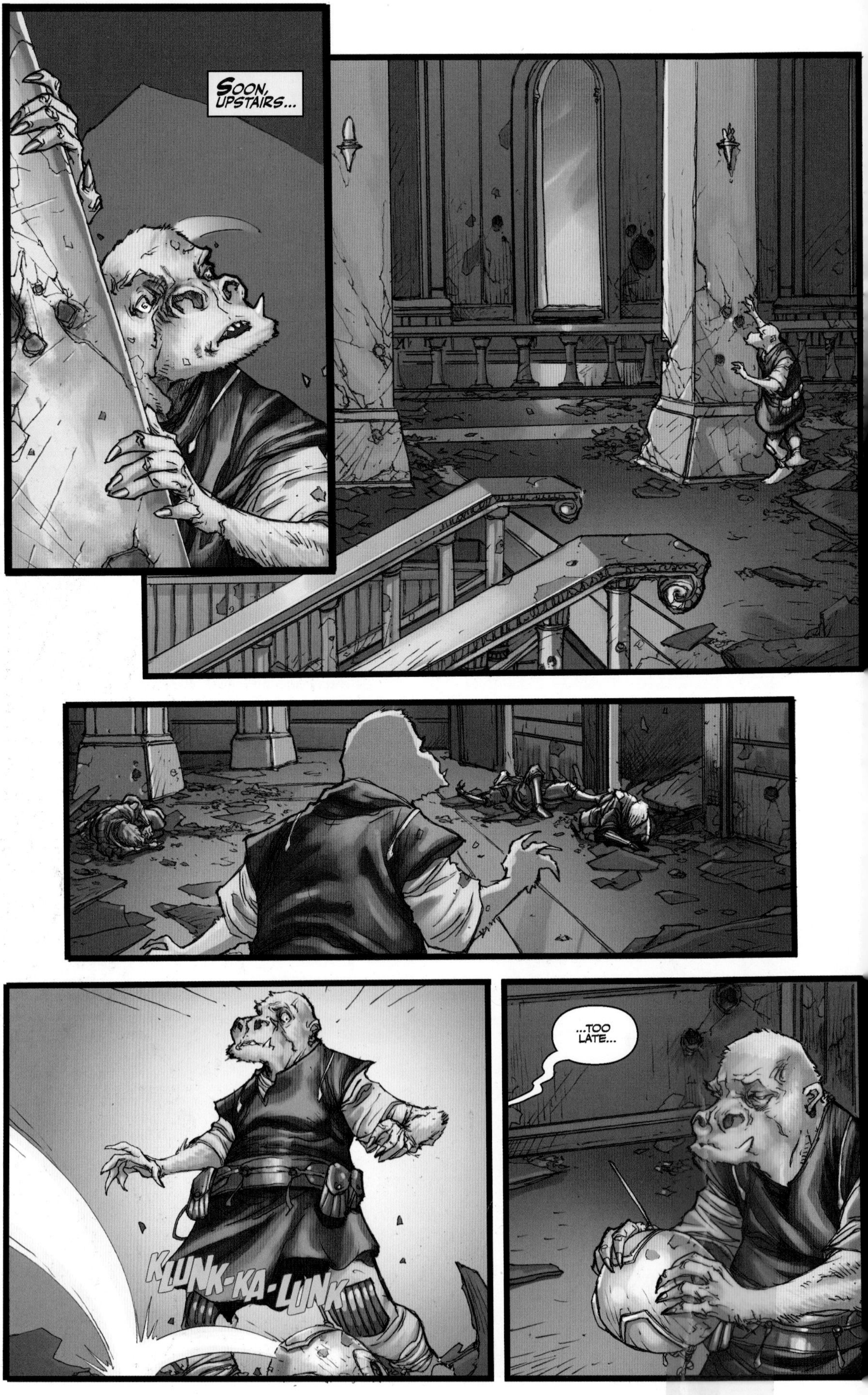
SOON, UPSTAIRS...
KLUNK-KA-LUNK
...TOO LATE...

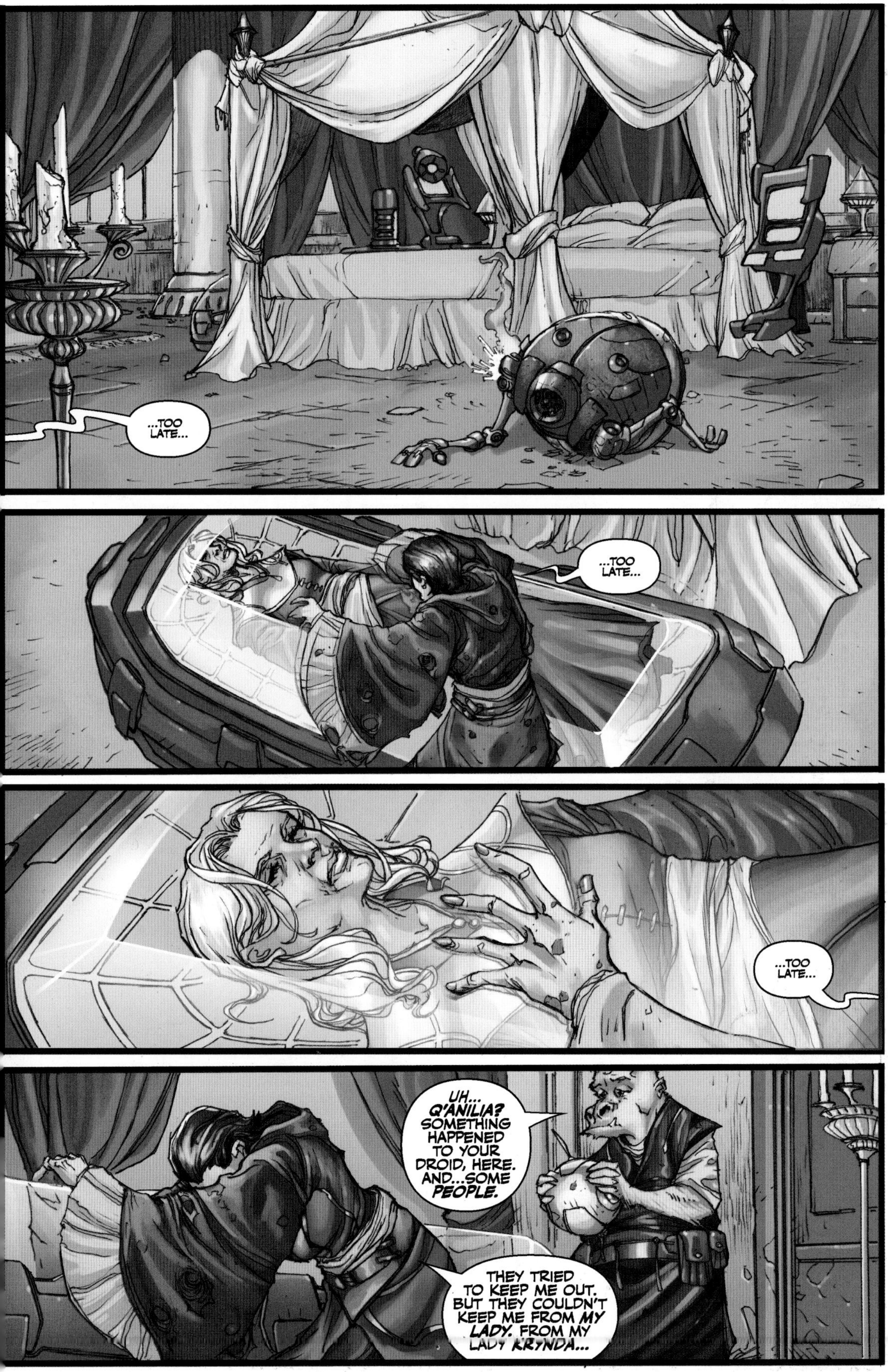
...TOO LATE...
...TOO LATE...
...TOO LATE...
UH... Q'ANILIA? SOMETHING HAPPENED TO YOUR DROID, HERE. AND...SOME PEOPLE.
THEY TRIED TO KEEP ME OUT. BUT THEY COULDN'T KEEP ME FROM MY LADY. FROM MY LADY KRYNDA...

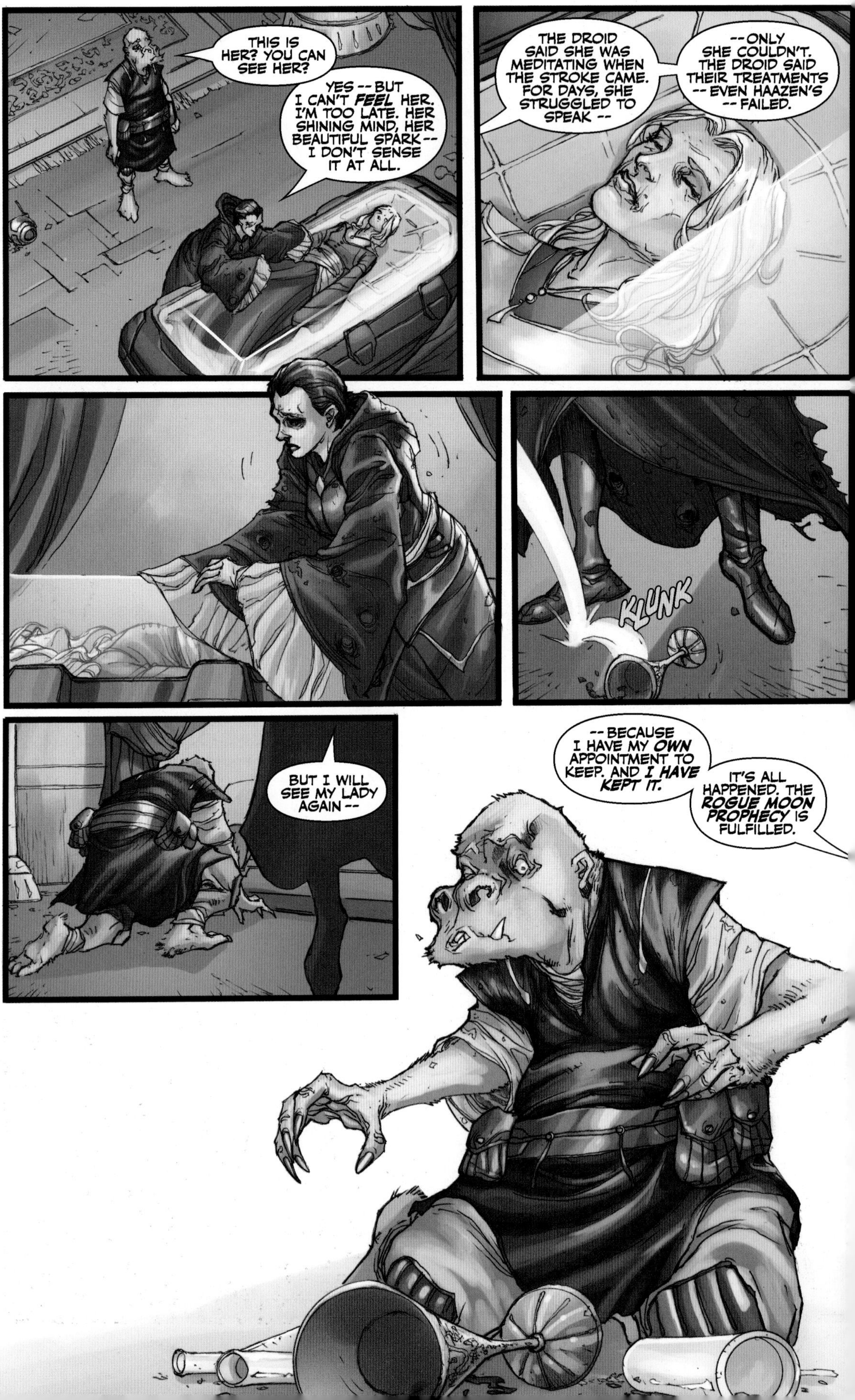
THIS IS HER? YOU CAN SEE HER?
YES -- BUT I CAN'T FEEL HER. I'M TOO LATE. HER SHINING MIND, HER BEAUTIFUL SPARK -- I DON'T SENSE IT AT ALL.
THE DROID SAID SHE WAS MEDITATING WHEN THE STROKE CAME. FOR DAYS, SHE STRUGGLED TO SPEAK --
-- ONLY SHE COULDN'T. THE DROID SAID THEIR TREATMENTS -- EVEN HAAZEN'S -- FAILED.
KLUNK
BUT I WILL SEE MY LADY AGAIN --
-- BECAUSE I HAVE MY OWN APPOINTMENT TO KEEP. AND I HAVE KEPT IT.
IT'S ALL HAPPENED. THE ROGUE MOON PROPHECY IS FULFILLED.

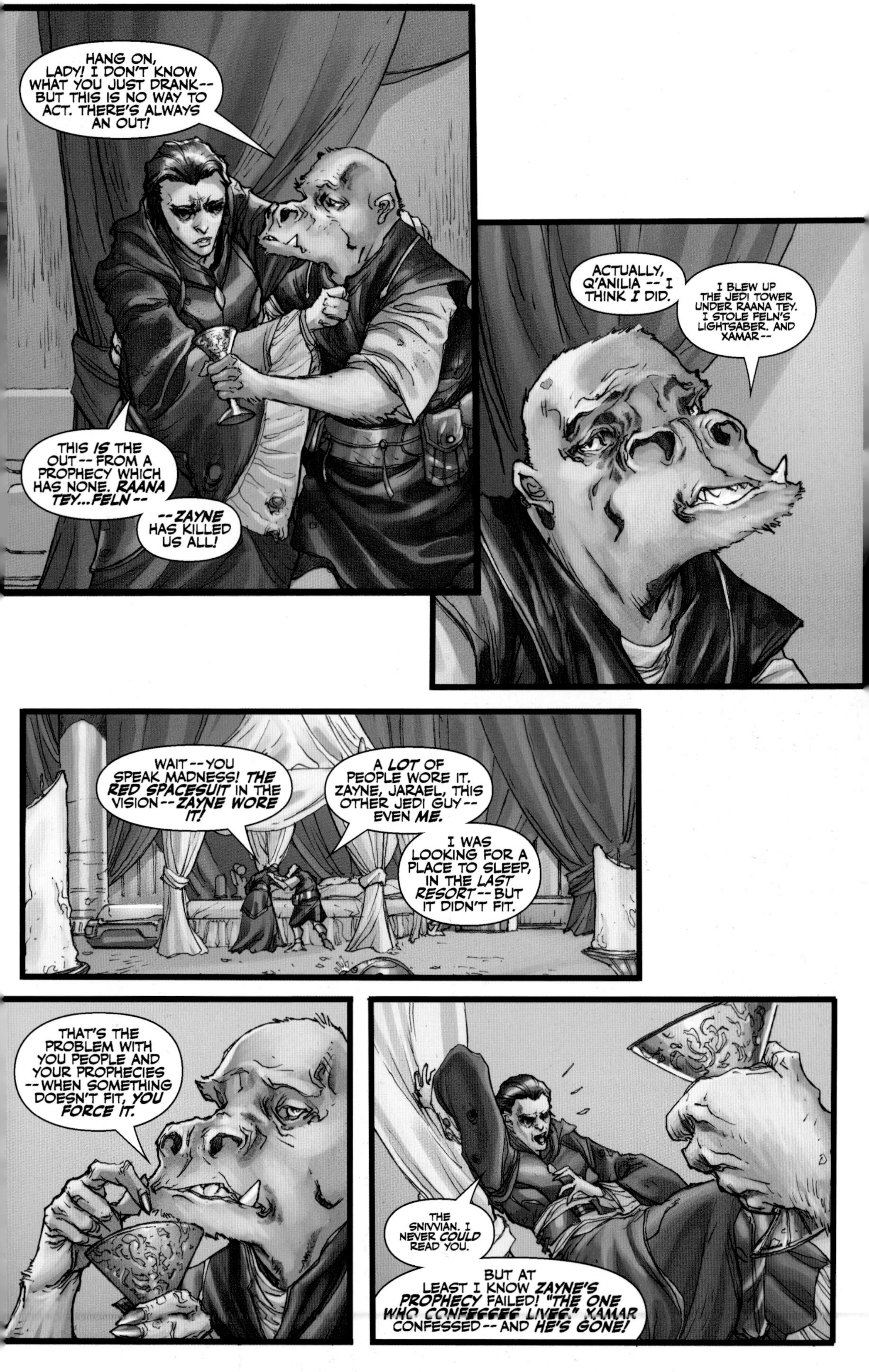
HANG ON, LADY! I DON'T KNOW WHAT YOU JUST DRANK-- BUT THIS IS NO WAY TO ACT. THERE'S ALWAYS AN OUT!
THIS *IS* THE OUT--FROM A PROPHECY WHICH HAS NONE. *RAANA TEY...FELN*--
--*ZAYNE* HAS KILLED US ALL!
ACTUALLY, Q'ANILIA -- I THINK *I* DID.
I BLEW UP THE JEDI TOWER UNDER RAANA TEY. I STOLE FELN'S LIGHTSABER. AND XAMAR--
WAIT--YOU SPEAK MADNESS! *THE RED SPACESUIT* IN THE VISION--*ZAYNE WORE IT!*
A *LOT* OF PEOPLE WORE IT. ZAYNE, JARAEL, THIS OTHER JEDI GUY-- EVEN *ME.*
I WAS LOOKING FOR A PLACE TO SLEEP, IN THE *LAST RESORT*--BUT IT DIDN'T FIT.
THAT'S THE PROBLEM WITH YOU PEOPLE AND YOUR PROPHECIES --WHEN SOMETHING DOESN'T FIT, *YOU FORCE IT.*
THE SNIVVIAN. I NEVER *COULD* READ YOU.
BUT AT LEAST I KNOW *ZAYNE'S PROPHECY* FAILED! *"THE ONE WHO CONFESSES LIVES."* XAMAR CONFESSED--AND *HE'S GONE!*

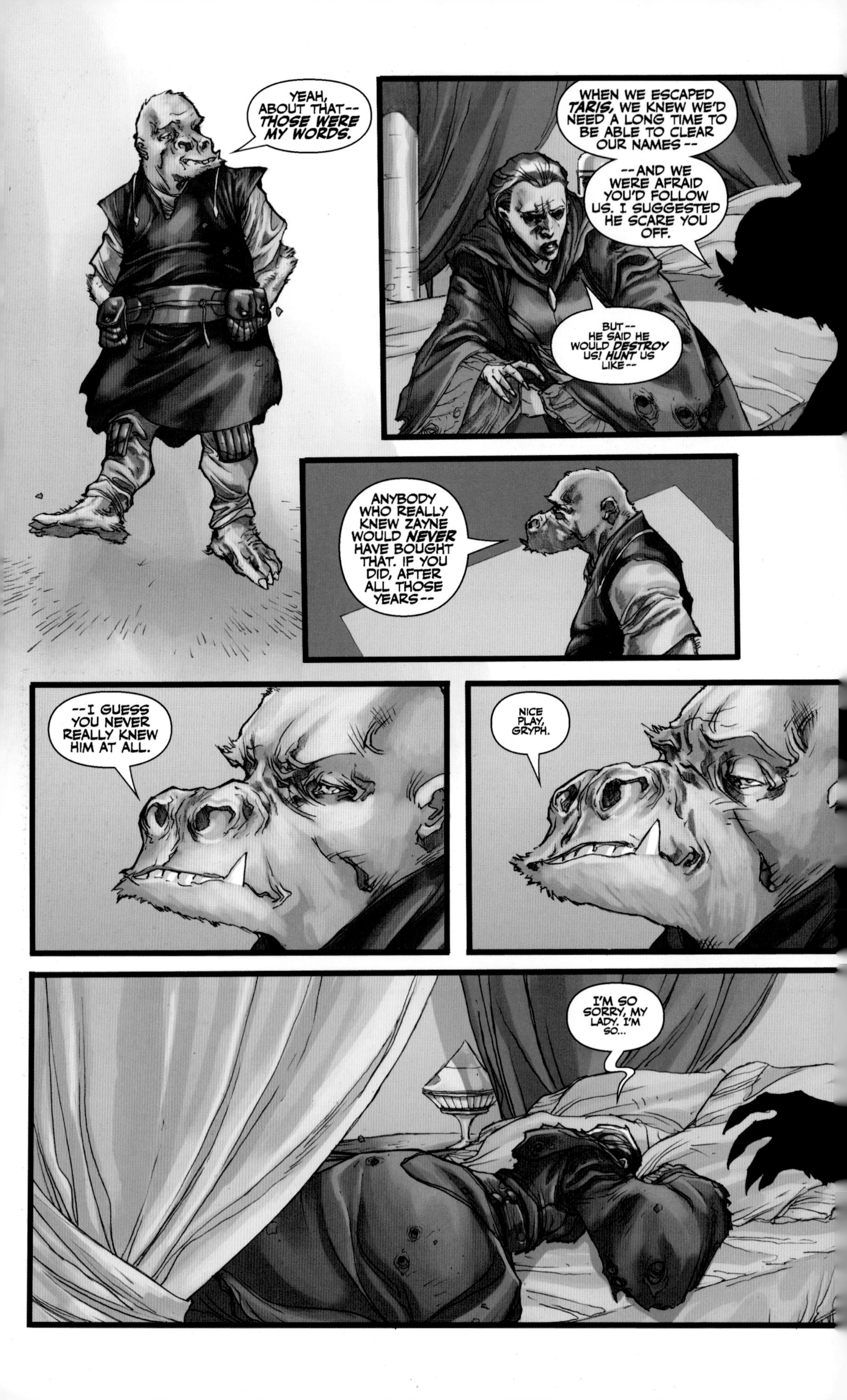
YEAH, ABOUT THAT-- *THOSE WERE MY WORDS.*
WHEN WE ESCAPED *TARIS,* WE KNEW WE'D NEED A LONG TIME TO BE ABLE TO CLEAR OUR NAMES --
--AND WE WERE AFRAID YOU'D FOLLOW US. I SUGGESTED HE SCARE YOU OFF.
BUT-- HE SAID HE WOULD *DESTROY* US! *HUNT* US LIKE--
ANYBODY WHO REALLY KNEW ZAYNE WOULD *NEVER* HAVE BOUGHT THAT. IF YOU DID, AFTER ALL THOSE YEARS--
--I GUESS YOU NEVER REALLY KNEW HIM AT ALL.
NICE PLAY, GRYPH.
I'M SO SORRY, MY LADY. I'M SO...

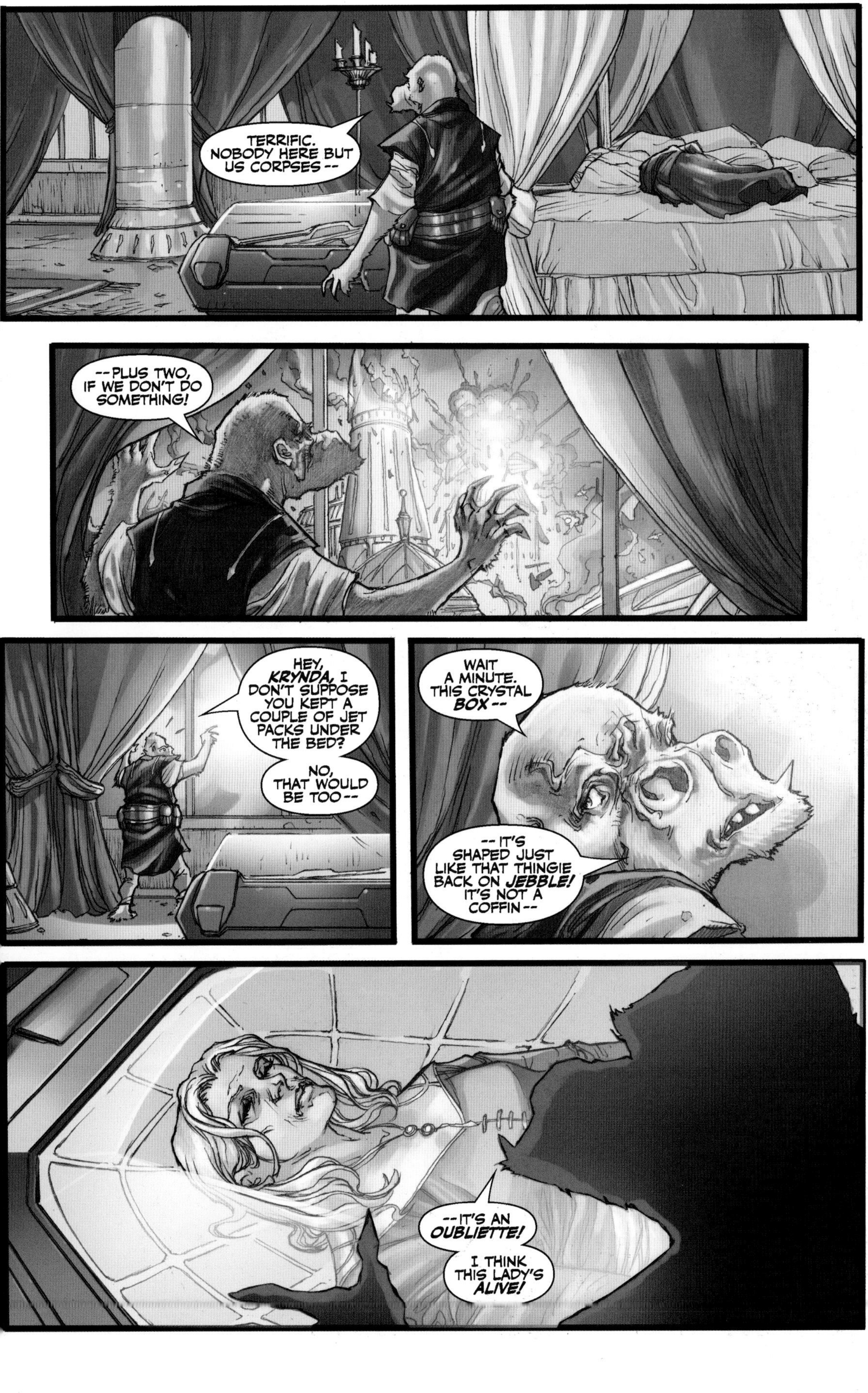
TERRIFIC. NOBODY HERE BUT US CORPSES --
-- PLUS TWO, IF WE DON'T DO SOMETHING!
HEY, KRYNDA, I DON'T SUPPOSE YOU KEPT A COUPLE OF JET PACKS UNDER THE BED?
NO, THAT WOULD BE TOO --
WAIT A MINUTE. THIS CRYSTAL BOX --
-- IT'S SHAPED JUST LIKE THAT THINGIE BACK ON JEBBLE! IT'S NOT A COFFIN --
-- IT'S AN OUBLIETTE!
I THINK THIS LADY'S ALIVE!

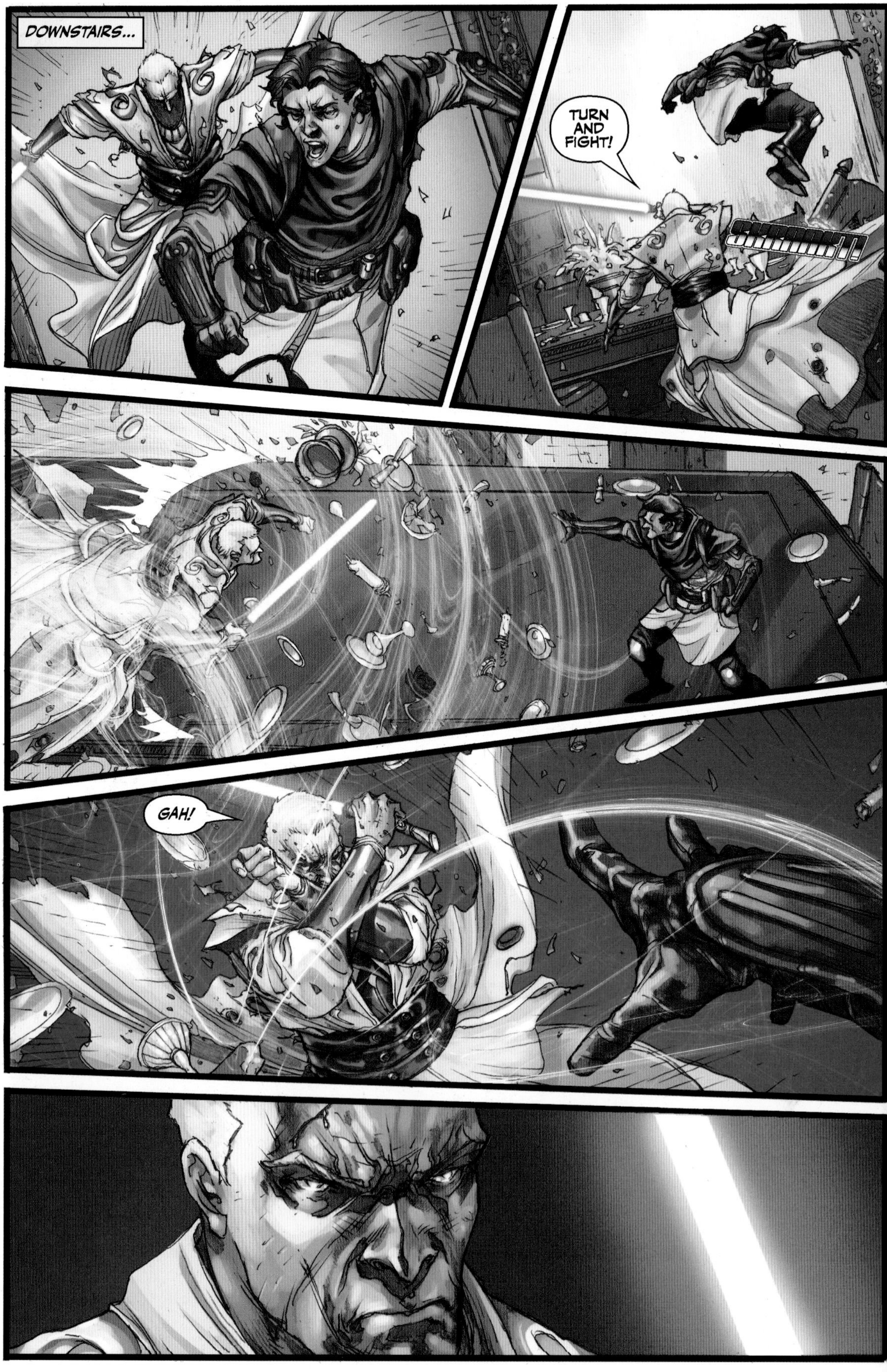
DOWNSTAIRS...
TURN AND FIGHT!
GAH!

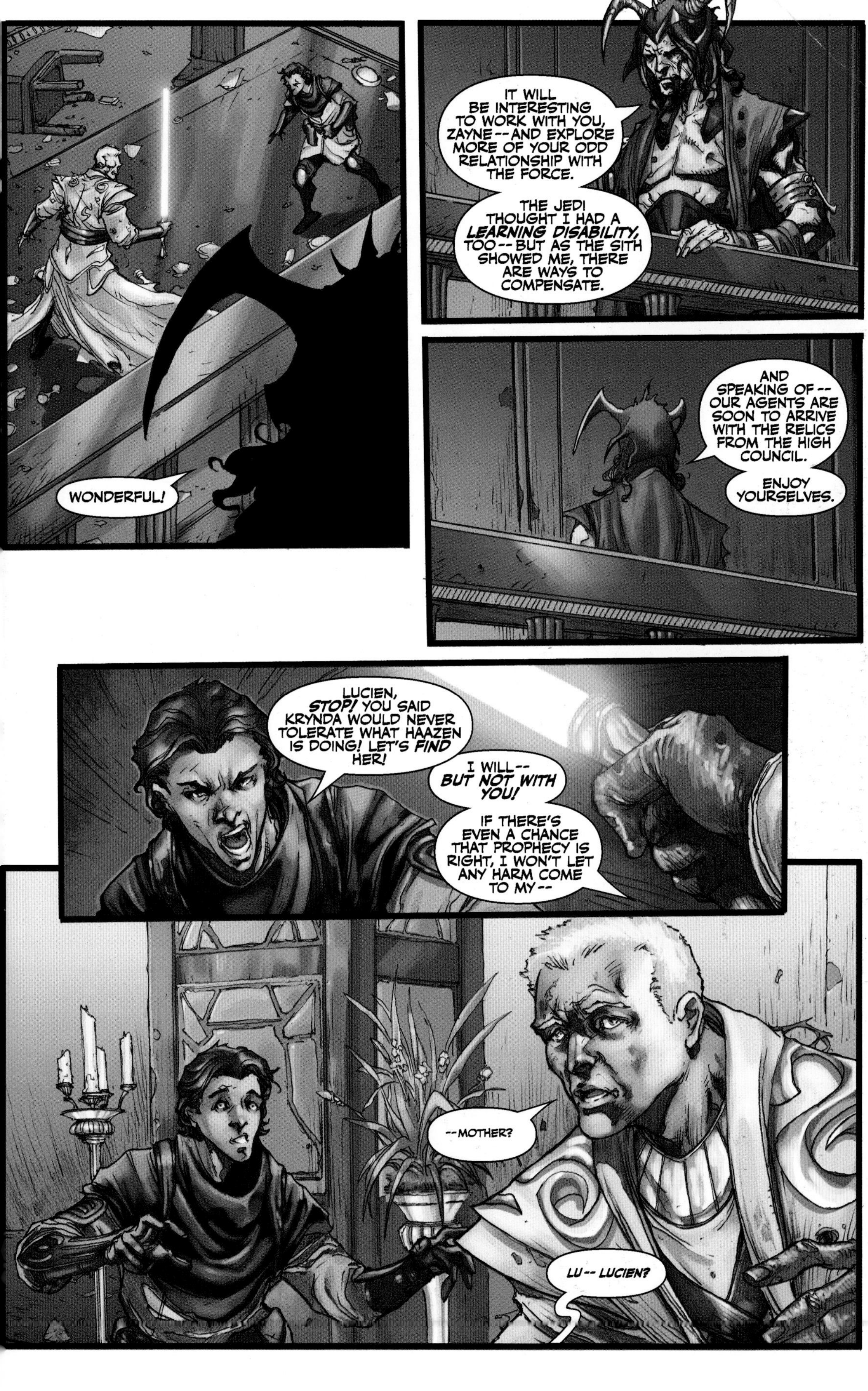
IT WILL BE INTERESTING TO WORK WITH YOU, ZAYNE--AND EXPLORE MORE OF YOUR ODD RELATIONSHIP WITH THE FORCE.
THE JEDI THOUGHT I HAD A LEARNING DISABILITY, TOO--BUT AS THE SITH SHOWED ME, THERE ARE WAYS TO COMPENSATE.
WONDERFUL!
AND SPEAKING OF--OUR AGENTS ARE SOON TO ARRIVE WITH THE RELICS FROM THE HIGH COUNCIL.
ENJOY YOURSELVES.
LUCIEN, STOP! YOU SAID KRYNDA WOULD NEVER TOLERATE WHAT HAAZEN IS DOING! LET'S FIND HER!
I WILL--BUT NOT WITH YOU!
IF THERE'S EVEN A CHANCE THAT PROPHECY IS RIGHT, I WON'T LET ANY HARM COME TO MY--
--MOTHER?
LU--LUCIEN?

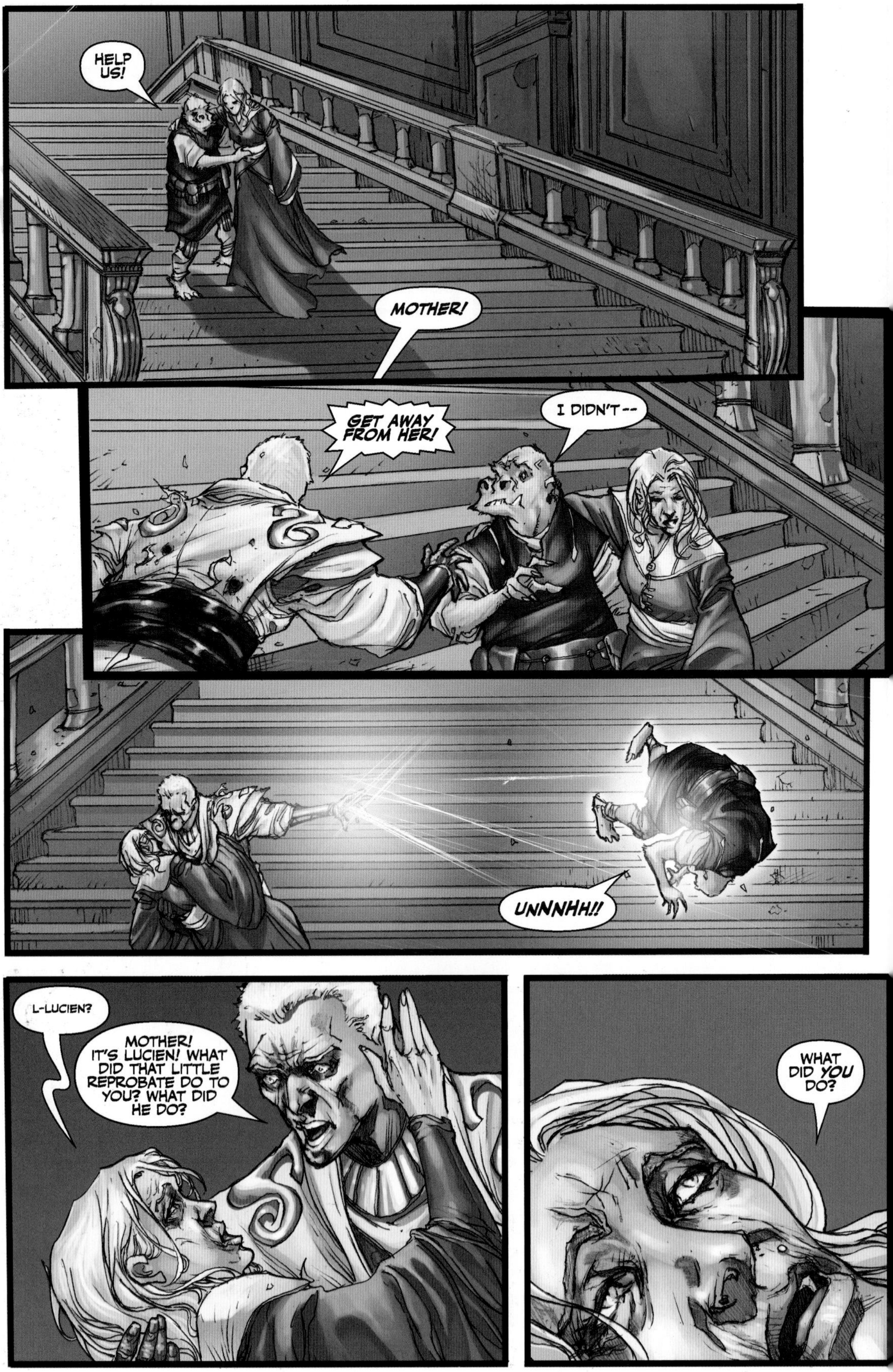
HELP US!
MOTHER!
GET AWAY FROM HER!
I DIDN'T --
UNNNHH!!
L-LUCIEN?
MOTHER! IT'S LUCIEN! WHAT DID THAT LITTLE REPROBATE DO TO YOU? WHAT DID HE DO?
WHAT DID *YOU* DO?

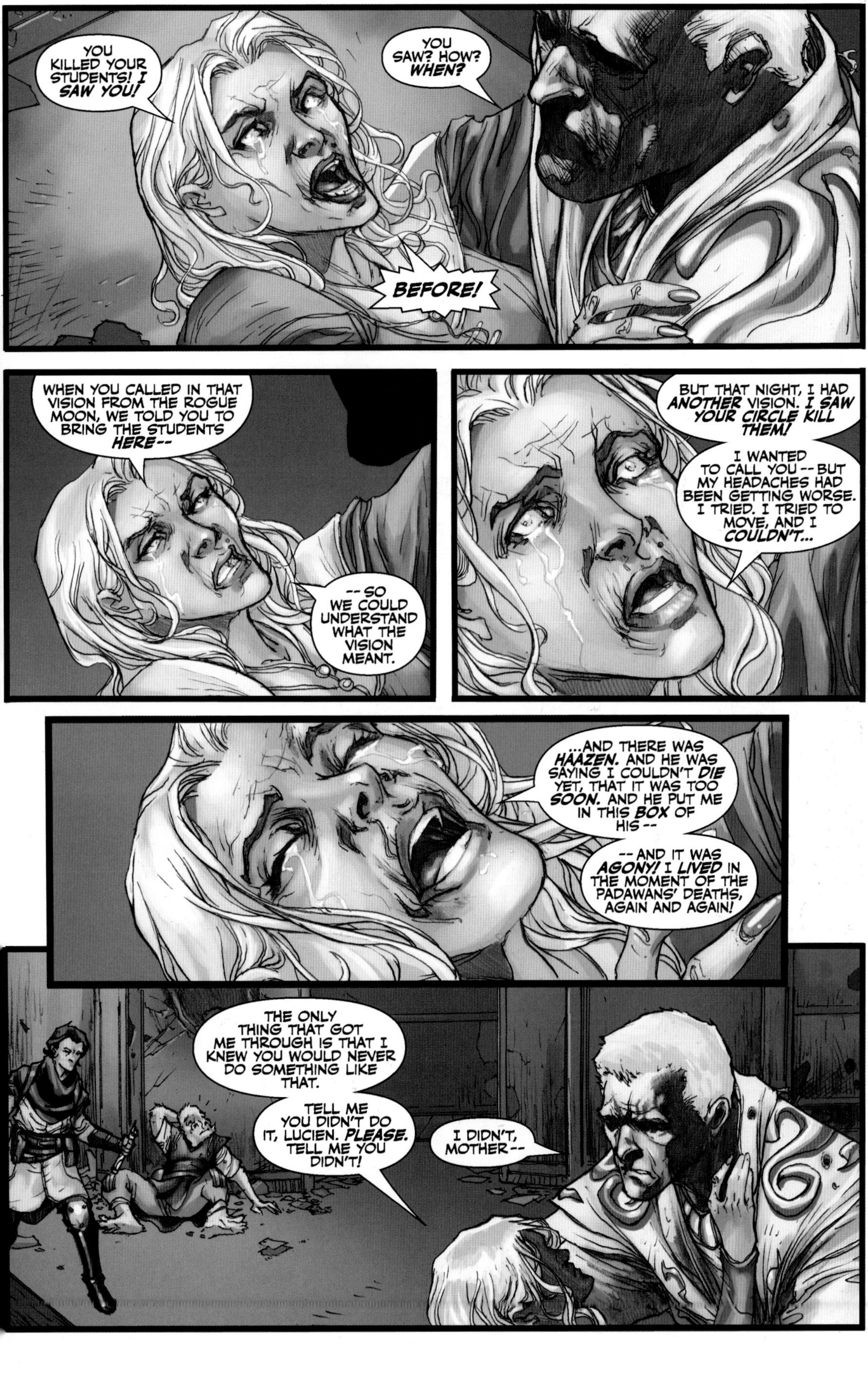

YOU KILLED YOUR STUDENTS! I SAW YOU!
YOU SAW? HOW? WHEN?
BEFORE!
WHEN YOU CALLED IN THAT VISION FROM THE ROGUE MOON, WE TOLD YOU TO BRING THE STUDENTS HERE--
--SO WE COULD UNDERSTAND WHAT THE VISION MEANT.
BUT THAT NIGHT, I HAD ANOTHER VISION. I SAW YOUR CIRCLE KILL THEM!
I WANTED TO CALL YOU--BUT MY HEADACHES HAD BEEN GETTING WORSE. I TRIED. I TRIED TO MOVE, AND I COULDN'T...
...AND THERE WAS HAAZEN. AND HE WAS SAYING I COULDN'T DIE YET, THAT IT WAS TOO SOON. AND HE PUT ME IN THIS BOX OF HIS--
--AND IT WAS AGONY! I LIVED IN THE MOMENT OF THE PADAWANS' DEATHS, AGAIN AND AGAIN!
THE ONLY THING THAT GOT ME THROUGH IS THAT I KNEW YOU WOULD NEVER DO SOMETHING LIKE THAT.
TELL ME YOU DIDN'T DO IT, LUCIEN. PLEASE. TELL ME YOU DIDN'T!
I DIDN'T, MOTHER--

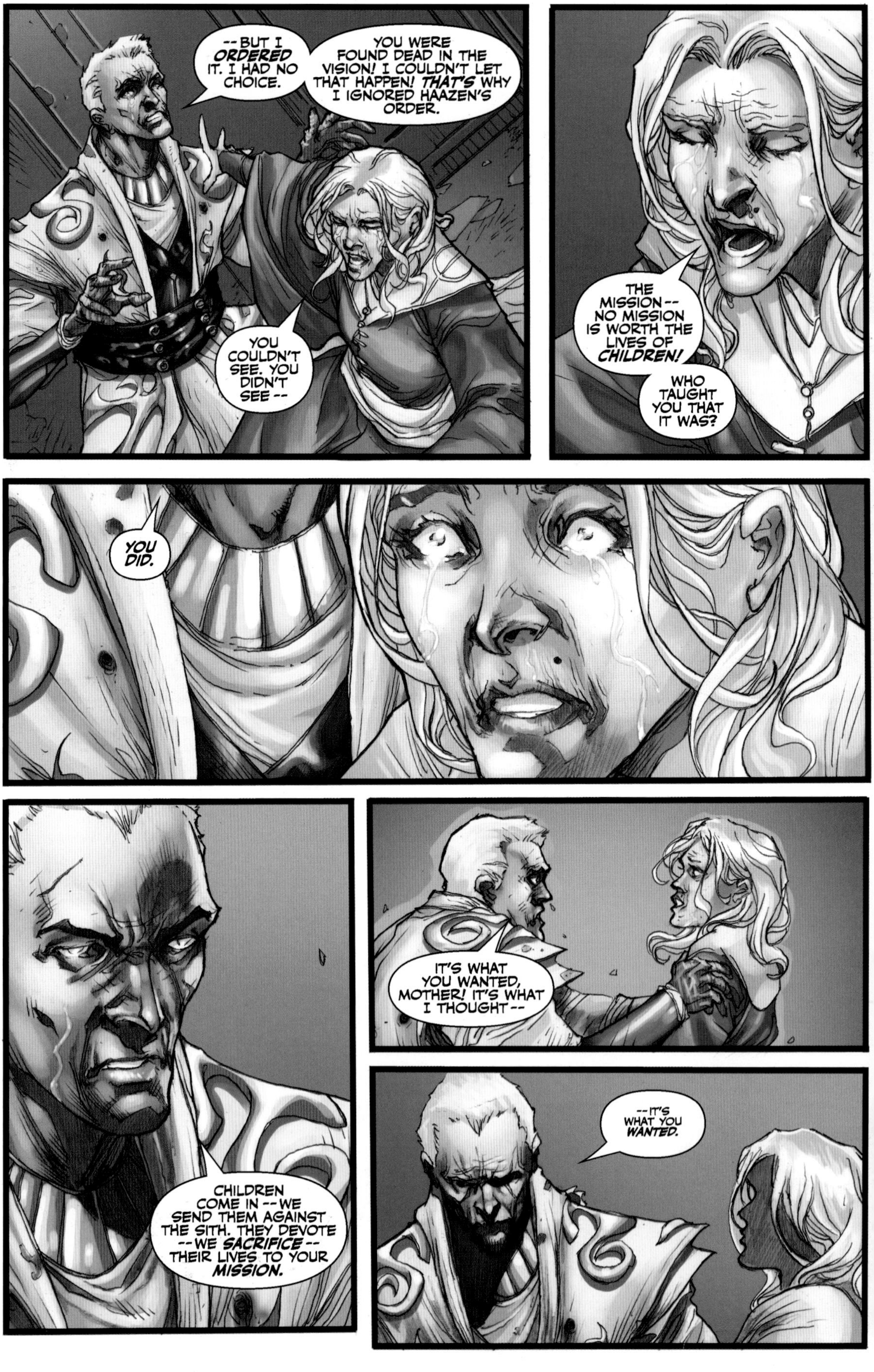
--BUT I *ORDERED* IT. I HAD NO CHOICE.
YOU WERE FOUND DEAD IN THE VISION! I COULDN'T LET THAT HAPPEN! *THAT'S* WHY I IGNORED HAAZEN'S ORDER.
YOU COULDN'T SEE. YOU DIDN'T SEE--
THE MISSION--NO MISSION IS WORTH THE LIVES OF *CHILDREN!*
WHO TAUGHT YOU THAT IT WAS?
YOU DID.
CHILDREN COME IN--WE SEND THEM AGAINST THE SITH. THEY DEVOTE --WE *SACRIFICE*-- THEIR LIVES TO YOUR *MISSION.*
IT'S WHAT YOU WANTED, MOTHER! IT'S WHAT I THOUGHT--
--IT'S WHAT YOU *WANTED.*

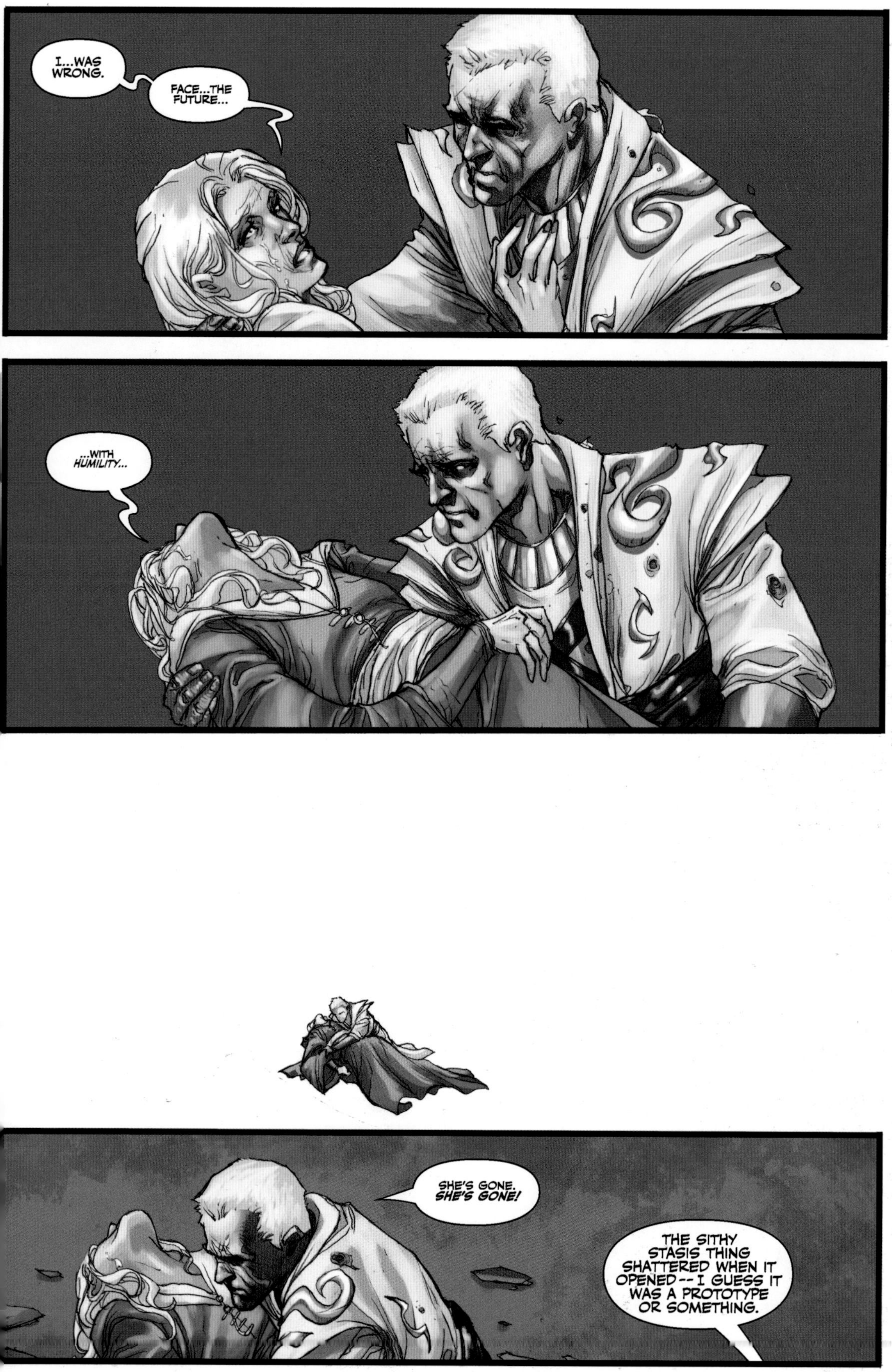

I...WAS WRONG.
FACE...THE FUTURE...
...WITH *HUMILITY*...
SHE'S GONE. *SHE'S GONE!*
THE SITHY STASIS THING SHATTERED WHEN IT OPENED-- I GUESS IT WAS A PROTOTYPE OR SOMETHING.

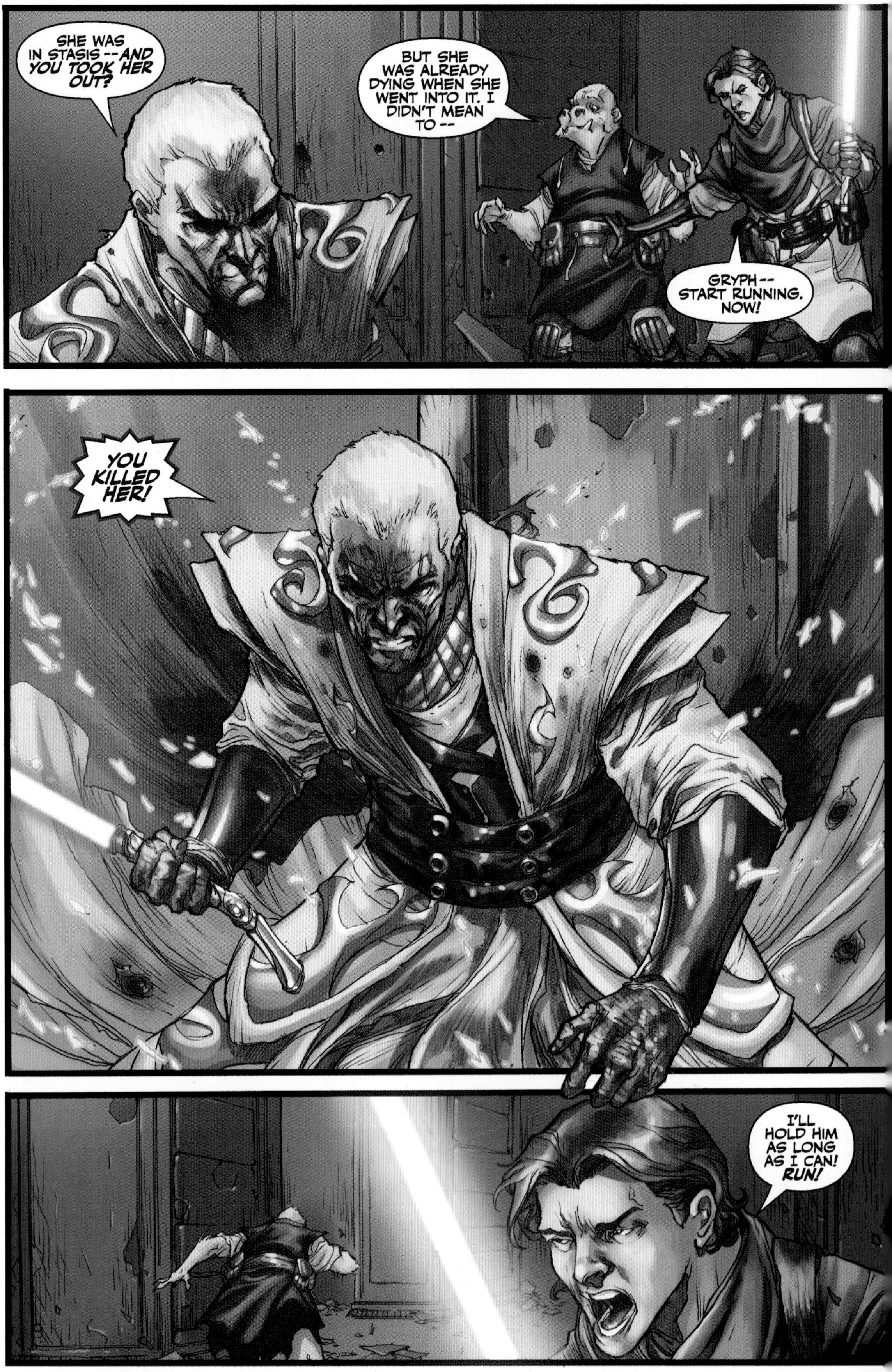
SHE WAS IN STASIS--AND YOU TOOK HER OUT?
BUT SHE WAS ALREADY DYING WHEN SHE WENT INTO IT. I DIDN'T MEAN TO--
GRYPH-- START RUNNING. NOW!
YOU KILLED HER!
I'LL HOLD HIM AS LONG AS I CAN! RUN!

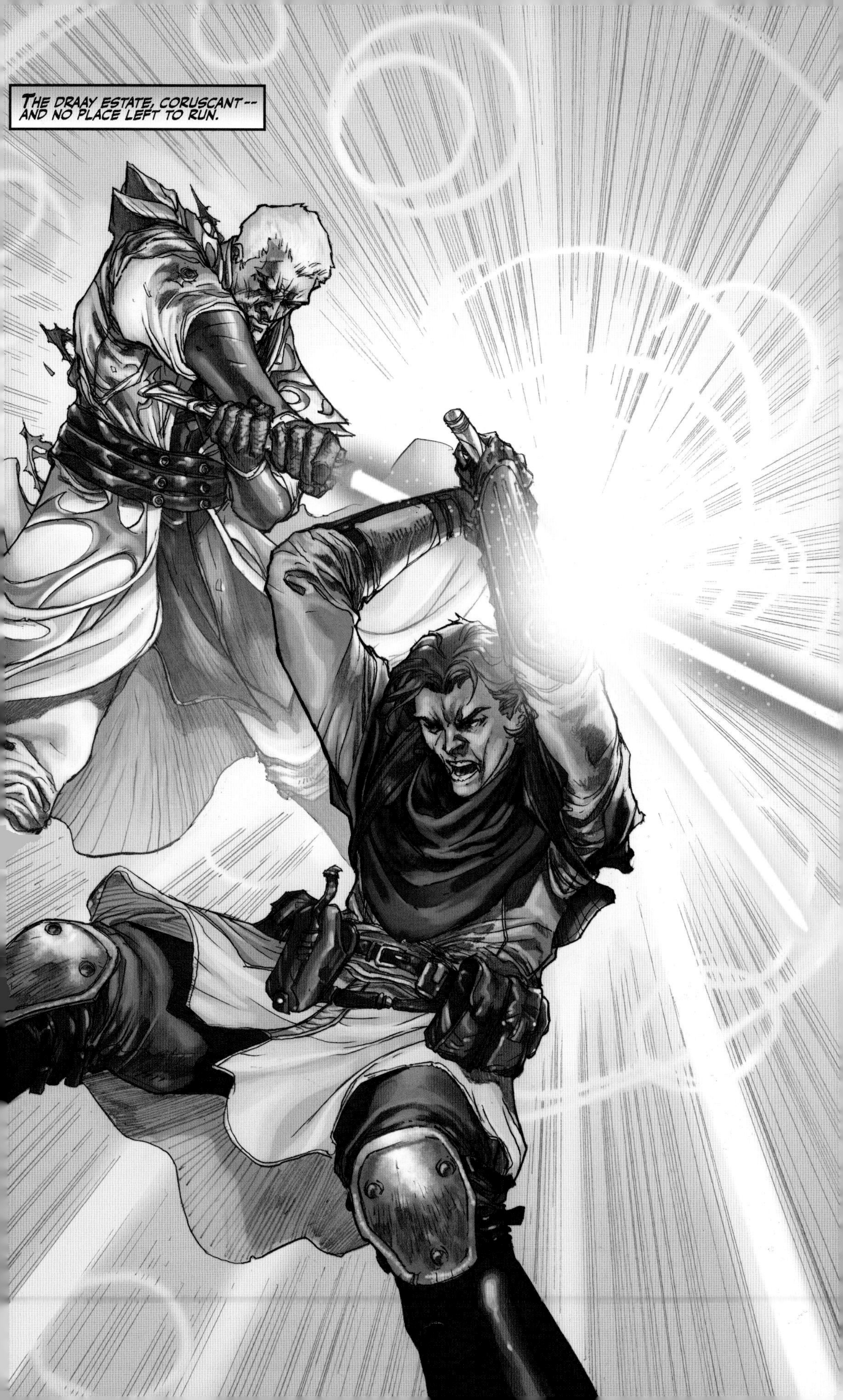
THE DRAAY ESTATE, CORUSCANT--
AND NO PLACE LEFT TO RUN.

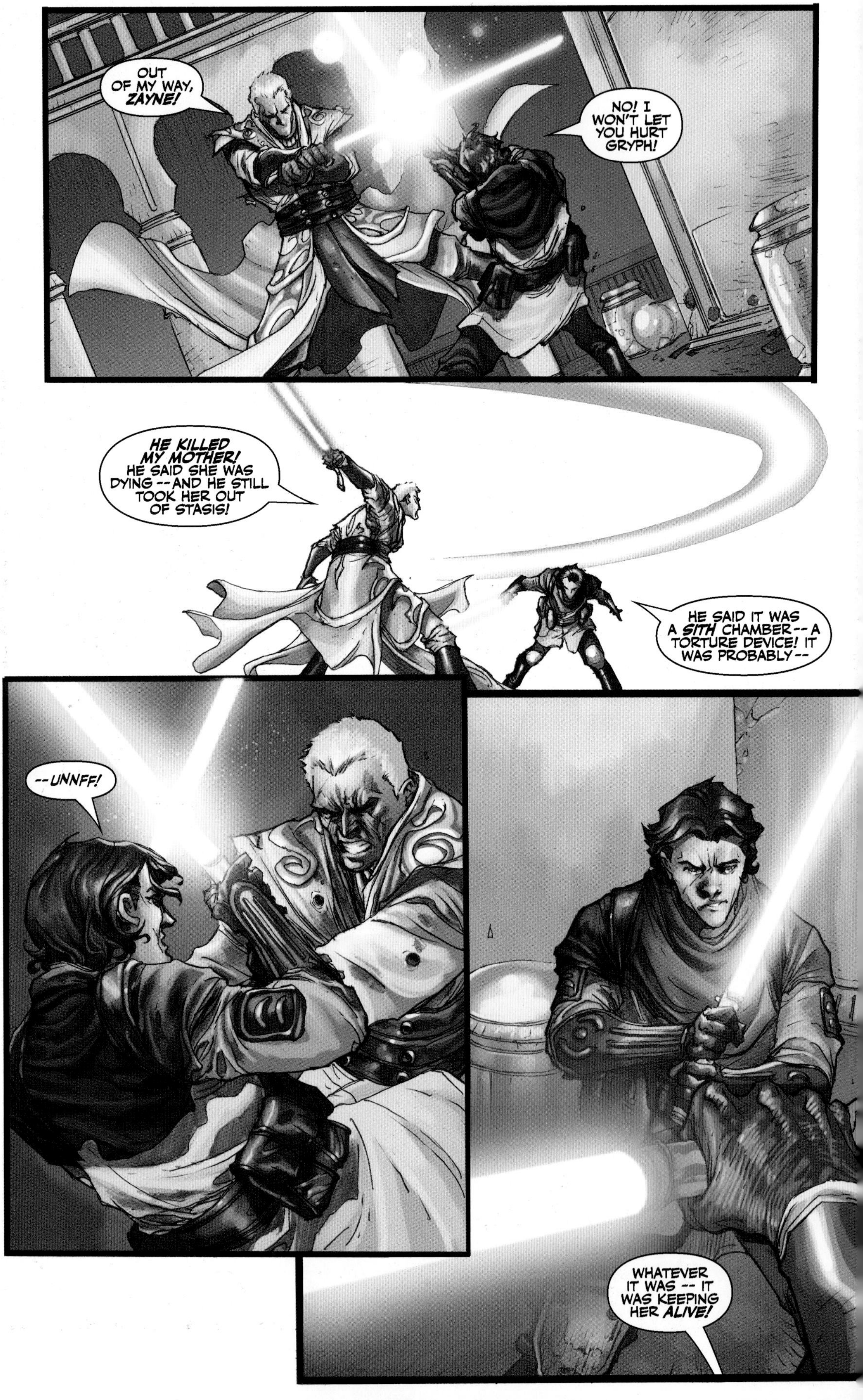
OUT OF MY WAY, ZAYNE!
NO! I WON'T LET YOU HURT GRYPH!
HE KILLED MY MOTHER! HE SAID SHE WAS DYING--AND HE STILL TOOK HER OUT OF STASIS!
HE SAID IT WAS A SITH CHAMBER--A TORTURE DEVICE! IT WAS PROBABLY--
--UNNFF!
WHATEVER IT WAS -- IT WAS KEEPING HER ALIVE!

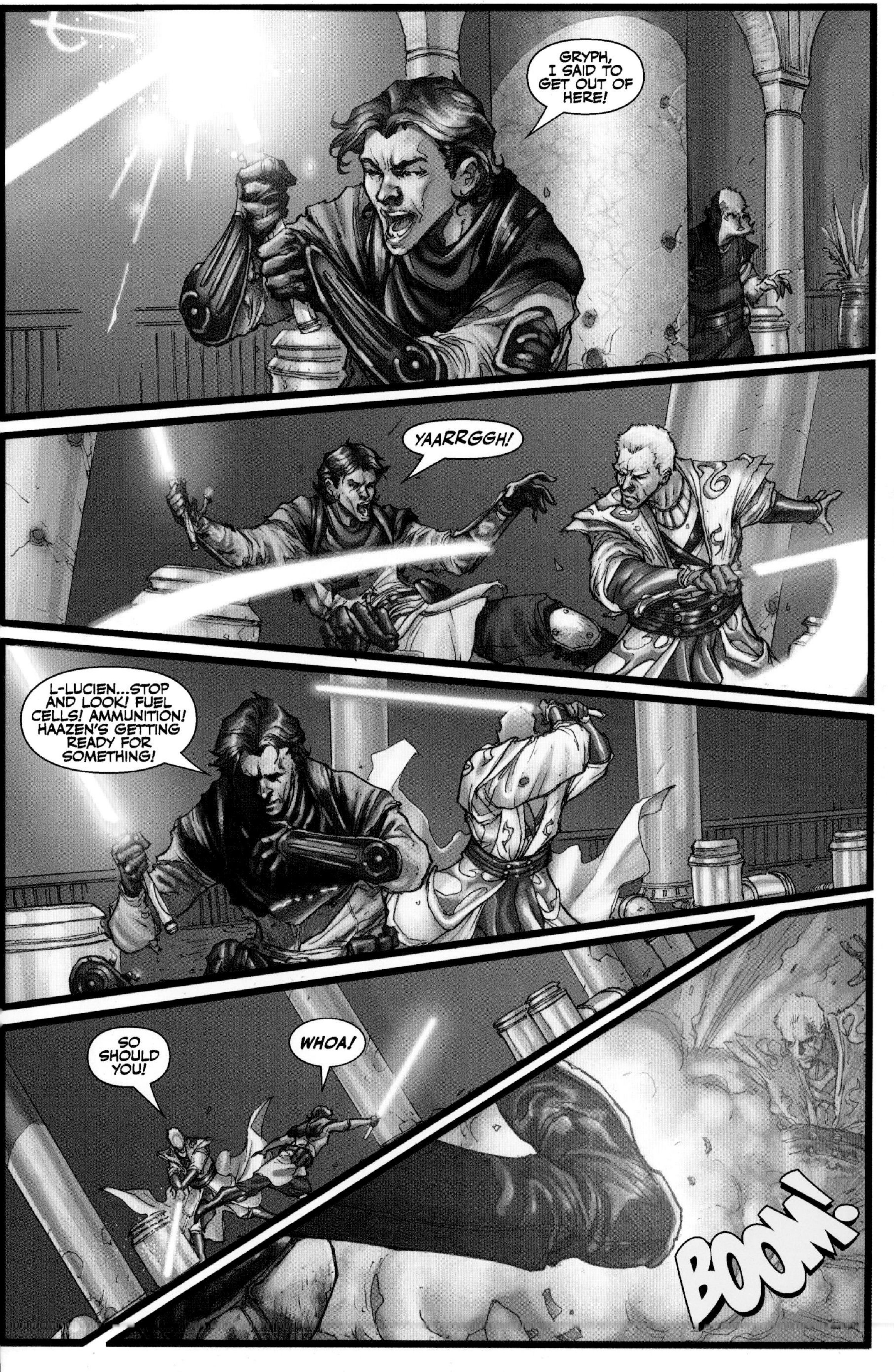
GRYPH, I SAID TO GET OUT OF HERE!
YAARRGGH!
L-LUCIEN...STOP AND LOOK! FUEL CELLS! AMMUNITION! HAAZEN'S GETTING READY FOR SOMETHING!
SO SHOULD YOU!
WHOA!
BOOM!

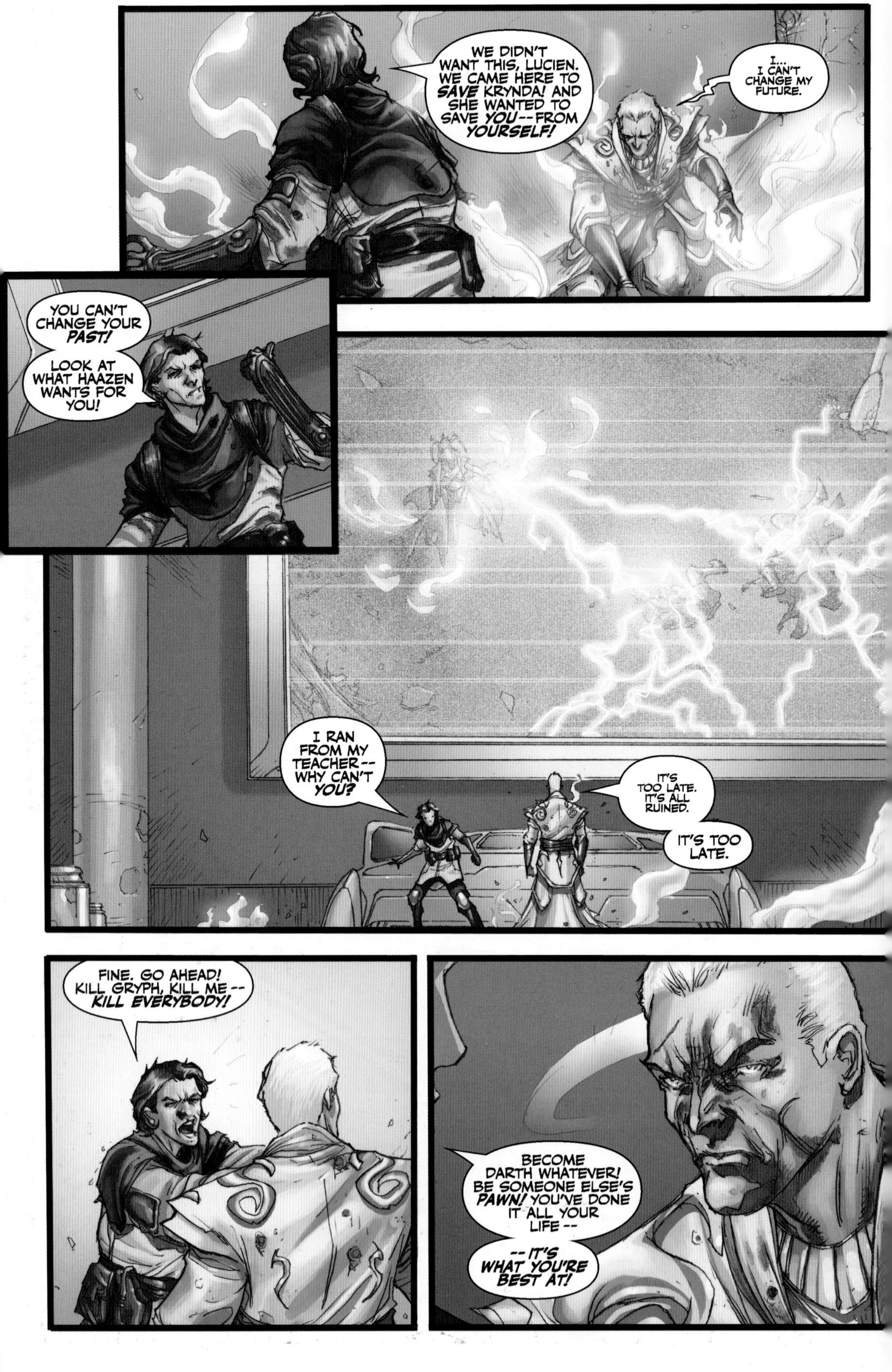
WE DIDN'T WANT THIS, LUCIEN. WE CAME HERE TO SAVE KRYNDA! AND SHE WANTED TO SAVE YOU--FROM YOURSELF!
I... I CAN'T CHANGE MY FUTURE.
YOU CAN'T CHANGE YOUR PAST!
LOOK AT WHAT HAAZEN WANTS FOR YOU!
I RAN FROM MY TEACHER-- WHY CAN'T YOU?
IT'S TOO LATE. IT'S ALL RUINED.
IT'S TOO LATE.
FINE. GO AHEAD! KILL GRYPH, KILL ME-- KILL EVERYBODY!
BECOME DARTH WHATEVER! BE SOMEONE ELSE'S PAWN! YOU'VE DONE IT ALL YOUR LIFE--
--IT'S WHAT YOU'RE BEST AT!

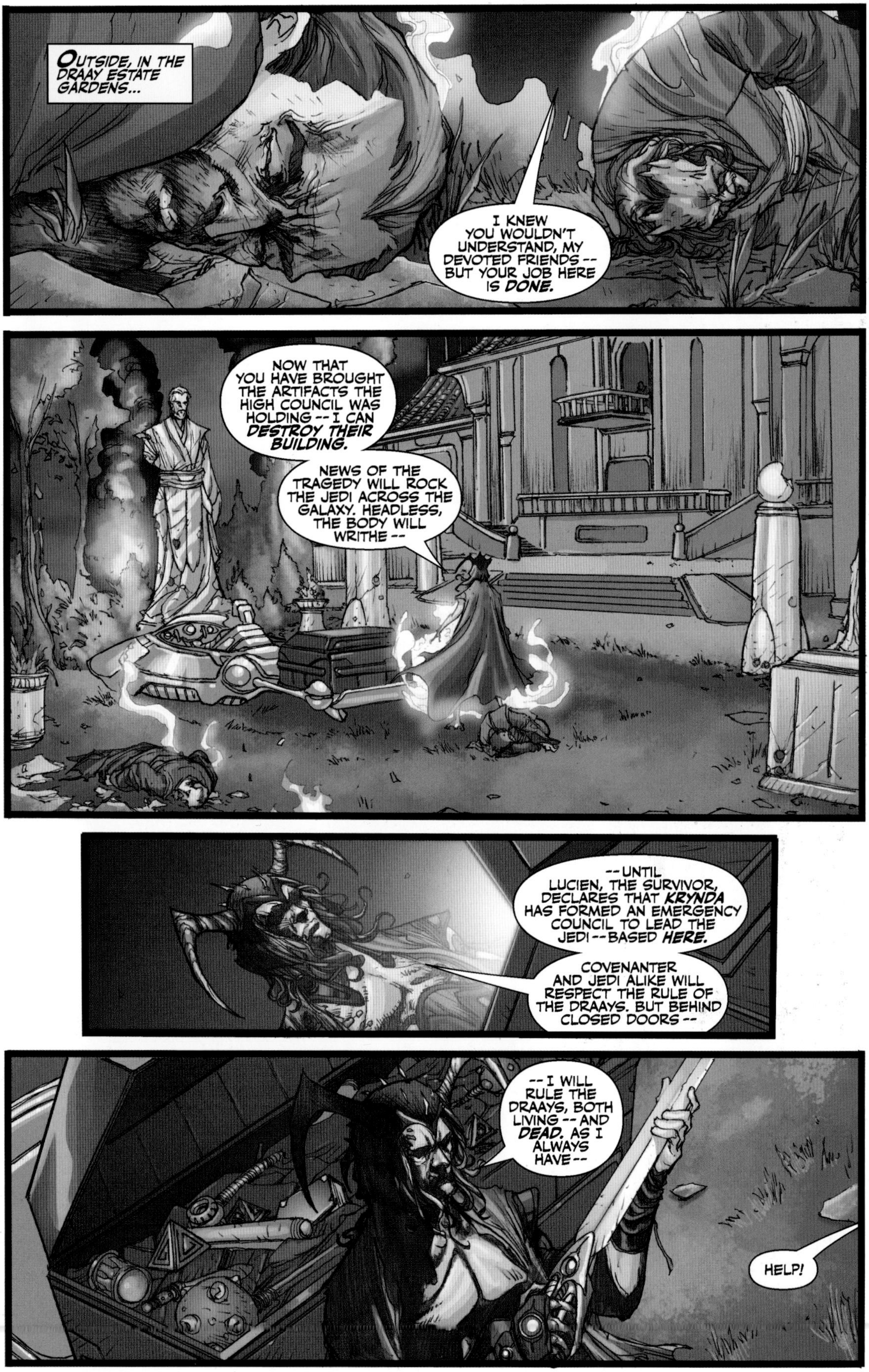
OUTSIDE, IN THE DRAAY ESTATE GARDENS...
I KNEW YOU WOULDN'T UNDERSTAND, MY DEVOTED FRIENDS -- BUT YOUR JOB HERE IS DONE.
NOW THAT YOU HAVE BROUGHT THE ARTIFACTS THE HIGH COUNCIL WAS HOLDING -- I CAN DESTROY THEIR BUILDING.
NEWS OF THE TRAGEDY WILL ROCK THE JEDI ACROSS THE GALAXY. HEADLESS, THE BODY WILL WRITHE --
-- UNTIL LUCIEN, THE SURVIVOR, DECLARES THAT KRYNDA HAS FORMED AN EMERGENCY COUNCIL TO LEAD THE JEDI -- BASED HERE.
COVENANTER AND JEDI ALIKE WILL RESPECT THE RULE OF THE DRAAYS. BUT BEHIND CLOSED DOORS --
-- I WILL RULE THE DRAAYS, BOTH LIVING -- AND DEAD, AS I ALWAYS HAVE --
HELP!

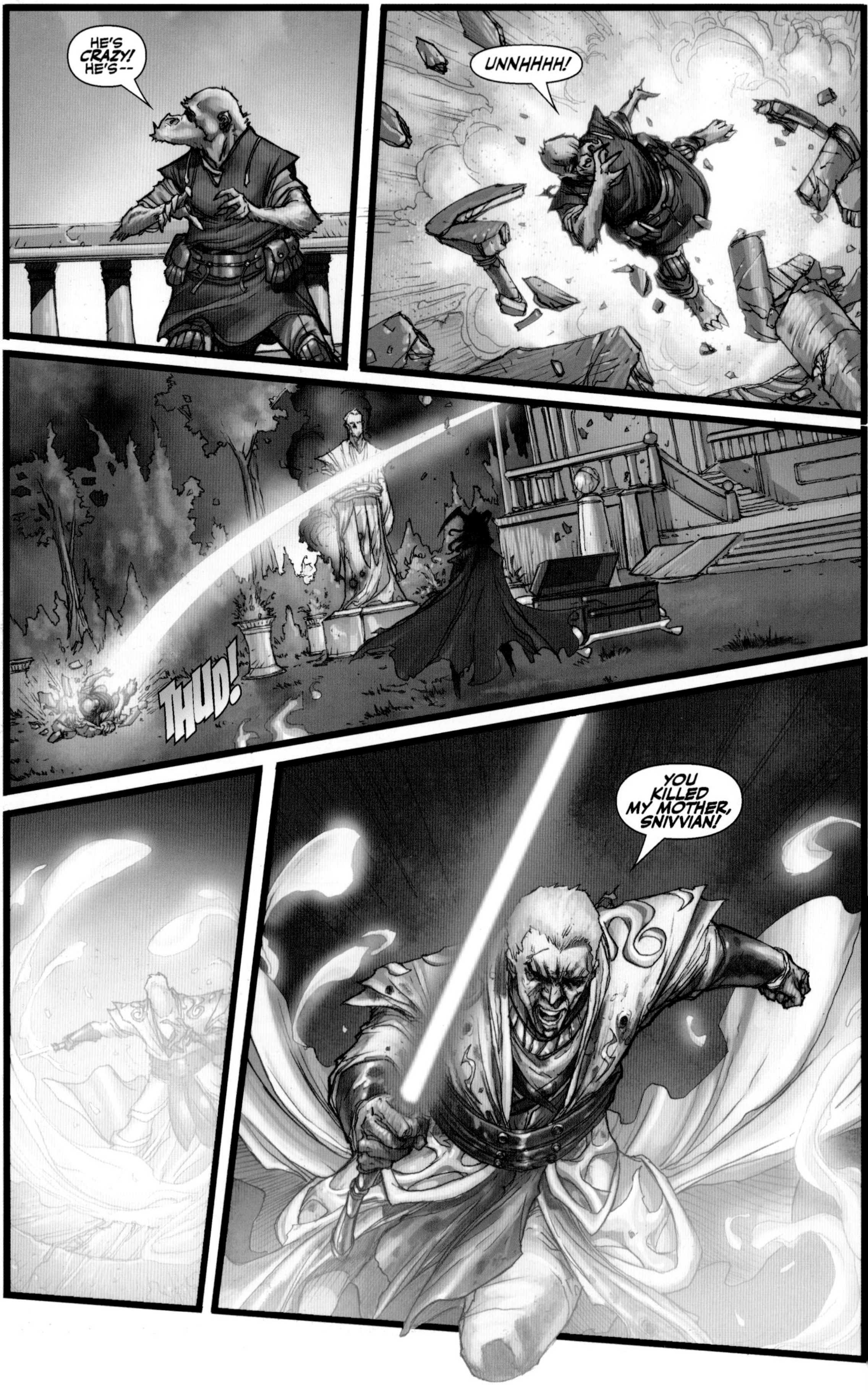
HE'S CRAZY! HE'S--
UNNHHHH!
THUD!
YOU KILLED MY MOTHER, SNIVVIAN!

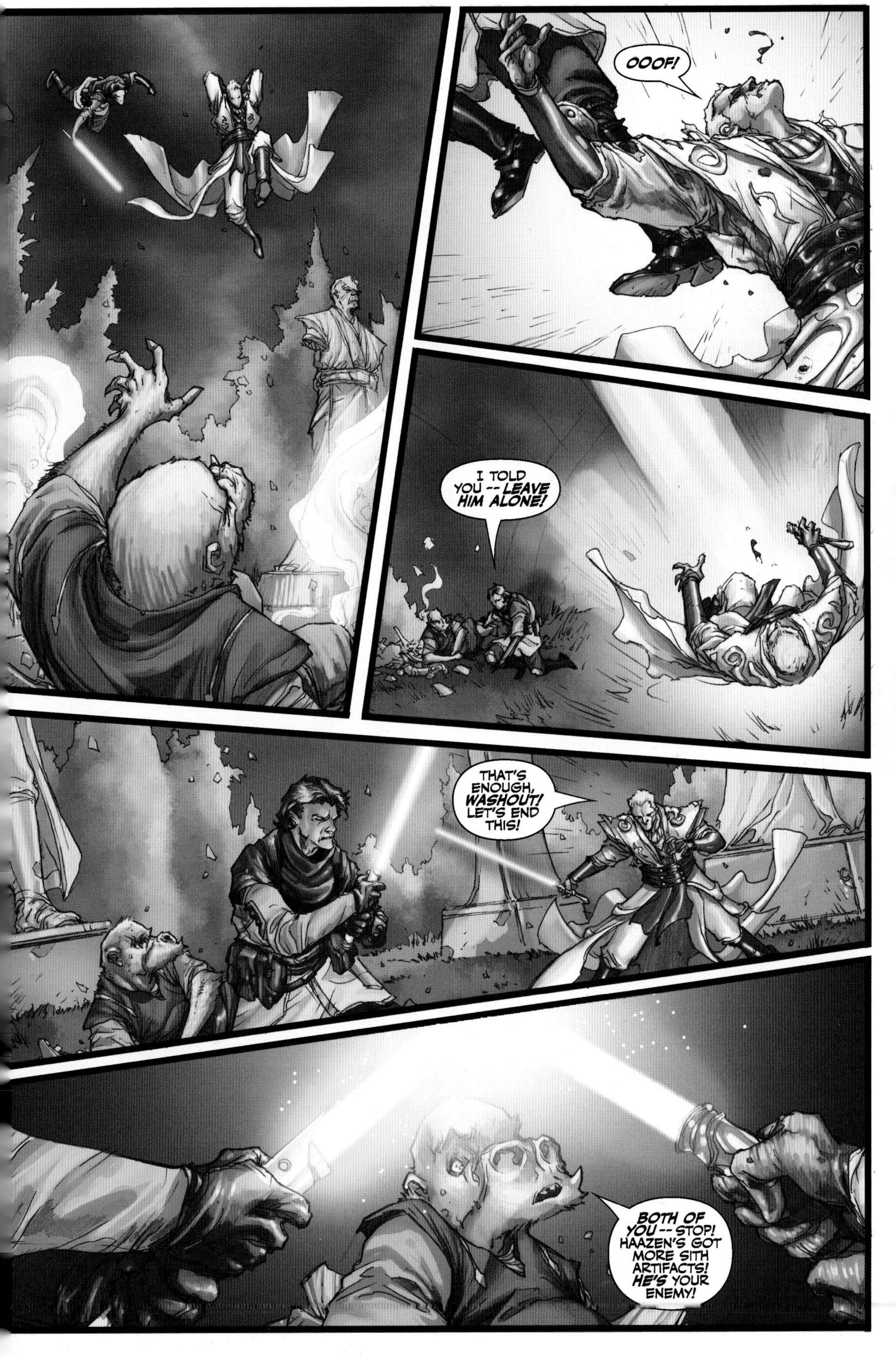
OOOF!
I TOLD YOU -- LEAVE HIM ALONE!
THAT'S ENOUGH, WASHOUT! LET'S END THIS!
BOTH OF YOU -- STOP! HAAZEN'S GOT MORE SITH ARTIFACTS! HE'S YOUR ENEMY!

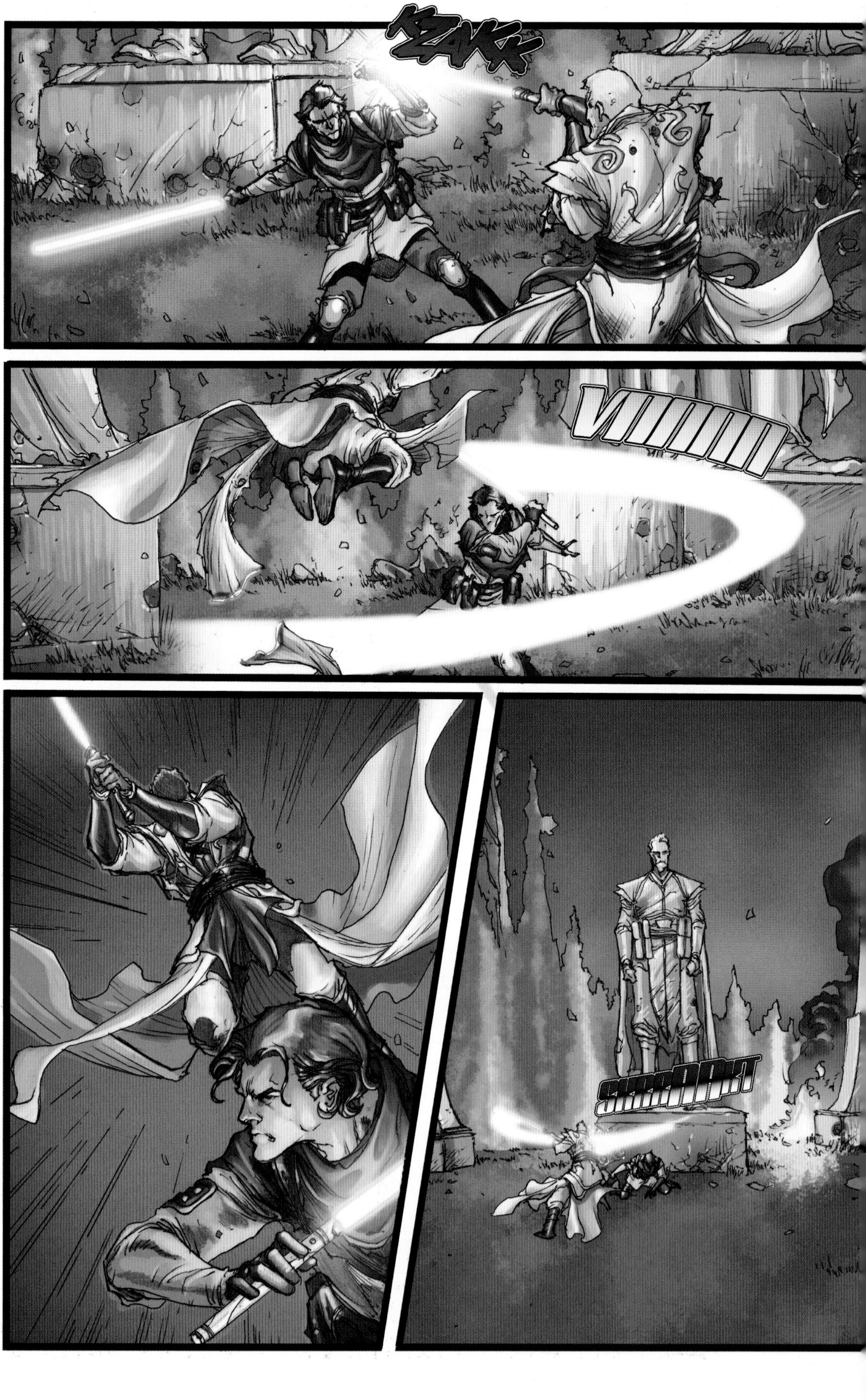
KZANKK

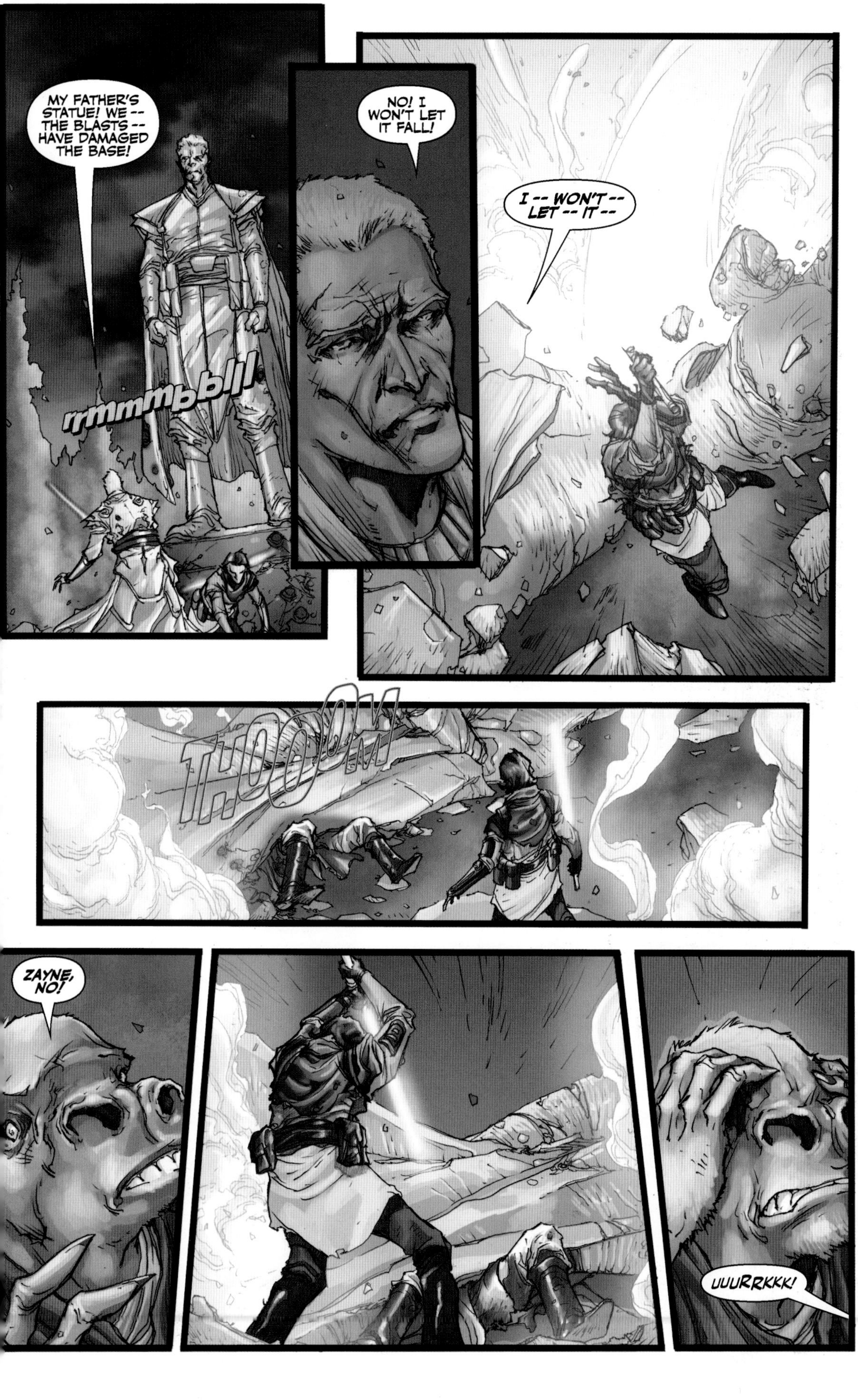
MY FATHER'S STATUE! WE -- THE BLASTS -- HAVE DAMAGED THE BASE!
rrmmmbblll
NO! I WON'T LET IT FALL!
I -- WON'T -- LET -- IT --
THOOOOM
ZAYNE, NO!
UUURRKKK!

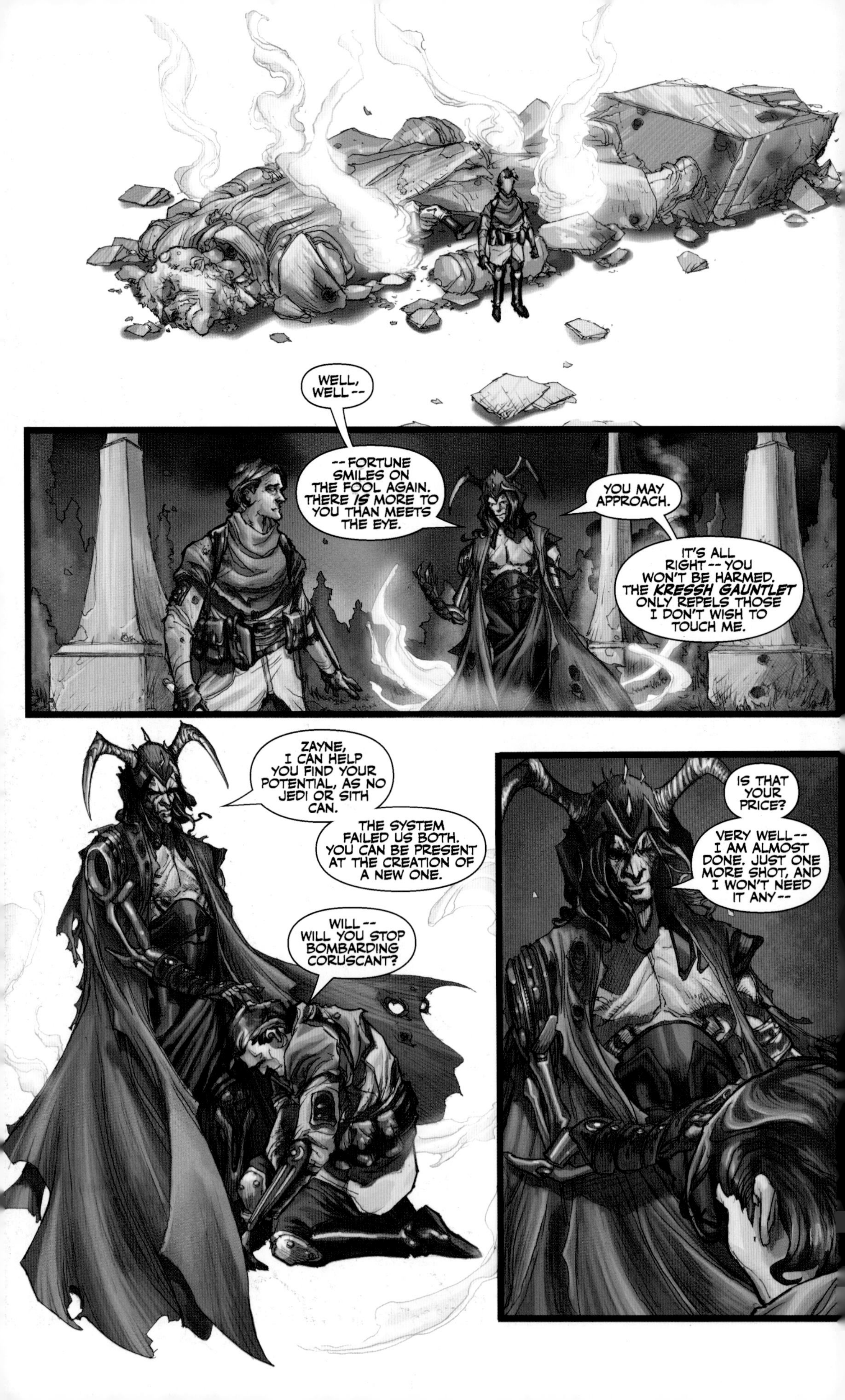
WELL, WELL--
--FORTUNE SMILES ON THE FOOL AGAIN. THERE *IS* MORE TO YOU THAN MEETS THE EYE.
YOU MAY APPROACH.
IT'S ALL RIGHT-- YOU WON'T BE HARMED. THE *KRESSH GAUNTLET* ONLY REPELS THOSE I DON'T WISH TO TOUCH ME.
ZAYNE, I CAN HELP YOU FIND YOUR POTENTIAL, AS NO JEDI OR SITH CAN.
THE SYSTEM FAILED US BOTH. YOU CAN BE PRESENT AT THE CREATION OF A NEW ONE.
WILL-- WILL YOU STOP BOMBARDING CORUSCANT?
IS THAT YOUR PRICE?
VERY WELL-- I AM ALMOST DONE. JUST ONE MORE SHOT, AND I WON'T NEED IT ANY--

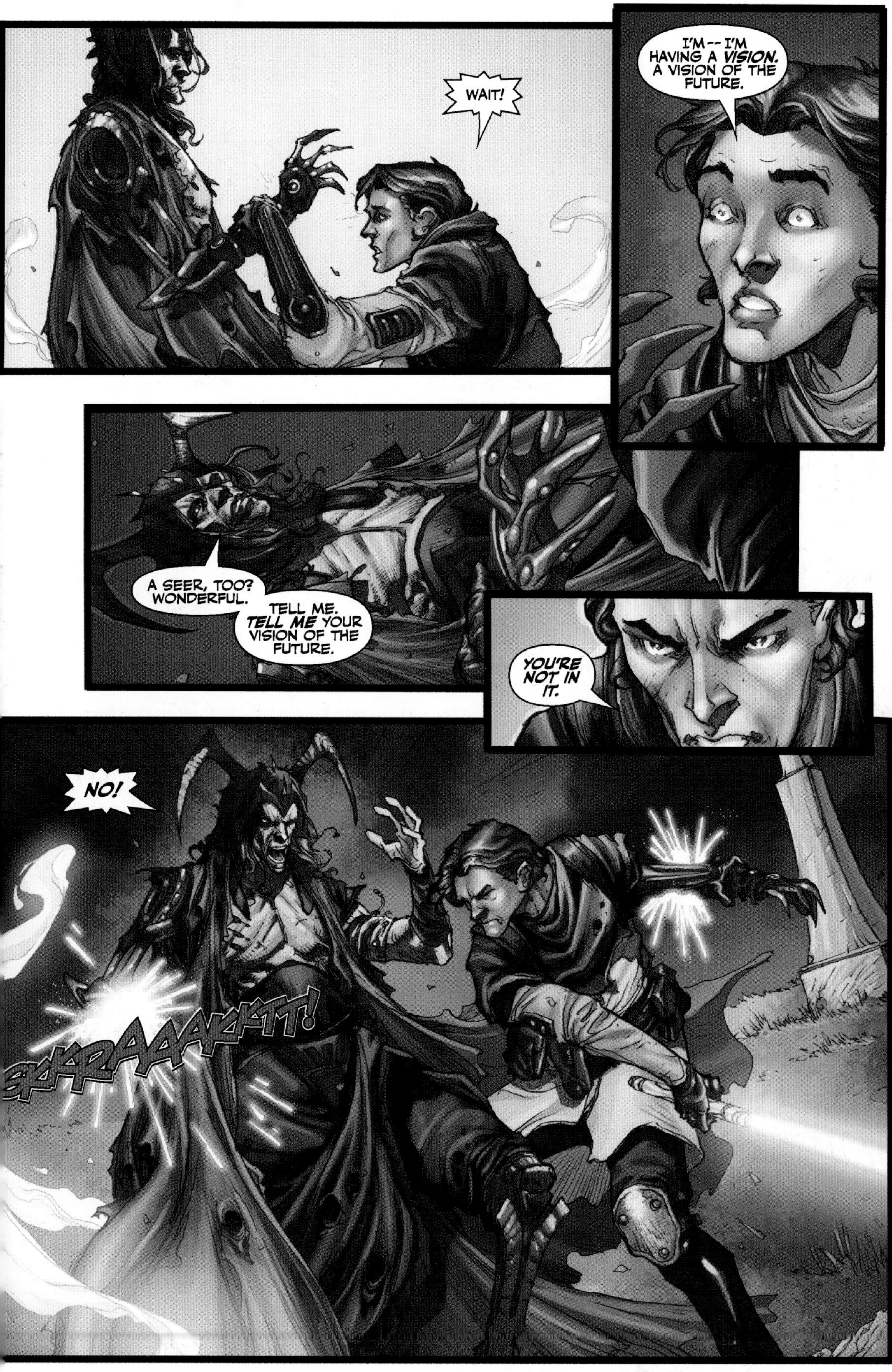
WAIT!
I'M -- I'M HAVING A *VISION.* A VISION OF THE FUTURE.
A SEER, TOO? WONDERFUL.
TELL ME. ***TELL ME*** YOUR VISION OF THE FUTURE.
YOU'RE NOT IN IT.
NO!
SKRAAAKKTT!

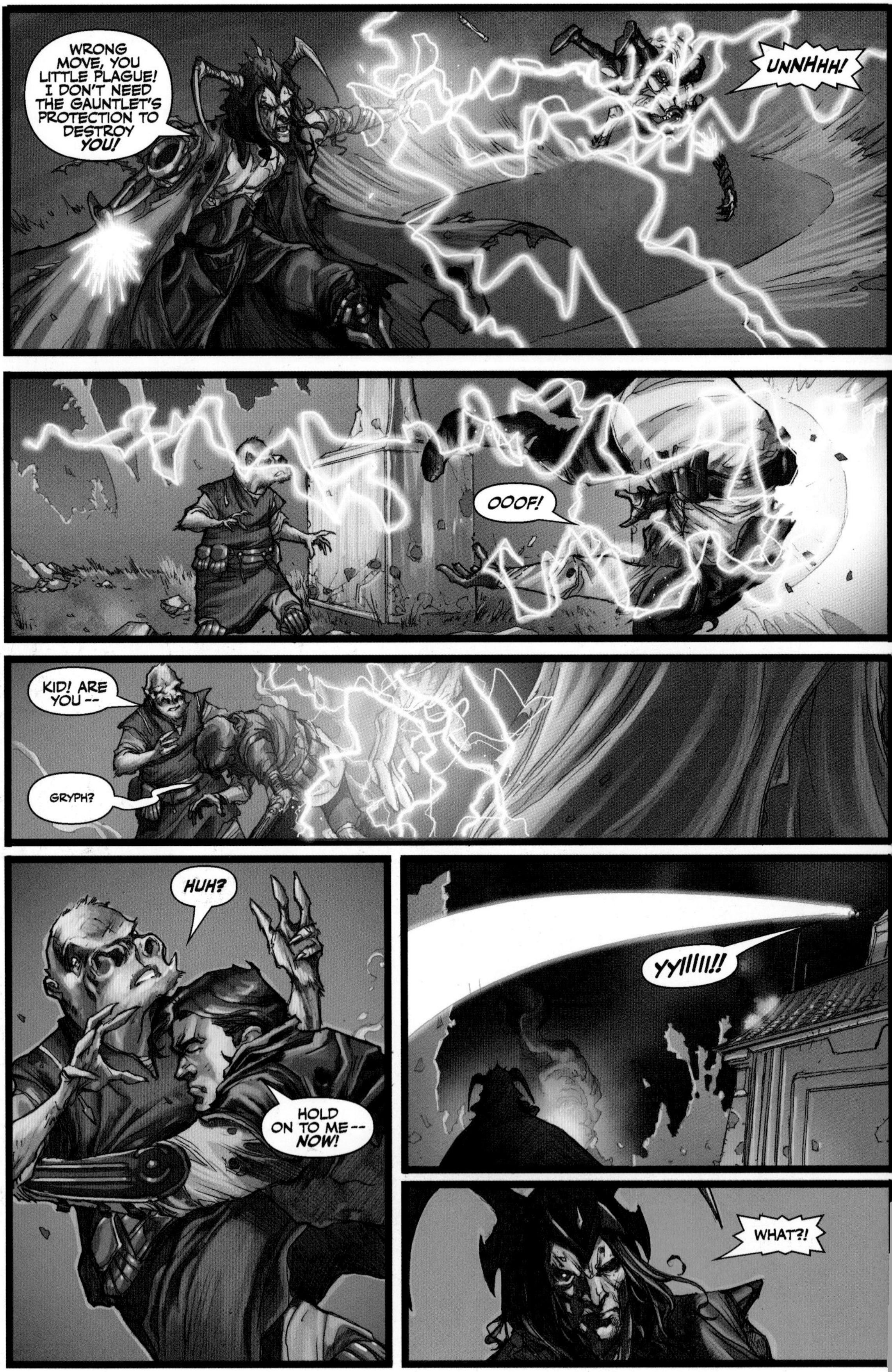
WRONG MOVE, YOU LITTLE PLAGUE! I DON'T NEED THE GAUNTLET'S PROTECTION TO DESTROY YOU!
UNNHHH!
OOOF!
KID! ARE YOU --
GRYPH?
HUH?
HOLD ON TO ME -- NOW!
YYIIIII!!
WHAT?!

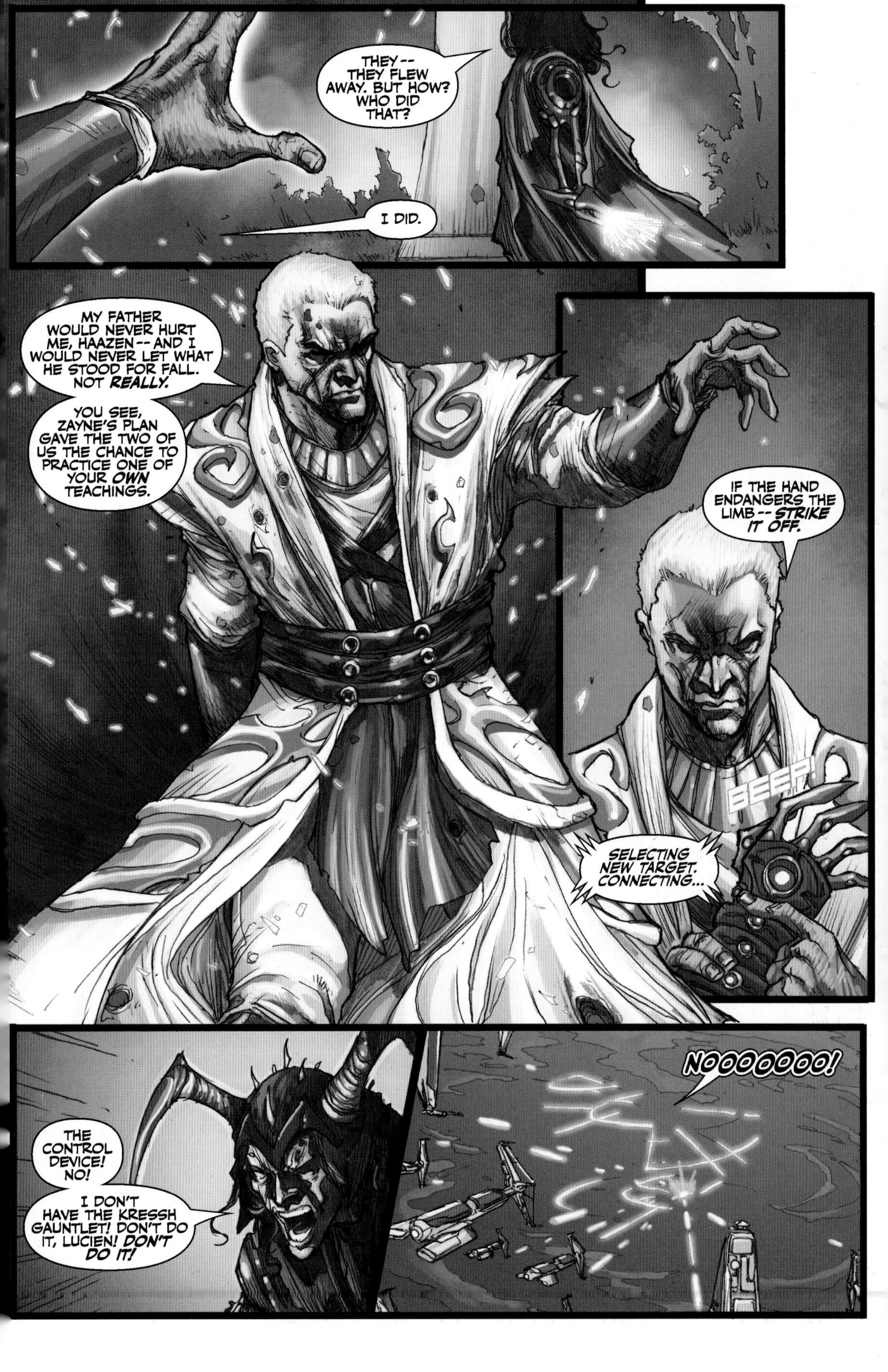
THEY-- THEY FLEW AWAY. BUT HOW? WHO DID THAT?
I DID.
MY FATHER WOULD NEVER HURT ME, HAAZEN-- AND I WOULD NEVER LET WHAT HE STOOD FOR FALL. NOT REALLY.
YOU SEE, ZAYNE'S PLAN GAVE THE TWO OF US THE CHANCE TO PRACTICE ONE OF YOUR OWN TEACHINGS.
IF THE HAND ENDANGERS THE LIMB-- STRIKE IT OFF.
BEEP!
SELECTING NEW TARGET. CONNECTING...
THE CONTROL DEVICE! NO!
I DON'T HAVE THE KRESSH GAUNTLET! DON'T DO IT, LUCIEN! DON'T DO IT!
NOOOOOOO!

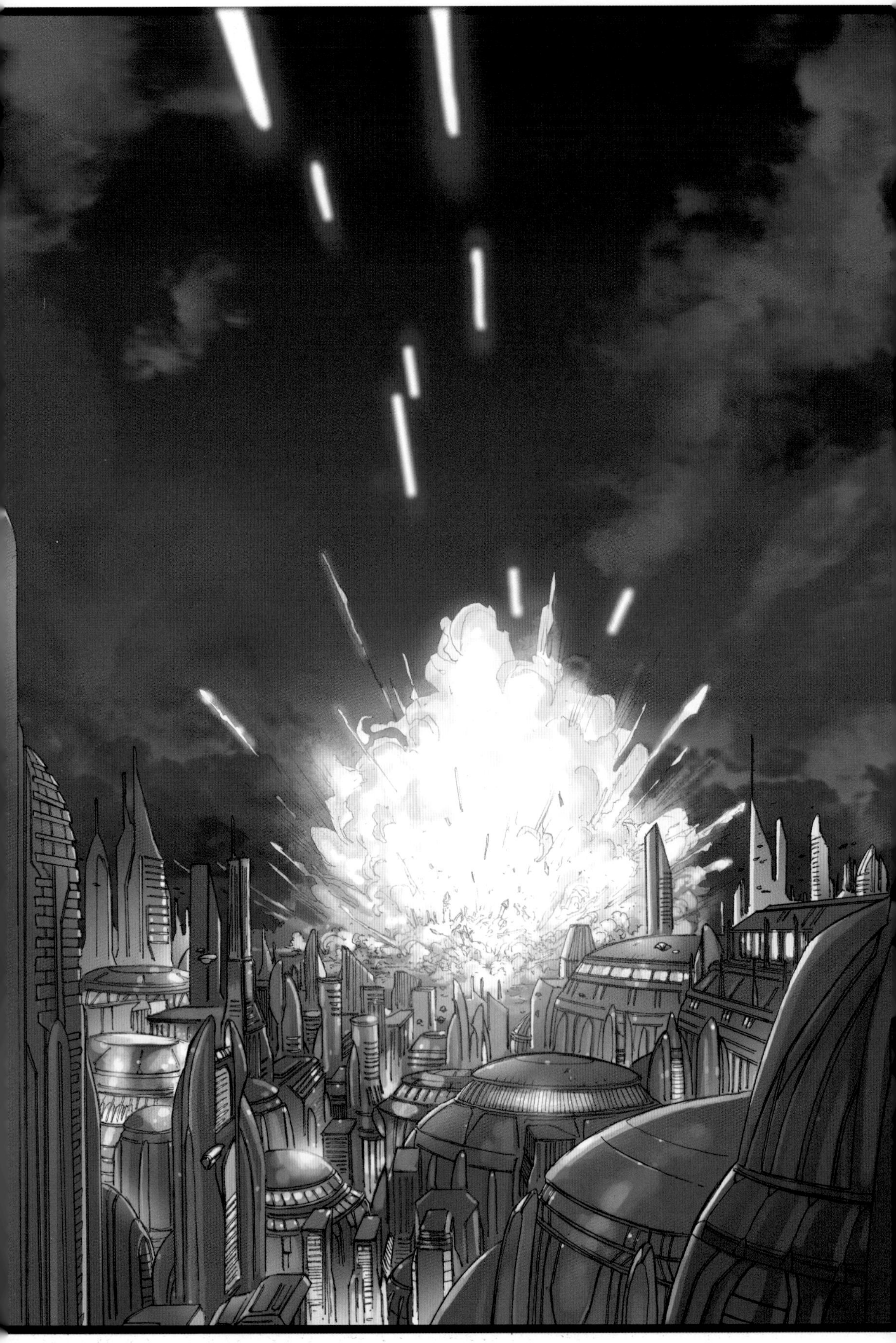

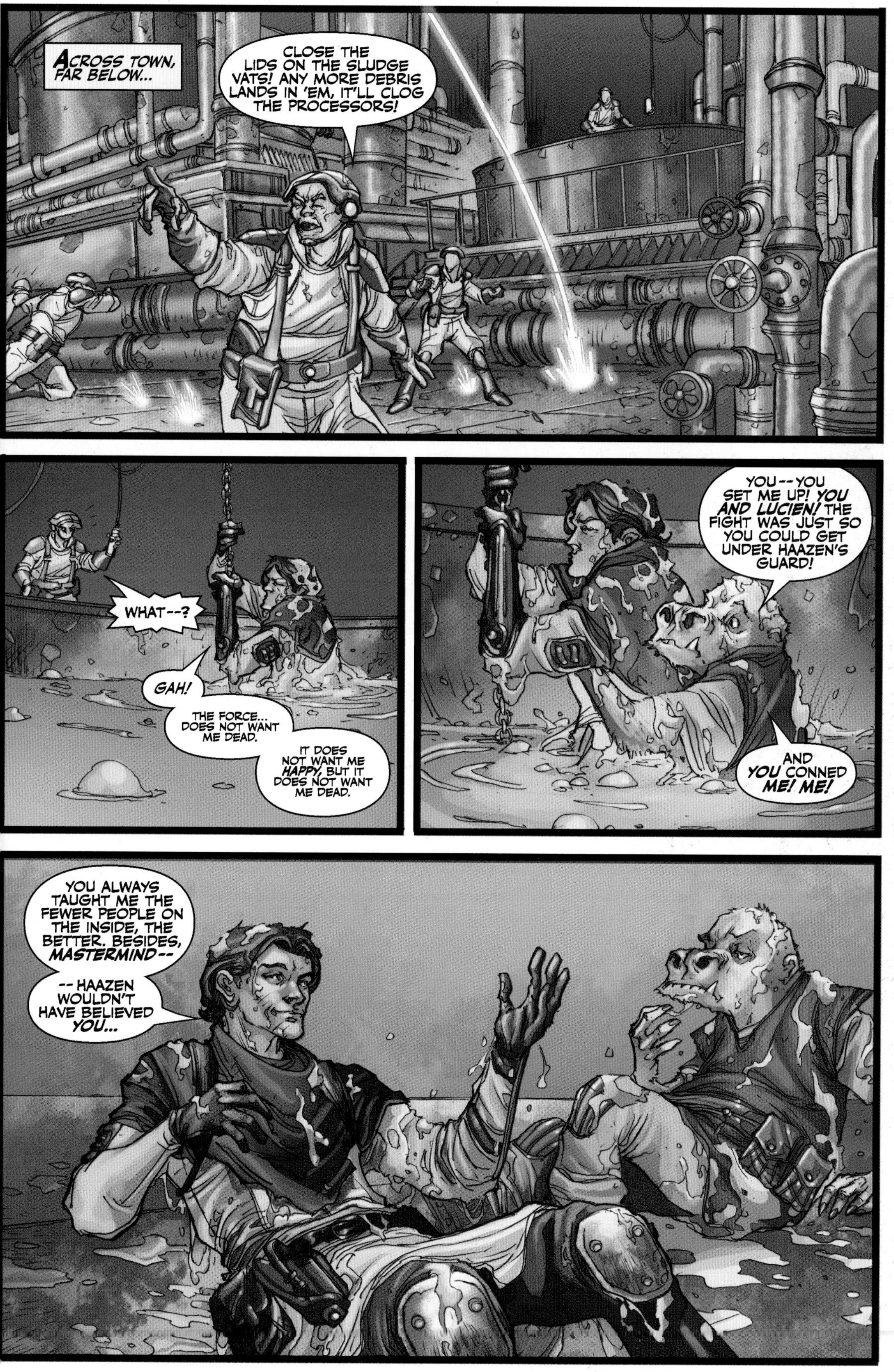
ACROSS TOWN, FAR BELOW...
CLOSE THE LIDS ON THE SLUDGE VATS! ANY MORE DEBRIS LANDS IN 'EM, IT'LL CLOG THE PROCESSORS!
WHAT--?
GAH!
THE FORCE... DOES NOT WANT ME DEAD.
IT DOES NOT WANT ME *HAPPY*, BUT IT DOES NOT WANT ME DEAD.
YOU--YOU SET ME UP! *YOU AND LUCIEN!* THE FIGHT WAS JUST SO YOU COULD GET UNDER HAAZEN'S GUARD!
AND *YOU* CONNED *ME! ME!*
YOU ALWAYS TAUGHT ME THE FEWER PEOPLE ON THE INSIDE, THE BETTER. BESIDES, *MASTERMIND*--
--HAAZEN WOULDN'T HAVE BELIEVED *YOU*...

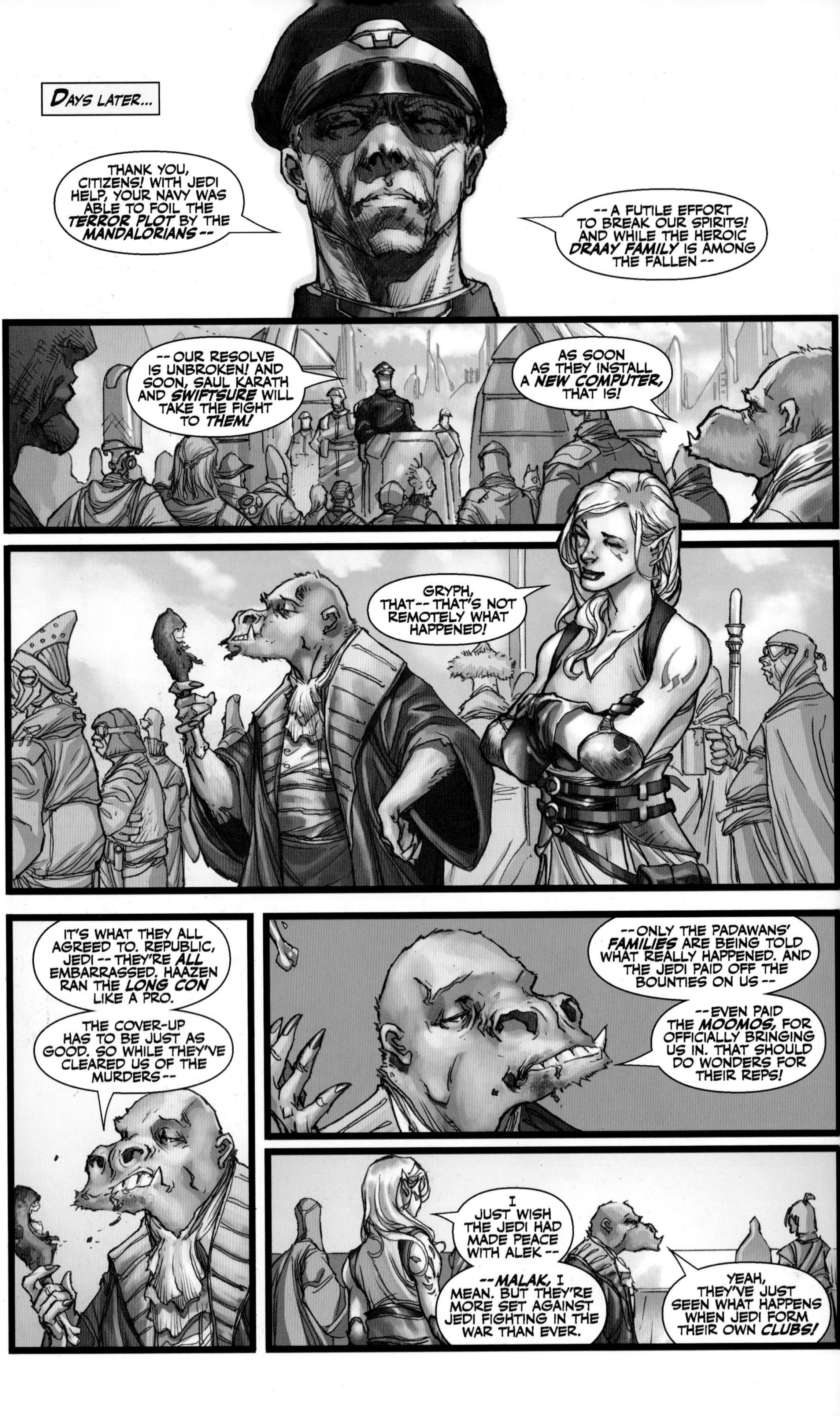
DAYS LATER...
THANK YOU, CITIZENS! WITH JEDI HELP, YOUR NAVY WAS ABLE TO FOIL THE TERROR PLOT BY THE MANDALORIANS--
--A FUTILE EFFORT TO BREAK OUR SPIRITS! AND WHILE THE HEROIC DRAAY FAMILY IS AMONG THE FALLEN--
--OUR RESOLVE IS UNBROKEN! AND SOON, SAUL KARATH AND SWIFTSURE WILL TAKE THE FIGHT TO THEM!
AS SOON AS THEY INSTALL A NEW COMPUTER, THAT IS!
GRYPH, THAT--THAT'S NOT REMOTELY WHAT HAPPENED!
IT'S WHAT THEY ALL AGREED TO. REPUBLIC, JEDI--THEY'RE ALL EMBARRASSED. HAAZEN RAN THE LONG CON LIKE A PRO.
THE COVER-UP HAS TO BE JUST AS GOOD. SO WHILE THEY'VE CLEARED US OF THE MURDERS--
--ONLY THE PADAWANS' FAMILIES ARE BEING TOLD WHAT REALLY HAPPENED. AND THE JEDI PAID OFF THE BOUNTIES ON US--
--EVEN PAID THE MOOMOS, FOR OFFICIALLY BRINGING US IN. THAT SHOULD DO WONDERS FOR THEIR REPS!
I JUST WISH THE JEDI HAD MADE PEACE WITH ALEK--
--MALAK, I MEAN. BUT THEY'RE MORE SET AGAINST JEDI FIGHTING IN THE WAR THAN EVER.
YEAH, THEY'VE JUST SEEN WHAT HAPPENS WHEN JEDI FORM THEIR OWN CLUBS!

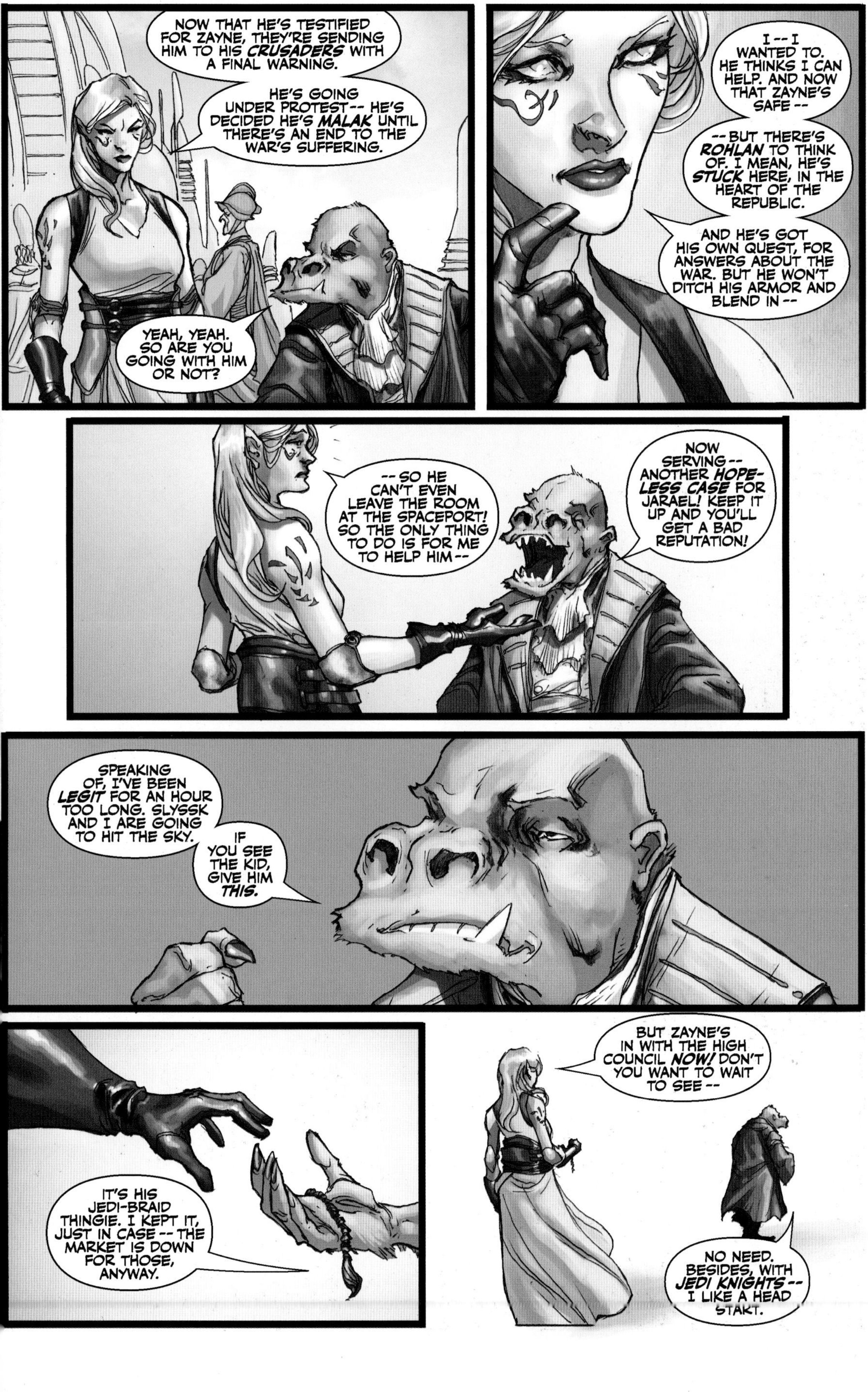
NOW THAT HE'S TESTIFIED FOR ZAYNE, THEY'RE SENDING HIM TO HIS CRUSADERS WITH A FINAL WARNING.
HE'S GOING UNDER PROTEST -- HE'S DECIDED HE'S MALAK UNTIL THERE'S AN END TO THE WAR'S SUFFERING.
YEAH, YEAH. SO ARE YOU GOING WITH HIM OR NOT?
I -- I WANTED TO. HE THINKS I CAN HELP. AND NOW THAT ZAYNE'S SAFE --
-- BUT THERE'S ROHLAN TO THINK OF. I MEAN, HE'S STUCK HERE, IN THE HEART OF THE REPUBLIC.
AND HE'S GOT HIS OWN QUEST, FOR ANSWERS ABOUT THE WAR. BUT HE WON'T DITCH HIS ARMOR AND BLEND IN --
-- SO HE CAN'T EVEN LEAVE THE ROOM AT THE SPACEPORT! SO THE ONLY THING TO DO IS FOR ME TO HELP HIM --
NOW SERVING -- ANOTHER HOPE-LESS CASE FOR JARAEL! KEEP IT UP AND YOU'LL GET A BAD REPUTATION!
SPEAKING OF, I'VE BEEN LEGIT FOR AN HOUR TOO LONG. SLYSSK AND I ARE GOING TO HIT THE SKY.
IF YOU SEE THE KID, GIVE HIM THIS.
IT'S HIS JEDI-BRAID THINGIE. I KEPT IT, JUST IN CASE -- THE MARKET IS DOWN FOR THOSE, ANYWAY.
BUT ZAYNE'S IN WITH THE HIGH COUNCIL NOW! DON'T YOU WANT TO WAIT TO SEE --
NO NEED. BESIDES, WITH JEDI KNIGHTS -- I LIKE A HEAD START.

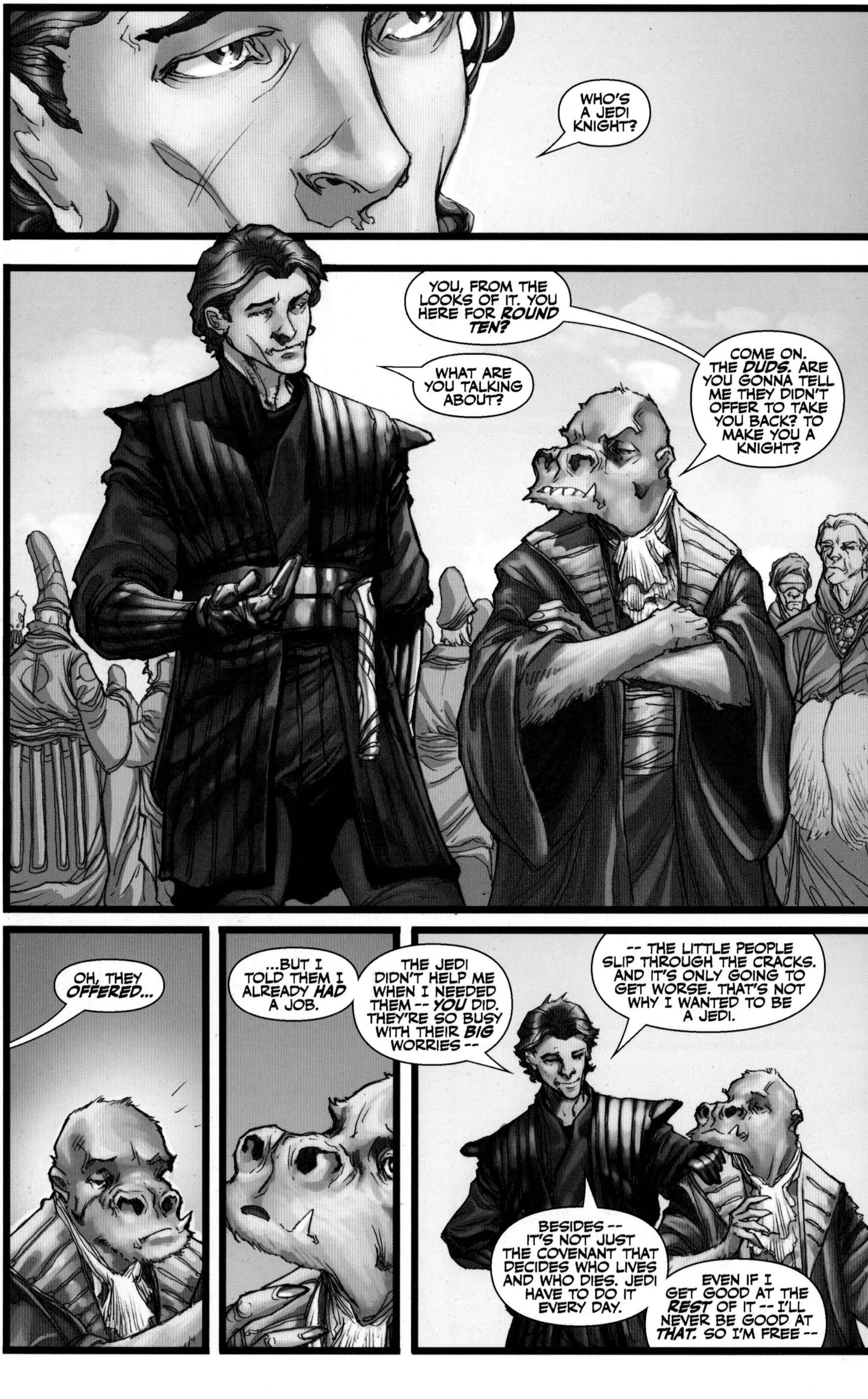
WHO'S A JEDI KNIGHT?
YOU, FROM THE LOOKS OF IT. YOU HERE FOR ROUND TEN?
WHAT ARE YOU TALKING ABOUT?
COME ON. THE DUDS. ARE YOU GONNA TELL ME THEY DIDN'T OFFER TO TAKE YOU BACK? TO MAKE YOU A KNIGHT?
OH, THEY OFFERED...
...BUT I TOLD THEM I ALREADY HAD A JOB.
THE JEDI DIDN'T HELP ME WHEN I NEEDED THEM -- YOU DID. THEY'RE SO BUSY WITH THEIR BIG WORRIES --
-- THE LITTLE PEOPLE SLIP THROUGH THE CRACKS. AND IT'S ONLY GOING TO GET WORSE. THAT'S NOT WHY I WANTED TO BE A JEDI.
BESIDES -- IT'S NOT JUST THE COVENANT THAT DECIDES WHO LIVES AND WHO DIES. JEDI HAVE TO DO IT EVERY DAY.
EVEN IF I GET GOOD AT THE REST OF IT -- I'LL NEVER BE GOOD AT THAT. SO I'M FREE --

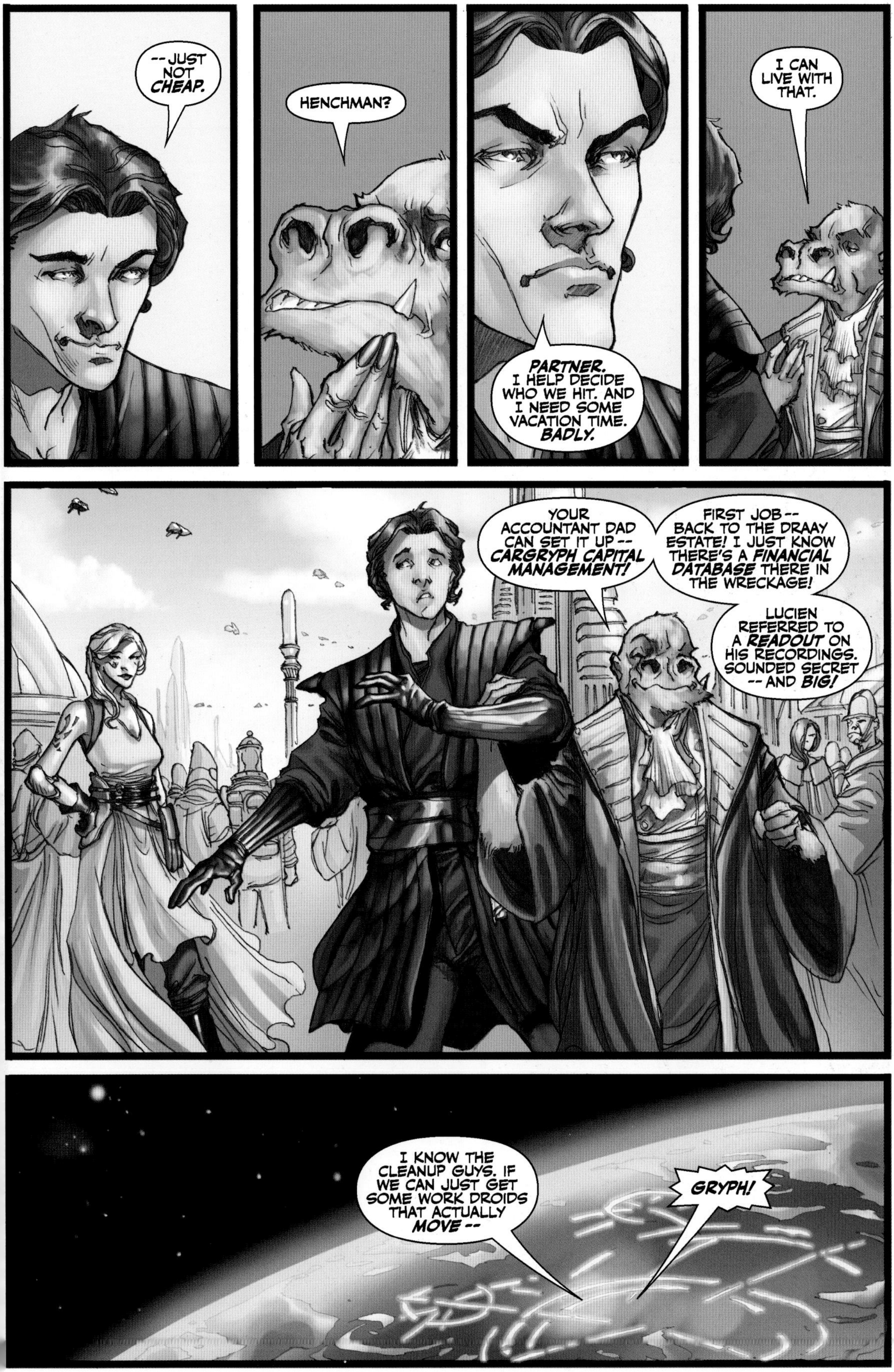

--JUST NOT *CHEAP.*
HENCHMAN?
PARTNER. I HELP DECIDE WHO WE HIT. AND I NEED SOME VACATION TIME. *BADLY.*
I CAN LIVE WITH THAT.
YOUR ACCOUNTANT DAD CAN SET IT UP-- *CARGRYPH CAPITAL MANAGEMENT!*
FIRST JOB-- BACK TO THE DRAAY ESTATE! I JUST KNOW THERE'S A *FINANCIAL DATABASE* THERE IN THE WRECKAGE!
LUCIEN REFERRED TO A *READOUT* ON HIS RECORDINGS. SOUNDED SECRET --AND *BIG!*
I KNOW THE CLEANUP GUYS. IF WE CAN JUST GET SOME WORK DROIDS THAT ACTUALLY *MOVE* --
GRYPH!

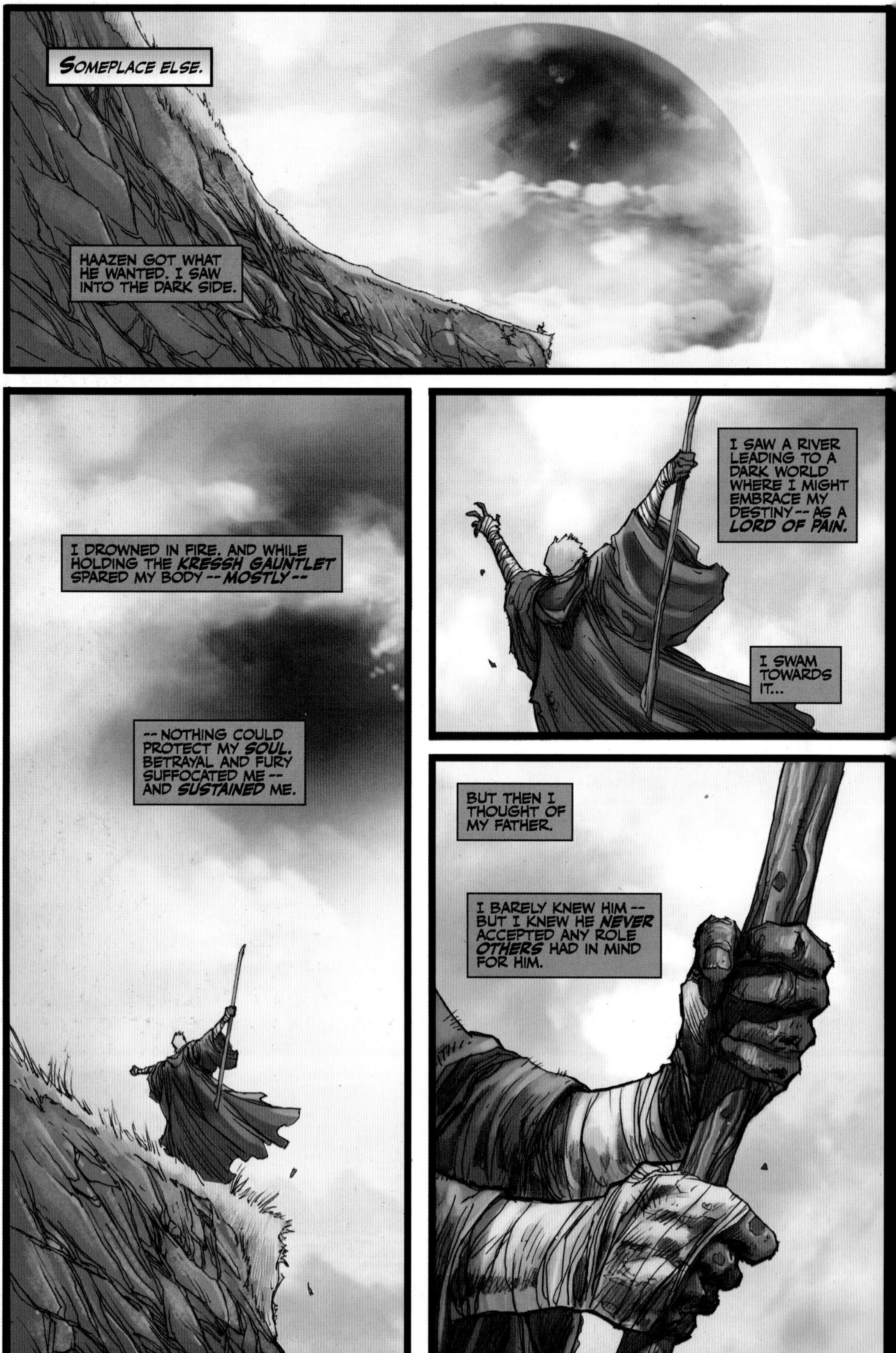
SOMEPLACE ELSE.
HAAZEN GOT WHAT HE WANTED. I SAW INTO THE DARK SIDE.
I DROWNED IN FIRE. AND WHILE HOLDING THE KRESSH GAUNTLET SPARED MY BODY -- MOSTLY --
-- NOTHING COULD PROTECT MY SOUL. BETRAYAL AND FURY SUFFOCATED ME -- AND SUSTAINED ME.
I SAW A RIVER LEADING TO A DARK WORLD WHERE I MIGHT EMBRACE MY DESTINY -- AS A LORD OF PAIN.
I SWAM TOWARDS IT...
BUT THEN I THOUGHT OF MY FATHER.
I BARELY KNEW HIM -- BUT I KNEW HE NEVER ACCEPTED ANY ROLE OTHERS HAD IN MIND FOR HIM.

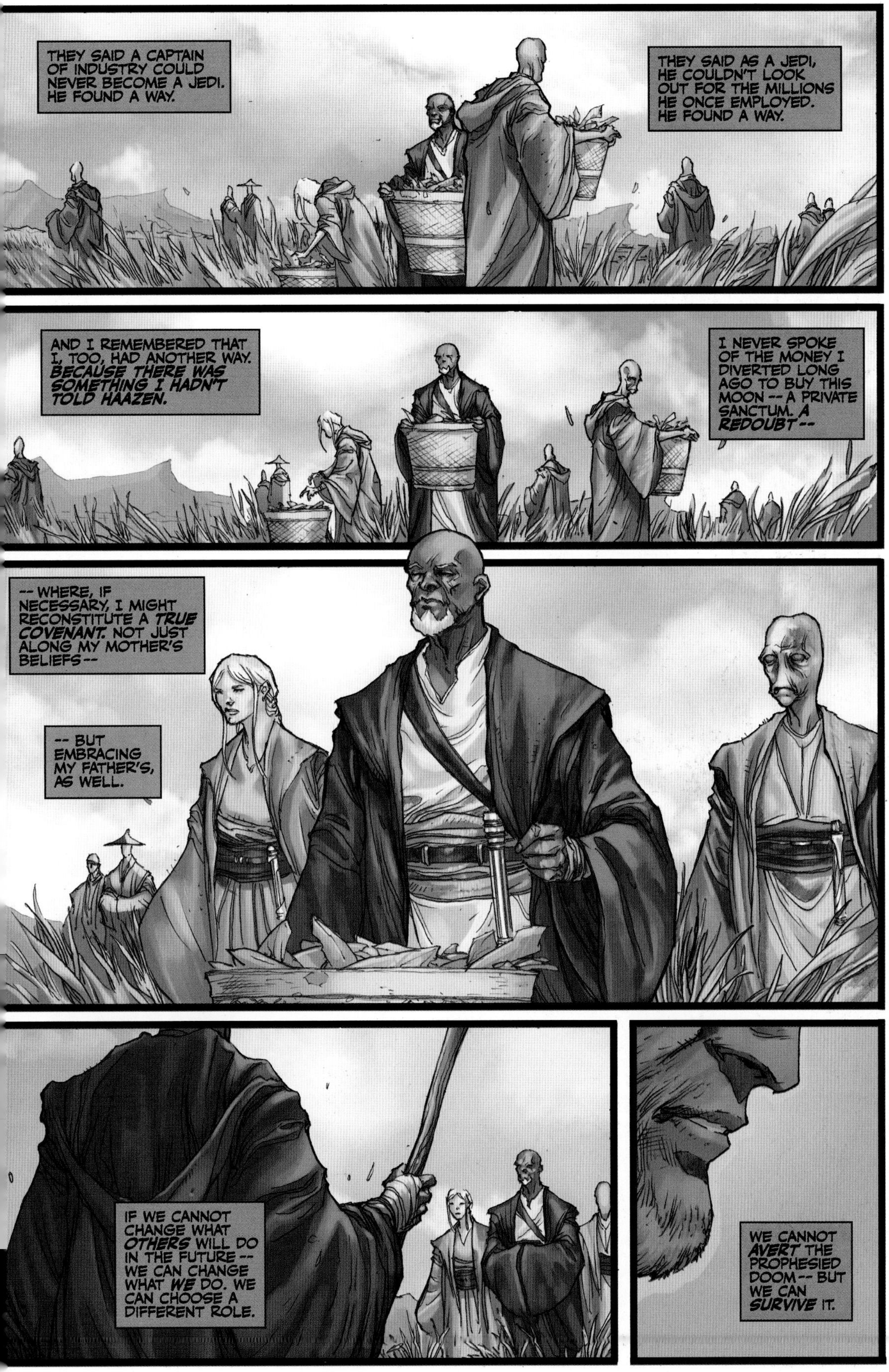
THEY SAID A CAPTAIN OF INDUSTRY COULD NEVER BECOME A JEDI. HE FOUND A WAY.
THEY SAID AS A JEDI, HE COULDN'T LOOK OUT FOR THE MILLIONS HE ONCE EMPLOYED. HE FOUND A WAY.
AND I REMEMBERED THAT I, TOO, HAD ANOTHER WAY. BECAUSE THERE WAS SOMETHING I HADN'T TOLD HAAZEN.
I NEVER SPOKE OF THE MONEY I DIVERTED LONG AGO TO BUY THIS MOON -- A PRIVATE SANCTUM. A REDOUBT --
-- WHERE, IF NECESSARY, I MIGHT RECONSTITUTE A TRUE COVENANT. NOT JUST ALONG MY MOTHER'S BELIEFS --
-- BUT EMBRACING MY FATHER'S, AS WELL.
IF WE CANNOT CHANGE WHAT OTHERS WILL DO IN THE FUTURE -- WE CAN CHANGE WHAT WE DO. WE CAN CHOOSE A DIFFERENT ROLE.
WE CANNOT AVERT THE PROPHESIED DOOM -- BUT WE CAN SURVIVE IT.

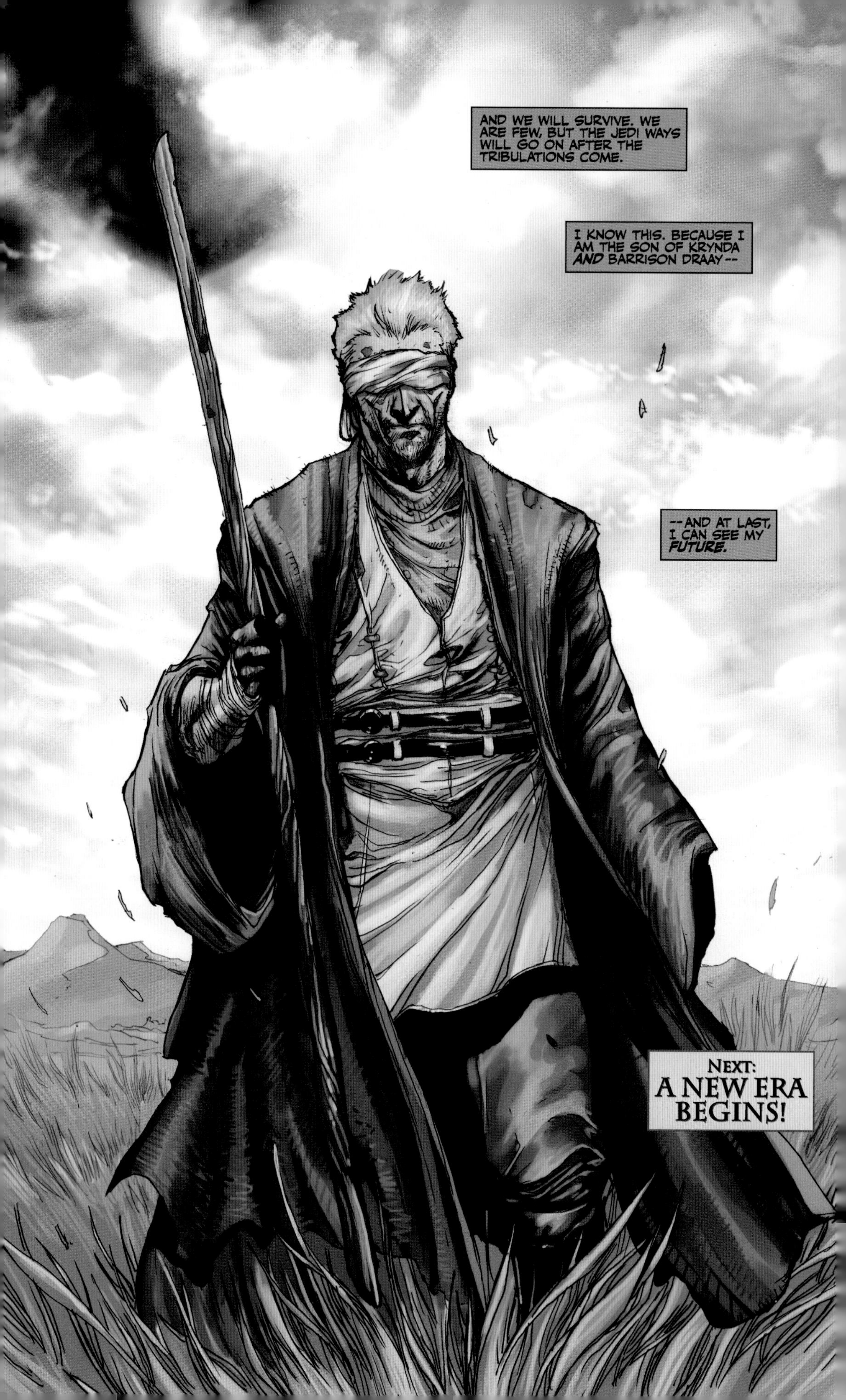
AND WE WILL SURVIVE. WE ARE FEW, BUT THE JEDI WAYS WILL GO ON AFTER THE TRIBULATIONS COME.
I KNOW THIS. BECAUSE I AM THE SON OF KRYNDA AND BARRISON DRAAY--
--AND AT LAST, I CAN SEE MY FUTURE.
NEXT: A NEW ERA BEGINS!

STAR WARS GRAPHIC NOVEL TIMELINE (IN YEARS)

Tales of the Jedi—5,000–3,986 BSW4
Knights of the Old Republic—3,964–3,963 BSW4
Jedi vs. Sith—1,000 BSW4
Jedi Council: Acts of War—33 BSW4
Prelude to Rebellion—33 BSW4
Darth Maul—33 BSW4
Episode I: The Phantom Menace—32 BSW4
Outlander—32 BSW4
Emissaries to Malastare—32 BSW4
Jango Fett: Open Seasons—32 BSW4
Twilight—31 BSW4
Bounty Hunters—31 BSW4
The Hunt for Aurra Sing—30 BSW4
Darkness—30 BSW4
The Stark Hyperspace War—30 BSW4
Rite of Passage—28 BSW4
Jango Fett—27 BSW4
Zam Wesell—27 BSW4
Honor and Duty—24 BSW4
Episode II: Attack of the Clones—22 BSW4
Clone Wars—22–19 BSW4
Clone Wars Adventures—22–19 BSW4
General Grievous—22–19 BSW4
Episode III: Revenge of the Sith—19 BSW4
Dark Times—19 BSW4
Droids—5.5 BSW4
Boba Fett: Enemy of the Empire—3 BSW4
Underworld—1 BSW4
Episode IV: A New Hope—SW4
Classic Star Wars—0–3 ASW4
A Long Time Ago . . . —0–4 ASW4
Empire—0 ASW4
Rebellion—0 ASW4
Vader's Quest—0 ASW4
Boba Fett: Man with a Mission—0 ASW4
Jabba the Hutt: The Art of the Deal—1 ASW4
The Force Unleashed—2 ASW4
Splinter of the Mind's Eye—2 ASW4
Episode V: The Empire Strikes Back—3 ASW4
Shadows of the Empire—3.5 ASW4
Episode VI: Return of the Jedi—4 ASW4
X-Wing Rogue Squadron—4–5 ASW4
Mara Jade: By the Emperor's Hand—4 ASW4
Heir to the Empire—9 ASW4
Dark Force Rising—9 ASW4
The Last Command—9 ASW4
Dark Empire—10 ASW4
Boba Fett: Death, Lies, and Treachery—10 ASW4
Crimson Empire—11 ASW4
Jedi Academy: Leviathan—12 ASW4
Union—19 ASW4
Chewbacca—25 ASW4
Legacy—130–137 ASW4

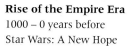

Old Republic Era
25,000 – 1000 years before
Star Wars: A New Hope

Rise of the Empire Era
1000 – 0 years before
Star Wars: A New Hope

Rebellion Era
0 – 5 years after
Star Wars: A New Hope

New Republic Era
5 – 25 years after
Star Wars: A New Hope

New Jedi Order Era
25+ years after
Star Wars: A New Hope

Legacy Era
130+ years after
Star Wars: A New Hope

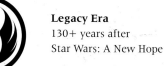

Infinities
Does not apply to timeline

Sergio Aragonés Stomps Star Wars
Star Wars Tales
Star Wars Infinities
Tag and Bink
Star Wars Visionaries

BSW4 = before *Episode IV: A New Hope*. ASW4 = after *Episode IV: A New Hope*.

PUBLISHER
MIKE RICHARDSON

EXECUTIVE VICE PRESIDENT
NEIL HANKERSON

CHIEF FINANCIAL OFFICER
TOM WEDDLE

VICE PRESIDENT OF PUBLISHING
RANDY STRADLEY

VICE PRESIDENT OF BUSINESS DEVELOPMENT
MICHAEL MARTENS

VICE PRESIDENT OF MARKETING, SALES, AND LICENSING
ANITA NELSON

VICE PRESIDENT OF PRODUCT DEVELOPMENT
DAVID SCROGGY

VICE PRESIDENT OF INFORMATION TECHNOLOGY
DALE LAFOUNTAIN

DIRECTOR OF PURCHASING
DARLENE VOGEL

GENERAL COUNSEL
KEN LIZZI

EDITORIAL DIRECTOR
DAVEY ESTRADA

SENIOR MANAGING EDITOR
SCOTT ALLIE

SENIOR BOOKS EDITOR, DARK HORSE BOOKS
CHRIS WARNER

SENIOR BOOKS EDITOR, M PRESS/DH PRESS
ROBERT SIMPSON

EXECUTIVE EDITOR
DIANA SCHUTZ

DIRECTOR OF DESIGN AND PRODUCTION
CARY GRAZZINI

ART DIRECTOR
LIA RIBACCHI

DIRECTOR OF SCHEDULING
CARA NIECE

STAR WARS VECTOR

An event with repercussions for every era and every hero in the *Star Wars* galaxy begins here! For anyone who never knew where to start with *Star Wars* comics, *Vector* is the perfect introduction to the entire *Star Wars* line! For any serious *Star Wars* fan, *Vector* is a must-see event with major happenings throughout the most important moments of the galaxy's history!

VOLUME ONE
(*Knights of the Old Republic* Vol. 5; *Dark Times* Vol. 3)
ISBN 978-1-59582-226-0 | $17.95

VOLUME TWO
(*Rebellion* Vol. 4; *Legacy* Vol. 6)
ISBN 978-1-59582-227-7 | $17.95

KNIGHTS OF THE OLD REPUBLIC
Volume One: Commencement
ISBN 978-1-59307-640-5 | $18.95

Volume Two: Flashpoint
ISBN 978-1-59307-761-7 | $18.95

Volume Three: Days of Fear, Nights of Anger
ISBN 978-1-59307-867-6 | $18.95

Volume Four: Daze of Hate, Knights of Suffering
ISBN 978-1-59582-208-6 | $18.95

REBELLION
Volume One: My Brother, My Enemy
ISBN 978-1-59307-711-2 | $14.95

Volume Two: The Ahakista Gambit
ISBN 978-1-59307-890-4 | $17.95

Volume Three: Small Victories
ISBN 978-1-59582-166-9 | $12.95

LEGACY
Volume One: Broken
ISBN 978-1-59307-716-7 | $17.95

Volume Two: Shards
ISBN 978-1-59307-879-9 | $19.95

Volume Three: Claws of the Dragon
ISBN 978-1-59307-946-8 | $17.95

Volume Four: Alliance
ISBN 978-1-59582-223-9 | $15.95

Volume Five: The Hidden Temple
ISBN 978-1-59582-224-6 | $15.95

DARK TIMES
Volume One: The Path to Nowhere
ISBN 978-1-59307-792-1 | $17.95

Volume Two: Parallels
ISBN 978-1-59307-945-1 | $17.95

www.darkhorse.com

AVAILABLE AT YOUR LOCAL COMICS SHOP OR BOOKSTORE
TO FIND A COMICS SHOP IN YOUR AREA, CALL 1-888-266-4226
For more information or to order direct: On the web: darkhorse.com
E-mail: mailorder@darkhorse.com • Phone: 1-800-862-0052 Mon.–Fri.
9 A.M. to 5 P.M. Pacific Time. STAR WARS © 2004–2009 Lucasfilm Ltd. & ™ (BL8005)

DARK HORSE BOOKS

STAR WARS OMNIBUS COLLECTIONS

STAR WARS
OMNIBUS
TALES OF THE JEDI
VOLUME 1

STAR WARS: TALES OF THE JEDI

Containing the *Tales of the Jedi* stories “The Golden Age of the Sith,” “The Freedon Nadd Uprising,” and “Knights of the Old Republic,” these huge omnibus editions are the ultimate introduction to the ancient history of the *Star Wars* universe!

Volume 1
ISBN 978-1-59307-830-0

Volume 2
ISBN 978-1-59307-911-6

STAR WARS
OMNIBUS
X-WING ROGUE SQUADRON
VOLUME 1

STAR WARS: X-WING ROGUE SQUADRON

Join Wedge Antilles and Rogue Squadron and learn the fate of the galaxy immediately after the events of *Return of the Jedi* as the Rebellion’s best pilots battle remnants of the Empire.

Volume 1
ISBN 978-1-59307-572-9

Volume 2
ISBN 978-1-59307-619-1

Volume 3
ISBN 978-1-59307-776-1

STAR WARS
OMNIBUS
DROIDS

STAR WARS: DROIDS

Before the fateful day Luke Skywalker met Artoo and Threepio for the first time, those two troublesome droids had some amazing adventures all their own!

ISBN 978-1-59307-955-0

STAR WARS
OMNIBUS
EARLY VICTORIES

STAR WARS: EARLY VICTORIES

Following the destruction of the first Death Star, Luke Skywalker is the new, unexpected hero of the Rebellion. But the galaxy hasn’t been saved yet–Luke and Princess Leia find there are many more battles to be fought against the Empire and Darth Vader!

ISBN 978-1-59582-172-0

STAR WARS
OMNIBUS
RISE OF THE SITH

STAR WARS: RISE OF THE SITH

Before the name of Skywalker–or Vader–achieved fame across the galaxy, the Jedi Knights had long preserved peace and justice . . . as well as prevented the return of the Sith. These thrilling tales illustrate the events leading up to *The Phantom Menace*.

ISBN 978-1-59582-228-4

STAR WARS
OMNIBUS
EMISSARIES & ASSASSINS

STAR WARS: EMISSARIES AND ASSASSINS

Discover more stories featuring Anakin Skywalker, Amidala, Obi-Wan, and Qui-Gon set during the time of Episode I *The Phantom Menace* in this mega collection!

ISBN 978-1-59582-229-1

$24.95 each

AVAILABLE AT YOUR LOCAL COMICS SHOP OR BOOKSTORE!
To find a comics shop in your area, call 1-888-266-4226
For more information or to order direct: • On the web: darkhorse.com • E-mail: mailorder@darkhorse.com
• Phone: 1-800-862-0052 Mon.–Fri. 9 AM to 5 PM Pacific Time